Democracy and Citizenship in Scandinavia

Democracy and Citizenship in Scandinavia

Jørgen Goul Andersen
Professor of Political Sociology
Aalborg University
Denmark

and

Jens Hoff
Associate Professor and Director of Studies
Department of Political Science
University of Copenhagen
Denmark

Published by PALGRAVE MACMILLAN
Houndmills, Basingstoke, Hampshire RG21 6XS and
175 Fifth Avenue, New York, N. Y. 10010
Companies and representatives throughout the world

PALGRAVE MACMILLAN is the global academic imprint of the Palgrave Macmillan division of St. Martin's Press, LLC and of Palgrave Macmillan Ltd. Macmillan® is a registered trademark in the United States, United Kingdom and other countries. Palgrave is a registered trademark in the European Union and other countries.

Outside North America
ISBN 0–333–67436–7

In North America
ISBN 0–333–67436–7

This book is printed on paper suitable for recycling and made from fully managed and sustained forest sources.

A catalogue record for this book is available from the British Library.

Library of Congress Catalog Card Number: 2001021193

Transferred to digital printing 2002

Printed and bound in Great Britain by
Antony Rowe Ltd, Chippenham and Eastbourne

Contents

List of Figures

List of Tables

Preface

The idea to provide a comprehensive overview of political participation and challenges to citizenship and democracy in Scandinavia was born out of our involvement in the Danish Citizenship Study which began in 1989. The study became much inspired by the Swedish Citizenship Study which was carried out by Oluf Petersson, Anders Westholm and Göran Blomberg shortly before, and the Danish study was also partly coordinated with a Norwegian Citizenship Study which ran simultaneously. This provided for the first time a comprehensive data set that was partly commensurable across the Nordic countries and much seemed to be gained by undertaking a comparative analysis on the basis of the data from these three studies. Accordingly we got a grant from the Nordic Social Sciences Research Council (NOS-S) to carry out such a comparative study. As it turned out, this was a much bigger job than anticipated as comparability was far from perfect, and as the data needed completion and updating. We are happy to be finally able to present the results in this book, which we hope can fill a void in the literature on citizenship and democracy in Scandinavia. More often than not, the largest nationwide studies of political participation in Scandinavia have been linked to broader studies of democracy and political power. And in accordance with what has almost become a Scandinavian tradition of empirical studies of political citizenship, we focus less on individual variations in political behavior, but rather apply a macro perspective which focus on the quality of democracy in the Scandinavian countries, and on contemporary challenges to citizenship in terms of labor market marginalization, Europeanization and immigration.

The comprehensive and comparative presentation not only elucidates the peculiarities of each country, but also brings forward more clearly a number of common trends that are easily overlooked when focusing only on one country at a time. As such, the book should be of broad scholarly interest. However, given this content the book should also be suited as a textbook for courses in Scandinavian politics at the university level, and we have tried to provide it with some useful overviews for this purpose, as far as possible updated to 2000.

We are indebted to a great many people for the completion of this work. Firstly, we would like to thank our colleagues in the original Danish Citizenship Survey: Johannes Andersen, Ann-Dorte Christensen, Birte Siim, and Lars Torpe, and our Scandinavian partners: Anders Westholm and Jan Teorell in Sweden and Helga Hernes, Nils Asbjørnsen and Torben Hviid Nielsen in Norway. Also we should like to thank the Social Sciences Research Councils in Denmark, Norway and Sweden who funded the original Citizenship

Surveys, and especially the Nordic Social Science Research Council (NOS-S) who made this study possible. Furthermore, the support of our own Departments, the Department of Economics, Politics and Public Administration at Aalborg University, and the Department of Political Science at the University of Copenhagen, has been indispensable for the completion of the book. Finally, we would like to thank colleagues who have commented on drafts, and students who have helped with all kinds of practicalities; in the last phase especially associate professor Marlene Wind and MA student Christian Elling.

JØRGEN GOUL ANDERSEN
JENS HOFF
Copenhagen

1
Introduction

The purpose of the book

The aim of this book is to provide a broad overview of political participation in Scandinavia but with the purpose of describing how democracy works from a citizenship point of view, rather than explaining variations in individual political behavior as such. In the first part of the book, we look at the major channels and patterns of political participation, and the changes that have taken place in them. More specifically, we want to examine the legacy of popular mobilization, in particular class mobilization, along with new forms of political participation associated with the Scandinavian welfare state. In the second part of the book, we address some of the core contemporary challenges to the ideals of full citizenship at the national level: marginalization in the labor market; European integration; and multi-ethnicity.

We have chosen the concept of citizenship (which will be defined below) as an overall perspective and as an umbrella for our analysis of political participation. As compared to other perspectives, it falls somewhere between instrumental approaches to political participation concerned with the articulation of interests or political equality on the one hand, and approaches concerned with the integrative effects of participation on the other. Directing attention to ideals of 'full citizenship', and more broadly to the quality and the nature of democracy, a citizenship approach provides a 'middle of the road' position which at the same time nicely points out the main challenges to citizenship. The concept of citizenship also covers what is usually referred to as 'political culture'. For data and space limitations, however, this is largely outside the scope of this book, although it will be addressed in the later chapters of the volume, which consider some challenges to the Scandinavian concept of citizenship.

When this book was first prepared in the mid-1990s, one of the purposes was to draw attention to some less reassuring aspects of the apparent success of citizenship in Scandinavia. In the intervening period, things have changed quite rapidly, and a number of problems have surfaced. It is tempting to speak now of a 'Danification' of Scandinavian politics in the sense that the decline in old structures and patterns that has been observed in Denmark for several years, has now become visible in the other countries as well. In fact it could seem that Denmark is still the most politically advanced nation in Scandinavia – as it was a century ago. At that time, Denmark was ahead in terms of political mobilization and the building of new institutions such as modern mass parties; in the last quarter of the twentieth century, Denmark appears as a forerunner in the demolition of the very same institutions. Still, this book is not really a story of declining citizenship; rather, it is a story of *changing* citizenship. Before we go on with the specification of research questions and hypotheses, however, we shall briefly discuss the concept of citizenship and the particular approach that is attached to it.

Citizenship, political participation and political culture

Citizenship is originally a legal concept which was turned into a sociological concept, first and foremost by Marshall (1950) in his famous essay on 'citizenship and social class' which discussed the ideal and the possibilities of 'full citizenship' in a capitalist society.[1] In many countries outside the Anglo-Saxon world, the concept has remained a predominantly legal concept, even in academic language. In other countries, citizenship, even in a sociological sense, mainly connotes social rights, broadly conceived. Thus there is much confusion about the meaning of citizenship. Another source of confusion over the concept derives from the fact that normative and analytical theories of citizenship are often conflated. In the following discussion, we shall try to distinguish more sharply between normative and analytical uses, and between the various dimensions of citizenship as an analytical concept.

To begin with the *normative* issue, there has been an intense discussion about the ideals of citizenship. Briefly, one may identify four or five traditions of such ideals:

- A liberal tradition (rarely formulated in the language of citizenship), emphasizing autonomy and freedom of choice;
- A social democratic tradition, emphasizing equality and social rights as a prerequisite for attaining this ideal;
- A heterogeneous republican tradition, stressing the virtues of political participation, political community, and orientation to the 'common good'; modern ideals of 'deliberative democracy' also belong mainly to this tradition;
- A communitarian tradition, emphasizing social integration and the building of social capital in civil society through participation and cooperation.[2]

Although these notions of citizenship may serve as useful inspiration for empirical studies, they address somewhat different problems than those we are concerned with here. The normative discussion may be relevant in pointing out some ideals and dimensions of measurement, but in this book, citizenship is used as an empirical and analytical concept. As such, citizenship has three main dimensions: a dimension of *rights* (and duties), a dimension of *participation*, and a dimension of *identities*. As can be seen from the description above, the normative discussion is concerned mainly (though not exclusively) with identities whereas our concern in this book is mainly with participation. Each of these three dimensions is briefly discussed below.[3]

Citizenship and political rights

At first sight, the dimension of (political) rights may seem fairly trivial when we speak of political participation within the democratic nation-state. However, even basic political rights such as the right to vote become far less trivial as soon as we address the questions of European integration, and of immigration. Furthermore, the question of rights reaches beyond the question of basic political rights. There is also the question of rights of citizens to act vis-à-vis public authorities, beyond the simple right of voting: *formal* rights to complain, to get access to information, to appoint members of boards of service institutions; and *informal* practices of accommodation and negotiation. In short, closely related to the rights dimension there is the question of institutional variations in opportunities of participation and influence, both within and between countries: Institutions may be 'empowering' in the sense that they provide many opportunities for participation and interest articulation, or they may be 'disempowering' to the extent that they deny such opportunities. This institutional perspective is particularly relevant when we consider opportunities for participation among welfare state users and clients.

Citizenship and political participation

The dimension of participation is obviously our main concern here, however. The basic question is to what extent the Scandinavian countries provide their citizens with the opportunities and resources for participating in politics and influencing political decisions, and to what extent these resources are evenly distributed among citizens. Furthermore, as will be spelled out in more detail below, from a citizenship perspective we are concerned not only with instrumental political behavior but also with the opportunities for full participation *in public life*, including participation in voluntary associations and in public discussions. From this perspective, participation in political discussions, political engagement and political efficacy are interesting in their own right and not only as resources for political participation; in principle, they might even be considered the key dependent variables.

Citizenship and political identities

The dimension of (political) identities is roughly equivalent to what has traditionally been labeled political culture if we follow Almond and Verba's (1963) classical definition of political culture as 'orientations – attitudes to the political system...and the role of the self in the system'.[4] However, one important aspect is missing from this definition: the orientation towards other citizens (that is, solidarity and tolerance). This relates to a classical distinction in the citizenship literature, namely the distinction between vertical and horizontal citizenship. Whereas the vertical dimension refers to the relationship between the individual and the political system, the horizontal dimension refers to the relationship between citizens. As indicated above, this last-mentioned distinction is also relevant for the participation dimension where we focus not only on instrumental activities to influence the decisions of public authorities but also on participation in debates in the public sphere broadly conceived.

As indicated, all three dimensions are relevant for a study of citizenship,[5] and all three dimensions will be included when discussing the challenges to citizenship in the second part of the book. However, in the first part, we focus on the dimension of participation, both because of lack of comparative data and because of insufficient space. Therefore, we have not elaborated very much on the identity dimension at this stage. For the same reason, we have chosen not to include any lengthy discussion about the normative theories of citizenship which are to a large extent focused on the identity dimension (this holds in particular for republican and communitarian theories, whereas the social democratic and liberal theories are more oriented towards participation and freedom of choice, respectively, both from a more instrumental perspective than the others).

Defining citizenship

To the extent that we focus on the participation dimension, we may follow the formal definition of citizenship in Turner (1993: 2) where citizenship is defined as 'a set of practices (juridical, political, economical and cultural) which define a person as a competent member of society, and which as a consequence shape the flow of resources to persons and social groups'. Civil, political and social rights and obligations define the formal status of citizenship and structure the connection between the individual and political institutions – that is, the political-institutional practices (the vertical dimension of citizenship). Political-cultural practices designate the relations between citizens as they meet or confront each other when discussing common affairs (the horizontal dimension of citizenship). Both types of practices contribute to the formation of political identities as citizens, or what is commonly referred to as political culture.

Citizenship in class-mobilized societies and beyond

Citizenship in the Scandinavian countries should be seen in the light of the strong tradition of collective mobilization of classes as well as other groups in these societies. The Scandinavian countries are ideal-typical examples of a very thorough mobilization along the basic cleavages of the industrial nation-state, in particular class cleavages. Very few other countries have witnessed as high levels of political mobilization in mass parties, in trade unions and farmers' associations and in cultural or religious associations as the Scandinavian countries,[6] and no other countries have ever reported as high levels of class voting. These factors have also contributed to a high and relatively evenly distributed mobilization among voters and a high degree of social equality in political participation. For instance, party membership was even negatively related to socioeconomic resources. This mobilization formed the basis of the classical model of 'Nordic Democracy' and the 'democratic class struggle'.

An important question is what happens when this cleavage structure is weakened and changed. Lipset and Rokkan (1967) traced the cleavage structures of modern industrial societies to two decisive events: the national revolution and the industrial revolution. Today, one often hears discussion of a *post*-industrial revolution and a *post*-national revolution that are likely to be followed by changing cleavages. The 'frozen' cleavage structures of the 1920s – of which the Scandinavian countries are, once again, prototypical (Damgaard 1974) – could be expected to melt, and class-based political institutions should erode. Indeed such processes may be identified. But the question is to what degree this has already taken place – and what the consequences are for citizenship: What happens to the equality in political participation achieved due to the fact that the collective resources of the dominated social classes used to compensate for the inequality in individual resources? Although one should have no illusions about the direction of influence between leadership and ordinary people in the classical 'associative democracy' of the Scandinavian countries, one may also ask what has happened to the traditional linkages between ordinary people and decision-makers, and to political trust. To what extent have alternative channels evolved, and do they provide equivalent opportunities for linkages and for having an influence on political decisions? Further, do they provide the same opportunities for social equality in participation?

Citizenship and the welfare state

Another important focus of this book is on the impact of the welfare state for citizenship. This is a discussion with classical roots – in fact older than the welfare state itself. Thus, Tocqueville (1835/40) criticized the individualizing and alienating effects of the benevolent welfare state he envisaged – as well as its negative effects on the level of solidarity in civil society. Similar thoughts have been echoed in the writings of, for example, Habermas (1981) and Wolfe (1989). From a right-wing perspective, a parallel criticism has been launched against the alleged tendency of the welfare state to generate moral hazard, rent-seeking or 'dependency'. However persuasive such ideas may appear, it has so far been impossible to provide convincing empirical evidence supporting such assertions (Goul Andersen 1998a: 275–308).[7]

The other mainstream position is the idea of the state 'empowering' citizens through the provision of social rights and economic resources. This position has its roots in J.S. Mill who was inspired by Tocqueville's ideas about the educational effect of participation but realized that a prerequisite for real freedom is not only autonomy but also resources and thereby a certain degree of economic equality. The first theorist to formulate this line of thinking in 'modern' terms was T.H. Marshall (1950) in his famous exposition of citizenship as both an ideal and a theory of social development. Today the premise of equality is echoed in most normative theories of democracy such as Dahl (1989). Also, as pointed out in Oldfield's (1990b) theory of citizenship as an 'unnatural practice', the welfare state plays a crucial role in granting civil, political and social rights; in providing economic and social resources; in creating open arenas for political decisions and public debates; and in educating citizens to democracy and participation (Oldfield 1990b: 27–8). These assumptions also enter the interpretations of this book, even though they can hardly be put to a critical empirical test.

A third important position is more readily testable: as indicated earlier, the institutions of the welfare state can be designed in more or less empowering or disempowering ways. And the argument put forward here is that the Scandinavian welfare states are prototypical examples of empowering welfare states. This holds both for the widespread universalism in the field of transfers and, in particular, for the responsiveness of public service institutions which is a core interest here (Petersson, Westholm and Blomberg 1989). This theme was first developed in Hernes' (1988) seminal article on 'Scandinavian Citizenship' where she discussed whether the modern Scandinavian welfare states 'imply fragmentation and alienation on the individual level.... or (whether) they develop intrapersonal pluralism and foster the growth of citizen competence...' (Hernes 1988: 212). She herself argued strongly in favor of the last-mentioned view and described Scandinavian social democratic welfare policies as a conscious attempt at a 'democratization of all areas of social life' (Hernes 1988: 203), not least public service institutions. Thus 'Scandinavian citizenship' is characterized as being 'activist, participatory and egalitarian' (Hernes 1988: 200).

Without necessarily accepting this 'social democratic construction of history', Petersson, Westholm and Blomberg (1989) developed the instruments of measurement of this sort of small-scale, everyday democracy which are also included in this study. An important question which cannot be tested empirically on hard data is whether such decentralization of influence can act as a remedy for the problems encountered in the traditional political and social associations, or whether this opportunity for influence on the outcome of the political system remains important only for people's own sense of control over their own lives.

A final question in relation to the Scandinavian welfare model concerns the effects of women's integration on the labor market which has been facilitated by the extensive provision of care facilities in the Scandinavian welfare state. On the basis of this labor market integration, it becomes interesting to examine to what extent the gender gap in political participation tends to disappear in general and to what extent women have been mobilized as wage earners and in trade unions in particular.

Broadening the concept of political participation

As already indicated, a citizenship perspective carries with it a somewhat different conception of political participation than more instrumentalist perspectives. Besides, even from an instrumentalist perspective, the definition of political participation has gradually been broadened. We begin with the general changes in the definition of political participation and then turn to the relationship between a citizen perspective and various alternatives.

In general, the concept of political participation has gradually been broadened, from narrow focus on elections, campaign and party activities (Milbrath and Goel 1977), to an ever-more encompassing list of activities. At the same time, the view on political participation as a unidimensional, cumulative phenomenon has been given up in favor of a multidimensional view (Verba and Nie 1972; Verba, Nie and Kim 1978). This followed more general changes in the perspectives of political science, which was highly 'input-biased' in the 1960s but discovered the implementation side in the 1970s (Pressman and Wildavsky 1973) and gradually became more oriented towards the output and outcome side. Thus, building on Verba, Nie and Kim (1978) who included 'communal activity' and 'particularized contacting' and Barnes, Kaase et al. (1979) who included political protest, Parry, Moyser and Day (1992) sought to avoid the input bias by defining political participation as actions aimed at influencing *policy outcomes*. They define political participation as: ' "taking part in the process of formulation, passage and implementation of public policies". It is concerned with action by citizens which is aimed at influencing decisions which are, in most cases, ultimately taken by public representatives and officials' (Parry, Moyser and Day 1992: 16). Operationally, this included voting, campaigning, individual contacts with public authorities, local groups and political protest (Parry, Moyser and Day 1992: 17). Similar operationalizations have been applied in earlier Scandinavian studies (Damgaard 1980; Hernes and Martinussen 1980).[8] The most controversial activity on the list is individual contacting. The argument is that even though such contacting may have purely non-political motives, it may nevertheless have the same aggregated impact upon implementation as collective activities.

Citizenship and the concept of participation

In the literature on political participation, one may distinguish between instrumentalist approaches on the one hand and approaches emphasizing the integrative aspects of political participation on the other. Rational choice theories and class (or group) theories belong to the first category: participation is about the articulation of interests of individuals and groups. From this perspective, only activities aiming at the promotion of such interests vis-à-vis political decision-makers may count as an act of political participation. In the other category, we find social capital theories which focus on the effect of political participation for the building of social capital – that is, conditions of interpersonal trust and cooperation (van Deth 1997). From this perspective, participation in, for example, voluntary associations, oriented towards interest articulation or not, becomes as relevant to study as voting and other straightforwardly *political* acts of participation. This holds also for another main tradition in this category: the tradition of participatory democracy or 'school of democracy'. From this perspective, the central interest is to what extent an act of participation contributes to the learning of political skills and to the achievement of civic orientations.

From a citizenship perspective, one would emphasize both the instrumental aspects of participation and the effects of participation, if not so much for the building of social capital, then at least for the building of 'political capital'. Thus all sorts of involvement in public life becomes relevant to include.

Secondly, one would also point at actions that contribute to strengthening the autonomy of individuals as citizens. This includes also the use of 'exit' (or 'choice') as an alternative or as a supplement to 'voice', and in particular it involves a distinction between what Petersson, Westholm and Blomberg (1989) have labeled the *'big democracy'* (influence on society) and *'small democracy'* (control over one's own life situation).[9] The most important new aspects added by the notion of 'small democracy' are workplace democracy and the formal or informal influence of users in public service institutions.

Bringing decisions as close as possible to those who are affected by these decisions, and giving these individuals and groups opportunities to influence, has served as a basic formula for democratization in the Scandinavian countries. Enhancing the opportunities for participating in influencing the outcome of decisions at the level of 'street-level bureaucracy' is often seen as a remedy also for the problems that are acknowledged on the input side of the political system – that is, the declining membership of political parties and professionalization of all sorts of associations. It is an important question, however, to what extent these forms of participation are commensurable, and to what extent participation and influence in the 'small democracy' may be a substitute for participation in the 'big democracy'. But regardless of the answers to this problem, participation at the 'small democracy' level remains important to study in its own right from a citizenship perspective.

It should be acknowledged that the above-mentioned activities may also be counted as political participation from more traditional perspectives on political participation. Participation in voluntary associations is generally acknowledged as a 'borderline case' (and, considering the political importance of trade unions and employers' associations in Scandinavia, participation in such associations must undisputedly be included). Next, as mentioned, 'communal activities' are frequently included in current definitions of political participation, and 'citizen contacting' includes quite a few 'small democracy' activities. Besides, some activities are mainly left out because of inadequate operationalizations. Thus if we recognize that the notion of implementation applies not only to public officials but also to 'street-level bureaucrats' (Lipsky 1980), the theoretical definition of Parry, Moyser and Day (1992) should obviously also include the informal interaction between users and (semi-)professionals in public service institutions. If citizens' contacts with public authorities have become more a matter of negotiation rather than simple rule application, this applies much more to interactions in service institutions. In short, if the phrase 'taking part in … the implementation of public policies' is taken seriously, it should operationally include most 'small democracy' activities (Hernes 1988; Petersson et al. 1989).

Finally, participation in public opinion formation is another classical borderline case: some operational definitions of political participation include this aspect; most definitions do not. From a citizenship perspective, this must obviously be included as political participation, but even from an instrumental perspective, this should also in principle be the case. As in the case of implementation, the stage of opinion formation in the broadest sense has increasingly been recognized as a central stage in the process of political decision-making. Thus, theories of political power and influence devote increasing attention not only to agenda setting but also to problem definition and preference formation (Petersson 1991; Flyvbjerg 1991).

The above-mentioned aspects may all be covered by the following theoretical definition of political participation: Political participation may be defined as *any activity which influences or seeks to influence, directly or indirectly, the decisions or the outcome of decisions of the political system or of such 'parapolitical systems' which immediately affect the citizens themselves.* The phrase 'parapolitical systems' (borrowed from Easton 1965) is necessary to include workplace democracy whereas the phrase 'any activity that influences...' takes account of the possibility that participation may sometimes have purely individual purposes. Finally, the term 'indirectly' makes it possible to include also activities of opinion formation which can only indirectly influence political decisions.

Data and design

As indicated, our task is not so much to explain variation in one or more dependent variables labeled 'participation' but, rather, to describe the quality and nature of democracy in the Scandinavian countries from a citizenship perspective. This also means that an explained variance of zero when we examine the correlation between social background variables and participation would be close to an ideal of 'full citizenship'. Even tracing out which objective and subjective variables actually *do* explain variations in participation is not always a key interest.

A key interest, on the other hand, would be cross-national comparisons of aggregate figures as well as comparisons over time. Wherever possible, we have sought to include such comparisons with countries outside Scandinavia but often, data do not easily lend themselves to such comparisons. Wherever possible, we have also sought to use time series, but in many instances, we have to rely only on cross-sectional data. Our core data consist of three Scandinavian citizenship surveys carried out by three separate research groups that have to some extent coordinated their efforts. On this basis, we have sought to make data as comparable as possible. As the fieldwork took place in 1987 in Sweden and in 1990 in the two other countries, we have put quite some effort into updating the material and supplementing with data from other sources wherever possible in order to ensure that the main conclusions remain valid.

Although comparisons between three fairly similar countries (Denmark, Norway and Sweden, occasionally supplemented with aggregate data from Finland) could speak in favor of a 'most similar design', this sort of design has only occasionally been applied – for example, in comparison of trade union participation and user participation in service institutions where institutional differences make such a design appropriate. More frequently, we simply try to describe as thoroughly as possible the Scandinavian countries, to identify *common* associations and trends, and using the information in the three country studies to complement each other. This is a more descriptive, more inductive, and more hypothesis-generating approach than we would have preferred, but this is what is possible with available data. Still, being able to identify similar characteristics, trends and associations in three countries does give the analysis a more generalizing ambition, both theoretically and empirically.

The plan of the book

As mentioned, the book is divided into two parts. Part I deals with the different channels of political participation in Scandinavian, both traditional and new. Part II deals with the some of the main current challenges to full citizenship: marginalization on the labor market; Europeanization; and the growing number of immigrants and refugees.

Chapter 2 analyses political involvement which is interesting in its own right but is also interesting to compare with actual participation: as traditional channels of political participation such as political parties appear to decline, one might envisage a discrepancy between high involvement and low participation (and in particular low commitment) which could be described as a 'spectator democracy' (Andersen et al. 1993). Chapter 3 deals with voter turnout which has traditionally been very high in the Scandinavian countries, due to a high level of mobilization in the lower classes. But does this pattern still hold in face of the weakening of class-based politics?

Chapter 4 analyses the 'crisis of political parties' and discusses whether these institutions have a future as a channel between the 'masses' and the political 'elites'. Besides, the chapter examines whether the differences in party membership in the Scandinavian countries are really as large as commonly believed. Chapters 5 and 6 complete the analysis of the 'traditional' channels of participation with a description of membership and activity in voluntary associations. Like the USA, the Scandinavian countries have traditionally been regarded as strongholds of voluntary associations, but what is the reality behind this folklore? Chapter 6 deals more specifically with participation in trade unions. Important questions here are whether Scandinavian trade unions have been resistant to the decline in trade unionism found in most European countries. And are there any costs of the unusually high (but perhaps less 'voluntary') unionization in Sweden and Denmark?

The following three chapters are concerned with 'new' forms of political participation. Chapter 7 analyses the reality of workplace democracy in the Nordic countries. Departing from the assumption that since the 1960s workplace democracy in Scandinavia, particularly in Sweden, has become an international 'role model', the model is scrutinized by looking at how the institutional arrangements for influence are actually used and perceived by Scandinavian wage-earners. The chapter also tests Pateman's (1970) hypothesis that the workplace is 'the primary classroom for transmitting patterns of political participation'.

Chapter 8 provides an overview of the uses of some major channels of user influence in the public sector. Using Hirschman's (1970) concepts of 'voice' and 'exit' the use and perceived importance of these modes of influence is analysed. Further, the chapter touches on the question of whether individual resources or institutional factors are most important in explaining user participation.

Chapter 9 deals with political protest, 'grass-roots participation' or, as we increasingly prefer to label it, single-issue participation. Whatever happened to the new social movements, and to what extent have social movements or 'grass-roots actions' become simple 'single-issue campaigning' and a part of routine politics?

In Part II, chapter 10 deals with labor market marginalization and its consequences. At the time of interviewing, this was a serious, long-standing problem only in Denmark but since then Sweden has also experienced this challenge to full citizenship often claimed to lead to social exclusion and a loss of citizenship. But to what extent is the welfare state able to remedy for this – may it rather aggravate the problems?

Traditionally, citizenship has been practiced within the frames of the nation-state but, increasingly, this is being challenged by European integration (as well as by globalization which is outside the scope of this book except for its implications for marginalization and immigration). To what extent are ordinary citizens able to relate to this, and does it generate new divisions between a social elite and the majority of the population? This question is treated in chapter 11 whereas chapter 12 deals with the consequences of immigration. In these two chapters, we explore not only political participation but also political rights and political identities, in accordance with the three dimensions of the concept of citizenship. Finally, chapter 13 summarizes the main findings and conclusions concerning the present state of democracy in the Scandinavian countries and the prospects for the future.

Part I

Political Participation and Citizenship

2
Political Engagement

Introduction: the problem and the concept

Political engagement is rarely considered to be an aspect of political participation as such. More typically, scholars (such as van Deth 1989: 277) distinguish between political interest or political engagement as a state of mind and political involvement or political participation as behavioral manifestations. Political engagement has frequently been considered *the* central intervening variable between socioeconomic status (SES) and political participation (Verba and Nie 1972), or at least a supplementary explanatory variable which, alongside political resources (such as skills, time, and money), links the world outside politics with political participation (Verba, Schlozman and Brady 1995: 272). Besides, it has served as measure of a 'natural' inequality in political participation that may be modified by institutional factors such as class-mobilizing organizations (Verba, Nie and Kim 1978).

However, even from an instrumental perspective political engagement may be seen as a source of indirect influence if government anticipates the possible reactions of citizens, and political discussions may be seen as a contribution to mass opinion formation and thus as part of the political process. From a citizenship point of view, however, participation in political discussions is a constituent part of full citizenship. As we are not much concerned here with explaining social psychological determinants of individual political behavior, we do not follow the tradition of treating political engagement as an independent or intervening variable; rather, citizens' political engagement is as such a central attribute of a democratic political system. In fact, the relationship between engagement and participation is more interesting at an aggregate level: do we find a development towards 'political detachment' (Kaase and Barnes 1979) or a 'spectator democracy' (Andersen et al. 1993) in the sense that citizens become increasingly engaged but participate less because participation is not considered possible or worthwhile – if not in general (which is clearly demonstrated not to

15

be the case in Topf 1995b), then in politics at the national level (that is, what may be termed 'big democracy')?

The potential of ordinary citizens for political engagement and competence is a classical, contested issue both in democratic theory and in electoral research. The belief that there are *basic, enduring limitations* in the capacity or willingness of ordinary citizens to engage in politics was one of the core premises of 'realist' democratic theory (Schumpeter 1944; Sartori 1987), and for a long time, empirical research seemed to support the idea that voters were unable to meet even the weakest criteria of political consciousness (Converse 1964). Later, this was challenged by increasing ideological consistency and political interest, suggesting that as politics become more salient, people engage in politics and become more politically conscious (Nie with Andersen 1974; Nielsen 1976). Not least in Scandinavia, rational models of 'issue voting' have become the dominant paradigm[1] for explaining voting behavior (for instance, Aardal and Valen 1989, 1995; Aardal 1999; Gilljam and Holmberg 1993, 1995, 2000; Nannestad 1989; Borre and Goul Andersen 1997; Andersen et al. 1999), although the dispute is far from settled (see, for example, Jenssen 1993).

The argument that engagement and competence increase when politics become salient bears resemblance to the classical argument of participatory democrats that engagement, competence and 'civic attitudes' may be enhanced by providing better opportunities of political participation (Pateman 1970; Barber 1984). However, there may also be other paths to political engagement. In a Scandinavian context, a central role has been ascribed to *class mobilization* (among farmers and the working class in particular), as well as to other forms of popular mobilization, in bringing people with relatively low levels of socioeconomic resources into politics. This argument applies not only to participation but also to political engagement because the mobilizing classes put a major emphasis on the enlightenment and education of their members.[2] The question is, however, if this class mobilization is still alive today. More recently, a similar role has been ascribed to *gender mobilization* (Togeby 1994) which is at least as distinctive of Scandinavian politics and may be analysed along the same lines: Have women in the Scandinavian countries succeeded in 'closing the gap' in political engagement (Karvonen and Selle 1995), and do the gender inequalities that remain derive from gender differences in political engagement, from institutional constraints, or both?

Next, researchers in the 'new politics' tradition have argued that the educational revolution, alongside increasing media exposure, contribute to a *'cognitive mobilization'* among citizens (Dalton 1988: 23; Inglehart 1990: 359). But to what degree has this happened in the Scandinavian countries? And how does that leave the minority among the younger generation who receive only a low level of formal education? Do we face an increasing polarization of engagement between higher- and lower-educated youth?

Finally, *the welfare state* may contribute to enhancing political engagement – and offset the marginalizing tendencies outlined above – (i) by reducing social inequality; (ii) by socializing children to active citizenship;[3] (iii) by providing new channels of participation; and (iv) by making politics more salient. Objectively speaking, Scandinavians have more stake in politics (as public employees, or as users of the social services and transfers) than the citizens of most other countries. Indeed, government's increasing share of the economy has been suggested as an explanation of the long-term increase in the levels of political interest in Western European societies (van Deth 1991), but this hypothesis has rarely been tested.

These are the major research questions that guide this chapter. First, however, we should specify how we have measured political engagement, and how the Scandinavian countries differ from other European countries in their level of political engagement.

Operationalization

Political engagement is typically used as an umbrella concept with little theoretical content, covering various aspects of people's attachment to politics: interest in politics, political information, political discussions, and political efficacy. We follow this line but include only 'internal' political efficacy (or 'political self-confidence') as an aspect of engagement; we consider 'external' efficacy or system 'responsiveness' to be more of an attitude to the political system.

Next, unlike some authors following a tradition of the 'Michigan school' (van Deth 1989), we do not include party identification as a measure of political engagement (it also tends to have low correlations with the other measures nowadays; see Verba, Schlozman and Brady 1995: 348), nor do we include attendance at political meetings. This would exclude the possibility of examining whether an increasing number of politically interested citizens are unable to identify with any party – or are interested in politics without showing any outward manifestations of that interest. Such questions relate to the scenario of a spectator democracy and seem very important for the interpretation of contemporary democracy.

Because of a shortage of data, we also have to exclude political information from our operational measures of political engagement. This leaves us with the following measures: interest in politics (all three countries); political efficacy (all three countries but using somewhat different measures); and political discussion with family, friends and colleagues (measured in Denmark and Norway only). Because the measures are different from country to country, we have to rely on single questions rather than composite indices.[4]

An overview: political interest in Scandinavia, in a comparative perspective

As some scholars have pointed out, few Scandinavian citizens declare themselves to be 'much' interested in politics (Jenssen 1993), and Norway has even been described as a 'distant democracy' (Martinussen 1977). The figures in Table 2.1 fall short of any normative ideals of participatory democracy and conform more with Almond and Verba's concept of a

Table 2.1 Political interest in Scandinavia and other Western countries, 1990 (percentages)

Country Citizenship surveys	Political interest, 1990				
	Much	Some	Little or none	Much/some, total	No interest in politics at all
Sweden (1987)	13	40	47	53	11
Norway	10	49	41	59	4
Denmark	22	40	38	62	9
European Community: *Eurobarometer*					
1. Denmark	20	47	33	67	6
2. United Kingdom	15	42	43	57	15
3. Germany (Western)	15	40	45	55	12
4. Greece	18	37	45	54	15
5. The Netherlands	13	40	47	53	10
6. Luxembourg	15	35	50	50	19
7. Ireland	10	33	57	43	26
8. France	9	30	61	39	24
9. Belgium	7	29	64	36	30
10. Spain	6	28	66	34	44
11. Italy	6	25	69	31	29
12. Portugal	6	25	69	31	29
EU-12, 1990	11	34	54	45	22
EU-12, 1994	9	34	56	43	20

Wording:
'Would you say that you are much, quite, only a little, or not at all interested in politics?' (Denmark)
'How interested are you in politics? Are you much, quite, only a little, or not at all interested in politics?' (Norway)
'Generally speaking, how interested are you in politics? (Which answer on this card...): Much interested, quite, interested, not very interested, not at all interested?' (Sweden)

Sources: Danish, Swedish (1987) and Norwegian citizenship surveys; *Eurobarometer. Trends 1974–1992* (average of two 1990 surveys, N=2000 in each country), and Eurobarometer 42, 1994 (last line only). More recent Eurobarometer data on political interest are unreliable (that is, exaggerated) in the Danish case as these data derive from a panel and reveal a panel effect.

'civic culture', at best. If we use comparative criteria rather than ideal standards, however, the picture is somewhat different. According to the Eurobarometer surveys, the Danes take a lead among the citizens of the European Union (EU). And even though the Norwegian and Swedish figures are lower, they are above the levels in most other EU countries. Now, the low average in the European Union derives in part from the very low level of political interest among Roman Catholic Southern Europeans (Italy, Spain and Portugal). The Scandinavians resemble the citizens of other Northern European countries, and the proportions of those 'highly interested' in politics in Norway and Sweden (10, respectively 13 per cent) are not much above the EU average. Only in Denmark, the proportion of those who describe themselves as 'highly interested' in politics is unusually high but similar figures have sometimes been encountered in American and German surveys (van Deth 1989: 283).

However, considering the possible effects of class and gender mobilization, and of expensive welfare states with emphasis on civic competence, the prediction is not that political interest should be particularly high. Rather, the expectation is that all these factors should contribute to low levels of political apathy. And this expectation is clearly confirmed. The distinctive characteristic of the Scandinavian countries is the low proportion of *'not at all interested'*, indicating the size of the entirely apolitical stratum. It ranges from 4 per cent in Norway to 11 per cent in Sweden;[5] in the other EU countries, the corresponding figure varied from 10 per cent (the Netherlands) to 44 per cent (Spain), with an average of 22 per cent. In short, *what distinguishes Scandinavia is the low level of total withdrawal from politics*, rather than a large proportion of highly involved citizens. In other words, political interest is rather equally distributed between individuals.[6] An important question is whether this may be attributed to class mobilization, to gender mobilization, to the size and nature of welfare states, or to quite different factors. Firstly, however, we shall look at longterm changes in the level of political interest. In several countries, such as France, Germany, Britain and the USA (data compiled in Dalton 1988: 23), there was a marked long-term increase in political interest from the 1950s to the 1970s.

The Eurobarometer time series (1983–1990) also show a minor increase – except in France (Eurobarometer, *Trends*, 1993), and time series on participation in political discussion reveal an increase in all countries except France and Italy (van Deth 1991). In the 1990s, however, the trend towards increasing subjective interest seems to have been reversed (Eurobarometer 42, 1994). This holds in particular for Germany, where only 8 per cent expressed much interest in politics; 59 per cent indicated little or no interest at all.

In Scandinavia, time series from election surveys dating back to around 1970 (Norway and Denmark) or 1960 (Sweden) indicate a clear upward

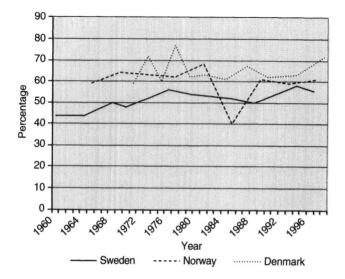

Figure 2.1   Political interest in Sweden, Denmark and Norway, 1960–1990. Proportions expressing 'some' or 'much' interest in politics (percentages)

Sources: Surveys from the Election Projects:
Sweden: Gilljam and Holmberg (1995: 169); Holmberg (2000: 54); Norway: Bjørklund (1999: 287); Aardal (1999: 202); Denmark: Goul Andersen (1984c: 30); data from election surveys.
Figures are uncorrected from sampling biases. Swedish calculations indicate that declining response rates may account for some 5–6 per cent of the long-term increase in political interest (Gilljam and Holmberg 1995: 169).

trend in Sweden and Denmark until the mid-1970s (Figure 2.1), perhaps even in the 1990s, whereas the Norwegian fluctuations are too large to allow any firm conclusions. When it comes to political efficacy (self-confidence), on the other hand, a long-term upward trend is also found in Norway (Aardal 1999: 174), equivalent to what is found in Denmark and Sweden (Goul Andersen 1984c). The next question is what explains the long-term trends in political engagement and the low level of political apathy in the Scandinavian countries, and whether there are trends towards decline of full citizenship among groups that are less mobilized than previously, or among the less-educated who could be the victims of technological, economic and social changes taking place in contemporary society. We begin with an overall picture of the social variations in political engagement.

Social variations in political engagement – an overview

Political interest, political efficacy and participation in political discussions are strongly correlated variables and reveal roughly the same social variations. There are, however, some significant differences between the various aspects and between countries (Tables 2.2 and 2.3). Beginning with gender, it is a uniform finding across indicators and between countries that men are more politically engaged than women. But regardless of which aspects we consider, gender differences are smaller in Norway than in the two other countries – even though Sweden and Denmark have been

Table 2.2 Social variations in political interest. Proportions interested in politics, and deviation from population mean, 1990 (1987) (percentage points)

	Interested in politics			N		
	Sweden	*Norway*	*Denmark*	*Sweden*	*Norway*	*Denmark*
Whole population	53	59	62	1987	1773	1968
Men	+8	+5	+7	1033	934	954
Women	−9	−4	−6	954	839	1014
18–29 years	−4	−4	−1	492	483	384
30–39 years	+1	+6	−2	377	383	414
40–49 years	0	+1	+5	359	349	390
50–59 years	+1	0	+4	279	212	257
60–69 years	+3	+2	−1	274	195	267
70 years or more	0	+1	−3	206	151	256
Low education	−7	−10	−8	1089	885	905
Medium education	+1	0	+1	385	330	662
High education	+14	+19	+17	512	532	400
Unskilled worker	−16	−16	−14	285	215	288
Skilled worker	−7	−9	−1	220	150	153
Lower nonmanuals	−6	−3	−3	362	280	341
Intermediary level	+8	+15	+15	266	189	251
Higher nonmanuals	+16	+18	+22	183	199	141
Farmers	+1	−1	+8	41	55	70
Self-employed	+13	+6	+8	111	108	103
Multiple Classification Analysis (MCA): beta values[1]	beta coefficients					
Gender	0.13	0.18	0.18			
Age	0.06[ns]	0.09*	0.14			
Education	0.14	0.25	0.17			
Class	0.17	0.16	0.18			
Explained variance (%) R^2	9.6	15.1	13.3			

Notes:
1. Political interest measured on a four-point scale. Education is school education. Interaction effects are ignored (they are typically insignificant).
*Significant at the 5 per cent level.
[ns]not significant; all other beta values are significant at the 1 per cent level.

Table 2.3 Social variations in political efficacy and participation in political discussions. Mean scores, and deviations from population means 1990 (1987)

	Efficacy				Political discussion	
	Sweden:		Norway	Denmark	Norway	Denmark
	Influence	Competence				
Whole population	4.10	4.87	2.48	3.20	1.09	1.09
Men	+0.17	+0.31	+0.11	+0.30	+0.07	+0.13
Women	−0.21	−0.35	−0.11	−0.26	−0.07	−0.13
18–29 years	0.00	−0.17	+0.13	+0.04	+0.03	+0.15
30–39 years	+0.18	+0.12	+0.26	+0.20	+0.08	+0.08
40–49 years	+0.40	+0.21	+0.07	+0.34	+0.07	+0.05
50–59 years	+0.17	+0.06	−0.24	−0.09	−0.05	+0.02
60–69 years	−0.50	−0.14	−0.27	−0.24	−0.12	−0.17
70 years or more	−0.71	−0.09	−0.49	−0.51	−0.29	−0.31
Low education	−0.53	−0.41	−0.33	−0.43	−0.11	−0.15
Medium education	+0.05	+0.01	+0.04	+0.12	−0.05	+0.02
High education	+1.02	+0.82	+0.53	+0.79	+0.22	+0.30
Unskilled worker	−0.65	−0.67	−0.33	−0.62	−0.18	−0.06
Skilled worker	−0.48	−0.45	+0.02	0.00	−0.06	+0.09
Lower nonmanuals	−0.07	−0.17	+0.08	+0.07	+0.03	0.00
Intermediary level	+0.71	+0.53	+0.42	+0.69	+0.20	+0.29
Higher nonmanuals	+1.45	+1.05	+0.41	+1.05	+0.30	+0.23
Farmers	−0.50	+0.08	−0.05	+0.34	+0.02	+0.11
Self-employed	+0.57	+0.60	+0.18	+0.22	+0.09	+0.17
MCA analysis: beta[1]						
Gender	0.09*	0.14	0.08*	0.18	0.15	0.13
Age	0.12	0.06ns	0.08*	0.11	0.05ns	0.03*
Education	0.10*	0.10*	0.22	0.19	0.12	0.18
Class	0.29	0.29	0.19	0.26	0.23	0.13
Explained variance R^2	15.0	15.8	8.7	18.7	11.0	7.5

Wording:
Sweden:
'Do people like you have more or less opportunity than others to make politicians take regard of your demands?'
'Do you have more or less opportunity than others to understand what is happening in politics?' (Measured on a scale 0 (much less)–10 (much more))
Norway:
'Politics often is so complicated that ordinary people cannot understand what's going on' (Measured on a scale 1 (quite agree)–5 (quite disagree))
Denmark:
'Politics usually is so complicated that people like me cannot really understand what's going on' (Measured on a scale 1 (quite agree)–5 (quite disagree))
Norway:
'Do you often, sometimes or never discuss politics with friends and people you know?'
Denmark:
'Do you often, only rarely, or never discuss politics with friends?'

Notes:
1. Interaction effects are ignored.
*Significant at the 5 per cent level;
ns not significant; all other beta values are significant at the 1 per cent level.

forerunners in terms of labor market integration of women. At this place, we can only speculate about the possible political explanations of this.

Age effects are fairly uniform across countries, but differ significantly across variables. Our data confirm the conventional finding that young people are less politically interested than the middle-aged but in all three countries, the association is weak and insignificant.[7] And when it comes to efficacy, young people do not feel less efficacious than the population average; on the contrary, citizens below 50 years are much more politically self-confident than citizens aged 50 years or more – the only exception being the Swedish question on competence. This tendency is even more clear when we move to political discussions; at this point the Danish data even reveal a monotonously declining participation with age. The question was not posed in the Swedish citizenship survey, but from a 1993 survey on Swedish youth (Vogel 1994: 350) it appears that exactly the same pattern is found in Sweden.

Finally, it is a uniform finding that education and class have much stronger effects upon political engagement than other variables, and there remain significant effects of both factors in the multivariate analyses.[8] In Denmark, we may notice that farmers score far above average on all measures, in contrast to Norway and Sweden, reflecting the legacy of the unusually strong mobilization of Danish farmers since the mid-nineteenth century.

Class and gender mobilization

The Scandinavian countries have been among the most strongly class-mobilized countries in the world (Elvander 1981; Korpi 1981), and the interesting question is whether this has deteriorated in recent years. As far as the effects of gender mobilization are concerned, these have been analysed in more detail elsewhere (Togeby 1994; Raaum 1999); we shall briefly comment on the results below.

As far as class mobilization is concerned, a classical argument runs that the mobilization of class consciousness is at the same time a mobilization of political interest. Accordingly, declining class consciousness would imply a similar decline in political interest. The premise of declining class identification is fulfilled (see, for example, Borre and Goul Andersen 1997: ch. 5) but the association between working-class identification and political interest among workers has become weak and insignificant.[9] However, we do find, in Denmark at least, a class-specific decline of political interest among workers: in 1971 and 1979, the working-class–middle-class difference in the proportion of politically interested amounted to 15–16 percentage points; in 1994 and 1998, the difference was 22–23 percentage points (source: Danish Election Program; data not presented).[10] At any rate, we observe from Tables 2.2 and 2.3 that class effects on political engagement in Scandinavia are strong, going far beyond what is explained by education,

Table 2.4   Gender difference in proportions interested
in politics (percentage points)

Gender Gap (Women–Men)	Sweden 1987	Norway 1990	Denmark 1994
18–29 years	−9	−3	−15
30–39 years	−19	−8	−16
40–49 years	−23	−18	−13
50–59 years	−8	−12	−9
60 years or more	−23	−8	−11
Education			
Low	−19	−4	−12
Medium	−16	−10	−10
High	−12	−17	−19

Note: Ns approximately identical for men and women.

and our preliminary analysis suggests that in the last quarter of the twentieth century, this class difference has increased, with workers becoming
relatively less engaged in politics.

If class mobilization has turned into class demobilization, the recent
history of gender mobilization is much more of a success. The reduction of
gender differences in political engagement and political participation is
among the most universal findings in Scandinavian social research. It is
linked to the emergence of a new gender gap in party choice where women
vote slightly more leftist than men; in this respect, the gender gap has not
only been closed but has even been reversed (Karvonen and Selle 1995;
Togeby 1994; Goul Andersen 1984a; Borre and Goul Andersen 1997).

As evidenced in Table 2.2 above, gender differences in political engagement have not disappeared, however. Although the gender gap has narrowed
slightly (Goul Andersen 1984a), men remain more politically interested than
women, especially in Denmark. Furthermore, the proportions expressing
'much' interest in politics is about twice as high among men as among
women in all three countries and across social or demographic categories.
Earlier findings that the gender gap will disappear with generational replacement and rising education is also disproved (see Table 2.4). With the exception of the youngest generation in Norway, the gender gap is *not*
systematically lower among the young, or among the better-educated (see
also Vogel 1994; Oskarson and Oscarsson 1994).

Cognitive mobilization

From micro-level correlations it is tempting to draw the macro-level inference that as more and more people achieve higher education, the level of
political interest is bound to increase. This is one of the main arguments

underpinning the 'cognitive mobilization' thesis which has found empirical support in a number of countries (Kaase and Marsh 1979: 36; van Deth 1989: 282).

Unlike class and gender mobilization, cognitive mobilization does not involve higher levels of equality. On the contrary, a corollary of cognitive mobilization may be an increasing polarization between the better-educated and the less-educated in the 'information society'. In earlier times, lack of education may have been compensated for by adult socialization where people became politically engaged as they gained more life experience and came into contact with different fields of society in general, as well as with the political system. In the information society, on the other hand, people who have only been educated to the statutory minimum may be much more severely handicapped and excluded from knowledge – perhaps even from jobs. However, such polarization may be counteracted upon by the welfare state if it provides education in civic competence.

This leaves us with four quite plausible hypotheses with different predictions. First, a 'cognitive mobilization' model predicts that at the aggregate level, political engagement increases as an effect of higher levels of education; at the individual level, the differences between educational groups remain constant over time. An 'adult socialization' model predicts that differences in political engagement between educational groups will decline over the life span. A 'polarization model' predicts an increasing polarization between the better- and the less-educated, especially among the younger generations. And finally, a 'welfare model' predicts the very opposite – that is, that the younger generations are the least polarized. Although the tests are restricted to Denmark[11] and not sufficiently strong to allow for strict theoretical inferences, they may at least guide the analysis and allow for some conclusions.

Beginning with the aggregate level, the cognitive mobilization thesis does not conform too well with historical data. As revealed by the sample sizes (N) for Denmark in Table 2.5, most of the educational revolution in Denmark has taken place in the 1980s and 1990s. In 1971, only 19 per cent of the adult Danish population had more than nine years of basic education, and only some 5 per cent had passed a high school exam ('gymnasium'). In 1994, the figures were 55 and 21 per cent, respectively. However, since the mid-1970s, there has been little – if any – increase in political interest in the three countries. Turning to the individual level, we may compare the association between education and political interest on the basis of the election studies (Table 2.5). Again, the mobilization thesis is contradicted by data as the association with education is weakened, from a difference between the highest and the lowest group of 37 percentage points in 1971 to 21 percentage points in 1998. These data also seem to contradict the polarization hypothesis. This hypothesis may still seem to be confirmed by the fact that educational differences in political interest

Table 2.5 Age, education and political interest, Denmark 1971–1998. Proportions interested in Politics (percentages)

Basic education	Interested in politics					N				
	1971	1979	1990	1994	1998	1971	1979	1990	1994	1998
Low: 7–9 years	55	55	54	56	64	1053	1201	905	905	705
Medium: 10 years	74	67	63	64	69	193	484	662	681	675
High: 12 years	92	85	80	79	85	50	229	400	434	613
High–low	37	30	26	23	21					

Source: Election surveys from the Danish Election Program

Table 2.6 Age, education and efficacy (subjective competence). Mean values on a 1–5 scale (Denmark and Norway 1990) and 0–10 scale (Sweden 1987)

Education	Denmark				Norway				Sweden			
	18–29	30–39	40–49	50+	18–29	30–39	40–49	50+	18–29	30–39	40–49	50+
Low	2.92	2.90	3.06	2.61	2.35	2.33	2.21	1.90	4.25	4.38	4.59	4.53
Medium	2.87	3.25	3.76	3.43	1.95	2.63	2.58	2.51	4.53	4.90	4.78	5.26
High	3.75	4.07	4.31	4.07	2.97	3.18	3.09	2.69	5.46	5.63	5.92	5.91
High–Low	.78	1.07	1.25	1.46	.62	.85	.88	.79	1.21	1.25	1.33	1.38

are highest among the young (data not presented). However, this finding has been consistent since 1971, indicating that this should rather be explained from an adult socialization model: The better-educated achieve political interest from education, the less-educated from life experience.

An even more surprising finding is the association between age, education and efficacy in the citizenship surveys, which is presented in Table 2.6. Although the interaction effect is statistically significant only in Denmark (at the 1 per cent level), all three countries reveal a common pattern, that is, the effects of education are smallest among the young. This is in line with the predictions from the 'welfare' model and contradicts the three others; but there are, of course, possible alternative explanations (such as, for example, media influence). Most importantly, perhaps, our data falsify the intuitively plausible assumption that there is a polarization among the young. The data indicate that within the Scandinavian welfare states, it has so far been possible to avoid such a polarization; but we cannot establish that this is *because* of the welfare state or because of the efforts of the school system to provide young people with a civic competence. Besides, more recent data indicates that vocational training has an increasing impact on efficacy, at least at the national and European level (Goul Andersen et al., forthcoming).

Welfare state mobilization?

The welfare states might play an important role in political engagement in yet another way, particularly in affecting the interest aspect (rather than efficacy). Objectively, citizens in the Scandinavian welfare states have more of a 'stake' in politics than citizens in most other countries. Not only are the Scandinavian welfare states universal ones with large 'constituencies'; they also assign unusually high priorities to welfare services. This enlarges the constituencies and furthermore means that nearly one-third of the workforce are employed in the public sector – that is, are directly dependent on political decisions. If political engagement is affected by having a stake in politics, this should be unusually strong in Scandinavia, and this might explain the relatively high level of political interest in these countries. If not, it questions a widespread assumption in the literature on political engagement.

A first test case is families with pre-school children in Sweden and Denmark.[12] By receiving child allowances and (in most cases) public child care, these families are among the main beneficiaries of the welfare state – and more so than in other European countries (Goul Andersen and Christiansen 1991). In addition, the Scandinavian programs of maternity leave are the most generous in the world. Thus, from the point of view of having a stake in politics, these families should be unusually interested in politics. From the point of view of resources, on the other hand, having small children is likely to deflect attention from other activities, including politics. However, such an effect should be larger on participation than on political engagement (Verba, Schlozman and Brady 1995 assume that time is a pure resource factor which does not affect motivation).

It turns out, however, that the effect of having pre-school children is insignificant when we control for age, education and social class. A further division between users and non-users of public child care adds nothing to the conclusion: In Denmark, users appear slightly more interested than non-users, in Sweden it is the opposite way around. But none of the recorded differences are significant (Table 2.7). Further divisions by number of children, or between persons having no children and persons having older children, do not change the result. And assumptions that there might be an effect among mothers which might be concealed by opposite effects among fathers (a well-known relationship when speaking of occupational career patterns) is also disproved. In short, unless positive and negative effects of having pre-school children balance each other, there simply are no effects. Apparently, political interest is not a matter of leisure time, nor is it a matter of having personal interests in the outcome of policies.

As stated above, the large proportion of public employees is another distinctive characteristic of the Scandinavian welfare states which adds another dimension to the sociopolitical cleavages in these countries (Goul Andersen and Borre 1997: 114–59), and in Denmark, there was also a marked political mobilization among public employees between the 1970s and the mid-1980s (Goul Andersen 1979; Svensson and Togeby 1986). But the impact upon political interest is very small (Table 2.8) and partly

Table 2.7   Political interest by having pre-school children and by use of public child-care facilities, among 20–44 years old. Denmark 1990 and Sweden 1987. Percentages expressing 'much' or 'some' political interest, and eta and beta coefficients (MCA analysis)

	Sweden	Denmark	Sweden N	Denmark N
Total	52	63	992	976
Without children 0–6 years	52	66	708	659
Having children 0–6 years	53	56	284	317
User of public childcare	50	60	216	213
Non-user of public childcare	63	49	68	104
Multiple Classification Analysis:[1]				
Eta	0.07	0.09		
Beta	0.06	0.05		

Notes:
1. Effect of family/childcare type: 0: No pre-school children; 1: Non-user of public childcare;
2. User of public childcare, controlled for gender, age, education, social class and employment, status.

Table 2.8 Sector variations in political interest. Proportions interested in politics. (percentages)

	Interested in politics			N		
	Sweden	Norway	Denmark	Sweden	Norway	Denmark
Empl. in private sector	50	58	65	848	730	715
Empl. in public sector	55	66	67	593	420	472
Manuals, private sector	42	48	58	350	250	253
Manuals, public sector	42	40	48	143	80	112
Nonman., private sector	53	63	69	347	328	288
Nonman., public sector	59	72	72	447	331	353
Employed or students	53	61	67	1506	1283	1314
Unemployed	37	51	41	27	53	111
Effect of unemployment (Beta)[1]	0.03	0.01	0.06			
Housewives	37	56	50	35	109	42
Pensioners, total	56	58	57	393	275	499
'disabled' (<60 years)	46	67	60	33	45	61
'early retired' (60–66 years)	61	58	53	94	36	117
old-age pensioners (67 years +)	56	56	58	266	194	321

Note: 1. MCA analysis, controlling for gender, age, education and social class. In Denmark $p = 0.036$; in the other countries, the effect is insignificant, due to small Ns.

explained by different composition of manuals and non manuals in the two sectors. In all three countries, non manuals in the public sector are a little bit more politically interested than their private sector counterparts; but the difference is negligible.

Finally, an increasing segment of the population receive their main income from the public sector as publicly supported – either being retired or unemployed. In all three countries, the official age of retirement was 67 years at the time of interviewing but the systems for early retirement were very different, Denmark being the only country with a system of early retirement allowance for the 60–66 years old. Nevertheless, other systems to some degree serve the same functions in the other countries, and to obtain as commensurable data as possible, we have chosen to distinguish by age rather than according to program. Citizenship and political participation among the unemployed is treated separately in chapter 10; here, it is sufficient to note that the unemployed are generally less politically interested than the employed, whereas there are only small deviations from population means among the various categories of retired people. Unsurprisingly from a consideration of political resources, we may thus note that having a stake in politics by being publicly supported does not lead to an increase in political engagement.

Conclusions

Political engagement may be a precondition of political participation but this is not the aspect which interests us here. What is more important for our analysis is the level and distribution of political interest and apathy, and the level of efficacy as characteristics of the Scandinavian political systems. At these points, the Scandinavian democracies can by no means be described as 'activist' democracies, but it nevertheless appears that political interest is relatively high, in particular in Denmark, and that political apathy is a rare phenomenon in all three countries. This does not seem to any considerable extent to be a consequence of people having a stake in politics as consumers of public services or as public employees, nor does it seem to be related to cognitive mobilization. Rather, gender mobilization may have an effect, and class mobilization may have left a legacy which does seem, however, to be in decline. What probably matters more is the relatively high degree of equality ensured by the welfare state, as well as the conscious attempt to teach children and young people to become active and critical citizens. At any rate, it seems that even some of the potentially weak groups among the young feel a relatively high degree of political efficacy and are very active as participants in political discussions. What is uncertain at present is whether this can survive in the 'knowledge society'.

3
Electoral Participation

Introduction: high levels of political engagement but declining electoral participation?

Until the mid-1990s, little attention was paid to nonvoting and non-voters in Scandinavia.[1] The reasons are obvious. In the first place, the social and other determinants of nonvoting were thought to be well known and stable (Korpi 1981; Valen and Aardal 1983) – apart from gender differences, which received some interest when the gender gap reversed in the 1980s. Secondly, survey data on the levels of abstention are not very reliable (Granberg and Holmberg 1991) and make it difficult to analyse nonvoting in general election studies.[2] But most importantly, studying nonvoting seemed of little relevance because of the high turnout rates. Unlike the USA, where studies of nonvoting mushroomed as a response to declining turnout in the 1970s (for example, Wolfinger and Rosenstone 1980; Burnham 1980; Boyd 1981; Abramson and Aldrich 1982; Avey 1989), Scandinavian figures were stable or even increasing when political trust declined in the 1970s. Thus, Scandinavia was only interesting as high-turnout countries in comparative studies of the determinants of nonvoting (Jackman 1987). What was to be explained was why turnout was so *high* in Scandinavia (Pettersen 1989).

However, by the end of the 1980s, there were signs of change, and in the 1990s, turnout in parliamentary elections has declined in all Nordic countries (Table 3.1). The most dramatic change has taken place in Finland, but the three other countries have also experienced a clear decline from the 1970s to the 1990s. In Norway, the participation rate of 75.8 per cent in 1993 was the lowest recorded since 1927. The Danish figure of 82.8 per cent in the 1990 election was the lowest since 1953. For a decade (four elections 1973–82), electoral participation in Sweden was above 90 per cent. But in 1998, it dropped to only 81.4 per cent.

The trend in Scandinavia resembles the general European trend where electoral participation, on average, has declined by some five percentage

Table 3.1   Average electoral participation in parliamentary elections, 1960s to 1990s (percentages of voting population)

	Average 1960s	Average 1970s	Average 1980s	Average 1990s
Denmark	87.3	87.7	86.0	84.5
Norway	82.8	81.6	83.1	77.1
Sweden	86.4	90.4	89.1	85.0
Finland[1]	85.0	81.1	78.7	70.8
Simple average	85.4	85.2	84.2	79.4

Note: 1. Finnish citizens living outside Finland have been omitted. Including these would bring the figure for the 1990s down to 67.5 per cent.

points from 1960–64 to 1985–89, with a downward trend continuing in the 1990s (Lane and Ersson 1991: 182; Topf 1995a; IDEA 1997; Franklin 1996; Lijphart 2000).

Until recently, these emerging trends were typically ignored (in Denmark) or interpreted as deviations explained by short-term factors relating to an individual election (Aardal and Valen 1995: ch. 3; Narud and Valen 1998). Only Swedish researchers were somewhat concerned about the long-term trends. However, this view has changed markedly in recent years, further stimulated by the low levels of participation in local and European elections, and attention is increasingly directed to long-term interpretations and explanations of the decline (Valen, Aardal and Berglund 1996; Bjørklund 1999: ch. 9; Teorell and Westholm 1999). It is clear that, it is now a pertinent research problem to examine whether we are facing a long-term trend, and to look for macro-level changes that could explain such a decline.

Macro-level explanations of declining turnout

Explaining nonvoting is a long-standing research tradition but at this place, we shall concentrate only on plausible macro-level explanations of declining turnout from which we try to spell out micro-level implications that can be tested against available data, leaving aside theories about institutional and country differences.

Beginning with *social change*, there are several factors that might lead to declining electoral participation (or declining political participation in general):

- A long-term trend towards increasing marginalization in the labor market;
- More single-person households;
- Class demobilization of the working class.

A second factor is *value change*. It is well known already from classical studies (Campbell et al. 1960) that voting depend on a feeling of civic obligation to vote. But a number of such values may be declining or changing. If people come to vote mainly for instrumental reasons, then they will also tend to recognize the 'voting paradox' so often discussed in rational choice theory.

Finally, there is *political change*. A first argument sounds that as politics becomes more complex, more people tend to withdraw entirely from politics; besides, the massive provision of entertainment and leisure activities makes it increasingly tempting to do so. However, as an explanation of decline in aggregate turnout, this argument can be ruled out from the very beginning; as we have seen in chapter 2, there are no signs that people become less politically engaged (cf. Bennulf and Hedberg 1999: 83).

Another classical political argument claims that if people become indifferent towards party alternatives, they may become less inclined to vote, even if they are politically engaged (Holmberg 1990: 215; Korpi 1981: 48–9, 76; Aardal and Valen 1995: ch. 3; Franklin 1996). For instance, a long-term feeling of indifference towards policy alternatives may develop if politics at the national level becomes less important, or if parties become increasingly similar, as they will be, according to new and classical variants of Kirchheimer's (1966) famous 'catch-all' party theory (see, for example, Pedersen 1989; Buksti 1989; Katz and Mair 1995). Finally, it may become increasingly difficult for parties to aggregate more complex cleavage structures and interest or value conflicts. One implication is that people may simply be cross-pressured. However, at least in the USA, cross-pressure does not seem to affect nonvoting at the individual level (Wolfinger and Rosenstone 1980: 35). Another possibility is that people may feel that they don't have any possibilities of being represented at all. Such a feeling of not being represented is normally associated with political distrust (Goul Andersen 1992b). In short, this explanation presupposes that nonvoting is a sort of protest among people who are not indifferent to politics as such.

These, then, are the leading hypotheses, which we examine along with a few ad hoc hypotheses below. From our overall perspective in this book, we would expect class demobilization, representation problems and value change to be the most plausible. The opposite holds for the theory of marginalization because this cannot explain why the trend is similar even in Norway, where unemployment has remained unusually low.[3] The hypotheses are listed alongside with their micro-level implications in Figure 3.1. To the degree that these implications are confirmed, we also become more confident in interpreting the decline in electoral participation as more than short-term fluctuations. Finally, since the citizenship surveys were conducted between elections, the information on nonvoting is likely to be quite unreliable; therefore, we have used data from election surveys as a supplement.

Type of explanation	Macro-level hypothesis	Micro-level implications	Comments
1. Social change	1.1 Class demobilization	Strong and increasing class differences	
	1.2 Labor market marginalization	Strong causal effect on unemployment	Difficult to explain similarities between countries
	1.3 More single-person households	Strong causal effect on marital status	
2. Value change	2.1 Declining sense of obligation to vote	Strong correlation between voting and perception of civic duty to vote	Difficult to determine the direction of causality
3. Political change	3.1 Politics becoming more complex because of internationalization and changing policy problems	Declining political engagement (including efficacy), and/or increasing social inequality in political engagement	Rejected. Predictions disproved in chapter 2
	3.2 Politics is becoming less relevant because parties are becoming increasingly alike (because of 'catch-all' strategies, or because of declining power)	Strong causal effect of the feeling that parties are alike	
	3.3.a Parties unable to aggregate and represent new interests: Cross-pressure 3.3.b Parties unable to aggregate and represent new interests: Distrust	Nonvoting widespread even among politically interested the same + a. strong effect of distrust c. Nonvoting related to policy (minority) position	

Figure 3.1   Macro-level explanations of declining electoral participation and their empirical implications at the micro level: an overview

Electoral mobilization and class mobilization

As high turnout rates are normally assumed to reflect small social differences and high-class mobilization (Korpi 1981; Rosenstone and Hansen 1993), we may begin by looking at the historical relationship between class mobilization and electoral mobilization. Figure 3.2 presents the turnout rates for the Scandinavian countries back to 1920. Although Norway was the first Scandinavian country to achieve a democratic constitution (1814) as well as parliamentary rule (1884), Denmark was the leading country in terms of the mobilization of voters.[4] Denmark had reached the 70 per cent

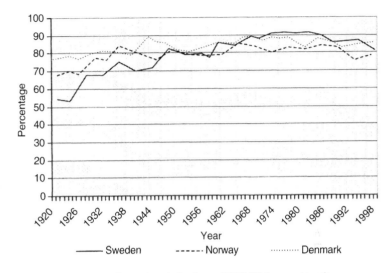

Figure 3.2 Turnout rates in national elections, 1920–98 (percentages)

Sources: Heidar (1983); Thomsen (1984); Holmberg (1990) and statistical yearbooks.

turnout threshold already by 1909 whereas Norway was to wait until 1930 and Sweden until 1936.

From 1970, Sweden took the lead, and in the four elections from 1973 to 1982, more than 90 per cent of all adult Swedes went to the ballot. Norway never reached that level but had a stable rate of participation until the sudden decline in 1993. In Denmark, turnout culminated in the six elections from 1966 to 1977 – a period of intense political conflict characterized by the emergence of several new parties (in 1973, the number of parties represented in the Danish parliament doubled from five to ten).[5] But in the 1980s and 1990s, participation has declined, as compared to that period.

Now, the question is how these figures relate to class mobilization and demobilization. It has usually been claimed that class differences disappeared only gradually alongside with the spread of wealth and the development of the welfare state (Korpi 1981; Holmberg 1990). However, we have reanalysed the unique Swedish statistical data, which contain detailed information on the occupation of voters and non-voters until the 1950s. Our analysis suggests that the relationship between class mobilization and electoral mobilization is more complex, and that class mobilization of workers is older than commonly believed. The existing analyses are based on too highly aggregated categories which means that the picture becomes blurred – by, for example, the social classification of maids as workers, the electoral mobilization of women, and by changes in the sectoral composition of the working class (Korpi 1981: 53). If the figures are disaggregated by gender and trade (Table 3.2), we observe that among *men*, except farm

Table 3.2   Electoral participation, by class, Sweden 1924–1991. 1924–1960: male voters; 1960–1991: men and women (abstention rates in percentages)

	1. Farmers	2. Self-employed	3. Nonmanual employees	4. (Other) Manual workers	5. Farm and Forest Workers	Class Difference: 4 − 3
1924	36.6	37.1	31.7	40.3	52.8	8.6
1936	16.3	21.0	18.4	21.9	28.0	3.5
1948	11.6	11.9	11.2	16.6	23.0	5.4
1960	9.6	8.9	8.4	12.4	19.1	4.0
1960 (s)	9.4	15.3	13.1	15.6	—	2.5
1970	7.8	11.2	9.4	13.5	—	4.1
1982	10.3	7.6	6.1	10.2	—	4.1
1991	13.3	15.5*	9.9	16.0	—	6.1
Change 1936–1991	3.0	5.5	9.5	5.9	—	−2.6

Note: By distinguishing between 'farm and forest workers' and 'other manual workers' we seek to leave out the effect of the changing composition of the working class. From 1960, 'farm and forest workers' cannot be identified but constitute a negligible group anyway. By including men only (1936–1958) we seek to leave out the effect of women's electoral mobilization. From 1960, the gender difference is insignificant anyway. That is, the 1991 figures would be roughly the same if they had only referred to male workers outside agriculture.

Sources: 1924–1960: *Statistical Yearbook*. Based on voter's registrar (or a 10 per cent sample). Recoded by the authors. The figures refer to men only. Sons working at their father's farm are excluded.

   1960–1991: Survey data; Proportions are weighted by correction factor. Quoted from Holmberg (1990: 209); Gilljam and Holmberg (1993: 67); and Statistika Centralbyrån (1993).

and forest workers, social class differences were already quite small in the 1920s, and at least from 1936. Thus, the difference between the male (urban) working class and the new middle class was only 8.6 percentage points by 1924 and as low as 3.5 percentage points in 1936 – that is, lower than the 6.1 percentage points we observe in 1991.[6]

This means that there has been a *general* mobilization of voters in the 1940s, 1950s and 1960s but not a *class-specific* mobilization of workers. It is the disappearance of maids and farm and forest workers (and to some degree the electoral mobilization of female workers) that accounts for the apparent reduction of class inequality since the 1930s. Briefly, this means that class mobilization even in Sweden is a relatively old phenomenon, which may have culminated already around 1960 when turnout rates were still quite modest.

This reinterpretation brings the Swedish data more in line with a Danish analysis of nonvoting in the 1960 election (Jeppesen and Meyer 1964) which concluded, on the basis of census data, that class differences were negligible – a finding that was later supported by ecological estimations (Thomsen 1987). This means that class mobilization does not seem very important for the increasing turnout after 1960 – or, alternatively, that class demobilization may have started earlier than previously believed.

Social structural variations

In Table 3.3, some of the analyses of the social variations in nonvoting from the Swedish Election Program are replicated for Denmark and Norway on the basis of election studies and the Norwegian citizenship survey, respectively. The Danish and the Norwegian data are based on respondents' information only, and are weighted to match the proportion of non-voters in the population.[7] This involves weights around 2.0 and 1.7, respectively, for non-voters. The Swedish data are more reliable because they are checked against voters' registers and subsequently weighted. At worst, the Danish data may give an exaggerated impression of nonvoting among groups where nonvoting is regarded as socially acceptable behavior.

Before returning to the question of class demobilization, we may notice that the gender gap in electoral participation has been closed or even reversed – although in Denmark, this apparently did not happen until the 1990s.[8] Age differences are more surprising since they seem to be increasing (although somewhat more convincingly in terms of percentage differences than in terms of odds ratios) both in Denmark and Sweden. All three countries reveal the conventional life cycle pattern of increasing electoral partic-ipation until about 50–59 years and a certain decline among the oldest citizens. But it seems that nonvoting in Denmark and Sweden is becoming more and more common among the young, to some extent even among those in the 30–39 years category.[9] The Norwegian 1990 data are inconclu-sive but Norwegian data from the 1990s also reveal an extraordinary decline among the young – without any signs of declining political interest among the young (Aardal 1999: 203–6). Even though most age differences are still to be explained by life cycle effects, there are relatively clear indica-tions of what can either be a period effect among the young, or the begin-ning of a generational change.

Differences between education groups are a little surprising from the point of view that lower participation is tantamount to increasing polarization. Danish and Swedish data show rather the opposite: at least as measured by odds ratios, the differences between education categories seems to be declin-ing rather than increasing. However, this is consistent with the decreasing polarization in political interest, which we observed in chapter 2.[10]

When it comes to class polarization, until recently the results were remarkably different. In Denmark, class polarization seems to be increasing dramatically. Especially among unskilled workers, nonvoting shows a marked increase. By 1994, some 29 per cent were abstainers – that is, about three times the rate among non-manual employees. Unfortunately, the Danish figures are the least reliable, due to strong weighting, but there is

Table 3.3   Social variations in electoral participation at the national level. Abstention rates (percentages)

	Denmark				Sweden				Norway
	1966	*1979*	*1990*	*1994*	*1976*	*1985*	*1994*	*1998*	*1989*
Gender:									
Men	10	12	15	15	8	11	14	20	18
Women	13	17	19	16	9	10	12	17	15
Age:[1] (years)									
18–29	13	21	23	26	12	16	16	26	25
30–39	11	12	18	18	8	8	14	20	14
40–49	10	9	13	12	3	7	10	20	12
50–59	11	7	11	6	7	7	11	13	17
60–69	12	11	11	8	7	8	10	9	10
70 or more		20	21	18	12	13	15	17	12
Education[2]									
Low	12	16	18	18	—	3	16	20	18
Medium	9	14	17	14	—	10	13	20	13
High	6	8	15	12	—	4	8	12	14
Occupation[3]									
Unskilled worker	12	21	24	29	10	15	17	25	21
Skilled worker	12	16	15	15					15
Nonmanual employee	7	10	13	10					15
Farmers	8	11	4	7	6	5	10	12	21
Other self-employed	11	8	20	12					11

Notes:
1. Sweden: 18–30 years (weighted average of 18–22 and 23–30), 31–40 years, 41–50 years, etc. Denmark 1966: 50–64 years and 65 years or more.
2. Denmark: Basic education; Figures for Sweden also include vocational training.
3. Sweden: Working class vs. middle class.

Source: Denmark and Sweden: Election Surveys. Norway: Citizenship survey 1990 (referring to 1989 election).

Sweden: Ns around 3000. Calculated proportions corrected by weight factor. Checked against voter's registers. *Source:* Bennulf and Hedberg 1999 (see also Statistika Centralbyrån (1993); Gilljam and Holmberg (1990, 1993)).

Denmark (approx. Ns for whole sample): 1966: 15000; 1979: 2000; 1990: 3000; 1994: 4000. Respondent's information only. Danish and Norwegian data are quite heavily weighted.

no doubt that class polarization has increased, as compared to the situation in 1960, when census data revealed virtually no class differences at all. The Swedish data do not include a distinction between skilled and unskilled workers. But for the working class as a whole, the figures in Table 3.3 reveal a significant change in percentage differences but less so in odds ratios. However, if we compare with the older data presented in Table 3.2, we certainly do observe an increased class polarization also in Sweden from the 1960s until now. Besides, a more comprehensive analysis of all elections 1976–98 (Bennulf and Hedberg 1999) reveal a clearer picture of change than the four elections selected for Table 3.3. Although our data do not allow any definite conclusions, we may hypothesize that in the last third of the twentieth century, class polarization in terms of voting has been increasing rather significantly at least in Denmark and Sweden.

Labor market marginalization and family change

As far as labor market marginalization is concerned, our data were collected at a time when this was only a serious problem in Denmark, and in Norway, it has remained a much smaller problem throughout the 1990s than in the other countries. At the same time, this means that marginalization can hardly explain the general trend across countries. However, the Danish data also indicate that the difference in abstention rates between the employed and those who are marginalized in the labor market is relatively small.

Table 3.4 reveals the effect of labor market position on nonvoting in Denmark in 1994 (based on weighted data from the Danish Election Program). We have not only distinguished between the employed and the unemployed but also sought to single out disablement pensioners. Because nearly all Danes are entitled to retire on an early retirement allowance from the age of 60, and since the type of retirement for this age group may depend on quite arbitrary factors, we have collapsed all groups living from transfer income other than unemployment benefits and simply divided by age so that all retired people aged less than 60 are classified as 'disabled' and those aged 60 years or more are classified as 'early retired'. The interesting group when we speak of marginalization is, of course, the former one.

The data in Table 3.4 confirm the appropriateness of this solution which maximize the inter-class variations (disablement pensioners and unemployed aged more than 60 years have very low levels of nonvoting), and since the sample is quite large, we are able to draw relatively firm conclusions. Further, it may be added that the survey was conducted just at the time when long-term unemployment was at its highest, both in absolute terms and as a percentage of total unemployment (Goul Andersen 1996a).

Table 3.4 Labor market position and nonvoting. Danish Election Study 1994

	Denmark 1994 *per cent non-voters*	*N*
Employed	15	2164
Unemployed < 60 years	23	300
Pensioners < 60 years ('disabled')	26	141
Transfer income, 60–66 years ('early retired')	6	238
Old-age pensioners	16	718

It turns out that the unemployed have significantly higher rates of non-voting that the employed, and among the 'disabled', 26 per cent abstain from voting. Among the early retired and among old-age pensioners, on the other hand, there are no signs of low participation. However, the unemployed and the disabled are recruited disproportionately from the ranks of the working class, in particular unskilled workers. We cannot control for former class position as far as the disabled are concerned, but it may be noticed that the proportion of non-voters remains below the level among unskilled workers. As far as the unemployed are concerned, we have made a large number of controls, which show that when we control for class, age and education, most of the effect of unemployment evaporates. Although a small but insignificant effect remains, we may safely conclude that labor market marginalization is not a relevant explanation of the macro-level changes in electoral participation in Denmark.[11]

Another social change, which could affect the level of nonvoting, is family change. Because of increasing divorce rates and aging populations, there is a growing proportion of single-member households. The association between marital status and nonvoting is indicated on the basis of results from the Norwegian citizenship survey and the Danish 1994 election survey in Table 3.5.[12] The results confirm the conventional finding that single persons are less inclined to vote, although in Norway, it is only among people aged 30 years or more.[13]

Now, as mentioned, we are not interested in explaining individual variations in electoral participation as such, and to the extent that marital status reflects some unmeasurable psychological characteristics that also affect political participation, it is not a very interesting variable since the causal effect on participation would be spurious. However, it turns out that, unlike voting, political engagement in the two countries is *not* affected by marital status. This strongly indicates that living together *as such* reinforces the propensity to vote – for example, because it strengthens

Table 3.5 Marital status, social network and percentage of non-voters in Denmark and Norway

	Denmark		Norway		N			
	Married	*Single*	*Married*	*Single*				
18–29 years	20	30	25	26	377	472	230	226
30 years +	10	20	10	25	2057	983	972	284
Total	11	23	13	26	2434	1455	1202	511
	Strong network	*Weak network*	*Strong network*	*Weak network*		*N*		
Total	13	17	14	21	1279	624	1187	526

compliance with the norm that one ought to vote (for Sweden, this is confirmed by an analysis of the behavior of spouses in Teorell and Westholm 1999). Thus, other things being equal, an increasing number of single-person (or rather single-adult) households is likely to lead to lower levels of electoral participation. However, until now there has not been a very great increase in single-person households in Scandinavia – in other words, this cannot explain much of the aggregate decline in turnout so far.

Much the same can be said about social network factors. The Danish and the Norwegian survey contained four nearly identical questions about social networks, which have been added to an index.[14] It turns out from Table 3.5 that such factors do have small but significant effects on electoral participation in Norway whereas in Denmark, the impact seems to be just below significance (on the unweighted data). In both countries, the effects on nonvoting were a bit strengthened when controlled for other factors such as class, age and education. However, there is nothing to indicate that social networks are weakening in the Scandinavian societies (rather the contrary, see Martinussen 1994) so this does not appear to be a possible explanation either.

Political change: representation, distrust and indifference

As mentioned, we can leave out the hypothesis that people abstain from voting because of the increasing complexity of politics. The implication that political interest and efficacy affect nonvoting may be correct but the premise that people should become less interested in politics or feel less efficacious was falsified in chapter 2. The remaining political hypotheses are more difficult to test. In particular, we have no way of testing the cross-pressure hypotheses: that people increasingly feel cross-pressured because parties are becoming more and more unable to aggregate issue positions. However, in general this hypothesis has found little empirical support (Wolfinger and Rosenstone 1980: 35), and in a highly plausible test case: The Norwegian 1993 election where voters were strongly cross-pressured by the EU issue, Narud and Valen (1998) concluded that cross-pressure was not a very relevant explanation.

The possibility of testing the propositions is a little better when it comes to the suggestions that people vote less because parties are becoming more alike, or because they increasingly distrust politicians.[15] Thus, in the Danish 1990 citizenship survey the respondents were asked whether they considered disagreements between parties as genuine or as tactically determined, and about their general trust in politicians. As demonstrated in Table 3.6, however, the perception that parties are different has only a negligible impact upon nonvoting. Political distrust, on the other hand, is associated with nonvoting (but even this uncontroversial finding vanishes if we control for feeling of civic duty to vote which is introduced in the

Table 3.6 Political interest, political distrust, political indifference and nonvoting. (abstention rate in percentages)

Danish Citizenship Survey 1990		*Political intrerest*	
		High (N)	*Low (N)*
High trust	Parties are different	4 (199)	16 (51)
	Parties are not different	6 (167)	14 (73)
Low trust	Parties are different	7 (302)	24 (122)
	Parties are not different	12 (386)	27 (312)

Wording: (trust): 'In general, how much trust do you have in politicians in Parliament?' (indifference): A says: 'All in all, there is little difference between what the large parties want. Disagreement between the parties is more attributable to their aspirations to be in office.' B says: 'There is considerable disagreement between what the political parties want. That's why it is sometimes difficult to reach agreement.'

following subsection). Although the validity of the question of indifference is questionable (as it may measure perceptions, rather than feelings of indifference), the data cannot confirm that distrust or indifference are major determinants of absenteeism. Even though this does not constitute a definitive test, the data do reduce the plausibility of the political explanations.

Value change: declining civic virtues

Even though some tests were not definitive, the social and political explanations of declining turnout discussed above did not appear very convincing. This leaves us with value explanations as a possibility, that is, the proposition that declining participation in elections reflect a decline in the norm that as a citizen, one should vote in elections. This assumption is consistent with our empirical data. Findings from the Danish citizenship survey presented in Table 3.7 indicate that the proportion of non-voters increases from 7 per cent among the huge majority who regard voting as an important civic virtue to 58 per cent among those who consider it less important or not important at all (values 1 to 5 on a scale from 1 to 10).

This result, however, which is in accordance with classic findings concerning duty to vote (Lewin 1970: 64–7), is open to all standard objections concerning the direction of causality: are abstainers simply legitimizing their behavior? At least, the weighted figures presented in Table 3.7 may be misleading. As it is likely that the propensity to give an incorrect answer is smaller among those who do not consider voting as a civic virtue, weighting may yield an exaggerated account of the effect. Therefore, the table also includes the unweighted results – which may, however, be biased in the opposite direction.

But can we interpret the correlation above as a 'value effect'? There are at least some observations which may justify such an interpretation. If we are

Table 3.7 Perception of voting as civic virtue and nonvoting (abstention rate in percentages), Denmark 1990

	Non-voters		N
	Weighted	*Unweighted*	
Not very important (values 1 through 5)	58	38	139
Rather important (values 6 through 8)	22	11	259
Very important (values 9 and 10)	7	3	1497

Source: Citizenship Survey 1990. Data refer to the 1988 election. Non-voters are weighted by 2.04; voters are weighted by 0.92. Unweighted Ns. As those who do not consider voting as a civic virtue may be more likely to report correctly on their voting behavior, unweighted proportions are also indicated.

Table 3.8 Age and perception of voting as a civic virtue (percentages)

Age	Very important virtue to vote[1]		Voting most important virtue[2]
	Denmark	*Sweden*	*Norway*
18–29 years	70	55	12
30–39 years	76	72	15
40–49 years	80	74	17
50–59 years	79	82	21
60–69 years	85	79	15
70+ years	82	82	21

Notes:
1. Values 9 or 10 on a scale from 0 (not important at all) to 10 (in Denmark 1 to 10).
2. Most important or second most important among eight listed virtues.

facing value change, it is natural to assume that it will appear as a generational difference, as seemed to be the case with nonvoting. It was noted above that there are no signs of a decline in political interest among the young. But, according to Table 3.8, young people are much less inclined to consider voting an important civic virtue than the elderly. In the absence of longitudinal data, such cross-sectional data are compatible with both a life cycle interpretation (people learn to appreciate the act of voting as they grow older) and a generational interpretation (among the younger generations, there are different values concerning civic duties and obligations). However, even though there may be a life cycle effect embodied in our data, we may infer from cohort analyses corncering value change (Gundelach and Riis 1992) that there has indeed been a value change towards more individualistic values during the 1980s. Thus, we feel a little more confident in interpreting at least some of the difference between age groups as a generational effect (see Topf 1995a for equivalent findings in other surveys).

Furthermore, a replication of the Swedish citizenship survey in 1997 confirms that also at the aggregate level, the perception of voting as a civic virtue has declined – and declined more than any of the other virtues that were listed. Furthermore, it turned out that not only did it have a strong impact on voting (in municipal elections), but that it was also able to explain most of the effect of other variables, except party identification (Teorell and Westholm 1999).[16] Now, this would also be the case if the causal order was the opposite, that is, if perception of voting as a civic virtue was a post hoc rationalization of nonvoting. However, from a mail follow-up of the 1997 citizenship study in relation to the 1998 election, it turned out that the perception of voting as a civic virtue was also a very good predictor of the propensity to vote in a subsequent election. Although this does not solve all conceivable problems of causality, this finding, in combination with the falsification of a large number of alternative hypotheses, strongly increases our confidence that value change may really be a core explanation of the declining long-term propensity to vote.[17]

Participation in local elections

Declining participation in local elections constitute a particular problem in the Scandinavian countries, especially in Denmark and Norway where participation is usually around 70 per cent, or even lower (see Table 3.9). By international comparison, such figures are by no means exceptional (Nieto 1994), but considering the exceptional degree of decentralization in the Nordic countries, and the use of decentralization as an instrument of democratization, low and declining participation in municipal elections constitute a particular problem.

The institutional structure is fairly similar: in all three countries, there are two levels of local government: county-level (secondary or county communes), and municipality-level (primary communes, or just: communes). Around 1970, the number of (primary) communes was dramatically reduced (to some 275 communes in Denmark and Sweden and about 450 in Norway) in order to strengthen local government and decentralize public services. The exact division of labor varies slightly, but in all three countries, communes and secondary communes are in charge of nearly all welfare services (including health care) and the payment (but to a much lesser extent financing) of most transfers. Although they are regulated by the national governments, the communes in all Scandinavian countries enjoy an unusually high degree of decentralization. Both primary and secondary communes also have the right to levy taxes of a quite considerable size.[18] In all three countries, the local election period is fixed (four years, in Sweden it was three years from 1970 to 1995). In Norway, local elections serve as a sort of mid-term election, whereas local and national elections have since 1970 been held concurrently in Sweden. In Denmark, the timing depends on when governments dissolve the parliament and call for an election (which most governments have tended to do at some point during the election period).

Table 3.9 Participation in local* and national elections, 1920–1999 (percentages)

	Denmark			Sweden			Norway		
	Nat.	Local	Diff.	Nat.	Local	Diff.	Nat.	Local	Diff.
1920–1939	79.0	78.4	0.6	63.3	56.2[1]	7.1	74.0	65.6	8.4
1945–1959	83.7	77.7	6.0	79.8	77.0	2.8	79.0	70.8	8.2
1960–1969	87.3	75.7	11.6	86.4	81.8	4.6	82.8	78.7	4.1
1970–1979	87.7	69.6	18.1	90.4	89.5	0.9	81.6	72.6	9.0
1980–1989	86.0	70.2	15.8	89.1	87.1	2.0	83.1	70.8	12.3
1990–1999	84.5	70.7	13.8	85.0	82.6	2.4	77.1	63.1	14.0

Notes:
*Commune level.
1. 1926–1939 (local elections were held in 1919, 1920 and 1922; participation rates were extremely low in 1920 and 1922).
Sources: As Table 3.1; Bjørklund 1999; statistical yearbooks.

In short, there is every reason to participate in local elections, and with the decentralization that has taken place since the 1960s, there have been increasing reasons to do so. The Swedish data conform with this expectation, as the original discrepancy between participation in local and national elections has disappeared. But in Norway, the discrepancy has increased rather than been reduced, and in Denmark, participation in national and local elections was the same in the 1920s and 1930s, whereas in the 1990s, it was 14 percentage points lower in local elections than in national elections. This is the same difference as is observed in Norway. In both countries, participation in local elections in the 1990s was even lower than in the 1920s and 1930s. It is difficult to explain these differences. Most probably the high turnout in Swedish local elections is explained by the fact that it is held concurrently with the national elections, even though it should be noticed that there was no big difference even in the 1950s and 1960s when this was not the case. One may at least suggest that this factor has contributed to the *maintenance* of high participation in local elections in Sweden.

There are many plausible explanations of declining turnout at the local level but most of them are incompatible with the empirical evidence. The argument that participation in local elections declines because regulations of central government makes the influence of local government illusory is simply wrong: in the first place, the real powers of local government have certainly increased in the last few decades. And, secondly, there is little difference between the degree of decentralization and autonomy between the Scandinavian countries.

Another explanatory factor could be the breakdown of a local public sphere due to the closure of local newspapers and the spread of national television. This would sound plausible in the Danish case, and it could also explain why the process has been delayed in Norway, where local newspapers are subsidized by the state, and where television was not nation-wide until the 1970s. But from this hypothesis, we should expect the Swedish trend to be somewhere between the Norwegian and the Danish. By the same token, the Danish and Norwegian data are compatible with the suggestion that the creation of larger communes, with less face-to-face contacts between the elected and the electorate, was responsible for declining participation in local elections. But this explanation is incompatible with the experience from Sweden where municipalities are even larger.

Now, these arguments rest on the premise that the Swedish participation rates would not be radically lower even if national and local elections were held separately. This may be too radical an extrapolation to make from historical findings. But there could be another institutional explanation that is compatible both with the trends in Denmark and Norway, and with the discrepancy between these two countries and Sweden: More that Sweden, Norway and in particular Denmark have gone very far in decentralizing influence over public service to the institution level. For instance, schools and childcare institutions are formally directed by boards elected by the parents whereas the city/municipal council has maintained control only over the aggregate budget. Thus, the sort of influence that is most important to people in their daily lives is effectively removed from the influence of the city council as well as from local parties (see further in chapter 8). Why should people care to vote when the decisions that are important to them are largely made elsewhere?

We cannot test this institutional (or 'saliency') explanation on our data but it does at least appear to be a plausible hypothesis. Further, it may lead to considerations about changing identity from citizens to users or even consumers, and from local political leaders to elected managers of the local welfare service apparatus. To the extent such changes of identity takes place, electoral participation becomes a quite 'unnatural' practice at the local level, as compared to more particularized practices in relation to concrete services.

However this may be, we may conclude that, at least in Norway and Denmark, political citizenship has become increasingly underdeveloped at the municipal level. Alongside with a long-term decline in turnout which we hypothesize is explainable mainly by class demobilization and decline of civic virtues in terms of feelings of 'duty to vote', the information about voting patterns in the Scandinavian countries paints a somewhat pessimistic picture of declining participation in conventional forms of politics which – along with the maintenance of a relatively high level of political interest – fits into the scenario of a 'spectator democracy' as far as the most fundamental and classical form of political participation is concerned. In the next chapters, we examine some further indications of class demobilization and the decline of conventional political participation before addressing the question whether 'new' forms of political participation and the empowering effects of the welfare state have been able to compensate for this decline.

4
Political Parties

The significance of political parties in Scandinavia and theories of party decline

Historically, Scandinavian political parties have played an extremely important role as agents of political mobilization. The traditional class parties were social movements, controlling huge numbers of members, most of the media,[1] and a large number of voluntary associations.[2] This holds not only for the social democratic parties and the labor movement but also for the farmers' parties and the organization of the rural population.[3] Membership of political parties in Scandinavia was among the highest in the world. In 1947, membership in Denmark peaked – at 27 per cent of the electorate – and around 1960, 22 per cent of the Danish and Swedish electorate belonged to political organizations, with Norway and Finland falling only a little behind. As can be seen from Table 4.1, only Austria and Switzerland have reached a similar level, whereas the typical figure was below 10 per cent.

This strong class mobilization has contributed to a reduction of inequality in political participation, and to strengthening linkages between the people and the political elite. Conversely, class demobilization and party decline could have severe consequences for citizenship. However, it is not always clear what is meant by crisis or decline of parties. One may distinguish between three levels, three types of tasks, and between corresponding perspectives (Figure 4.1):[4]

- the electoral level/the electoral perspective
- the organizational level/perspective on parties as organizations
- the parliamentary-governmental level/perspective on policy formation and leadership.

This also serves to clarify various meanings of 'party decline'. At the *parliamentary/governmental level*, party decline means declining influence on policy outcome and less control over recruitment of political leaders – a classical debate which is outside the scope of this book. *At the electoral level,* the *'frozen cleavages'* pointed out by Lipset and Rokkan (1967) are claimed to have melted, being replaced by new cleavages and/or increasing volatility – a subject to which we return below. However, most important here is of course the *change or decline of party organizations*. With Kirchheimer's (1966) famous article on 'catch-all parties' and Epstein's (1975) theory of party decline as forerunners, much scholarly interest in the subject was directed towards describing membership figures, financial conditions and

Table 4.1 Party members as percentages of the electorate in various countries

	First election in 1960s	*Last election in 1980s*
Denmark	21.1	6.5
Norway	15.5	13.5
Sweden	22.0	21.2
Finland	18.9	12.9
Iceland	—	(34)
Austria	26.2	21.8
Switzerland	—	(24)
Germany (Western)	2.5	4.2
Netherlands	9.4	2.8
Belgium	7.8	9.2
France	—	(4)
Italy	12.7	9.7
UK	9.4	3.3
Ireland	—	5.3
Portugal	—	(5)
Greece	—	(4)
Spain	—	(2)

Source: Katz et al. (1992); figures in parentheses are estimates quoted from Gallagher et al. (1992).

At the electoral level:	– *articulation* of interests – *aggregation* of interests – *structuring the vote*
At the organizational level:	– political *mobilization* – political *education* – people–elite *communication* – political *agenda-setting*
At the parliamentary/governmental level:	– recruitment of political *leaders,* – *policy formation,* – *organization of government*

Figure 4.1 Tasks of political parties

so on. (Djupsund and Svåsand 1990; Wiberg 1991; Katz and Mair 1992b; Bille 1997; Widfeldt 1995). This also involved theorizing over the successor of Duverger's (1954) 'mass party' – be it 'centrally directed mass parties' (Andersen 1980), 'electoral-professional parties' (Panebianco 1988), 'media parties' (Pedersen 1989), or 'cartel parties' (Katz and Mair 1995).

As illustrated in Figure 4.2, there are three basic questions to be asked. To what extent is there really a decline of parties as channels of participation? Why has this occurred? And what are the consequences? In a Scandinavian context, all three questions have been contested issues. Figure 4.2 sketches how competing interpretations can be tested. In the first place, it has been discussed whether declining party membership is at all a general trend. Thus, the first task, of course, is to provide a comprehensive overview of membership figures and participation.

Among *explanations* of declining party membership, we may distinguish between institutional and societal explanations. As explanations in terms of declining political interest are ruled out by the results in chapter 2, the main societal explanation is the postmodernity hypothesis, which argues that parties face increasing difficulties in articulating and aggregating the changing and complex conflicts of postmodern society. Among the relevant indicators are changes in party systems, increasing volatility, declining partisanship, and unwillingness to take a party stand on issues. As representation problems undermine the collective identities that are a precondition of mass party membership (Panebianco 1988: 9–11), this leads to membership problems.

Societal explanations are rather deterministic: that is, they regard parties as victims of social change without much chance of improving their position. This is also the case for a mixed societal/institutional explanation which suggests that political parties are no longer viable as channels of communication and participation: In the first place, mass parties are based on local organizations often preoccupied with local problems while citizens are more interested in national political issues. Secondly, salient local interests are articulated more effectively through other channels: Protesting, contacting, user participation and so on.

The remaining explanations are institutional and contingent: that is, they assume that declining membership may be avoided or at least strongly modified by appropriate institutional measures. A popular explanation thus claims that parties experience membership problems because they devote too little influence to their members. This explanation has frequently been accepted by the parties themselves, and several European parties have taken steps to improve the influence of rank- and file-members (Mair 1994). Another explanation suggests that country differences in state support and in availability of public offices affect the parameters of costs and benefits of party membership and thus determine the level of membership (Sundberg 1987). Both explanations rest upon the assumption that

Basic question	Explanatory factor	Type of explanation	Description	Implications/test
I. Is there really a decline of parties as channels of participation?			Description of decline of membership and participation	
			Parties not interested in members	Not tested: Based on false premises (see text)
II. What explains decline of party membership?	Institutional explanations: Parties as organizations	Contingent explanations: Parties may change the situation	Democracy problems: Too little influence	Present, former or potential members feel they (will) have too little influence
			Cost/benefit problems: Too high costs, too few benefits	Party decline contingent on institutional factors: State support and availability of public offices
	Institutional/ societal explanations	Determinist explanations Parties are victims of change	Parties obsolete: more appropriate opportunities for participation and influence	Increase in alternative forms of participation Inefficiency: membership takes too much time
	Societal explanations		Postmodernity: Changing and more complex cleavages	Declining commitment Dealignment Increasing volatility Party system change
			Declining interest in politics	Not tested: Based on false premises (see chapter 2)
III. What are the consequences of decline in party membership?			Consequences for social and political representativeness, political communication and education, and for political distrust	

Figure 4.2   Hypotheses concerning party decline and its explanations

people join parties mainly in order to obtain influence. However, as will be demonstrated below, this assumption is less plausible than it may sound. Finally, it might be suggested that members are becoming less important to parties, as they are increasingly financed by the state and prefer the mass media as channels of communication. However, this idea is based on false premises as parties give quite high priority to recruitment of members, be it for reasons of legitimization (Mair 1994: 13–15) or simply out of democratic ideals.

Finally, a third set of problems concern the consequences of declining party membership for the social and political representativeness of party members, for political linkage, and for political equality. These questions are addressed in the last section of the chapter.

Decline of party membership in Scandinavia, 1960–2000

For a long time, there was a discrepancy between nearly unanimous theories of decline of party membership and highly ambiguous empirical evidence (Gallagher et al. 1992). Although data collected in the early 1990s (Katz et al. 1992; Katz and Mair 1992a) did indicate a general trend (Table 4.1), there remained quite a few exceptions, and the differences between the Scandinavian countries became a strong argument against theories of 'inexorable' party decline (Selle 1991). From a societal perspective, Denmark seemed prototypical – party membership declined from 27 per cent of the electorate in 1947 to less than 5 per cent in 2000 (Table 4.2).[5] However, from an institutional perspective, Denmark was the deviant case as membership in the other countries remained quite stable (Sundberg 1987). Based on an assumption that membership depends on individual incentives (Elklit 1991), it has been argued that institutionally determined differences in costs and benefits for party members could explain variations between the Scandinavian countries. Thus, Sundberg (1987, 1989a) argued that the *costs* of membership (subscription, payment for arrangements, and so on.) were affected by the level of public party support. In Denmark, party support was not introduced until 1987 and remained quite low until 1995. Consequently, Danish parties were 'poor' whereas the 'well-to-do' parties of Norway and Finland received more than twice as much (per capita), and the 'rich' parties in Sweden about six times as much. On the *benefit* side, there are differences in the availability of office positions.

Table 4.2 Institutional variations: number of candidates in local (municipal) elections and public party support in the 1980s

	No. of candidates	Public support
Denmark	23 789 (1981)	30 mio Dkk (1987)
Sweden	56 426 (1979)	370 mio Skr (1988)
Finland	66 776 (1980)	60 mio FMk (1986)
Norway	102 339 (1983)	63 mio Nkr (1983)

Source: Sundberg (1989: 294–5, 300).

In Norway and Finland, an immense number of local boards recruit their members mainly from the candidate lists for the local elections. Accordingly, these lists tend to be very long. In Denmark, less than 25 000 members were candidates in local elections around 1980; in Norway, the figure was more than 100 000. Sweden and Finland fell in between. In short, with high costs and few benefits to offer their members, Danish parties were disadvantaged.

Until the 1990s, Sundberg's theory appeared plausible because it correctly predicted the ranking between the Scandinavian countries as well as the absence of any discernible trend in party membership in Norway and Sweden. However, the implicit argument that party members are eager to candidate for public office positions is questionable. And on the cost side, the data presented in Bille (1992), Sundberg and Gylling (1992) and Pierre and Widfeldt (1992) suggest that differences in membership fees are small which at least tends to weaken the cost argument. However this may be, the alternative hypothesis that declining membership is in fact 'inexorable' has gained more credibility in the 1990s. Even though the decline is less dramatic, it seems that the other Scandinavian countries follow the Danish course, only with some delay (Table 4.3). When collective membership of the Swedish Social Democratic Party was abandoned in 1990, total party membership immediately dropped to 9 per cent of the electorate. At that time, most Swedish parties, except the Social Democrats and the Conservatives, had already suffered from a steady decline in membership for a some time, and in the 1990s, the decline continued in nearly all parties, bringing total membership down to 6.6 per cent by 1999. Finland has been a little more resistant to change as the proportion of (individual) party members has only declined from 19 per cent in 1962 to about 10.1 per cent in 1999 (9.6 per cent if we include Finns living abroad). In Finland, however, the Center Party has been resistant to change and organized nearly 60 per cent of all party members in the country by 1995 (or more than 45 per cent of

Table 4.3 Party membership in Scandinavia (percentage of electorate)

Demark	1947	1960	1971	1979	1984	1990	1992	1995	1999
Social Dem.	11.8	9.1	5.0	2.9	2.6	2.4	2.3	1.7	1.5
Liberals	7.9	6.8	3.6	2.5	2.3	2.0	1.9	2.1	2.1
Rad. Liberals	1.3	1.1	0.6	0.4	0.3	0.2	0.2	0.1	0.1
Conservatives	3.2	4.0	3.3	1.2	1.3	1.0	0.8	0.7	0.6
Soc. People's Party	—	0.1	0.2	0.1	0.2	0.2	0.2	0.2	0.2
Communists	1.8	0.5	0.3	0.2	0.2	0.1	0.0	—	—
Christians	—	—	0.2	0.3	0.3	0.2	0.2	0.2	0.2
Progr. Party	—	—	—	0.2	0.1	0.2	0.2	0.1	0.1
Others	0.5	0.2	0.1	0.1	0.1	0.1	0.1	0.1	0.2
Total	26.6	21.8	13.2	8.0	7.4	6.5	5.8	5.2	5.0

Table 4.3   (Continued)

Sweden	1960	1970	1979	1985	1991	1992	1995	1999
Social Dem.[1]	14.7	14.8	18.9	18.6	4.1	4.1	3.5	2.7
Center P.	2.4	2.1	2.3	2.0	1.6	1.5	2.1	1.6
Liberals	1.8	1.4	0.9	0.7	0.6	0.5	0.4	0.4
Conservatives[2]	2.7	1.1	1.1	1.5	2.2	2.0	1.5	1.3
Comm./Left Party	0.4	0.3	0.3	0.3	0.2	0.2	0.2	0.2
Christians	—	—	—	0.4	0.4	0.4	0.4	0.4
Environm.	—	—	—	0.1	0.1	0.1	0.1	0.1
Others	—	—	—	—	—	—	—	—
Total	22.0	19.6	23.5	23.6	9.2	8.8	8.2	6.6

Norway	1953	1961	1969	1979	1985	1989	1992	1995	1999
Social Dem. (indv.)[3]	3.9	3.9	3.7	3.6	4.0	3.0	2.8	2.2	1.8
Center P.	—	2.6	2.8	2.0	1.7	1.5	1.5	1.4	1.0
Liberals[4]	—	1.0	0.6	0.3	0.4	0.4	0.3	0.2	0.2
Conservatives	3.5	4.2	4.3	4.1	5.5	4.9	3.7	2.6	1.9
Christians	—	1.3	1.6	2.0	1.9	1.8	1.7	1.6	1.4
Soc. Alliance	—	0.1	0.1	0.4	0.4	0.4	0.3	0.3	0.3
Communists	—	—	—	—	—	—	—	—	—
Progr. Party	—	—	—	0.2	0.4	0.5	0.4	0.3	0.4
Others	—	—	—	—	—	—	—	—	—
Total[3]	—	13.1	13.1	12.6	14.2	12.5	10.7	c.8.5	c.7.1

Finland	1962	1970	1979	1987	1991	1992	1995	1999
Social Dem.	1.7	2.0	2.6	2.2	2.0	1.9	1.8	1.6
Center P.	10.0	9.3	7.9	7.0	6.8	6.7	6.5	5.7
Swedish PP.	1.9	1.6	1.1	1.2	1.0	1.0	1.1	1.0
Conservatives	3.2	2.6	1.9	1.8	1.6	1.5	1.2	1.1
Christians	—	—	0.4	0.4	0.4	0.4	0.4	0.4
Comm./Left P.	2.2	1.7	1.4	0.8	0.6	0.4	0.4	0.3
Others[5]				—	—	—	—	—
Total	18.9	17.2	15.3	14.3	12.4	11.9	11.6	10.1

Notes:
1. Collective membership abandoned in 1990. Figures 1960–85 include collective members.
2. 1960–1985: Data 'cleaned' for ancillary members; 1991–1992: official data.
3. Individual members only. Figures for collective members of the Social Democratic Party 1953–1977 have been calculated from linear interpolation of collective member's share in 1952 and 1979 and subsequently deducted.
4. 1961–1969 linear interpolation from Heidar (1983).
5. Liberals/Young Finns, Rural Party/True Finns, Environmentalists (around 1000 members) and others.

Sources: Katz et al. (1992); Heidar (1983); information from party secretariats. Older Danish data was kindly provided by Lars Bille, University of Copenhagen and Jørgen Elklit, University of Aarhus.

the party voters). In Norway, party membership used to be lower, if we exclude the collective members of the Social Democratic Party. Furthermore, individual membership reached its peak as late as 1985. However, 15 years later, the proportion of party members had been halved to 7 per cent. This in not far from the 5 per cent in Denmark by 1999.

In short, at the beginning of the twenty-first century, Sweden and Norway have converged towards the Danish level, and the Finnish figure of 10 per cent derives only from the success of the Center Party. Thus, in terms of membership, Nordic parties can no longer be described as strong, even by European standards. These figures do not rule out the possibility that institutional factors may account for the difference that remains. However, even this modified theory appears problematical. Thus, one should expect that the introduction of state funding for political parties in Denmark in 1987 would affect the decline in membership. But this is not the case. By 1982, there were 300 000 party members in Denmark. The figure later fell 272 000 (1987), to 231 000 in 1992, then to 210 000 (1995), before finally declining to 200 000 in 1999. The increase in party support to nearly four times the previous level in 1995 has not improved the situation, nor did a common membership campaign have any effect.

From an institutional argument, one might also argue that decentralization to non-political user boards in public service institutions reduce parties' control over local politics; as this has gone further in Denmark and Norway than in Sweden, incentives to party membership would seem to be greater in Sweden. But nothing indicates that this makes Swedish parties more resistant to decline of membership. By the same token, members' influence on elected representatives should improve the incentives of membership. However, among left wing parties, who have always placed much more emphasis on members' influence than the other parties, membership is invariably low (Table 4.3).

As in all other European countries, *Communist parties* have suffered from declining membership (Katz et al. 1992) or even been dissolved, and in Denmark, Norway and Sweden, the *Social Democrats* are also among the main victims.[6] But for partly different reasons: In Denmark, (individual) membership has declined from 11.8 per cent of the electorate in 1947 to 1.5 per cent in 1999. In Sweden, elimination of collective membership counts the most, and also in Norway, individual membership has 'only' declined from 3.9 per cent in 1953 to 1.8 per cent in 1999.

Among the non-socialist parties, the *Liberal parties* have managed equally badly: in Finland, the Liberals are even eliminated in Parliament; in Sweden and Norway, relative membership has declined by three-quarters since 1960; and in Denmark, the 'Radical Liberals' now have less than 6000 members. Surprisingly, the *farmers' parties* (the right-wing liberal 'Venstre' in Denmark, Center Parties in the other countries) have the best record. The Danish Venstre even had a small increase in membership in the 1990s and has become the largest member party. In the other countries, absolute figures have been fairly constant, and in Finland, the Center Party is the only large party left. In the 1980s, the Scandinavian *Conservative* parties mobilized ideologically and experienced a certain increase in membership. In Norway, the Conservatives even became the largest member party. But in the 1990s, Conservatives have invariably suffered a decline.

To conclude, in spite of some short-term successes, long-term decline seems to be a common destiny of nearly all parties, and it is also worth noting that no new parties founded after 1945 has ever managed to organize more than 0.5 per cent of the electorate. Most significantly, the successful Finnish Environmentalists have never commanded more than 1500 party members, and in spite of twenty years in Parliament, the Danish Center Democrats have typically counted less than 2000 members. With the partial exception of the Christian parties, new parties that have emerged since the era of popular mobilization in mass parties have not been able to build up strong party organizations. This confirms rather determinist theories of party decline and suggests that large membership parties simply belong to another historical period.

The reality of party membership

As a next step we may notice that institutional hypotheses about the benefits of party membership implicitly refer mainly to the motives of active and engaged members. However, party membership may vary from a 'way of life' among some *party activists* to little more than *passive support membership*. Whereas party activists may be concerned with public office positions (or with influence opportunities), subscription rates is the only cost/benefit factor that seems relevant for passive support members; and since such fees are fairly stable and similar, this does not explain much variation over time or between countries. This leaves us with the benefit factor, which applies mainly to committed members. Consequently, we should expect to find the most significant country differences in the number of party activists. The postmodernity hypothesis leads to the very opposite implications: it is the commitment to parties among 'ordinary people' that is likely to change over time, and to differ between countries. The distinctive characteristic of traditional class/mass parties is their ability to mobilize large numbers of relatively passive supporters mainly on the basis of group loyalties, and as such loyalties are undermined in 'postmodern' societies, party membership becomes an increasingly 'unnatural' practice for ordinary people. From this perspective, country differences are mainly a matter of inertia and thus a matter of time.

To test these propositions, we compare party activity in Denmark and Sweden. Our measures are not entirely identical but roughly equivalent.[7]

As Table 4.4 reveals, this gives another impression of country differences. Now, survey-based figures usually exaggerate membership – and more so in Denmark than in the other countries.[8] But our data nevertheless indicate that the proportion of *active* party members among the entire electorate in Denmark at the time of interviewing was quite close to Sweden. Comparisons with older Danish data produce similar results: Thus our data reveal no change at all from 1979 to 1990 in active party membership. Even when compared with 1971, the figures indicate only a moderate decline.

Table 4.4 Party activity in Sweden (1987) and in Denmark (1971, 1979 and 1990) (percentages)

	Party member	*Active*[1]	*Office holder*[2]
Denmark 1971	16.7	8.1[3]	2.0[4]
Denmark 1979[5]	11.7	6.1	2.0
Denmark 1990[6]	9.4	5.8	2.7
Sweden 1987	15.1	6.4	2.6
Norway 1990	13.0	n.a.	n.a.

Notes:
1. Active: Participate in 'most' or 'some' meetings (Denmark); Being a party member and having attended a political meeting within the last year (Sweden).
2. Office holder: Holds office in the party, or as representative for the party e.g. on local board.
3. 'Usually' attends meetings (1971 only).
4. Only positions within the party (1971).
5. Survey among 18–70 years old only.
6. Figures reported for the 18–69 years old, to achieve comparability with 1979 sample. For the entire sample, the figures were 10.6 per cent, 6.0 per cent and 2.4 per cent, respectively.

Sources: Citizenship surveys, Danish Participation Survey 1979 and Danish election survey 1971.

Table 4.5 Political interest among party members in Denmark, Norway and Sweden (percentages)

Political interest	*Denmark 1971*	*Denmark 1990*	*Norway 1990*	*Sweden 1987*
Much	27	53	21	27
Some	50	34	59	51
Little or none	23	13	20	22
N	228	207	226	299

Source: As Table 4.4.

Table 4.6   Proportions being member of a political party, by political interest (percentages)

Political interest	Denmark 1971	Denmark 1990	Norway 1990	Sweden 1987
Much	33 (N = 180)	25 (N = 430)	28 (N = 173)	32 (N = 247)
Some	18 (N = 591)	9 (N = 798)	15 (N = 873)	19 (N = 801)
Little	9 (N = 531)	4 (N = 580)	7 (N = 627)	8 (N = 705)
None	.	1 (N = 154)	4 (N = 74)	4 (N = 227)

Source: As Table 4.4.

Thus the data do not confirm the institutional explanation but at the same time contribute to a slightly more complex interpretation of membership decline in Denmark. To some degree, the declining membership simply reflects the exit of passive supporters, and crude membership figures thus give an exaggerated picture of the decline in participation.

Unfortunately, the Norwegian survey did not measure party activity. But we may compare the level of political interest among party members in the three countries. At this point, Table 4.5 reveals a marked difference between Denmark and the two other countries. 53 per cent of the Danish party members were highly interested in politics, as compared to only 21 per cent among the Norwegian members and 27 per cent among the Swedish. Again, this does not confirm the institutional hypothesis. It furthermore emerges that in 1971 Danish party members had about the same level of political interest as party members in the two other countries around 1990.

In Table 4.6, we compare the propensity to be a party member among the politically interested segment of the population. Even though this segment, according to respondents' own information, is largest in Denmark, the proportion of party members among the politically interested is almost as large in Norway and Sweden. What distinguishes Denmark from the two other countries is the low proportion of party members among people with only 'some' or 'little' interest in politics. The same difference is found when we compare with the 1971 Danish figures. In short, party membership among people with a more limited interest in politics seems to be the key variable in differences over time and between countries. This confirms the postmodern explanation but disproves the institutional explanation. It also indicates – in accordance with later developments – that parties in the other countries were in a more vulnerable position than at first appeared.

Another ambiguity is that party membership is seldom for life. Norwegian panel data indicate that about one-third of all party members are replaced from one election to another (Selle and Svåsand 1991: 464). This means that quite a few people are engaged in party political activity at

Table 4.7 Present party members, former members and potential party members, Denmark 1979 and 1990 (percentages)

	Proportions		Cumulative proportions	
	1979	*1990[1]*	*1979*	*1990[1]*
Actual party member	12	9	12	9
Former party member	15	9	27	18
Consider membership[2]	14	7	37	23

Notes:
1. 18–69 years old only (because of comparability with the 1979 survey).
2. 1990: Considered membership within the last year.

Source: Participation survey 1979; citizenship survey 1990.

some stage in the life cycle. A Danish survey in 1979 indicated that 27 per cent described themselves as actual or former party members, and a further 10 per cent had considered becoming members (Table 4.7). Even by 1990, nearly one-quarter of the electorate were actual, former or would-be party members.

From a perspective of parties as linkage between the people and the political elites, the declining membership figures in Denmark may mean more in terms of political communication than in terms of political participation. By 1990, Danish parties were still able to attract quite a few members among the most politically interested.[9]

The motivational bases of party membership

The motivational base of party membership provides another opportunity to test the propositions about member influence and postmodernity. An institutional perspective predicts that insufficient member influence is a main source of declining membership, whereas the postmodernity hypothesis predicts that unwillingness to commitment is decisive. Finally, the societal/institutional hypothesis about the viability of parties is basically a macro-level argument. However, at the motivational level, we may expect lack of time and preference for other types of political activity to be decisive.

In an earlier Danish participation survey from 1979, party members were asked why they were members, and former members were asked why they had left the party. As it is unlikely that these motives have changed, the Danish and Norwegian citizenship survey applied a third strategy; namely to ask nonmembers about their reasons for remaining outside (a problem that was not explored in the Swedish survey).

To begin with the Danish findings from 1979, 80 per cent indicated that they 'wanted to give the party extra support by becoming members', and 78 per cent answered that they wanted to 'have influence on society'

Table 4.8 Motives not to be a party member. Percentages answering 'much' or 'some importance'. Norway and Denmark 1990

	Norway	Denmark	Denmark, potential members (N = 125)
1. Too little time for politics	55	45	60
2. Family more important	57	—	—
3. Don't want to spend leisure time	65	—	—
4. Don't want to be committed to the political views of a particular party	75	59	56
5. Prefer to express political views in other ways	52	—	—
6. My interests are better represented by interest organization	36	22	19
7. Prefer to organize in grass-roots movements	—	12	12
8. No influence for ordinary party members	48	34	27
9. Not interested in politics	—	36	16
10. Politics uninteresting and boring	37	—	—
11. Party political activities are boring and uninteresting	—	38	30
12. Politics too complicated	53	—	—
13. Politics not important in my life	55	—	—
14. I would be of no use as a party member	37	—	—

Source: Citizenship surveys.

(Kristensen 1980). The answers may be rationalized, and open-ended questions might have been more appropriate; still, it is remarkable that the motive of support was mentioned more frequently than influence. The answers of former party members were based on open-ended questions and pull in the same direction. The typical answers were 'not enough time', 'declining interest' and 'passivity' (61 per cent of all answers). The next major group of answers referred to political disagreement (33 per cent). Only 3 per cent indicated that they left the party because of 'lack of influence' (Goul Andersen 1993c: 53).

Dissatisfaction with member influence was also a rare phenomenon among party members in the Danish 1990 survey. Only 11 per cent declared that they were 'not too satisfied' or 'not at all satisfied' with their influence on the party; 89 per cent were 'very satisfied' or 'fairly satisfied'. The assumption that member influence is not the core problem is also confirmed by the motives of nonmembers. The most important motive, both in Norway and Denmark, was unwillingness to feel committed to the political views of any particular party (item 4 in Table 4.8). This was followed by various indicators of insufficient time (items 1–3) and lack of political engagement (items 12–14); member influence (item 8) comes far down the list.

Now, it might be more relevant to examine motives among potential party members, or among the politically interested. However, the answers of these two overlapping groups almost coincide, and it becomes even clearer that the decisive motives are lack of time and unwillingness to be committed to the political views of a particular party. Only 27 per cent of the potential members pointed at insufficient member influence.

As far as the 'viability' argument is concerned, data are ambiguous: Most potential members find party activity too time consuming, but only 30 per cent see party politics as 'boring' and almost nobody refers to a preference for grass-roots activities. At least at the *social psychological* level, such activities do not seem to be important alternatives to party activity. Most basically, the data seem to confirm that the problems of mass parties are rooted in societal change, which makes it more difficult for ordinary citizens to identify strongly with particular parties. If this is the case, we should expect to find related, and similar, changes in all countries when looking at other aspects of the relationship between parties and citizens – that is, party system change, electoral volatility, and changes in party identification.

Party system change

The Scandinavian party systems were traditionally based on class cleavages between the working class, the bourgeoisie, and the farmers, and to a lesser extent on cultural conflicts between center and periphery (Rokkan 1970). Somewhat paradoxically, as these conflicts were highly mobilized, party choice in the consensual Scandinavian countries was nearly the most class-divided in the world. With few variations, the Scandinavian countries were dominated by five parties from the 1920s: Social Democrats, Conservatives, Liberals, an Agrarian party, and a small Communist party.[10] Since the 1970s, this has changed fundamentally. For a long time, the stability of the Swedish party system seemed to contradict the notion of change. But in 1991, new parties entered the Swedish parliament for the first time in more than 60 years, and also Sweden came in line with the general trend. By 1995, seven parties were represented in the Swedish parliament, eight parties in Norway and Denmark, and 11 parties in Finland.[11] Two Communist parties and one Liberal party had disappeared, and another Liberal party survived with a single seat.[12]

The new parties have been quite similar from country to country (Figure 4.3). First, *Christian parties* have spread from Norway to all other countries. After nearly 30 years of unsuccessful attempts, the Swedish Christian party finally broke through the 4 per cent threshold in 1991. In Norway, the Christians became a major party shortly after the war whereas it remains a small party in the other countries. The Danish party even dropped out of parliament in 1994 after 21 years of representation but regained 4 seats in the 1998 election.

	First election	Electoral break-through	Highest support	Average since break-through	Last election before 2000[1]
1. Christian Parties					
Norway	1933	1945	13.7 (1997)	9.8	13.7
Finland	1966	1970	4.8 (1979)	3.0	4.2
Denmark	1971	1973	5.3 (1975)	2.9	2.5
Sweden	1964	1991	11.7 (1998)	5.6	11.7
2. Left-Libertarians					
a. New Left Parties: SF/SV[2]					
Denmark	1960	1960	14.6 (1987)	8.3	7.6
Norway	1961	1961	11.2 (1973)	6.2	6.0
b. Green Parties[3]					
Sweden	1982	1988	5.5 (1988)	4.6	4.5
Finland	1987	1987	7.3 (1999)	6.2	7.3
c. Left Radical					
Denmark (Unity List)[2]	1990	1994	3.1 (1994)	2.9	2.7
3. Right-Wing Populists					
Finland (Rural Party/ True Finns)	1970[4]	1970	10.5 (1970)	5.6	1.0
Denmark (Progr. Party)[5]	1973	1973	15.9 (1973)	8.9	2.4
Denmark (Danish People P.)	1998	1998	7.4 (1998)	7.4	7.4
Norway (Progr. Party)[6]	1973	1973	15.3 (1997)	7.1	15.3
Sweden (New Democracy)	1991	1991	6.7 (1991)	4.0	1.2
4. Other Parties[7]					
Denmark (Center Democrats)	1973	1973	8.3 (1981)	4.7	4.3

Figure 4.3   Major new parties in Scandinavia, 1960–2000

1. Norway 1997; Sweden and Denmark 1998; Finland 1999.
2. The Danish Socialist People's Party (SF) was formed by defectors from the Communist Party, the Norwegian SF by dissatisfied Social Democrats. In Denmark, a splinter from SF, the 'Left Socialist Party' was represented 1968–71 and 1975–87. It later united with Communists and others to form a 'Unity List' which broke through in 1994. In Norway, a 'Red Election Alliance' won a single seat in 1993.
3. A Green party obtained some 1.5 per cent in the Danish elections of 1987, 1988 and 1990. Green lists in Norway have been equally unsuccessful.
4. In 1962 and 1966, it was represented as a 'Smallholders' party'. Decisive breakthrough in 1970.
5. In 1995, the party broke, and the previous leader (with three other MPs) formed a new party – the 'Danish People's Party'.
6. In 1973 as Anders Lange's Party.
7. Other new parties have a maximum of one seat by 1999.

Next, *'left-libertarian' parties* (Kitshelt 1988) have emerged in all countries. In Denmark and Norway, Communists were replaced by a Socialist People's Party already around 1960. In the 1970s, these parties absorbed the wave of postmaterialism and exchanged their working-class supporters for new middle-class voters (Goul Andersen and Bjørklund 1990). In Norway and Denmark, there have also been left-radical parties within this party family.

This pre-empted the base for other green parties, which broke through in Finland and Sweden in 1987 and 1988, respectively. In Sweden, the Greens dropped out of Parliament in 1991 but they returned in 1994.[13]

All four countries have also witnessed the entrance of *right-wing populist parties*. The Finnish Rural Party (renamed to True Finns in 1999) began as an agrarian populist movement (Sänkiaho 1971) whereas the Danish and Norwegian Progress Parties began as tax protest parties. In the 1980s, however, they converged on protest against immigration and refugee policies. To a lesser extent, but only temporarily, this was also the case for the Swedish 'New Democracy' which appeared out of nowhere in the 1991 election. These parties are unusual in having the same working-class base as the Social Democrats, or even more so (Goul Andersen and Bjørklund 2000; Gilljam and Holmberg 1993). By 1999, however, New Democracy and FRP/True Finns have almost collapsed because of internal conflicts (the Finnish party won a single seat in 1995 and 1999), whereas in Norway the Progress Party has survived for more than 25 years. This is also the case in Denmark where the former leader of the Progress Party, Pia Kjaersgaard, broke away in 1996 to form a new Danish People Party of her own which soon cemented its position as the successor of the Progress Party.

Finally, the Danish *Center Democrats* is a Danish party 'speciality' which does not belong to any Scandinavian party family. Rather, it has 'belonged' to the Jacobsen family that founded the party. Beginning as a protest against leftist and postmaterialist tendencies in the Social Democratic party, it developed into a center party with a very unusual combination of a liberal stand on immigration and materialist orientations on other issues. This has made the party dependent on single issues and upon the charisma of its founder and of his daughter who took over leadership in the 1990s. The party has participated both in centre-right and centre-left governments.

The emergence of new party families *is* a significant change, even though their electoral support is unstable and some parties have already collapsed. Some might argue that in a long-term perspective, the new parties are only a minor disturbance. Thus, in the latest elections (1997–99), the five old parties from the 1920s still accounted for 72.7 per cent of the vote in Denmark, 61.7 per cent in Norway, 81.1 per cent in Sweden and 77.4 per cent in Finland. If we add the Christian parties and the Socialist People's Parties, this brings the Norwegian, Danish and Finnish figures to above 80 per cent and the Swedish figure to above 90 per cent. However, these figures should be seen against other indicators of weakening of the old parties: electoral volatility and changes in party identification.

Electoral volatility and declining partisanship

In relation to discussions about political system crisis in the 1970s, increasing electoral volatility also came into focus (Pedersen 1979; Borre 1980).

Table 4.9 Electoral volatility, indicated by net gains (percentage points)

	Norway	Sweden	Denmark	Finland	Average
1920–39	13.3 (6)	7.5 (6)	5.3 (7)	8.8 (8)	8.7
1940–49	12.6 (2)	9.4 (3)	13.4 (3)	15.8 (2)	12.8
1950–69	4.3 (5)	4.6 (6)	7.1 (8)	5.4 (5)	5.4
1970–95	13.8 (6)	8.3 (9)	13.5 (11)	9.5 (7)	11.3
1990–99	15.9 (3)	13.5 (3)	12.0 (3)	11.1 (3)	13.1
1920–99	11.2 (20)	7.5 (25)	9.8 (30)	8.9 (24)	9.4

Source: As Figure 4.4. Number of elections in parentheses.

Although there is little to support a notion of system crisis (Svensson 1996), volatility is nevertheless a signal about societal change, which we suggest is at the core of parties' membership problems. From the post-modernity hypothesis, we would expect a common trend towards increasing volatility. But is there such a trend? First, we analyse aggregate measures (indicated by net gains), under the assumption that there is a long-term correspondence between gross and net volatility.[14]

The results in Table 4.9 clearly falsify the thesis of Bartolini and Mair (1990) that European party systems have been stabilizing ever since 1885.[15] In the period 1920–39 there was an average volatility of 8.7 per cent in the Nordic countries. The Second World War and its aftermath generated substantial unrest, and in the 1940s, average volatility reached 12.8 per cent. Then followed the most stable period from 1950 to 1969, when volatility was as low as 5.4 per cent. But in the elections in the period 1970–95, volatility reached an average of 11.3 per cent. The elections in the 1990s even revealed a Nordic average of 13.1 per cent – that is, above the level in the 1940s. Thus the trend since 1970 is clearly towards destabilization. There are interesting country differences, however. For the entire period 1920–99, the Norwegian party system is the most unstable whereas the Swedish is the most stable. Denmark appears as the most politically advanced country: both stabilization and destabilization of the party system took place earlier than in the other countries. In Denmark, 1920–39 was the most stable period, and the Danish party system was the most stable in Scandinavia. This reflects early industrialization in Denmark which is also observable from the historical figures on electoral participation in chapter 3 and on unionization in chapter 6: The main social forces of industrial society were fully mobilized at an earlier stage but postmodern change also took place earlier than in the other countries.

Thus, Denmark also took the lead in destabilization: the 1950s and 1960s were less stable than in the other countries, and less stable than the interwar period. The 'earthquake' in 1973 was unique but was followed by substantial unrest throughout the 1970s. The same pattern is found in Norway but not in the other countries. Probably the EC issue served to

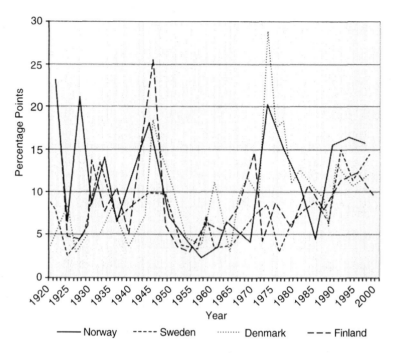

Figure 4.4 Electoral volatility, indicated by net gains (percentage points)

Sources: Heidar (1983); statistical yearbooks, various issues; *Yearbook of Nordic Statistics*. Figures may ocasionally be a little deflated as it has not always been possible to identify 'others'. These are all very small parties collapsed into the category.

destabilize the party systems in Denmark and Norway (Goul Andersen and Bjørklund 1990), and so did the 'new left' mobilization among the better-educated (Goul Andersen 1984c; Svensson and Togeby 1986; Borre and Goul Andersen 1997: 160–89). In the 1990s, however, Sweden has exceeded the Danish level. It may be noted that a high threshold of representation is no safeguard against instability. In the elections of the 1990s, Finland that has no threshold at all, stands out as the most stable country, followed by Denmark with a very low threshold. Briefly, the Nordic countries seem to follow a common destiny towards high instability, and the mobilization around new cleavages so far does not typically entail a new stability but rather genuine dealignment.

Now, net volatility need not reflect gross volatility. But the gross volatility figures in Figure 4.5 confirm the trends even more convincingly. The Swedish data reveal an almost monotonous increase in gross volatility since 1956. In the 1990s, volatility in Sweden and Norway has reached

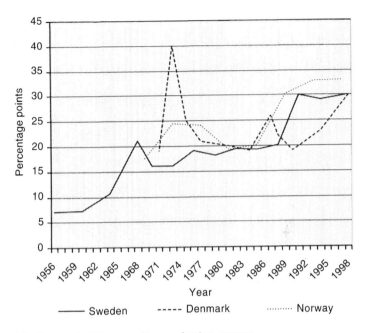

Figure 4.5 Gross volatility, according to election surveys.

Notes:
1. Includes only those who voted in both elections (not nonvoters). Average 1970–2000: Sweden 21.8, Denmark 23.8, Norway 26.3.
Norway: Panel data. Denmark: recall except panel in 1973 and 1988
Sweden: recall until 1970, since 1973 half recall, half panel.

Source: Gilljam and Holmberg (1995: 31); Aardal and Valen (1995: 33); (Aardal 1999: 35); Holmberg (2000: 19); Sauerberg (1992: 102). Tonsgaard (1989: 143); Nielsen (1999a).

quite impressive levels approaching the Danish 1973 election when 40 per cent changed party. Since then, Danish data have been based on recall and thus tend to underestimate volatility; still, they confirm that volatility has stabilized at a high level at least.

Now it must be acknowledged that most party shifts take place within the same party bloc i.e. within the socialist or non-socialist blocs, respectively. However, even at this point, Gilljam and Holmberg (1995: 32) report new records, and in Norway, 'bloc volatility' increased almost monotonously – from 6 per cent in 1969 to 16 per cent in 1993 (Aardal and Valen 1995: 33).[16]

A final standard indicator of volatility is time of voting decision. Again, the evidence is unambiguous (Figure 4.6). In Sweden, the proportion which did not decide until the election campaign has been increasing regularly

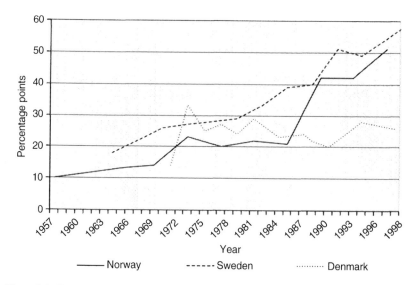

Figure 4.6   Time of voting decision. Proportions deciding during the election campaign (percentages)

Sources: Listhaug (1989: 115); Aardal (1999: 16); Gilljam and Holmberg (1993: 44); Holmberg (2000: 22); Sauerberg (1992: 102); Aardal (1999: 16). Information from the Norwegian election project provided by Tor Bjørklund, and the Danish election surveys 1994 and 1998.

from 18 per cent in 1964 to 51 per cent in 1991, 49 per cent in 1994 and 57 percent in 1998. In the 1997 election, Norway reached a similar level, departing from only 10 per cent in 1957. In the 1990s, Danish voters are the most stable although the figure has increased from 14 per cent in 1971 to 26 per cent in 1998.

To sum up, Denmark was the first country to experience declining party membership, considerable changes in the party system, and dramatic increases in volatility. But in all these respects, Denmark now appears as a prototypical forerunner, not as a deviant case. A similar pattern is found when we turn to party identification.

Party identification

The Scandinavian evidence on party identification leaves little doubt that party identification has declined along with party membership. Unfortunately, we have no Danish data on party identification before 1971 when 55 per cent were party identifiers. Much depends on how we interpret this figure. If it is interpreted as a baseline, one could claim with quite some justification, at least until recently, that developments were very different in the Scandinavian countries: A strong downward trend in Sweden, fluctuations in

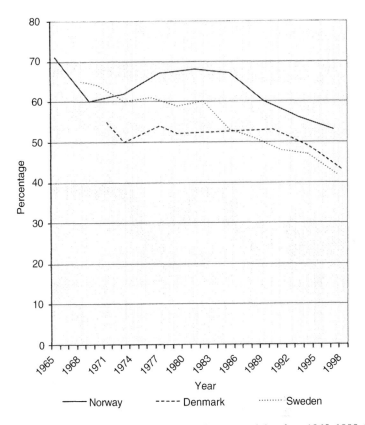

Figure 4.7 Party identification in Denmark, Norway and Sweden, 1965–1998 (percentages Identifying with particular party)

Sources: Pedersen and Weber (1983: 86); Goul Andersen (1984); Aardal and Valen (1989: 282); Listhaug (1989: 147); Aardal (1999: 149); Holmberg (1992); Gilljam and Holmberg (1995: 67); Holmberg (2000: 41); Danish election surveys 1994 and 1998.

Note: 1. Danish and Swedish wordings are almost identical and was posed in accordance with the classical Michigan format. In 1998, a wording identical to the Norwegian one and in accordance with CSES prescriptions was also applied in the Denmark and Sweden surveys. According to this question, there were 49 per cent party identifiers in Denmark and 52 per cent in Sweden in 1998.

Norway, and little change in Denmark. This could support a hypothesis of Swedish exceptionalism (Holmberg 1992).

However, if we take into account the evidence above which indicated that Denmark was a forerunner in terms of volatility and so on, and acknowledging that party identification in both Norway and Sweden declined from the 1960s to the early 1970s, it seems likely that some decline in party identification had already taken place before the first Danish measurement in 1971. From this assumption, and including the latest Norwegian evidence, it seems reasonable to conclude that the Scandinavian countries are converging towards a low level of party identification – just as they seem to be converging on other aspects of party decline. The latest figures read as follows: 53 per cent in Norway (1997); 43 per cent in Denmark (1998); and 47 and 42 per cent in Sweden (1995 and 1998, respectively). The proportion of strong identifiers in Sweden was 24 per cent in 1995 and 19 per cent in 1998 – half or less of the proportion in the 1960s – in Denmark and Norway, it was 26 and 28 per cent, respectively, in 1994 and 1997.[17] With the possible exception of the Swedish 1998 election, Sweden in the 1990s looks much the same as Denmark or Norway. Thus, rather than Swedish exceptionalism, we would stress Swedish normalization.[18] Finally, the data are equivalent to the data on party membership in yet another sense: the Swedish surveys show that it is mainly the group of politically uninterested party identifiers that has declined (by 13 percentage points 1968–94) whereas the larger group of politically interested party identifiers has only declined by 5 percentage points (Gilljam and Holmberg 1995: 69; Petersson 1977).

To sum up: As long as we take each factor separately, the data were open to interpretations – at least until recently: Party membership had declined, but until recently, mainly in Denmark; party identification had declined, but mainly in Sweden; party systems had changed, but until recently mainly in Denmark and Norway; volatility had increased but this might be attributed to short-term factors. However, reading this information together, including the most recent data and adding the observations that party identification seems to be converging at a low level; and that party membership and party identification seems to have declined especially among the less politically interested, it is difficult to escape the conclusion that fundamental and basically similar changes have taken place in all Scandinavian countries. All this seems to reject the institutional explanations of party membership in favor of the postmodernity hypothesis: All Scandinavian countries seem to converge towards a situation where party membership and party attachment is much lower than previously whereas volatility is higher. The analysis of changes in the party systems confirms that more complex conflicts are among the basic underlying changes.[19]

Thus we disagree with the conclusion in Holmberg and Schmitt (1995: 123) that 'the parties themselves, more than any anonymous processes of socio-structural change, are in a position to determine the future of partisanship in Western Europe'. On the contrary, we believe that Scandinavian parties are precisely victims of such processes, without much chance of influencing their situation. Individual parties may reverse the trends (as was the case with the mobilization of the Scandinavian Conservative parties and the Danish Liberals in the 1980s and 1990s, respectively), but only temporarily.

This does not mean, however, that parties are simply declining; we do agree with Schmitt and Holmberg (1995: 122) that 'parties will prove to be far more tenacious than many expect'. But parties are not simply parties. Parties are not declining, they are changing (Mair 1994). What is declining is the type of class-mobilizing mass party of which the Scandinavian parties, along with the Austrian parties, have been prototypical, and which have been considered fundamental to citizenship in the Scandinavian countries (Korpi 1981). Parties will survive, even with considerable active membership, but they will not survive as popular *movements*. And from the traditional picture of Scandinavian politics, one would expect this to have far-reaching consequences for citizenship, not the least for inequality in participation. This brings us to the question of the consequences of party decline.

Consequences of declining party membership

Low participation is traditionally believed to be associated with social inequality in participation (Korpi 1981). What used to distinguish the Scandinavian countries was a zero or even negative association between socioeconomic position and party membership as party membership was mainly based on collective resources. Even in 1988–89, Denmark was in fact the single EU member country where educational attainments did not have a positive effect on party membership (Widfeldt 1995: 159).[20] A central question is whether this pattern of social equality in participation in political parties is maintained. One should expect that party membership would gradually come to follow the conventional socioeconomic pattern – that is, become highest among the better-educated in the upper middle class. So far, this seems to have happened only to a limited degree, however (Table 4.10). In all three countries, we still find a zero or negative relationship between education and party memberships in the citizenship surveys.[21] Now, this negative association is mainly spurious, caused by higher membership rates among the old who have, in general, lower educational attainments. But control for age does not bring forward a positive relationship. One might then imagine that education would be positively related to party membership among the young but negatively related among the old. But this is also not confirmed by our data.

At one point, however, we do find evidence of significant change: In Denmark and Norway, party membership is markedly lower among workers than among other social groups, and, at least in Denmark, this deviates strongly from earlier findings. Thus in 1971, party membership was at least as widespread among manual workers as among nonmanual employees (or even more), in 1979 nonmanual employees had just taken the lead, and in 1990, party membership was about twice as high among nonmanuals. As late as in 1987, there was no evidence of a similar class demobilization of the working class in the Swedish citizenship survey, nor was it found in the

Table 4.10   Social variations in party membership (party members in percentages)

	Denmark 1971[1]	Denmark 1979[2]	Denmark 1990[3]	Norway 1990	Sweden 1987
Total	17	12	10	13	15
Men	21	14	12	14	18
Women	13	8	7	12	12
18–29 years	7	5	4	7	8
30–39	13	8	6	12	13
40–49	18	13	9	13	14
50–59	23	17	14	21	20
60–69	26	15	11	18	22
70 years or more	21	15	16	17	21
low education	18	12	11	13	16
medium education	16	10	8	15	13
high education	8	11	8	11	14
unskilled worker	14	7	8	7	14
skilled worker			4	7	16
lower level non manual			8	10	9
medium level non manual	10	10	12	17	15
higher level non manual			13	2	13
farmer	60	44	41	38	49
other self-employed	27	9	12	22	18

Notes:
1. 1971 election survey (N = 1302).
2. 1979 participation survey and 1979 election survey (pooled samples, N = c.4000).
3. 1990 citizenship survey pooled with 1991 distrust survey, except on class (N = c.4000).

1988 election survey (Widfeldt 1995: 156–7); however, in the Swedish 1994 election survey, the proportion of party members among workers does seem to have climbed a little below that of non manual employees (Gilljam and Holmberg 1995: 182).

Among farmers, however, there is only little sign of a class demobilization: in all three countries, farmers remain far the best organized social class. Even though there may be a decline, between one-third and one-half of the farmers in Scandinavia have remained members of a political party. This confirms the unique strength of political mobilization of farmers in Scandinavia. The demobilization of the working class, on the other hand, is not a particular Scandinavian phenomenon but is found in social democratic parties all over Europe (Hine 1986). Sweden has been an exception, at least until recently (Widfeldt 1995: 157). But Denmark and Norway fall into the general pattern. According to the citizenship surveys, only 26 per cent of the Social Democratic party members in Norway were workers, as compared to 43 per cent among the party's voters. In Denmark, the equivalent figures are 33 and 49 per cent, respectively.[22] This represents a dramatic decline, as compared to two Danish surveys conducted in 1969 and 1971[23] which indicated that the proportion of workers among Social Democratic party members was 68 and 76 per cent respectively. This is also confirmed by the fact that 57 per cent of former Social Democratic party members in the 1990 citizenship survey were manual workers.

This brings us to the question of the representativeness of party members, including the question of the representativeness of active members and members with office positions. At this point, we find significant differences between Denmark and Norway, on the one hand, and Sweden on the other (Table 4.11). In Sweden, workers are slightly over-represented among party members, and even among those who are active in parties, 38 per cent are manual workers. In Denmark and Norway, only 16 per cent of the party members are workers, and among those who are active and among office holders, the proportion declines to 11 per cent. Another illustration of the difference in class mobilization is the fact that in Denmark and Norway, self-employed constitute twice the proportion of manual workers; in Sweden, it is the other way around, and among office holders, the country difference is even more marked. In short: class demobilization of the working class has gone very far in Denmark and Norway; however, in Sweden, there were no genuine signs of class demobilization by 1987. Otherwise the data confirm that people in a higher socioeconomic position tend to be more active and in particular have better chances of being appointed to office positions. Still, these biases in participation are small. Apart from the working-class demobilization, which took place in Norway and Denmark in the 1970s and 1980s, the Scandinavian parties have maintained a high social representativeness as far as socioeconomic position is concerned.

However, the Scandinavian parties are far less representative on other dimensions. As pointed out in Westerståhl (1981), parties are strongly male-dominated, and they are dominated by the middle-aged and the old. In Denmark and Sweden, nearly two-thirds of the party members are men, and parties are the only institutions of participation where the gender patterns have remained nearly unchanged. This holds in particular for Denmark whereas the gender distribution of party members in Norway is more equal. According to more recent Swedish figures, this seems to take place also in Sweden (Gilljam and Holmberg 1995: 182). In Denmark, on the other hand, the young have, objectively, strong incentives to become party members, as their proportion of offices is twice their proportion of members. However, the number of office holders in these samples is too low to allow any firm conclusions.

Because of class demobilization and age and gender biases, Danish parties do not contribute much to the achievement of more general equality in political participation; the Norwegian parties are more representative, at least in the gender dimension, and the Swedish parties remain very

Table 4.11   Social representativeness of party members (percentages)

	Norway 1990		Denmark 1990				Sweden 1987			
	Citizens	Members	Citizens	Members	Activists	Office holders	Citizens	Members	Actives	Office holders
	N: 1773	N: 226	N: 1968	N: 208	N: 126	N: 56	N: 1987	N: 300	N: 128	N: 51
Total	100	100	100	100	100	100	100	100	100	100
Men	53	57	49	64	66	77	52	63	61	61
Women	47	43	51	36	34	23	48	37	39	39
18–29 years	27	15	20	9	10	18	25	14	14	12
30–39	22	20	21	13	14	11	19	16	13	20
40–49	19	19	20	21	24	27	18	17	16	23
50–59	12	19	13	21	19	21	14	19	23	27
60–69	11	15	14	14	17	14	14	20	23	16
70 years or more	9	12	13	22	16	9	10	14	11	2
low education	51	51	46	55	51	43	55	60	55	47
medium education	19	22	34	26	29	29	19	16	18	22
high education	30	27	20	19	20	28	26	24	27	31
unskilled workers	18	9	21	12	9	7	19	19	19	13
skilled workers	13	7	11	4	3	4	15	17	19	22
low non manuals medium	23	19	26	20	22	24	25	15	16	20
non manuals	16	21	19	21	26	24	18	19	20	16
high non manuals	16	15	10	13	13	20	12	11	13	20
farmer	5	14	5	21	19	15	3	9	10	5
self-employed	9	15	8	9	8	6	8	9	3	4

Source: Scandinavian citizenship surveys.

Table 4.12 Left–Right polarization[1] by party membership and party activity. Denmark 1979 and 1990 (standard deviations and means)

	Standard deviations		Means		N	
	1979	1990	1979	1990	1979	1990
Not party member	1.93	2.12	5.56	5.36	1480	1629
Party Member	1.97	2.57	5.82	5.61	212	202
Active member	2.08	2.61	5.69	5.74	111	117
Office holders	(2.50)	2.58	5.00	5.40	26	48
Much interested in politics (whole population)	2.35	2.50	5.02	5.36	317	417

Note:
1. As measured by self-placement on a scale from 0 (extreme left) to 10 (extreme right). In 1979, the scale was from 1 to 10. This explains why the mean was lower in 1990.

Source: Danish Participation Survey 1979; Citizenship Survey 1990.

representative even in the socioeconomic dimension. But does this social representativeness have any impact on ideological representativeness?

In the first place, one might suggest that, as membership declines, the remaining members will be increasingly 'extremist', as compared with the voters – that is, parties may become inhabited by people with strong ideological commitments. At worst, such organizations *may* become an *obstacle* to representation, and to communication between the elite and the people. Thus, one may compare left–right self-placements of voters and supporters in various parties, or – as a more summarized measure – the standard deviations. At this point, Eurobarometer data suggest that party members are a bit more polarized than the voters are but that the difference is by no means dramatic (Widfeldt 1995). However, this may be a simple effect of political interest as the less politically interested are inclined to place themselves close to the center on a left–right scale.

From Danish data in 1979 and 1990, we are able to examine whether membership decline implies a larger polarization (as indicated by standard deviations), and we may furthermore examine whether this change in polarization is more dramatic than among the politically interested segment of the population in general.

The data presented in Table 4.12 confirm the polarization thesis at all points. Party members are equally representative in 1979 and 1990 (members were slightly more to the right in both years, reflecting the low organization among left-wing voters). But party members were more polarized in 1990 than in 1979. In 1979, party members were not significantly more polarized than nonmembers ($s = 1.93$ and 1.97, respectively). But in 1990 we encounter a much larger polarization among party members ($s = 2.57$). Although polarization has also increased a little among the

Table 4.13   Attitudinal correlates of party membership. Percentage Difference Indexes (PDIs), and mean values. Denmark 1990

	Denmark 1990			
	Citizens	Members	Activists	Office holders
	N: 1968	N: 208	N: 126	N: 56
Politics not so complicated+	+8	+39	+51	+73
Trust in politicians*	−38	−6	+4	+29
Trust in local politicians*	−2	+37	+45	+57
Parties are different*	−16	+13	+23	+36
Denmark should not give up EU membership	−33	−48	−50	−50
Immigrants not a threat to Danish culture	+1	+11	+19	+41
Mean values (scale 1–10)				
Political tolerance a virtue	7.7	8.0	8.1	8.1
Ethnic tolerance a virtue	6.5	6.9	7.2	7.7
Participation in associations a virtue*	5.7	7.1	7.8	7.8

*Significant (at the 0.01 level) when controlled for gender, age, education and political interest. +significant at the 0.05 level.
Source: Danish citizenship survey 1990.

electorate at large (partly because of a change of scale), the change among party members is significant. It also emerges that in 1990, polarization has become higher among party members than among the politically interested segment of the population.[24]

Still, there is nothing dramatic about these figures. In a sense, it is only 'natural' that party members are as polarized as those who are much interested in politics and, so far, there is nothing to suggest that this constitutes any serious problem of representativeness. Even from the classical perspective of class mobilization it was assumed natural that the organized party members were a sort of 'vanguard' that could point out new political goals.

However, there may be other aspects: (a) policy attitudes, which do not follow the ordinary left–right scale; (b) civicness; and (c) efficacy and trust. Representativeness along such dimensions is revealed in Table 4.13.

To begin with attitudes, anti-EU attitudes and anti-immigration attitudes are seldom found among the political establishment in Denmark, and such attitudes are strongly correlated with political distrust (Goul Andersen 1992b). It would therefore be interesting to examine whether party members were representative of such issues. At the EU issue, they in fact do seem to be quite representative; even among office holders, the minority who are against EU membership is almost as large as among the electorate at large. On the immigration issue, however, we find a different pattern as these attitudes are far more widespread in the population than among party members, in particular among office holders.

Now, this could be an effect of 'political education' taking place within the parties, which might in this way contribute to more civic attitudes (Togeby 1992). However, when we control for political interest, education, gender and age, the effect of party membership entirely evaporates. This holds also for effects on other 'civic virtues' such as ethnic and political tolerance; the only significant effect that remains is the quite self-evident effect on the perception of association membership as a virtue.

In short, the decline of 'political education' via party membership will probably have a certain effect on political trust, and perhaps also on political efficacy. Nothing indicates that party membership otherwise is important for 'civic virtues' such as political or ethnic tolerance but it remains that party members, because of their social composition and political engagement , are more tolerant towards immigrants, and as such less representative of the population at large.

In the case of efficacy and political trust, it is misleading to speak about representativeness. Rather, efficacy and political trust may at once be causes of party membership, and at the same time reinforced by it. Not surprisingly, it is here we encounter the most significant associations between attitudes and party membership; among ordinary citizens, nearly one-half find politics 'so complicated that people like myself cannot really understand what is going on' (PDI = 8); among office holders, virtually nobody think politics is so complicated (PDI = 73). Still, if we control for political interest, age, gender and education, it in fact turns out that two-thirds of the effect disappears; what remains is a significant, but weak, effect. As to the political trust variables, on the other hand, party membership is a decisive factor with strong, non-spurious effects. This holds also for the perception that parties are different.

Conclusions

The conclusions from this chapter are quite clear. Political parties, which have been responsible for the political mobilization and integration of the broad masses of Scandinavian citizens, are changing, and as member parties, they are declining. We found little support to any institutional explanations that could give parties much hope of reversing the trend. Basically, the problems of the parties are the same in all Scandinavian countries, although it seems that there is still much more left of the class-mobilizing function in Sweden than in Norway and Denmark.

This does not mean that parties are declining, only that they are losing the mass-mobilizing and mass-integrating character they used to have in Scandinavia, unlike in most other countries. The period of Scandinavian exceptionalism is coming to an end. Other things being equal, as party declines as a channel of participation, this leads to greater social inequality in political participation, even if it turned out that the participation that has remained in political parties is less socially biased than might be feared. On the other hand, parties in Sweden and Denmark have not managed to become representative on the gender dimension, and they are certainly no longer representative on an age dimension.

As far as the consequences in terms of communication are concerned, decline of party membership probably does mean a decline of a trust-generating apparatus, and to a lesser degree a decline of political efficacy. The assumption that parties are generators of civic virtues, on the other, found no support in the Danish material. It emerged that party members in fact *were* more tolerant than nonmembers but that this was not *because* of their party membership. This means, however, that politicians do not have many opportunities to get in contact with people having less civic attitudes via the political parties.

5
Participation in Voluntary Associations

Introduction: the significance of voluntary associations in Scandinavia

Alongside political parties, voluntary associations[1] have played a central role in citizens' political mobilization, and many of the tasks ascribed to political parties could be ascribed to voluntary associations as well. As 'intermediaries' between the people and the elite, and as agencies of political education, they have been regarded as a 'school of democracy', as safeguards against an alienating 'mass society' (Kornhauser 1960; Tocqueville 1835/40), and as a core contribution to social capital formation (Putnam et al. 1993). In Scandinavia, mobilization of classes and counter-cultures was particularly strong (Klausen and Selle 1995), and the systems of interest organizations were as 'frozen' as the party systems from the 1920s. Below, we examine membership of voluntary associations in general – trade unions are treated separately in chapter 6. The main concern here is a 'mapping' based on a typology and discussion of measurement problems, but we also deal with three leading theoretical questions. First, are voluntary associations still vital as *movements* – that is, are they able to engage and mobilize active members, or are they victims of some sort of 'institutional sclerosis' like political parties (Micheletti 1994)? Secondly, is widespread membership and participation an indicator of high social equality (Korpi 1981)? And finally, are active members and office holders representative of the general population?[2]

To begin with the question of membership, it is a common assumption in the Scandinavian countries that these are the countries of voluntary associations par excellence. Unfortunately, there are few aggregate accounts of voluntary association membership, and most survey estimates are unreliable. Still, even when estimates of *levels* are flawed, *comparisons* may be reliable, and the combination of various estimates in Table 5.1 in fact confirms the assumption above. From the citizenship surveys, we know that the Danish and Swedish figures are nearly identical; as Sweden has the

Table 5.1   Membership of voluntary associations in various countries, according to the World Values Survey (1981–1983) and Eurobarometer (1987/1990). Percentages reporting Membership of at least one Association

| | World values survey | | | | Eurobarometer | |
| | Membership | | Working membership[1] | | | |
	Total[2]	Excluding unions	Total[2]	Excluding unions	1987	1990
Sweden	65	39	20	18	—	—
Norway	60	40	21	18	—	—
Denmark	—	—	—	—	83	86
Netherlands	49	44	20	20	71	74
UK	44	31	16	16	61	61
Belgium	38	25	18	17	51	56
Germany	43	38	17	15	47	57
France	25	20	14	12	44	42
Italy	23	14	11	9	36	38
Ireland	34	26	17	16	65	56
USA	47	41	19	19	—	—

Notes:
1. Working membership defined as doing unpaid work for the association.
2. Excluding churches (in religiously homogeneous countries people belong to the state church whereas they have to belong to a religious association in heterogeneous countries. This would introduce a bias in our material as membership of the state church is not counted in).
Sources: Curtis, Grabb and Baer 1992: 139–52; Tchernia 1991: 367; Aarts 1995: 232.

highest ranking among the countries in the World Values Survey and as Denmark has the highest ranking in the Eurobarometer surveys, we feel safe to conclude that the Scandinavian countries indeed do have exceptionally high levels of membership.[3]

However, excepting trade unions, the Netherlands, the USA and Germany reveal equally high rates of membership, and when it comes to 'working memberships' (defined as doing unpaid work for the association), national differences are even smaller. Thus, membership and activity in non-union associations seems to be high in Scandinavia but probably not unique.

It is questionable whether participation in voluntary associations should count as 'political'. As most associations articulate demands towards welfare state governments, it may be argued that they are all 'political'. More often, they are seen as providing resources for political participation. A 'middle solution' is to see economic associations such as trade unions as political, the rest as unpolitical (Johansen 1980). Finally, members' awareness of political activities could serve as a criterion (Verba, Schlozman and Brady 1995).[4] Still others do not find the distinction very important, either because they are interested in social participation in general, or in social capital formation. Whatever the research interest may be, however, the discussion would benefit from a more systematic classification of associations.

A typology of voluntary associations

Poor classifications are a source of both bad measurement and theoretical confusion about voluntary associations. Some of the most widely used classifications in literature (for example, Verba and Nie 1972; Barnes, Kaase et al. 1979; see also Parry, Moyser and Day 1992) were apparently developed on an inductive, ad hoc basis and perpetuated in subsequent surveys in order to ensure comparability. However, a typology can be elaborated from very simple criteria (see Figure 5.1).

Like much of the literature, we distinguish between *interest groups* (those organized around a particular interest) and *promotional groups* (those organized around a particular cause). For simplicity, leisure associations are included among the last mentioned. As pointed out by Rasmussen (1971), the operational criterion of this distinction is membership rather than purpose: Promotional groups are open to everybody whereas interest groups organize people sharing a particular characteristic.[5] Among *interest groups*, the most important subcategory is organizations representing *basic interests of income maintenance* (*'primary economic associations'*), that is, organizations for employers/self-employed, for employees (*'class organizations'*), and for

---

1. Interest groups
    1.1. Primary Economic Associations
        1.1.1. Class Organizations
            1.1.1.1. Trade Unions
            1.1.1.2. Business, farmers', employers' associations
        1.1.2. Client associations
    1.2. Other Role Associations
        1.2.1. Community and Housing Associations
        1.2.2. Users of Public Services
        1.2.3. Others (e.g. car owners' associations)
2. Promotional groups
    2.1. Political Associations
        2.1.1. Environmental Associations
        2.1.2. Moral and Religious Associations
        2.1.3. Other (e.g. international) associations
    2.2. Humanitarian Associations
    2.3. Leisure and Cultural Associations
3. Consumers' Cooperatives

Figure 5.1 A typology of interest associations[1]

1. An operational classification is presented in Asbjørnsen, Hoff and Goul Andersen (1995).

publicly supported groups (*'client organizations'*). These associations are by far the most important, not only in terms of membership, staffing and influence, but also from a perspective of political equality: are the interests of the various social groups equally well-organized? Do citizens have equal access to influence through associations? The residual category of interest groups (*'other role associations'*) may be subdivided on a more inductive basis; in Scandinavia it seems relevant to distinguish between *community and housing, users of welfare services*, and *others* (for example, car owners' and shareowners' associations).

Among *promotional groups*, we distinguish between *political associations* (dealing with controversial issues), *humanitarian associations* (dealing with uncontroversial, charitable purposes)[6] and *leisure or cultural associations* (where people are typically members only in order to participate in some sort of leisure activity). Inductively, the political associations may be further subdivided into environmental associations, moral and religious associations[7] and others (such as associations dealing with international issues).

Finally, *consumers' cooperatives* constitute a separate group. They are not easily grouped into any of the categories above, and their membership numbers are so large that it would give an entirely biased picture to collapse this type of organizations into any other category.

Some of these groups are more clearly political. With the exception of some community and housing associations, nearly all *interest groups* are political because they make demands on behalf on a particular group. Among *promotional groups*, the 'political associations' may be viewed as an alternative or as a supplement to political parties.[8] As such, they resemble nation-wide action groups (chapter 9). Humanitarian, and leisure and cultural associations are at the borderline. From an instrumental point of view, such associations may be judged political (i) because they compete for public money; (ii) because they are well integrated in quasi-corporatist networks; and (iii) because they are sometimes even in charge of public programs. From a citizenship point of view, a sharp distinction is not very relevant since participation in such associations is also constitutive to full citizenship. This holds even more from a social capital point of view, and applies even to consumers' cooperatives. Even when they function like conventional firms, they do provide channels of participation.

Membership and activity in voluntary associations: an overview

Measuring membership of voluntary associations by survey techniques is extremely difficult because people often forget their memberships unless they are explicitly reminded by presenting a showcard or by reading the detailed coding categories. Furthermore, the categories must be sufficiently specific and disaggregated to ensure that people are reminded – and to avoid multiple memberships of associations belonging to the same category.

In most of the literature, these criteria are not met, and some of the most widely applied standard questions are flawed as they lead to serious under-reporting (Baumgartner and Walker 1988). In Scandinavia, there has been a tradition of using detailed showcards and coding, derived from archive lists of nation-wide associations (Buksti and Johansen 1978; Hernes and Martinussen 1980; Goul Andersen, Buksti and Eliassen 1980; Goul Andersen 1981; Petersson et al. 1989). In the Swedish and Danish citizenship surveys, some 30 and 45 types, respectively, were presented on showcards (alongside with several examples within each type). Whereas the Danish and the Swedish data are comparable, the Norwegian survey used only 15 types and few examples. Some types of associations were entirely

Table 5.2 Membership and activity in voluntary associations in Denmark, Norway and Sweden. Number of memberships, activities and office positions. Percentages and Means

Number of organizations[1]	Membership			Active Participation			Office Position[2]	
	Denmark[3]	Sweden	Norway	Denmark	Sweden	Norway	Denmark	Sweden
0	7.4	5.7	29.6	58.4	42.3	47.2	87.6	64.9
1	18.1	15.0	29.8	23.8	27.8	31.5	9.7	24.1
2	20.2	20.2	22.3	10.3	15.3	15.0	2.0	7.1
3	19.9	20.0	10.0	4.0	7.8	3.9	0.6	2.4
4	13.6	14.6	5.5	2.2	4.0	1.8	0.2	1.0
5	8.4	10.9	1.7	0.7	1.5	0.3	0.1	0.3
6	5.0	5.8	0.5	0.5	0.6	0.1	—	0.2
7	2.9	3.6	0.5	0.2	0.2	0.1	—	0.1
8 or more	4.5	4.2	0.2	0.1	0.5	—	—	0.1
Mean	*3.08*	*3.27*	*1.43*	*0.73*	*1.15*	*0.83*	*0.16*	*0.52*
Standard Deviation	2.24	2.16	1.41	1.13	1.42	1.01	0.49	0.90
N	1968	1987	1773	1968	1987	1773	1890	1987

Denmark 1979/1990: 18–70 years old

At least	1979	91		64			22	
one assoc.	1990	94		44			14	
Mean	1979	2.9		1.3			0.3	
	1990	3.2		0.8			0.2	
N	1979	1858		1858			1858	
	1990	1712		1712			1712	

Notes:
1. The figures refer to number of *types* of associations (some 45 in Denmark, some 30 in Sweden and 15 in Norway). Community associations, consumers cooperatives, and so on, were not included in the Norwegian survey.
2. Norwegian data are omitted as they include *former* office holders.
3. The Danish sample includes people aged more than 80 years. This affects the proportion of members and active members by up to one percentage point in this and the following tables.

Source: Scandinavian Citizenship Surveys and Participation Survey 1979.

Table 5.3 Membership and activity in voluntary associations in Denmark, Norway and Sweden. Selected, aggregated types. Number of memberships and active memberships. Percentages and means

Number of organizations[1]	Membership			Active participation		
	Denmark	Sweden	Norway	Denmark	Sweden	Norway
0	12.2	11.1	30.2	63.8	46.9	48.2
1	29.0	29.8	31.5	26.4	35.2	32.4
2	32.2	35.8	23.6	7.9	13.2	14.9
3	16.8	15.6	9.2	1.5	3.5	3.2
4 or more	9.8	7.6	5.5	0.4	1.2	1.3
Mean	*1.87*	*1.82*	*1.31*	*0.48*	*0.77*	*0.77*
Standard deviation	1.23	1.15	1.22	0.75	0.91	0.91
Mean excluding unions	1.27	1.20	0.99			

Note:
1. Number of *types* of associations. The types were: trade unions, trade and employer associations, client associations, environmental associations, religious or abstinence associations, humanitarian associations, leisure, sports and cultural associations, and other associations.

omitted, and worst of all, a filter question asked people if they were members of any associations before reminding them of the categories. Thus the Norwegian data on membership are seriously underestimated but data on *active* membership are more comparable as people are more likely to remember memberships that are salient to them.

Our detailed questions confirm that voluntary association membership is widespread. Table 5.2 shows that, on average, Danes and Swedes hold membership in just above three (types of) associations, and only some 6–7 per cent are not member of any association. Three-quarters are members of two or more associations, and, because of multiple memberships, these figures are lower limits.[9] The reported average for Norway is only one-half but this is probably a function of the difference in wording and question format.

To obtain comparability on *active* membership, we have aggregated the Danish and Swedish data to match the Norwegian categories of associations (Table 5.3). There remains a gap in membership but level of *active* membership in Sweden and Norway now becomes nearly identical whereas the Danes appears to fall below. As seen from Table 5.2, 58 per cent of the Swedes have participated in some association meeting within the last year, as compared to 42 per cent of the Danes.

It is frequently argued that partly because of hierarchical organizational structures, and partly because of oligarchy coupled with corporatism, voluntary associations change from popular movements to professional-bureaucratic institutions with passive members (Micheletti 1994). Although it is wrong to speak of a 'golden age' of associations, a comparison with Danish data from 1979 in Table 5.2 seems to confirm the argument: Membership has increased, from an average of 2.9 to 3.2 memberships per respondent, but active memberships has declined from 1.3 to 0.8 on average. The decline is exaggerated because of comparability problems[10] but a similar trend was found in a replication of the question in a Swedish survey from 1997 (Petersson et al. 1998: 62–9). In Denmark, the trend is confirmed by data on trade union participation (Goul Andersen 1993c: 62) but otherwise, the trend is uncertain (Torpe 2000; Fridberg 1994, 2000). At any rate, the ratio of active to passive membership is declining, and, even in absolute terms, activity may be moving in the same direction.

Variations between types of voluntary associations

Membership of various types of voluntary associations is described in Table 5.4. From an instrumental perspective, the most important question is whether citizens' basic economic interests are organized, including those who are outside the labor market. Such interests seem unusually well organized in Denmark and Sweden. Nearly 75 per cent of the *entire* adult population are members of at least one such an association defending basic economic interests (that is, a 'primary economic association'). In Denmark, this represents an increase of some 10 percentage points during the 1980s, mainly because of continued unionization and higher organization rates among pensioners. Norwegian figures are lower, not only because of lower union membership (which is real but also reflects measurement problems) but also apparently because of lower levels of membership among the self-employed.

Figures on the organization of target populations in such associations (Table 5.5) reveal quite high organization rates also among retired and unemployed people – except for the unemployed in Norway (a difference to which we return in chapter 6). Since these data were collected around 1990, both the proportion of union members and membership in pensioners' associations have increased among the retired (Petersson et al. 1998; Torpe 2000). But organization of the disabled remain rather weak in all three countries whereas public employees are the best organized.

Alongside primary economic associations, some 50 per cent of the Danes and Swedes hold membership in other role associations (see Table 5.4) defending group interests of homeowners, tenants, local communities, users of public services, car owners, shareholders, and other interest groups. This means that 83 per cent of the entire population are members of *some* interest association.

Table 5.4   Membership of various associations (percentages of whole population)

	Denmark: 18–70 years old		Whole population 1987/90		
	1979	*1990*	*Denmark*	*Sweden*	*Norway*
1. Trade Unions	52.4	66.5	61.9	62.0	32.0
2. Employers'/trade Associations	13.4	8.9	8.7	12.0	7.0
3. Class Org. (1+2)	62.2	71.8	67.3	68.5	37.7
4. Client Associations	9.1	11.2	13.4	10.5	8.7
5. Primary economic Associations (3+4)	66.7	77.1	74.8	74.3	42.8
6. Housing and community	37.1	44.0	43.0	30.1	—
7. User of public services	5.6	5.9	5.4	10.1	—
8. Others (for example, car owners)	12.1	10.5	10.2	20.8	(4.2)
9. Other role, total (6+7+8)	46.9	51.0	49.7	48.0	—
10. Interest groups, total (5+9)	79.4	85.8	83.2	83.0	(44.6)
11. Environmental	8.1	21.5	20.6	8.1	6.6
12. Religion, absenteeism	3.9	3.1	3.1	11.6	7.4
13. Other political associations	11.5	10.1	10.1	4.1	4.2
14. Political, total (11–13)	19.9	30.1	29.3	20.7	16.0
15. Humanitarian	15.9	19.5	19.8	9.6	13.4
16. Leisure and Culture	47.3	50.9	48.1	55.9	35.9
17. Other associations	5.0	4.5	4.6	7.8	15.5
18. Promotional groups, total (11–17)	60.7	69.0	66.1	66.8	55.6
19. Consumers' Cooperatives	31.1	25.5	24.8	43.2	—
Average number of associations	2.90	3.24	3.14	3.27	1.43
N	1858	1712	1968	1987	1773

Turning to promotional groups, we may notice that two-thirds of the adult population in Denmark and Sweden are members of a least one such group – political, humanitarian or leisure/cultural. The last-mentioned group counts one-half of the Danes and Swedes as members, and (at least) some 36 per cent in Norway – in other words, Scandinavians are not 'bowling alone'. Membership of humanitarian associations is also widespread: some 20 per cent of the

Table 5.5 The organization of target populations (1987/90). Percentages who are members of primary economic organization (class or client organization)

	Member of primary economic organization			N		
	Denmark	Sweden	Norway	Denmark	Sweden	Norway
Wage earners[1]	86	85	52	1177	1316	1033
Farmer, fisherman	84	71	54	70	41	55
Other self-employed	64	66	32	103	111	108
Disabled[2]	44	58	41	61	33	46
Early retired[2]	70	61	42	111	94	36
Old age pensioner[2]	51	49	40	316	266	180
Out of labor force, incl. housewives	52	49	28	661	519	570
Unemployed	82	82	19	117	27	53
Private sector	81	78	40	718	848	730
Public sector	92	91	70	472	593	420
Basic education 7–9	71	71	38	905	1089	885
10 years	80	81	50	662	385	330
12 years	72	77	46	400	512	532
Men	79	75	44	954	1033	934
Women	69	73	42	1014	954	839
18–29 years	68	72	27	384	492	483
30–39 years	88	83	49	414	377	383
40–49 years	81	88	54	390	359	349
50–59 years	77	82	50	257	279	212
60–69 years	67	62	46	267	274	195
70 years +	52	47	39	256	206	151

Notes:
1. Including apprentices.
2. To overcome differences in retirement systems and question wordings, we have distinguished between pensioners aged less than 60 years ('disabled'), pensioners aged 60–66 years ('early retired'), and pensioners aged 67 years or more ('old age pensioners'), regardless of programs.
Source: Scandinavian Citizenship Surveys.

Danes and 10 per cent of the Swedes hold membership in such associations, with the Norwegians falling in between.

From an instrumental perspective, 'political associations' are particularly interesting. It is obvious that they tend to articulate interests which have been more or less beyond the scope of routine politics and the dominant cleavages: environmental, religious and moral, or various other purposes stretching from consumers' interests to international solidarity. This type of associations has most members in Denmark, mainly because of effective membership campaigns of the major environmental movement. In Norway and Sweden, on the other hand, religious and moral associations are considerably stronger than in Denmark. Finally, the consumers' cooperative movement has always been strong in Scandinavia, and 25 per cent of the Danes and 43 per cent of the Swedes hold membership of this association. In Norway, it was not included in the questionnaire.[11]

From a social capital or school of democracy perspective, the level of active membership is of course much more interesting than raw membership figures. The proportion of active members as a percentage of the population is shown in Table 5.6. In all three countries, leisure and cultural associations are the most important in terms of activity, followed by trade unions. It is noteworthy also that political associations, apart from religious associations in Norway and Sweden, are far less important in terms of activity than in terms of membership which is mainly passive support membership: even though more than 20 per cent of the Danes are members

Table 5.6 Active participation in various associations (percentages of whole population)

	Denmark: 18–70 years old		Whole population 1987/90		
	1979	1990	Denmark[1]	Sweden	Norway
1. Trade unions	25.6	13.2	12.3	.15.4	19.3
2. Employers'/ trade Associations	8.1	2.5	2.3	3.6	3.7
3. Class organizations. (1+2)	30.5	15.4	14.5	18.2	22.6
4. Client associations	4.3	3.3	3.9	4.5	5.4
5. Primary economic Associations (3+4)	33.6	18.1	17.9	21.9	27.0
6. Housing and community	19.1	9.8	9.7	9.1	—
7. User public services	5.0	3.5	3.2	4.5	—
8. Others (e.g. car owners)	3.9	1.2	1.2	7.7	(3.4)
9. Other role, total (6+7+8)	25.8	13.1	12.8	19.0	—
11. Environmental	2.0	1.0	1.0	1.1	2.5
12. Religion, absenteeism	3.2	2.0	2.0	7.5	6.6
13. Other political associations	3.4	1.3	1.2	2.0	1.2
14. Political, total (11–13)	7.6	4.1	3.9	9.8	9.8
15. Humanitarian	3.7	1.8	1.8	9.6	5.8
16. Leisure and Culture	31.1	25.0	23.4	36.3	24.2
17. Other associations	2.9	1.4	1.5	3.6	9.0
18. Promotional groups, total (11–13)	38.1	28.7	26.3	47.4	39.0
19. Consumers' cooperative	7.3	2.9	2.9	6.0	—
N	1858	1712	1968	1987	1773

Notes:
1. Average of 18–99 years old and 18–74 years old.
(not fully comparably)

Source: Scandinavian Citizenship Surveys.

of an environmental association (that is, four times the proportion of party members), only one per cent are active members (that is, little more than a quarter of active party members).

As to country differences, the Norwegians stand out as the most active on nearly all fully comparable measures, even in trade unions. Denmark is lagging significantly behind the two other countries. As mentioned, part of this difference hinges on measurement problems in the Danish survey. But we may note that the difference is disproportionately large when it comes to religious and humanitarian associations where most Danes do nothing beyond paying their membership fees, whereas Swedes, and in particular Norwegians, are much more active. Thus, 10 per cent of the Swedes have participated actively in some humanitarian association, as compared to only 2 per cent among the Danes. When it comes to leisure and cultural associations, on the other hand, the differences between countries are smaller – the Swedes stand out as the most active, and the Danes seem to be the most active in housing and community associations which, however, are usually very narrowly oriented in the Danish case. In short, Denmark and Norway stand out as the two poles: There is much voluntary association membership in Denmark but such associations seem to have lost much of their character of *movements*. In Norway, and to a somewhat lesser extent in Sweden, one finds active membership and a lot of voluntarism. It thus seems that roughly the same aggregate figures on membership in the Nordic countries conceal quite some differences in the real life of associations.

Social and political representativeness

As mentioned, it is a widespread assumption that high participation is also socially equal participation (Korpi 1981), and that in particular trade unions contribute to reducing social differences. But to what extent is this confirmed when it comes to voluntary association activity in Scandinavia? And, more generally, how are the social and demographic variations in membership? Table 5.7 reveals a rather similar and well-known pattern. Membership is most widespread among the middle-aged, among the better-educated, among medium- or higher-level employees, and among farmers. Public employees hold by far the largest number of memberships. Variations in active participation are roughly similar, but less pronounced. In the absence of comparable data from other countries, it is difficult to determine whether the above social variations should be characterized as large, moderate or small. Still, as the largest social variation amounts to 1.43 memberships (the difference between the adjusted effects of unskilled workers and higher non-manuals in Denmark controlled for third variables), as compared to a mean of 3.49, it does seem reasonable to characterize the social differences in membership as quite moderate.

Table 5.7 Social variations in the number of voluntary association memberships. Multiple Classification Analysis. Deviations from means, eta and beta coefficients. labor force only[1]

	Unadjusted deviations from mean; eta coefficients			Adjusted deviations from mean; beta coefficients		
	Denmark	Sweden	Norway	Denmark	Sweden	Norway
A. All associations						
Grand mean	*3.47*	*3.51*	*1.61*	*3.47*	*3.51*	*1.61*
Unskilled worker	−.69	−.78	−.41	−.43	−.51	−.21
Skilled worker	−.35	−.76	−.43	−.01	−.42	−.13
Lower non manual	.07	−.13	−.08	.00	−.10	−.11
Medium non manual	.75	.71	.53	.27	.41	.26
Higher non manual	.76	1.21	.44	.36	.70	.15
Farmer, fisherman	.06	.27	.07	.49	.50	.31
Other self-employed	−.13	.15	−.18	−.02	.14	−.02
Eta/Beta	.23	.32	.25	.12	.20	.12
Unemployed	−.87	−1.29	−.65	−.47	−.82	−.43
Privately Employed	−.26	−.30	−.25	.24	−.23	−.20
Public Employees	.57	.49	.46	.45	.37	.37
Eta/Beta	.21	.20	.24	.16	.15	.19
18–29 years	.69	−.83	−.48	−.60	−.62	−.35
30–39 years	.14	.30	.14	.08	.18	.07
40–49 years	.20	.63	.23	.18	.47	.19
50–59 years	.31	.14	.16	.36	.17	.16
60–69 years	.12	−.21	.08	.10	−.12	.02
70 years or more[2]	(−1.22)	−.79	(−1.03)	(−1.22)	−1.01	(−.78)
Eta/Beta	.17	.26	.20	.15	.20	.15
Men	.03	.08	-.02	.10	.18	.06
Women	−.03	−.09	.02	−.10	−.21	−.09
Eta/Beta	.01	.04	.01	.04	.09	.05
7–9 years' basic education	−.44	−.47	−.33	−.34	−.27	−.19
10 years	.05	.06	.16	.08	.16	.02
12 years	.61	.73	.36	.41	.34	.26
Eta/beta	.18	.24	.22	.13	.13	.14
Explained variance (R²)				.105	.177	.132
B. Excl. Class Organizations				*Beta coefficients*		
Occupation				.20	.19	.13
Sector				.14	.12	.10
Age				.13	.18	.13
Gender				.01	.09	.04
Education				.13	.14	.15
Explained variance (R²)				.126	.166	.098

Notes:
1. Interactions (e.g. occupation, sector) are ignored.
2. There are few respondents in this category because only the active members of the labor force are included.

However, the assumption that high membership and participation equates to a high level of social equality is not confirmed. Thus it emerges that of all three countries Sweden has the largest class differences in participation. Even more surprisingly, the assumption that trade unions promote equality in participation is also disproved. It emerges from section B of Table 5.7 that the effect of social class and education is nearly unaffected by the inclusion or exclusion of trade unions. This indicates that the mobilization of class interests no longer plays any significant role for maintenance of political equality. It is also 'disturbing', from a class-mobilization point of view, that Norway (which has the weakest trade union membership) has in fact smaller class variations in participation than Sweden.

Representativeness: a 'power' analysis of positions

As mentioned, the question of inequality of participation may also be addressed from a representativeness perspective. Which social and political groups control the system of voluntary associations? Who occupy the *positions* – as members, as active members, and as office holders – and to what degree do the occupants of these positions deviate from the population at large?

From a *resource perspective*, one would imagine that the social distribution becomes increasingly biased in favor of the better-off groups as we move from members to office holders – that is, from the lowest to the higher levels of power within the associations. From what might be labeled a *'Scandinavian democracy model'*, one could expect that the lower classes were able to maintain considerable control over power positions within the associations. Furthermore, we would expect that the political parties were able to maintain control over power positions within the associations. Finally, it would also be interesting to examine whether particular parties or party groups had more power than others in the system of interest associations. As mentioned, the focus here is on *positions* rather than individuals. Thus the unit of analysis is positions that is, the distribution of the 12–15 million positions as members of interest associations among the 4 million adult Danes and so on. Technically, we have weighted individuals by their number of memberships, number of active memberships and number of office positions, respectively.

As far as *gender* is concerned, Table 5.8 shows that men have maintained a high level of control over the interest association system in Denmark and Sweden whereas the gender gap has nearly disappeared in Norway. Not surprisingly, *education* enhances membership and participation in all three countries. But the association is weaker than might be expected, and even more surprisingly, higher education does not promote access to office positions. On the contrary, in all three countries, the better-educated are more represented at the active participant level than at the level of office

Table 5.8 Distribution of population and positions in voluntary associations. (percentages)

	Whole population (N = 1968)	Composition of positions (weighted)		
		Members (N = 6053)	Actives (1432)	Office holders (N = 320)
Proportion of Men				
Denmark	49	+2	+8	+15
Sweden	52	+2	+5	+11
Norway	53	+1	+1	+3
Proportion of 18–29 years old				
Denmark	19	−2	0	−7
Sweden	25	−5	−5	−8
Norway	27	−6	−6	−11
Proportion of 60 + years old				
Denmark	7	−6	−8	−7
Sweden	24	−4	−4	−5
Norway	19	−1	−2	0
Proportion with 12 years school				
Denmark	20	+5	+10	+8
Sweden	26	+7	+9	+8
Norway	30	+9	+7	+8
Public employees[1]				
Denmark	24	+8	+9	+5
Sweden	29	+7	+7	+8
Norway	24	+10	+10	+10
Proportion of workers[2]				
Denmark	32	−6	−7	−9
Sweden	34	−7	−10	−12
Norway	31	−9	−9	−13
Proportion of party members				
Denmark	10	+3	+5	+10
Sweden	15	+5	+8	+10
Norway	13	+6	+7	+10
Proportion of socialists				
Denmark	51	−2	0	−1
Sweden	52	−3	−2	−2
Norway	44	0	−2	−1

Notes:
1. As proportion of sample.
2. As a proportion of those gainfully employed.

Source: Scandinavian Citizenship Surveys.

positions. It thus seems that there is a legacy left of the class-mobilized 'Scandinavian democracy model', even though class mobilization as such has declined. In all three countries, *public employees* are far more active than the population at large, but they have been most successful in Norway – where the proportion of public employees increases gradually by some 10 percentage points from the general population to the composition of office holders. In Denmark, on the other hand, public employees have a lower share of office positions than among the actives. Thus in Denmark, public employees appear less powerful than could be expected from level of active participation

Finally, the *political* composition at all levels is almost the same as for the population at large at least in the sense that there are no significant deviations from the overall balance between socialist and non-socialist parties. The *proportion of party members*, on the other hand, is increasing with level of activity – in Denmark from 10 per cent members in the general population to 20 per cent among office holders, to mention the most significant difference. The fact that the difference in the two other countries is the same or even lower indicates that political parties no longer have much influence on voluntary associations and that the correlation should probably rather be interpreted in accordance with a 'school of democracy' point of view.

The question is, then, whether the data confirm the 'resource model' or 'the Scandinavian model'. To some degree, they provide evidence which seems to support each of the hypotheses. The observation that the better-educated are less over-represented than might be expected, in particular at the level of office positions, is surprising and may be seen as a confirmation of the Scandinavian model. Furthermore, although there are obvious inequalities of representation, these must be described as relatively moderate. The most surprising in this respect is perhaps the significant under-representation of women among actives and office holders, in particular in Denmark and, to a lesser extent, in Sweden.

Conclusions

Voluntary associations have played a more important role in Scandinavia than in most other countries. From its early beginnings in the counter-cultural movements, in particular in Norway and Sweden, it developed through the class mobilization of workers and farmers and finally led to a strong level of organization around sports and physical exercise activities. This has left a legacy whereby Scandinavian citizens hold an unusually large number of association memberships, probably even when compared to the USA. The Swedes seem to take the lead as far as association membership is concerned but the Norwegians seem to be the most active in associations. Both in Denmark 1990 and more recently in Sweden

(Petersson et al. 1998), there are signs of a certain weakening of active participation. Both from a social capital perspective and from a citizenship perspective, such trends are a cause for concern.

From an instrumental perspective on political participation, on the other hand, one would rather stress that not all associations are equally important politically. Of particular interest (also from a citizenship perspective) is the membership of associations which are organized to protect people's basic source of income ('primary economic associations'). It is remarkable that some 75 per cent of *all* citizens (including those who are not economically active) are members of such an association in Sweden and Denmark. Not only the economically active population (including the unemployed) but also most groups outside the labor market are well organized. Norway falls a little behind on primary economic associations, whereas measurement problems may account for much of the difference in membership of other associations.

As far as *promotional groups* are concerned, special interest is directed towards 'political associations', which deal with controversial political issues such as the environment. Although these associations were growing dramatically in membership in the 1980s and early 1990s – especially in Denmark – they are far less important in terms of participation. It seems mainly to be a matter of passive support for causes that are perceived to be too weakly represented in politics. It is in accordance with this interpretation that membership in environmental associations in Denmark declined markedly in the second half of the 1990s in correspondence with increasing government activities to improve the environment.

Finally, we have examined the social and political representativeness of voluntary association members, of active members, and of office holders taking *positions* rather than individuals as units of analysis. Not surprisingly, we find most of the conventional socioeconomic and demographic biases here. But, generally speaking, they are not very strong, and somewhat surprisingly, there are signs that participatory equality has been increasing. Among the significant differences between the Scandinavian countries, we find that the Norwegians have gone far towards closing the gender gap in participation and representation in voluntary associations, a fact that stands in sharp contrast to Denmark where it seems that little has changed, in particular at the level of office holders. Another interesting finding – this time common to all three countries – is the absence of significant left–right political biases in the voluntary association system: the political distribution of citizens, members, active members and office holders – or more precisely of these positions – is nearly identical in all three countries. Besides, only a minority of 20 per cent or less of office positions are occupied by party members.

6
Participation in Trade Unions

The strong unions in Scandinavia and theories of union decline

Alongside political parties and farmers' associations, Scandinavian trade unions have been a cornerstone in class mobilization of the lower social strata and in the achievement of relatively high levels of political participation with small differences between social classes (Korpi 1981). But today, trade unions are claimed to be subject to much the same pressures as political parties – to differentiated interests and aggregation problems, problems of representativeness and member loyalty (Müller-Jentsch 1988; Bild et al. 1993), organizational obsolescence (Hancke 1991), and declining influence on public policy (Hyman 1991: 625–7).

Nevertheless, trade union membership in Scandinavia continued to increase in the 1970s and 1980s, at a time when the decline of unionization almost became an international research discipline. As revealed by Table 6.1, in the 1990s, some 85 per cent of all employees in Denmark and Sweden were trade union members; Finland fell only slightly below this level, and in Norway, 56 per cent were organized. In most other countries, the figure was below 50 per cent. Scandinavian unions have not always been in this exceptional position. Around 1920, only Denmark was among the highly unionized countries. But in the 1930s, Sweden took the lead, and since the Second World War, only Austria and Belgium have had rates of unionization comparable to Scandinavia. Since 1970, the gap has widened even further. For instance, Denmark and Austria had roughly the same level of unionization until 1970, but in 1988, the Austrian figure was only 46 per cent.

The purpose of this chapter is to explore the nature, causes and consequences of unionization in Scandinavia. Why did membership continue to increase to this level? Have Scandinavian unions been able to avoid the pressures experienced in other countries? What explains the difference between Norway and the other Nordic countries? And are trade unions

Table 6.1   Trade union density[1] in various countries (percentages)

	Gross density					Net density		
	1920	*1930*	*1940*	*1950*	*1960*	*1970*	*1980*	*1988/89*
Denmark[2]	47	37	46	53	62	62	79	84
Sweden	24	32	48	59	63	68	80	85
Finland	13	7	12	36	34	51	70	71
Norway	20	19	37	50	63	51	57	57
Austria	42	44	40	56	55	60	54	46
Switzerland	26	24	26	38	35	31	31	26
Germany (Western)	53	34	—	33	37	33	37	34
Netherlands	36	30	29	42	39	37	35	25
Belgium	40	29	39	56	61	46	57	53
France	7	7	—	—	—	22	19	12
Italy	—	—	—	40	22	36	49	40
UK	48	26	33	44	44	45	51	42
Ireland	—	—	—	—	—	53	57	52
USA	17	10	20	28	29	26	23	16

Notes:
1. Gross density is defined as *all union members as proportion of the wage-earning labor force.* Net density is defined as the *proportion of union members among employed wage-earners.*
2. The Danish figures for the period 1970–90 are based on own computations as Visser's (1991) labor force estimate for Denmark is heavily affected by unusually large numbers of children, pupils and students in Denmark who work part time little in their summer holidays and count as member of the labor force. (Visser seems to believe that the difference between gross and net union density in Denmark derives from low unionization among the unemployed; the real explanation is the large number of retired union members).

Sources:
1920–1960: Pedersen (1989: 24) – gross density (union members in proportion of labor force).
1970–1988/89: Visser (1991: 101) – net density (the proportion of union members among employed wage earners). Other accounts may be found in Bain and Price 1980; Kjellberg 1983; Freeman 1989; Griffin et al. 1990; and various country studies.

still social movements – do they still generate participation, identities and a sense of efficacy among the lower classes? The Nordic citizenship surveys give an opportunity to approach such questions by means of comparative individual-level data.

This is not the place for a full account of the literature about unionization and union decline (for an overview, see Goul Andersen 1996); we may just sum up that most theories crystallize into four major types: Social structural, institutional, conjunctural and ideological. *Social structural theories* focus on the *changing labor force composition* (Troy 1986, 1990; Green 1992) and claim that unionization declines in post-industrial service societies along with the most unionized groups, such as manual workers, manufacture and construction workers and full-time male workers. However, such changes may be less harmful to Scandinavian unions. In the first place, the large public service sector in Scandinavia has a crowding-out effect on the private service sector, which is among the smallest in the rich countries, without any signs of convergence (Goul Andersen 1994c). As public employees are highly unionized, this sort of service sector growth is not a threat to unionization. Secondly, as women are integrated in the labor market, gender differences in unionization are likely to evaporate. Finally, white-collar unionization is facilitated by the structure of unions where most of the new middle class is organized outside the main confederation of unions. By 1985, the largest confederation of unions, the LO (equivalent of the British TUC), accounted for less than 70 per cent of union membership in Denmark, 64 per cent in Norway, and 60 per cent in Sweden (Visser 1990: 16–17).[1] Equivalent figures for Austria, the UK and Germany were 100, 89 and 82 per cent, respectively.

In short, the effects of social change are likely to diverge between countries with similar labor force compositions. Such *country variations* are the frame of reference for *institutional theories*. The most important institutional factor is the unemployment benefit system: Under the so-called 'Ghent system', where unemployment benefits are based on membership of unemployment insurance funds de facto controlled by the unions, there are much stronger incentives to union membership than in state-organized systems (Neumann et al. 1991; Pedersen 1989, 1990; Western 1993; Rothstein 1992).[2] However, we shall also examine whether there is a down side to the Ghent system: It may contribute to a level of institutionalization where trade unions are really no longer 'voluntary' associations. From a citizenship perspective, however, the Ghent system may also have important side-effects for the status of the unemployed who are likely to be organized and to constitute a quite significant proportion of trade union members. In state-controlled systems, on the other hand, trade unions often tend to be associations mainly for the employed. As such, they aggravate 'insider'/'outsider' divisions in the labor market.

As to *conjunctural theories*, a classic proposition argues that unionization follows the business cycle – positively correlated with inflation, negatively correlated with unemployment (Ashenfelter and Pencavel 1969; Jones 1992). In the early phase of unionization, such a correlation was observable in most countries. However, an institutional perspective suggests that this is a contingent relationship: under the Ghent system, we should rather expect the opposite.

Finally, *ideological theories* point at the impact of individualism (Lipset 1986), employer or government hostility (Freeman 1988), the strength of left parties (Wallerstein 1989; Korpi 1981; Przeworski and Sprague 1986) or strike militancy (Griffin et al. 1990). Such variables will also interact with social structural change. Thus, early recognition of unions as legitimate counterparts and consensual traditions in the labor market (Galenson

1952) facilitate middle-class unionization and make unions less vulnerable to individualist value change.

However, these theories have little to say about the role of unions as social movements – that is, about participation in unions, about their identity-shaping functions, and about efficacy and trust among members. These questions are treated in the subsequent section whereas the last section discusses the social and political representativeness of Scandinavian trade unions.

Union membership: institutions and social change

Among institutional factors favoring unionization, two are particularly plausible: union control over unemployment insurance (the Ghent system) and tax deductions for membership fees. The first factor turns out as decisive but tax deductions also seem to have a small impact. Thus it emerges from Table 6.2 that countries with such inducements had higher levels of union-ization and better records of change from 1970 to 1989. Denmark and Finland, the only two countries having both inducements, had the largest increase in union density in the period 1970–89 among all the listed nations. Historically, centralized bargaining and corporatism may also have contributed to high unionization, but more decentralized bargaining and declining corporatism in the 1980s did not appear to have any impact (Ahlen 1989; Western 1993).

This macro-level observation could lead to oversimplified inferences about individual motivations and selective incentives, however. On the one hand, survey data confirm that unemployment insurance is important. In the Danish 1979 participation survey, membership was 94 per cent among wage-earners who had been unemployed within the last two years, as compared to an average of 80 per cent, and 23 per cent answered that they would leave the union if they could obtain unemployment benefits otherwise (Goul Andersen 1984a: 205).[3] Furthermore, in a Danish survey of LO members in 1992, unemployment insurance was the strongest motive (Table 6.3). On the other hand, it is not the only motive. It was mentioned by 90 per cent, but 73 per cent also felt an obligation to be a union member, 74 per cent indi-cated defense of their own interests, and 87 per cent believed that trade unions are necessary to protect the interests of wage-earners.[4] Closed shop arrangements – a selective incentive alongside unemployment insurance – was referred to by only 57 per cent. On the other hand, the keyword 'soli-darity' was also referred to by only 58 per cent. To sum up, even though unemployment insurance system is a decisive factor in union membership, and even though motives frequently fall short of 'solidarity', most members also have motives that are in line with traditional trade union ideology.

But how have Scandinavian unions so far been affected by the growth of new middle-class and service occupations? And does lower unionization in

Table 6.2 Trade unions' control over unemployment insurance, tax deductions for membership fees, increase in trade union density, and Union Density 1989

Country	Control over unemployment insurance	Tax deductions for union membership fees	Increase in trade union density, 1970–89	Increase in trade union Density, 1980–89	Trade Union Density, 1989
Denmark	+	+	+22	+5	84
Finland	+	+	+20	+1	71
Sweden	+	+/−[1]	+17	+5	85
Belgium	+	−	+7	−4	53
Average 4 countries			*+16*	*+3*	*73*
Norway	−	+[2]	+6	0	57
Austria	−	+	−14	−8	46
Average 2 countries			*−4*	*−4*	*52*
Ireland	−	n.a.	−1	−5	52
UK	−	(−)[3]	−3	−9	42
Italy	−	−	+4	−9	40
Germany(W)	−	−	+1	−3	34
Netherlands	−	(−)[4]	−12	−10	25
USA	−	−	−10	−7	16
France	−	−	−10	−7	12
Average 7 countries			*−4*	*−7*	*32*

Notes:
1. Low ceiling; abolished by 1992.
2. Ceiling of 1800 NoK (1992).
3. Not for typical trade unions.
4. Normally included in standard deductions.

Source: Table 6.1; Visser 1991; and information collected by the authors from embassies and tax authorities in various countries (1994). Tax values of deductions from membership fees in Denmark has been reduced (but in an invisible way) during the 1990s.

Norway mean that union membership is more concentrated in the traditional 'core' working class? To begin with the changing class composition, it turns out that *the gap between white-collar and blue-collar unionization has evaporated in the Scandinavian countries.* The suspicion that trade union membership might be concentrated among 'core' workers in Norway is also falsified; on the contrary, unionization seems highest among nonmanuals (Table 6.4).[5] This is a quite recent trend (Visser 1990: 51–6): In Denmark, the collar gap had narrowed in the 1930s but widened during the prosperous 1960s. Between 1970 and 1982, however, the gap virtually disappeared (Pedersen 1979; Plovsing 1973; Scheuer 1984, 1989; Danmarks Statistik 1992: table 12.8), and at the start of twenty-first century, white-collar workers are at least as organized as blue-collars.

Table 6.3   Motives of Danish LO members, 1992 (percentages)

	Strongly agree	Agree	Neither agree nor disagree	Disagree	Disagree strongly	Agree, total
'Trade unions are necessary to safeguard the interests of the wage-earners'	65	22	9	2	2	87
'Why are you a member of your union?'						
'Because I think one should be member of a union'	56	17	12	5	10	73
'Because of solidarity with my work mates'	40	18	20	7	15	58
'In order to have my interests attended to'	53	21	16	4	6	74
'In order to be insured against unemployment'	78	12	4	1	4	90
'Because it is mandatory at my workplace'	48	9	14	4	25	57

Source: Jørgensen et al. 1993: 239–41 (survey of LO (TUC) members, 1992).

This is related to the large numbers of public employees among nonmanual workers. As in most countries, unionization is highest among public employees. In Norway, public employees appear to be twice as frequently organized as the privately employed. This explains why the collar gap has reversed: within both sectors, unionization among manuals and non manuals is the same. This also means that membership is very low among manuals in the private sector (although the figures are too low, due to inadequate measurement, see note 5). At any rate, the comparatively high unionization in Norway hinges upon the existence of a large public sector. In Denmark and Sweden, sector and class interact: in the public sector, the collar gap is reversed but in the private sector we find the conventional class pattern where only some 70–75 per cent of the non manual employees (62 per cent among higher non manuals) are organized. But even here, the collar gap is narrowing.

To assess the impact of private service growth, we have examined private sector differences in Denmark in Table 6.5. This would seem to have an

Table 6.4 Trade union membership, by class and sector (percentages)

	Percentages of union members				N			
	Denmark		Sweden	Norway	Denmark		Sweden	Norway
	1979	1990	1987	1990	1979	1990	1987	1990
Total	80	86	83	46	1120	1128	1276	1018
Manual workers	83	88	82	39	529	435	489	361
Non manual employees	77	85	84	50	591	681	787	657
Unskilled workers	81	85	76	40	352	286	277	211
Skilled workers	86	93	90	37	177	149	212	150
Lower nonmanual	78	88	83	46	499	376	355	279
Medium nonmanual		86	88	55		162	253	180
Higher nonmanual	74	74	77	52	92	143	179	198
Private sector	78	82	77	32	683	548	675	558
Worker	86	90	81	33	400	254	336	245
Nonmanual	67	74	72	32	283	287	339	313
Public sector	83	91	90	68	434	469	574	405
Worker	73	87	84	68	129	112	141	78
Nonmanual	87	92	92	68	305	357	433	327

Source: Scandinavian Citizenship Surveys and Danish Participation Survey 1979.

Table 6.5 Unionization in Denmark 1990, by occupation and sector (percentages)

	Percentages of union members			N		
	Manual workers	Nonmanual employees	Total	Manual workers	Nonmanual employees	Total[1]
Manufacture & construction	95	75	89	188	84	273
Private services	78	73	74	59	198	261
Public sector	87	92	91	112	357	469

Note: 1. Including respondents with no information on occupation.

Source: Scandinavian Citizenship Surveys.

impact; among manual workers in manufacture and construction, 95 per cent were organized by 1990; among non manuals and/or service workers in the private sector, the figure is only around three-quarters. Still, this is high by international standards (Troy 1990), and until the 1990s, unionization continued to increase within all categories.

The decline of working-class communities and the declining size of the average firm have also been suggested as sources of union decline (Even and Macpherson 1990; Beaumont and Harris 1991). But this also seems to be contingent on institutional factors (see Table 6.6). In Norway, our data confirm earlier findings from Norway and elsewhere that firm size is important (Tøssebro 1983; Bain and Elsheikh 1979; Visser 1990: 60–1). In Denmark, however (see also Visser 1991: 117–18), firm size has become unimportant – as only the smallest firms (those with 1–4 employees) deviate from the general pattern. This is logical: workers in small firms may not be covered by collective wage agreements, but they need unemployment insurance like anyone else. From an institutional perspective, one would exactly expect to find negligible differences in Denmark but larger differences in Norway. As to socialization, the Swedish and Norwegian data indicate that contact with colleagues in private life has no effect upon unionization. Interestingly, the data also show that few wage-earners have such contacts: one out of three in Sweden, one out of five in Norway. By implication, even the disintegration of working-class communities does not seem to affect the levels of unionization.

In short, *changes in class structure and class structuration do not seem important for union membership in Scandinavia*. The same holds for the entry of women into the labor market. Until recently, it was a universal finding that women had lower unionization (see, for example, Visser 1991: 115–17), and female labor market participation was seen as a source of

Table 6.6 Trade union membership, by plant size (private sector employees only) and contact with colleagues in private life (percentages)

Plant size	Percentages of union members			N		
	Denmark	Sweden	Norway	Denmark	Sweden	Norway
1–4	74	—[1]	14	42	—	115
5–9	90	—	24	61	—	84
10–19	81	—	26	72	—	97
20–49	87	—	42	82	—	94
50–99	82	—	35	61	—	58
100–499	80	—	56	136	—	70
500 +	86	—	58	70	—	31
Contact with colleagues outside work						
Yes	—[1]	84	43	—	420	194
No	—	83	50	—	833	742

Note: 1. Question not posed.

Source: Scandinavian Citizenship Surveys.

declining unionization (Moore and Newman 1988). This was explained by women sector distribution, part-time labor or lower attachment to the job role (Even and Macpherson 1992; Bertl et al. 1988; Hirsch and Addison 1986). But these theories are obsolete (Goul Andersen 1984a). *In all three Scandinavian countries, women now have higher rates of union membership than men.* Although the gender gap is narrowing in all countries (Visser 1991: 115–17), the reversal of the gap is unique. But it follows logically from gender differences in class position: few women occupy leading positions in the private sector, and around one-half are employed in the public services. Employees with very short working hours (8–24 hours a week) remain less likely to unionize but such short working hours have nearly disappeared in the Scandinavian countries which were the first to introduce part-time labor on a massive scale in the 1960s and 1970s; since 1980, however, the trend is strongly towards full-time or almost full-time employment (Goul Andersen 2000). In Denmark, the sharp increase in unionization among women in the 1970s was frequently interpreted as an effect of the Ghent

Table 6.7 Trade union membership among wage-earners, by gender, employment, age and education (percentages)

	Percentages of union members				N			
	Denmark		Sweden	Norway	Denmark		Sweden	Norway
	1979	*1990*	*1987*	*1990*	*1979*	*1990*	*1987*	*1990*
Men	83	85	82	42	617	562	655	594
Women	76	86	84	52	503	566	621	424
Working hours:								
Short-time (8–24 h)	67[1]	78	65	41	242	74	116	140
Part-time (25–32 h)		85	86	49		118	147	81
Full-time (33 h +)	83[1]	87	85	49	793	824	979	751
Employed	80	86	83	47		1017	1249	974
Unemployed	85	81	82	18	52	111	27	44
Low basic education	84	88	84	41	614	391	615	458
Medium	74	86	86	51	390	464	282	213
High	79	81	79	50	107	272	379	335
18–29 years	79	78	77	33	340	259	374	258
30–39 years	83	91	84	49	337	356	315	292
40–49 years	78	87	91	56	227	305	299	252
50–59 years	82	84	86	43	171	168	205	140
60–69 years	67	75	68	51	45	40	79	70

Note: 1. Respondent indicated whether he/she was in part-time or full-time employment.

Source: Scandinavian Citizenship Surveys, and Danish Mass Participation Survey 1979.

system; however, the identical patterns in the Scandinavian countries show that this is *not* the case: changing gender roles was the explanation.[6]

To sum up, our findings confirm the conventional institutional explanation of high unionization but contradict most generalizations about social variations. Most significantly, both the gender gap and the collar gap in unionization have been closed or reversed; and under the Ghent system, even firm size and unemployment is unimportant. Other things being equal, high unionization of the unemployed makes unions less 'insider'-dominated – and the unemployed less politically marginalized. As will be demonstrated below (Table 6.16), the unemployed actually feel that they have more influence on their union than do the employed.

However, this analysis does not necessarily indicate a promising future for the unions. One could imagine that increasing unionization was an effect of generational replacement, like unionization among part-time employed women in the 1970s. But, as revealed by Table 6.7, union membership has increased in all age groups in Denmark from 1979 to 1990 *except* among the young. Thus, the trade unions may be more vulnerable than they seem at first glance. And data on participation and attitudes do not look too promising, either.

Unions as movements

As Colin Crouch has put it: 'Unions may have a long-term future, but do union *movements*?' (Crouch 1990, quoted in Hyman 1991: 630). This question seems particularly relevant to ask in a Danish and Swedish context where union membership does not express much of a choice. We shall focus in this section on three factors: engagement and participation among members; solidarity and identity formation; and efficacy and trust. Participation is important in its own right, but is probably also a precondition of identity formation and trust among members. And without such diffuse support, nourished by participation, even union *membership* may rest on less solid grounds. If membership is based on purely instrumental motives, unions become dependent on their ability to provide selective incentives (Olson 1965) and vulnerable to changes in the calculation of costs and benefits among individual members. Professionalization and bureaucratization, not to mention oligarchical leadership, are likely to have a negative impact upon trust and identity formation. However, in the life span of social movements, bureaucratization frequently accumulates (Touraine 1986; Micheletti 1994), and if membership can be taken for granted, union leaders may have fewer incentives to be responsive to members' wants. This is the down side to the medal of the Ghent system – in other words, the Danish and Swedish unions may run the risk of becoming victims of their own success.

First, we examine *union participation*. As to country differences, the question is whether Norwegian unions have been able to maintain higher levels of participation. As to social variations, one could imagine that the working-class–middle-class divide would surface instead as variations in *participation* in countries where membership is more of a fact than a choice. We only have one comparable activity measure: participation in union meetings within the last year (for more detailed accounts of activity, see, for example, Jørgensen et al. 1993). From the Danish survey, interest in union politics serves as a control. Our data confirm that activity is low among Danish and Swedish union members where only 21 and 26 per cent, respectively, had participated, as compared to 65 per cent among the Norwegians (Table 6.8). And in this case, the Danish 1990 figures seem reliable (Goul Andersen 1993c).

In Denmark, comparable data from 1979 indicate that active participation halved between 1979 and 1990.[7] Still, this conclusion should not be pushed too far. In the first place, the 1970s were a period of industrial unrest. Secondly, *interest* in trade union politics has not changed much (Table 6.8), and participation in union activities at the *workplace* has not declined (chapter 7). Finally, even in 1990, nearly 30 per cent of *all* members have had the experience of holding an office position in the union. This remains a high figure when compared to other associations.

Still, the trend does fit the prediction of decline, and one might imagine that this reflects the changing class structure towards individualist middle classes. But in all three countries, non manuals are more active than blue-collar workers (Table 6.9). This pattern is sector-specific, however: In

Table 6.8 Active[1] union members, as proportion of (a) members and (b) all employees in Denmark, Sweden and Norway, and interest in trade union politics[2] (Denmark only) (percentages)

	Percentages of active members			N		
	Denmark	Sweden	Norway	Denmark	Sweden	Norway
	1979 1990			1979 1990		
(a) Proportion of trade union members	46 21	26	65	896 964	1060	470
(b) Proportion of all wage-earners	37 18	22	30	1120 1128	1276	1018
Interest in trade union politics (members only)	58 56	—[3]	—[3]	896 964	—	—

Notes: 1. Have participated in at least one meeting within the last 12 months.
2. Much or some interest in the activities of the union.
3. Question not posed.

Source: Scandinavian Citizenship Surveys and Danish Participation Survey 1979.

Table 6.9   Trade union activity, by class and sector (percentages of members)

	Denmark		Sweden Partici- pation	Norway Partici- pation	N Denmark	Sweden	Norway
	Interest	Participation					
Manual workers	53	17	19	57	382	402	141
Nonmanual employees	60	24	31	69	576	658	329
Unskilled workers	51	14	15	57	243	211	85
Skilled workers	53	22	22	59	139	191	56
Lower non-manual	54	19	27	66	331	297	128
Medium non-manual	73	37	34	77	139	223	99
Higher non-manual	61	21	34	64	106	138	102
Private sector	49	16	27	57	447	519	180
Worker	52	19	21	60	229	274	80
Nonmanual	46	14	33	55	213	245	100
Public sector	66	28	27	71	427	519	276
Worker	56	15	13	55	97	119	53
Nonmanual	69	31	30	75	330	400	223

Source: Scandinavian Citizenship Surveys.

Denmark and Norway, manual workers are in fact the most active in the private sector, whereas nonmanuals are by far the most active among public employees, and the most active of all groups. In Sweden, nonmanuals are even the most active among the privately employed.

In accordance with the interpretations above, we find that gender differences in participation have nearly disappeared (Table 6.10); and female unionization has been followed by steadily increasing interest in trade union politics (Goul Andersen 1984a: 202–26) so that women are now slightly more interested in trade union politics than men.

Briefly, the country differences do confirm that there is a down side to the Ghent system: What is gained in membership may be lost in participation. The assumption that social change as such leads to lower participation, on the other hand, is falsified: the gender gap is almost closed, and non manuals are more active than manual workers. Thus it is not least among manual workers that unions face participation problems. Although interest in union politics has remained, it seems that members increasingly assume the role of spectators – albeit interested and critical spectators.

Table 6.10 Trade union activity, by gender, employment, education and age (percentages of members)

	Denmark		Sweden	Norway	N		
	Interest	Participation	Participation	Participation	Denmark	Sweden	Norway
Men	56	24	28	66	479	537	251
Women	58	19	25	65	485	523	219
7–9 years basic education	54	17	24	59	344	518	187
10 years	54	20	27	70	401	242	109
12 years or more	66	29	29	69	219	300	169
18–29 years	48	12	16	59	203	291	86
30–39 years	62	25	27	68	323	266	145
40–49 years	58	24	31	70	266	273	142
50–59 years	58	21	35	65	142	176	60
60–69 years	43	20	26	53	30	54	36

Table 6.11 Feeling of affinity with various movements. Whole population (percentages expressing 'some' or 'much' affinity)

	Denmark[1]	Sweden[1]	Norway
1. Labor movement	45	46	46
2. Environmental movement	58	68	68
3. Peace movement	41	67	57
4. Women's movement	26	46	37
5. Int. solidarity movement	—	61	60
6. State church	—	38	75
7. Temperance movement	—	30	19
Average 1–4	43	57	52
Average 1–7	—	51	52

Note:
1. In Denmark and Sweden measured by on a scale 0–10. Recoded as follows: 0–4 No affinity; 5–8, Some affinity; 9–10 much affinity.

Source: Scandinavian Citizenship Surveys.

The second set of questions is whether unions have maintained their *identity-shaping capacities*, whether this problem is larger in Denmark and Sweden, and whether it is related to participation. Our measure here is *feeling of affinity with the labor movement*. Among the population at large, the proportion that express affinity with the labor movement is virtually identical in all three countries (at around 45–46 per cent; see Table 6.11).[8] As compared to identification with other movements, these figures are rather low. In Sweden and Norway, feeling of affinity with other movements is larger, whereas the Danes are less enthusiastic about movements altogether. Among union members, however, the feeling of affinity with the labor movement is much greater in Norway than in the other two countries (Table 6.12). In Denmark and Sweden, only about one-half of the trade union members identify with the labor movement, and in all three countries, even union members feel more affinity with the environmental movement than with the labor movement.

Table 6.12   Affinity with labor movement (percentages feeling 'some' or 'much' affinity)

Affinity with labor movement	Whole population	Employees			N			
		Total	Members	Nonmembers				
Denmark	45	49	51	35	1968	1128	964	164
Sweden	46	43	47	25	1936	1254	1045	209
Norway	46	49	61	39	1736	1018	470	548

Source: Scandinavian Citizenship Surveys.

Table 6.13   Affinity with the labor movement, by age. Whole population (percentages feeling 'much' or 'some' affinity)

Age (years)	Denmark	Sweden	Norway	N		
				Denmark	Sweden	Norway
18–29	42	32	44	384	478	470
30–39	54	46	49	414	372	380
40–49	46	44	47	390	350	344
50–59	44	49	50	257	275	211
60–69	41	65	46	267	268	191
70 or more	40	58	41	256	193	145

Source: Scandinavian Citizenship Surveys.

Table 6.14   Affinity with the labor movement, by participation. Employees only (percentages feeling 'some' or 'much' affinity)

	All employees			Manual workers			Nonmanuals		
	Denmark	Sweden	Norway	Denmark	Sweden	Norway	Denmark	Sweden	Norway
Nonmember	34	25	40	44	29	48	30	22	34
Passive	48	42	59	53	49	68	44	38	53
Active	65	60	61	75	73	77	61	55	55
N	192	212	555	59	85	222	133	127	333
	776	797	165	318	331	60	458	466	105
	209	283	312	64	78	83	145	205	229

Source: Scandinavian Citizenship Surveys.

In Denmark and Norway, age differences are small (Table 6.13). But in Sweden, affinity is nearly twice as high among the old as among the young. It is tempting to suggest that this may indicate generational change, reflecting the fact that the hegemonic position of the labor movement in Swedish politics has come to an end. Finally, the assumption that affinity with the labor movement is related to participation is confirmed by Table 6.14. In Denmark and Sweden, activity is at least as important for the feeling of affinity as membership, whereas membership seems most important in Norway.

Efficacy and trust in unions

Other things being equal, a high level of unionization means strong unions. But if membership can be taken for granted, it may also mean less responsiveness. Thus we should expect Norwegian members to feel more efficacious vis-à-vis the unions but at the same time to consider the unions to be less powerful than in the two other countries. Analogous differences may be expected when comparing blue-collar and white-collar members: Blue-collar unions may be strong, but less responsive. In the citizenship surveys, perception of the union's influence at the workplace was measured alongside with feeling of whether members could influence the union.

The most remarkable finding from Table 6.15[9] is that a large proportion of the union members, and in Denmark and Sweden even a large majority, feel they have little or no influence upon their own unions. Next, the country difference in efficacy is as predicted: Norwegian union members are much more inclined to feel they can affect the unions than the Danes and the Swedes. This holds even if we include nonmembers – in other words, it is not explained simply by the fact that membership is more voluntary in Norway. The expectation that Norwegians consider unions less powerful, on the other hand, is falsified: One-half of the Norwegian members consider their unions to be powerful, as compared to one-quarter of the Swedes and the Danes. It is likely that the answers reflect not only perceptions of union power but also the level of overall confidence in the unions. At the individual level, this interpretation is confirmed by a clear *positive* correlation between the feeling of influence and the feeling that the union is powerful (Pearson correlations between 0.20 and 0.30).

As far as social differences are concerned, our data confirm that manual workers consider unions to be more powerful but at the same time feel more powerless vis-à-vis the unions than non manual employees. This is especially true in the cases of Norway and Sweden (Table 6.16). One might expect that public employees would consider their unions more powerful and feel more efficacious than those privately employed, but there are no aggregate sector differences. However, when we control for manual vs non manual labor, we find an interesting interaction effect. In all three countries,

Table 6.15 Perceived trade union power at workplace and influence upon trade unions. All employees, and trade union members only (percentages)

	All employees			Trade union members		
	Denmark[1]	Sweden	Norway	Denmark	Sweden	Norway
A. *Trade union power at workplace*						
Much	(27)	24	40	27	26	49
Little	(56)	52	39	56	56	46
None	(13)	13	5	13	10	3
Don't know[2]	(4)	11	16	4	8	2
N (=100%)	933	1276	971	933	1060	461
PDI: Much minus none[3]	(14)	11	35	14	16	46
B. *Influence on trade union*						
Much	(5)	4	4	5	4	7
Some	(29)	27	30	29	31	44
Little	(38)	36	30	38	39	37
No influence at all	(21)	21	13	21	16	8
Don't know	(7)	12	23	7	10	4
N (=100%)	933	1276	1276	933	1060	461
PDI: Much/some minus little or none	−25	−26	−9	−25	−20	+6

Notes:
1. Trade union members only (the Danish question was only posed to trade union members).
2. Including 'Not relevant'. Nineteen per cent of all employees gave this answer, but only 1 per cent of trade union members.
3. Percentage difference index: Difference between the indicated proportions (in percentage points).

Source: Scandinavian Citizenship Surveys.

manual workers in the public sector consider their unions less powerful and feel less efficacious than those privately employed workers. Among non manuals, public employees feel more efficacious and consider unions more powerful than private employees. Finally, age differences are surprisingly small; the only large variations are low efficacy among young Swedes and older Norwegians.

It comes as no surprise that those who are active in union politics are much more inclined to feel efficacious and to feel that the union is powerful. But in Denmark, even the active members are not inclined to think they can influence the union (Table 6.17). The difference in efficacy between Swedes and the Norwegians, however, is to a large extent explained by the fact that Norwegians are more active.

Table 6.16 Union Power at workplace and influence upon trade unions. Trade union members only (PDIs)

	Influence on union			Union power			N		
	Denmark	Sweden	Norway	Denmark	Sweden	Norway	Denmark	Sweden	Norway
Manual workers	−27	−33	−16	23	19	52	373	402	135
Nonmanual employment	−23	−12	16	9	13	45	561	658	326
Private sector	−33	−21	5	11	16	44	432	519	180
Manual	−28	−31	0	27	20	59	225	274	80
Nonmanual	−37	−9	9	−7	13	33	203	245	100
Public sector	−18	−19	11	18	15	49	422	519	275
Manual	−32	−39	−39	16	19	42	95	119	53
Nonmanual	−14	−16	19	18	14	51	327	400	222
18–29 years	−25	−35	8	16	12	61	198	291	85
30–39 years	−23	−13	22	16	15	44	316	266	139
40–49 years	−20	−12	10	16	18	43	258	273	141
50–59 years	−34	−19	−3	4	17	50	137	176	60
60–69 years	−30	−17	−40	7	22	40	30	54	35

PDI influence on union: 'Much' or 'some' versus 'little' or 'none'.
PDI union power: 'Much' versus 'none'.

Source: Scandinavian Citizenship Surveys.

Table 6.17 Trade union activity, evaluation of union power at workplace and feeling of influence upon trade unions. Trade union members only (PDIs)

	Influence on unions			Union power			N		
	Denmark	Sweden	Norway	Denmark	Sweden	Norway	Denmark	Sweden	Norway
Passive member									
Manual	−33	−34	−17	12	11	38	792	782	158
Nonmanual	−34	−42	−32	23	16	42	308	327	56
	−31	−29	−8	4	7	34	427	455	102
Active members									
Worker	5	20	19	23	29	52	200	278	303
Employee	6	7	−5	23	35	57	65	75	79
	5	24	27	23	27	50	134	83	224

Source: Scandinavian Citizenship Surveys.

To conclude, whereas Danish and Swedish unions have been unusually successful in recruiting members, they are less successful as social movements. Low participation, low identification with the labor movement, low efficacy and low evaluations of union influence reflecting low trust are some of the keywords that recur in the analysis. Norwegian unions, on the other hand, appear healthier as social movements.

Representativeness

Since the birth of the Scandinavian labor movement, there has been a close cooperation and much overlapping membership between the trade unions and the Social Democratic parties in all countries. The first question is how much remains of this, especially among office holders. Next, one may ask whether the political biases of office holders constitute a problem as the members have become politically more heterogeneous, both because of declining class voting and because of increasing membership.

As to the first question, it turns out that the association between party and unions has become rather weak. Only 22 per cent of the trade union office holders in Denmark and Sweden are party members, and only 9, respectively 8 per cent, hold an office in a political party. Even among workers, the proportion of party members among office holders in Sweden is 'only' 37 per cent (the sizes of the Danish samples are too small, but the figures are almost certain to be lower).

In Denmark and Sweden, office holders furthermore turn out to be politically representative of the active members, regardless of class. Passive members are less socialist (Table 6.18) but the main discrepancy is between members and nonmembers (who constitute a politically deviant minority). The proportion of socialists among union members is 60 per cent in Denmark and 58 per cent in Sweden, as compared to 36 per cent and 33 per cent, respectively, among nonmembers. One could imagine that in less unionized Norway, union members would be more politically homogeneous. But the opposite turns out to be the case – the proportion of socialists among union members was only 53 per cent in 1990, as compared to 36 per cent among nonmembers. This also means that the attitudes of Norwegian union members described above is not a spurious effect of more socialist orientations.

The party political biases of the top union leadership may certainly still constitute a problem for members but otherwise the political biases are surprisingly small. Furthermore, we know from other studies that office holders are in line with the members when it comes to the far more relevant question of priorities between tasks (Jørgensen et al. 1993). With actives and office holders being fairly representative of the members, socially and politically, however, it may also be suggested that trade unions

Table 6.18 Party composition of union members, active members and office holders
(percentages, voting socialist)

Per cent socialist[1]	All employees		Workers		Nonmanual	
	Denmark	Sweden	Denmark	Sweden	Denmark	Sweden
Nonmembers	36	33	51	50	30	22
Members[2]	60	58	69	75	54	47
Active members[3]	73	63	85	84	68	54
Office holders	73	64	(86)	92	65	54
	143	163	39	64	104	99
	822	876	309	331	513	545
	183	237	53	70	130	167
	48	135	14	38	34	97

Notes:
1. Denmark: Party choice in latest election; Sweden: Preferred party. Data are not weighted.
2. Including actives and office holders.
3. Including office holders.
Source: Scandinavian Citizenship Surveys.

are increasingly becoming simple interest associations rather than movements: They do not contribute much to political equality as movements
(at best, participation is less socially biased than in other movements), and
they probably no longer give much of a socialist interpretation to members' experiences. Thus despite high rates of membership, the Scandinavian
trade unions fit well into the picture of class demobilization that we have
seen earlier.

Scandinavian unions: conclusions

The decline of trade unions is a significant aspect of class demobilization in
many countries but in Scandinavia – and in particular in Denmark and
Sweden – unions have remained strong. Unionization continued to rise
until around 1990 and is by far the highest among the Western industrial-
ized countries. Although this is not the only motive for membership, it is
beyond doubt that the trade unions' control of the unemployment insurance system plays a major role in its current success. This has made the
unions immune to social and ideological change, as well as to economic
recession, and it provides an opportunity for the unemployed to have
some influence on the unions. An interesting characteristic is that both the
gender gap and the collar gap in unionization and participation have been
closed or even reversed.

From an instrumental and even from a citizenship point of view, the
thorough organization of citizens' economic interests is important (we

return to the unemployed in chapter 10). But comparison with Norway indicates that there is also a down side to the apparent success – that is, that unions are performing very poorly as social movements in Denmark and Sweden. The Scandinavian countries seem sufficiently alike to allow the conclusion that the difference in unemployment insurance system is probably the major source of the country differences.

It must be acknowledged that interest in union politics has remained at a relatively high level and that unions continue to play a role in mass political mobilization in Scandinavia. But the role of the unions does seem to be declining, and although there remains a basic support for unions among members, unions seem increasingly vulnerable to institutional change. A change in the unemployment benefit system could undoubtedly reduce figures of membership dramatically, perhaps to a level below those in Norway, because there is far less enthusiasm about unions in Denmark and Sweden. Although the Norwegian figures show that participation at the workplace level does not rule out the possibility that participation in unions may also be high, and although strong unions may be a precondition of workplace participation there is little doubt that employees in modern companies are seeking other ways to obtain influence than through unions, partly through more individualized and informal channels. This is the subject of the next chapter.

7
Workplace Democracy in Scandinavia

Introduction

Democracy at work – whether in the form of workplace democracy, industrial democracy or economic democracy[1] – has been discussed by numerous scholars as well as pursued by numerous social movements and political parties ever since the breakthrough of democracy in the spheres of politics and civil society. Scholars from the neo-pluralist school of democracy (Dahl 1986), those with an orientation towards participatory democracy (Macpherson 1977, 1985; Pateman 1970), and scholars from socialist theories of democracy (Horvat 1977; Markovic 1982) have all – albeit from different perspectives – advocated the idea of democracy in the sphere of work. The topic has been subject to discussion between the American and the English tradition of democratic thinking (Dahl 1986: 111–35). Furthermore, trade unions and socialist as well as social democratic parties have, with varying degrees of intensity and conviction, pursued this idea for over a hundred years. These thoughts and the struggles carried out by unions and parties have – though similar in nature – resulted in very different institutional arrangements and positions of power for employees in different countries (Walker 1977; Potterfield 1999).

Whereas the institutional arrangements – the laws, collective agreements and so on – are quite well described in the literature, empirical studies of the actual influence of employees on their workplace through these arrangements are largely neglected. The purpose of this chapter is therefore to shed some light on this question on the basis of survey data from the Scandinavian citizenship studies. More concretely we shall look at: (i) the attempts of individual wage-earners at exercising power through initiatives to change conditions at their workplace by contacting union representatives, supervisors or management, and through their own work as union representatives; (ii) wage-earners' (collective) attempts at exercising power at their workplace through their unions; and (iii) whether participation at the workplace is of importance for wider political participation.

The data at hand allows us to analyze these questions in some depth for the three Scandinavian countries, thereby illustrating similarities and differences between them. However, comparisons with countries outside Scandinavia are very difficult because of the lack of comparable data. We shall, none the less, make certain assumptions about the uniqueness of the 'Scandinavian case' after our short historical sketch below. As these assumptions are consequential for the hypotheses we shall pursue, the hypotheses will be spelled out in detail only after the sketch.

Another limitation of our analysis is that we shall limit ourselves to an analysis of workplace democracy. By workplace democracy we shall understand participation at the shop-floor level; that is, the extent to which employees, as individuals, are able to influence their own working conditions through both formal and informal channels. The formal channels here will include influence through union representatives or other employees', representatives, through formal complaints or grievance procedures,

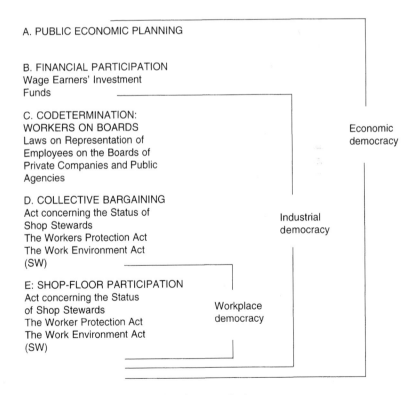

Figure 7.1 Workplace, industrial and economic democracy

Source: Inspired by Åsard 1986
(SW = Swedish examples)

and through work councils at the level of the workplace. Informal channels include individual initiatives towards supervisors or management.

We thus make a distinction between workplace democracy and industrial and economic democracy. This distinction is quite common in the literature on democratization of enterprises, and is tied to the distinction between 'participatory' and 'representative' democracy. Workplace democracy is seen as representing 'participatory democracy' whereas industrial and economic democracy are seen as 'representative' variants (see, for example, Pateman 1970; Elden 1981). However, most writers on this subject seem to agree that industrial democracy, which adds the dimensions of collective bargaining and codetermination in the form of worker representatives on company boards, also encompasses what we have defined here as workplace democracy. Finally, economic democracy designates the situation where unions and political parties have moved on to engage in macroeconomic policies through proposals and laws on redistribution of profits – especially through wage-earners' funds – with possible considerable long-term effects on overall investments and employment. As economic democracy has workplace and industrial democracy as a prerequisite, and deal in- or explicitly with these levels of democracy, we see economic democracy as also embodying these two concepts. Our conception of the relation between the three concepts is illustrated in Figure 7.1.

Historical background

In order to understand properly the special character of workplace democracy in Scandinavia, and thus the background for the hypotheses set forth below, it is necessary to locate it in its historical context.

Industrial democracy has its roots in French syndicalism and English guild socialism (Sturmthal 1977), and was further developed by Marxist/socialist/anarchist ideas of 'council socialism' (Gramsci 1971; Pannekoek 1946). In Scandinavia, the debates about workplace democracy date back to the beginning of the century, and seem to have emerged in waves. In Denmark, for example, there was a first wave of interest in workplace democracy in the period 1919–27, a second wave just after the Second World War, and a third wave in the period 1964–73 (Dalgaard 1992). These waves seem to coincide with periods of working-class strength,[2] and each of the waves has resulted in some cumulative progress concerning the question of workplace democracy, at least institutionally.

Drawing again on primarily Danish experiences it is clear that already in the first wave different ideas about workplace democracy as well as industrial and economic democracy were discussed in the Social Democratic party and the unions. The Social Democratic party launched a law proposal on works councils (1924), and the unions (the Danish DsF being the equivalent of the Swedish LO) pursued the question of consultative workplace committees in collective bargaining (1920). Whereas the legislative proposal foundered due to labor movement infighting between social democrats and the revolutionary left, and to staunch opposition from employers and bourgeois parties, the unions were able to establish consultative shop-floor committees in some industries. However, the committees were solely of a consultative nature.

A new wave of working-class radicalism emerged immediately after the Second World War. However, this time the social democratic parties, being either ruling parties or the biggest national parties, had to be more sensitive to employers' interests, and towards the task of stimulating production to promote reconstruction. Cooperation was the order of the day, and collective bargaining resulted in agreements establishing work councils with equal representation for management and employees in 1945 (Norway), 1946 (Sweden) and 1947 (Denmark).

However, the councils soon came under fire for having no real power. If one looks, for example, at the Danish agreement this criticism seems justified. The councils dealt with questions concerning work conditions; for example welfare, security and health. They also aimed to stimulate employee interest in the workplace, and to promote rational management. However, the councils had no decision-making authority in any of these areas. Furthermore, the councils were not allowed to engage in matters of collective bargaining or arbitration. In Norway and Sweden the work councils had much the same tasks, and the Scandinavian work councils of the 1940s were therefore rather similar to the type of 'paternalist' work councils established in for example the Netherlands in 1950 (Visser 1993).

In the third wave towards the middle/end of the 1960s, new collective agreements gave employees the right to exert an influence over safety rules, workplace welfare arrangements and long-term personnel policies (Schiller 1977). This new phase is interesting because it was preceded by/went hand-in-hand with experiments in workplace democracy. Especially interesting and encompassing are the Norwegian experiments that started as early as 1962 as a joint research effort by the LO and the Employers Federation (Elden 1979; Gustavsen and Hunnius 1981). The findings of the experiments resulted, through the so-called Aspengreen Committee (1963–65),[3] in proposals on: (i) expanded consultations among employers, local union representatives and work councils; (ii) education of workers to prepare them for participation; and (iii) changes in company legislation in order to enable workers to take part in decision-making in the workplace.

Over the next decade, these proposals found their way into collective agreements. The greatest resistance from the employers was over the idea of worker representatives on company boards. None the less, this was enacted (partly by law) between 1972 and 1975. As a result, any company with more than 200 employees was to have a corporate assembly of at least 12 members – two-thirds being elected by the shareholders, and one-third by the employees. Similarly, employees are entitled to not less than two representatives on the board of companies with more than 50 employees.

The same development was seen in Sweden and Denmark, and in 1973–74 legislation was passed in these countries which gave employees the right to appoint two members to company boards. Elements of industrial democracy were now in place to support and complement workplace democracy. In Sweden the attack on employers' prerogatives went further, and resulted in the passing of the Law on Codetermination ('Lag om Medbestämmande i Arbetslivet') in 1976. This law requires the employer to negotiate before making decisions on important matters such as reorganizations, expansions or shutdowns. Employees also acquired the right to strike over codetermination issues even after an agreement on wages has been concluded (Schiller 1977; Dokras 1990).

The last part of the third phase represents the move from workplace and industrial democracy towards economic democracy. While this might represent a highpoint of the strength of organized labor in Scandinavia, it probably also represents, as Dalgaard (1993) puts it: 'the last reform from the socialdemocratic movement with a systems-transforming perspective'. Best known and internationally discussed are the different Swedish proposals and finally the Law on Wage Earners Funds in 1983 ('Lag om löntagerfonder'; see Pontusson 1992). This law developed from the Meidner proposal in 1976, whose purpose was to: (i) complement the solidaristic wage policy; (ii) counter the concentration of private property; and (iii) increase the influence of wage-earners. This purpose was to be realized through the establishment of a number of wage-earners' funds financed by a percentage of corporate profits. These funds were to be transformed into shares in the company from where the profit came originally,[4] with no upper limit to the percentage of shares the funds could hold. This rather radical proposal was, however, watered down, partly due to the electoral defeat of the Social Democratic Party in the 1976 election, and partly due to an all-out campaign by Swedish employers in the 1981 election campaign against a new joint proposal by the Swedish LO and social democracy.

As a result, the final Law on Wage Earners Funds, proposed in Parliament in 1983, and passed with a slim majority, was moderate compared both to the 1976 and the 1981 proposals. The main changes from the 1981 proposal was that the number of funds was reduced to five, and that there was to be a ceiling on the percentage of shares the funds could hold in any single company (8 per cent), and of total joint-stock capital (10 per cent). The board on each fund would consist of nine members appointed by the government. Of these, five should represent 'wage-earners' interests'.

The Danish debate and proposals on economic democracy had its background in the campaign on workplace democracy which the LO started in 1967. However, the Danish debate deviated markedly from the Swedish in that the Social Democratic Party did not dominate the debate to the same extent as its Swedish sister party. Thus, in Denmark both the Radical Liberal Party, and the Socialist People's Party pursued their own proposals. The Socialdemocrats could not automatically count on the support of either of these parties, and therefore had to maneuver between the center and the left. The party put forward a proposal for a law on economic democracy in 1973, which contained only one (big) wage-earner fund. The fund was to be financed by a payroll tax, and the proceeds were to accrue to the individual wage-earners after a period of 5–7 years. The ceiling on shares that the fund could own in any one company was set at 50 per cent. However, the law proposal fell in Parliament because the People's Socialist Party chose not to support it. None the less, the debate on economic democracy/profit-sharing continued throughout the 1970s and 1980s, though with less vigor. It finally came to an end in 1991, when the Social Democratic Party and LO abandoned their common work committee on the issue.

To conclude this short sketch of the debate on economic democracy in Sweden and Denmark one can say that both proposals were at the outset very ambitious, having both a power, a participatory, and a welfare political aspect. However, during the negotiations and deliberations the power and participation aspects were gradually watered down, and the welfare political aspect became more prominent (that is, the question of creating enough capital for future investments, thus preserving jobs and incomes).

This short historical sketch has aimed to demonstrate that whereas the Scandinavian countries did not deviate much from other European countries concerning workplace democracy before the 1950s, they took a different route from the 1960s. Generally speaking, we think it possible today to distinguish between an English/American, a continental European and a Scandinavian type of workplace/industrial democracy. The English/American type is based exclusively on collective bargaining, with an emphasis on the shop-floor level, and on the importance of the shop steward system. As pointed out by, for example, Derber (1977) collective bargaining in these countries often covers more than in the other types, and workplace/industrial democracy is therefore by no means absent from these systems. However, because the bargaining is focused at plant level there tends to be large variations in the standard of workplace/industrial democracy between plants and between industries.

The continental European type is also to some extent based on collective bargaining. However, here the emphasis is on industry-wide negotiations between organizational leaders; often with weak links to the plant level. Codetermination is normally implemented by law, which means that there is not necessarily a direct link between unions and work councils (even though most elected council members are normally union members). Germany (Fürstenberg 1977), the Netherlands (Albeda 1977; Visser 1993), and France (Delamotte 1977) are good examples of this type.

By contrast, the Scandinavian type is based on both collective agreements and laws. Collective bargaining on issues related to workplace/industrial democracy takes place at both the industry and the plant levels, with an emphasis on the role of elected union representatives and the local union(s). Work councils are normally established by collective agreements, whereas other forms of codetermination, such as employee representation on boards, are established by law. Given the large variations between industries and between countries, it might be difficult to determine which type gives wage-earners the biggest influence in their own workplace and work conditions. However, we will claim, or at least put forward as a hypothesis, that since the end of the 1960s the Scandinavian type has been leading in this respect. Due to high rates of unionization and strong social democratic parties, an institutional framework has been built (work councils, numerous laws to protect the wage-earner, codetermination arrangements, and so on) which underpins the power positions of the wage-earners. Sweden stands out here, and has for years internationally been seen as a 'role model' as to wage-earner influence, due to its unique law on codetermination, and its experiment with economic democracy.

The hypotheses

As mentioned above, this postulated or real position of the Scandinavian wage-earners forms the background for a number of hypotheses that we shall test in the following paragraphs. Firstly, we expect to see high levels of democratic participation at the workplace (hypothesis #1), because the organizational framework is geared for this. The underlying assumption here is that there is a positive correlation between institutional arrangements for participation and actual participatory behavior.[5] Secondly, we expect to see high levels of job satisfaction (hypothesis #2), because Pateman (1970) and others postulate a (positive) correlation between participation and job satisfaction (hypothesis #3). Thirdly, as the general conditions for participation and some form of influence are considered as good, we also expect to find both high levels of experienced efficacy at the individual level (success with initiatives) at the workplace (hypothesis #4), as well as high levels of perceived individual efficacy (hypothesis #5). Finally, we shall pursue a hypothesis (#6) put forward by Pateman (1970), and tested by among others Elden (1981) and Greenberg (1981). The hypothesis has two parts. The first part postulates a positive correlation between a high level of self-determination in one's own work – that is, self-managed/autonomous work conditions and high levels of participation in work place democracy as well as high levels of job satisfaction and perceptions of efficacy. The second part postulates a positive correlation between these factors; especially a high level of participation in work place democracy, and a high level of efficacy, and wider political participation and efficacy. Thus Pateman (1970: 66), drawing on texts by John Stuart Mill,

Rousseau and E.D.H. Cole, refers to the workplace, as 'the primary class-room for transmitting patterns of...political participation' (see also Karasek 1978: 76 and Elden 1981: 55).

Participation and job satisfaction

In order to measure the degree of participation at the workplace, the Scandinavian Citizenship Surveys asked four questions. The respondents were asked whether they have been in contact with: (i) the union representative or any other elected employee representative, or (ii) supervisors or managers, concerning conditions at their workplace within the last year. The respondents were also asked (iii) whether they have themselves been a union representative, or had any other elected position at the workplace within the last year. Finally, the respondents were asked (iv) whether they had taken any (other) initiative to improve conditions at their workplace within the last year. The percentage of respondents answering these questions in the affirmative can be seen in Table 7.1.

Two features are notable about Table 7.1. Firstly, the extent of participation (the high percentages). Secondly, the similarity between the three countries. Concerning the extent of participation, we note that *in Scandinavia approximately one in six wage-earners have held an elected position in his/her workplace within the last year.* The extent of contacts with union representatives or other elected representatives (25–50 per cent), and contacts with management (50–70 per cent), are also impressive; both being indicators of what has been called the 'low power distance' of Scandinavian societies (Hofstede 1984).

Concerning the similarities between the countries these are also striking, insofar as we can observe exactly the same pattern in all three countries.

Table 7.1 Participation at workplace (percentages)

	Sweden	Denmark	Norway
Contact with union repr. or other worker repr.	49	34	26
Contact with management concerning work conditions	69	79*	46
Is/have been union repr. or other elected repr. within last 12 month	18	17	15
Other individual initiative	60	57	53
N	1310	1013	1184

*The question combines two questions in the Danish questionnaire, the sums of which are added here. Because there might be some overlapping, the percentage presented is probably somewhat exaggerated.

However, the Swedish percentages are generally a little higher than the Danish, which are again a little higher than the Norwegian. These differences are exactly as we would expect, given the more elaborate institutional framework for participation in Sweden, and the greater union density in Sweden (and Denmark) than in Norway. *The differences therefore lends credibility to Stymne's hypothesis about a positive correlation between institutional arrangements for participation and actual participatory behavior.* In sum, we will conclude that hypothesis #1 is verified, even though we lack internationally comparable data.

Turning to job satisfaction (Table 7.2) we also find very high percentages; here of wage-earners who say that they are very or rather satisfied with their job (75–90 per cent). Again, 'high' is a relative term, and we know from other data that when asking about job satisfaction in this general way, high levels of job satisfaction are usually found. We also know that the level of satisfaction reported is highly dependent on the scale used to measure satisfaction (see note to Table 7.2). None the less, we are so confident about the validity of the data reported here, that we will regard hypothesis #2 as also verified.

One of the assumed correlations in Pateman's (1970) work on participatory democracy is a positive correlation between participation (at the workplace) and (job) satisfaction. The assumption is that the more people are able to form the parameters of their own life by participating in, for example, the planning of their work environment, the happier they will be about it. This assumed correlation is in stark contrast to the way the relationship

Table 7.2 Job satisfaction (percentages)

	Sweden*	Denmark	Norway
Very/rather satisfied	75	85	91
Neither/nor	5	5	2
Very/rather dissatisfied	20	10	7
N	1310	1013	1184

*While the Danish and Norwegian surveys used a five-point scale similar to the one shown in this table to register the responses, a scale from 0 to 10 was used in the Swedish survey. The scale was constructed in such a way that only 0 would count as 'satisfied', whereas 1–10 would count as varying degrees of 'dissatisfied'. In order to obtain full comparability with the Swedish data, half of the Danish questionnaires were designed in the same way. When using this scale, 'satisfaction' is measured at only 27 per cent in Sweden and 44 per cent in Denmark. However, the Danish survey design also made it possible to 'translate' from one scale to the other, and showed that the Swedish scale was probably often misunderstood by the respondents as having a midpoint around 5. Therefore we have translated the Swedish scale in the following way: 0 to 5 = 'very'/ 'rather satisfied', 6 = 'neither/nor', 7 to 10 = 'very'/ 'rather dissatisfied'. For a further discussion of this survey design problem, see Asbjørnsen, Andersen and Hoff 1995.

Table 7.3 Correlation between job satisfaction and participation (Pearson's r)

	Sweden	Denmark	Norway
Contact with union repr. or other worker repr.	−.21	−.17	−.14
Contact with management to change work conditions	−.18	−.11*	−.17
Is/have been union repr. within last 12 months	−.09	−.08	−.01
Other individual initiative	−.43	−.30	−.16

*This figure is an average of two other figures, as the question combines two items in the Danish questionnaire (cf. Table 7.1). All figures are significant at the 0.001 level.

between participation and satisfaction is seen in the Swedish Citizenship study. Here the causality is reversed, and it is assumed that one of the main reasons for people to participate in democratic decision-making processes at the workplace or elsewhere is dissatisfaction. Petersson et al. (1989: 40) goes so far as to state that: 'The demands fostered by dissatisfaction with one's living conditions is the essential fuel (for action, (eds.)) in social life'.

If we look at the ways in which we have registered workplace satisfaction in this study the data seem to lend more credibility to Petersson et al.'s interpretation than to Pateman's (see Table 7.3). Thus, nowhere in the table do we see a positive correlation between participation and job satisfaction. On the contrary, all the correlations are negative, *indicating instead a correlation between job dissatisfaction and participation*. However, except for 'other individual initiatives' the correlations are weak. It is especially noteworthy that the weakest correlations are found between dissatisfaction and 'is or have been a union representative within the last 12 months'. Thus, job dissatisfaction does not seem to be a motivating factor for persons who chose to become union representatives.

Summing up, we can say that high levels of job satisfaction were found (Table 7.2). However, these high levels of job satisfaction were not found to be positively correlated with the high levels of participation also found (Table 7.1), and hypothesis #3 was therefore falsified. Also, even though a consistent correlation between job dissatisfaction and different forms of participation was found, these correlations were not very strong except concerning the more informal individual initiatives to change work conditions (strongest in Sweden; less so in Denmark and Norway).

Individual and collective efficacy

In this section, we shall consider how wage-earners in Scandinavia experience and perceive their own personal efficacy at their workplace. This is in contrast to chapter 6 were we looked at the collective resource which the unions constitute, and the perceived efficacy of this collective resource at the workplace. In the Swedish Citizenship Study, Petersson et al. (1989) approached the question of experienced efficacy as a question of citizens' 'power' in a number of social arenas, among them the workplace. By combining the questions on satisfaction/dissatisfaction, initiative/no initiative and success/no success, it is, according to Petersson et al., possible to distinguish between *power, powerlessness* and *apathy*, as illustrated in Figure 7.2.

As the figure illustrates, there are four possible ways in which power/ powerlessness is expressed: (i) the wage-earner is satisfied, and therefore takes no initiative; (ii) he/she can also (none the less) take an initiative and be successful. *This is the successful exertion of power.* The same option is, of course, open to the dissatisfied wage-earner; (iii) the wage-earner can also take an initiative, and be unsuccessful. This is the bitter experience of *powerlessness*; and (iv) finally, the wage-earner can be dissatisfied, and still not take an initiative. This is what Petersson et al. (1989) call *apathy*. Thus, the point with the figure is, that is possible, also empirically, to distinguish between *power, powerlessness* and *apathy*. The workplace power profiles for Sweden, Denmark and Norway are shown in Figures 7.3a, 7.3b and 7.3c. Numbers in the figures are percentages of N.

There are two striking features about these profiles. Firstly, concerning the exertion of power we notice that a very high proportion of the persons who take an initiative to change things at their workplace are successful.

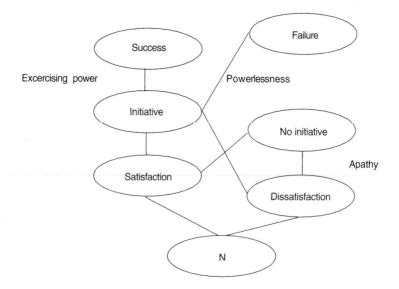

Figure 7.2   Workplace power profile

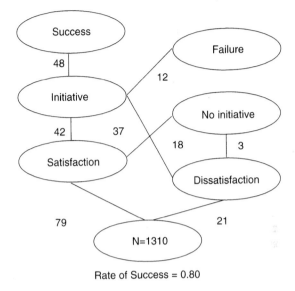

Figure 7.3a Workplace power profile. Sweden

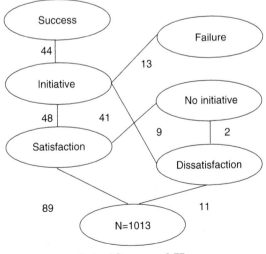

Figure 7.3b Workplace power profile. Denmark

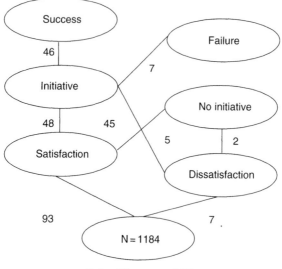

Figure 7.3c   Workplace power profile. Norway

Thus, in all three countries, more than 50 per cent of the wage-earners have taken an initiative within the last year, and of these between 44 and 48 per cent have been successful according to their own judgement. *This gives a probability of success ranging between 0.77 and 0.87.* In other words, persons who take an initiative experience a high level of individual effi-cacy, and *we will thus regard hypothesis #4 as verified.* Secondly, *apathy is low.* Only 2–3 per cent of the wage-earners are dissatisfied, and have not taken an initiative to change the source of their dissatisfaction. By far the largest proportion of the dissatisfied wage-earners have taken an initiative; rates of initiative ranging between 0.71 and 0.86. Even though wage-earners are seen to experience a high level of personal efficacy at the workplace when they take initiatives of various kinds, they might not – for reasons having to do with, for example, organizational culture, working class ideology, and so on – perceive their own efficacy to be very high. The Citizenship Surveys have therefore asked a question about how the wage-earner perceives his/her possibility to influence his/her general work conditions.[6] The results are seen in Table 7.4.

As we can see from Table 7.4, 54 per cent of the Swedish and 87 per cent of the Danish wage-earners think that they have 'high' or 'some' efficacy when it comes to influencing their general work conditions.[7] Conversely, 46 per cent of the Swedish and 13 per cent of the Danish wage-earners think their efficacy is 'small' or non-existent ('none'). These figures seem to

Table 7.4 Wage-earners' perception of own efficacy at workplace (percentages)

	Sweden*	Denmark**
High	17	24
Some	37	63
Small	22	9
None	24	4

* For Sweden the scale used has been translated as follows: 0 = none, 1–4 = small, 5–8 = some, 9–10 = high.
** For Denmark the scale used have been translated as follows: 'meget gode' = high, 'gode' + 'hverken gode eller dårlige' = some, 'dårlige' = small, 'meget dårlige' = none.

match the levels of experienced efficacy (percentage being successful) found in the power profiles quite well (see below for correlations), and *we will therefore also regard hypothesis #5 as verified*. However, it is surprising that the Danish wage-earners perceive their efficacy as somewhat better than the Swedish wage-earners. Given the Swedish wage-earners' better formal channels for influence one might expect the reverse to be true. While one should not probably pay too much attention to the distribution of the figures between the categories 'high', 'some' and 'small', as the distribution might be affected by the different response categories used (see note to Table 7.2), the category 'none' should be identical. Here, as many as 24 per cent of the Swedish wage-earners have answered that they have no chance whatsoever of influencing the general conditions at their workplace, while this only goes for 4 per cent of the Danish wage-earners.

Different explanations of this difference are possible. One explanation might be that the size of workplace is generally bigger in Sweden, and that wage-earners at large workplaces might feel less efficacious than wage-earners at small workplaces. Another explanation might be that the composition of the workforce is different in the two countries, and that, for example, manual workers perceive their efficacy differently (lower) than non-manual employees, who might have easier access to management or important decision-making. We have tested both of these explanations by controlling both experienced and perceived efficacy for size of workplace,[8] and composition of workforce.[9]

The results of these analyses are quite clear. Concerning experienced efficacy neither size of workplace nor composition of the workforce is of importance in accounting for the differences found between the countries. Concerning perceived efficacy size of workplace was not of importance in accounting for the variations. *However, composition of the workforce was found to be of importance in Sweden, where as much as 40 per cent of manual*

Table 7.5 Correlation between experienced and perceived efficacy. Percentage saying they have 'some' or 'high' possibility for influence

	Sweden	Denmark
No initiative	40	84
Initiative + success	66	98
Initiative + uncertain	51	85
Initiative + failure	41	57
Pearson's r	.23	.26
N = (no initiative/ initiative)	502/790	414/574

workers said they had no possibility of influencing general working conditions at their workplace, against only 18 per cent of non-manual employees. In Denmark no such difference was found. The reason why a substantial amount of manual workers in Sweden hold such a negative perception of their own efficacy is not entirely clear. One possible explanation might the difference in industrial structure.

Above, we noticed that there is a possible relationship between experienced and perceived efficacy. A likely hypothesis concerning such relationship is that if a wage-earner tries to influence his/her working conditions, and has success in doing so, then he/she is likely to perceive his/her efficacy as higher than wage-earners who have tried to influence and failed, or than wage-earners who have not tried at all. As Table 7.5 shows, such a relationship exists. *Both in Denmark and Sweden we find a clear correlation between perception of efficacy, and the experience of success with an initiative.* This result is interesting, since it shows that probably a process of social learning is at work here, and that this process might be more important for the perception of efficacy than a number of background variables (cf. above).

The workplace as a 'classroom for democracy'

In a broader political perspective one of the most interesting things about participation in decision-making in the workplace is whether such participation has a positive effect on participation in other social arenas; most notably in more traditional politics. Above we noted that such a hypothesis has both been formulated on theoretical grounds (Pateman 1970) and tested empirically (Elden 1981; Greenberg 1981). In particular Elden has taken pains to specify the different elements in Pateman's original hypothesis.[10] He stresses that the hypothesis essentially has two parts. The first part postulates a relationship between the organization of work and participation in workplace democracy, whereas the second part postulates a relationship between this kind of participation and political participation in general.[11]

More concretely the first part of the hypothesis postulates a positive correlation between high levels of self-determination in one's own work (self-managed/autonomous work conditions) and high levels of participation in workplace democracy as well as high levels of job satisfaction and perceptions of efficacy. The second part postulates a positive correlation between these factors; especially participation and efficacy and wider political participation and efficacy. Figure 7.4 shows the relationship between the different elements in Elden's hypothesis, as well as the indicators we have used to operationalize it. Since we have already dealt with the relationship between participation and job satisfaction, the latter is left out of the hypothesis here. Also, due to a lack of data, the first part of the hypothesis could not be tested in Denmark. In Norway, because there is no data on wage-earners' perceived efficacy at their workplace, data on experienced efficacy have been used instead. The shortcomings caused by these data problems should appear in Tables 7.7 to 7.9.

Concerning the first part of the hypothesis – the correlation between self-managed work conditions and participation and efficacy at the workplace – the only variable we have which examines self-managed work conditions is a question on job autonomy. The respondents were thus asked about how they saw their possibilities to plan and regulate their own work. The distribution of answers is found in Table 7.6.

As we can see from Table 7.6, more than 50 per cent of Swedish and Norwegian wage-earners consider their possibilities of planning and regulating their own work to be 'high'. These percentages seems promising for Elden's hypothesis, which we shall now scrutinize in more detail.

Organization of work →	**Participation at workplace** →	**Political participation**
Self-managed work conditions	High level of participation. Perception of high efficacy.	High level of political participation. High level of political efficacy.
Indicator: Autonomy in job	**Indicators:** participation: Own initiative. been union repr.	**Indicators:** participation: Party membership. Participation in demonstration.
	efficacy: Own efficacy at workplace. Efficacy in union.	efficacy: Perception of power(lessness).

Figure 7.4 Elden's (Pateman's) hypothesis

Table 7.6   Autonomy in own job
(Percentages)

	Sweden*	Norway
High	54	53
Some	24	33
Small	22	14

*Scale used: 0–3 = small; 4–7 = some;
8–10 = high.

Table 7.7   Elden's hypothesis, Part 1. Correlation between job autonomy and participation and efficacy at the workplace (Pearson's r)

	Sweden	Norway
Own efficacy at workplace	.53	*
Success with initiative	—	.23
Efficacy in union	.18	.13
Taken own initiative	.18	.14
Been a union representative	.13	.04

*Question not asked in the Norwegian 1990 Citizenship Survey.

Considering the first part of the hypothesis, we find quite strong correlations between autonomy in job and the feeling of efficacy (measured by perceived success with initiative(s) in Norway for the lack of a better measure).[12] We also find positive correlations between autonomy in job, and the two indicators we have chosen to represent participation at the workplace: taking an initiative to change work conditions, and the question about whether the respondent is or has been a union representative within the last twelve months. However, these correlations are rather weak (between .04 and .18). *On this basis we will conclude, that the first part of hypothesis #6 is verified; at least concerning a positive correlation between autonomous work conditions and efficacy at the workplace.*[13]

Looking at the second part of the hypothesis we generally find very disappointing correlations. Thus, the correlations between the indicators we have chosen to represent participation and efficacy at the workplace, and the indicators we have chosen to represent broader political participation and efficacy, range between the insignificant and (±) .20 (Pearson's r). Even though almost all the correlations are in the hypothesized direction, this is hardly an impressive result. Concerning the second part of the hypothesis we must therefore conclude, that it cannot be verified. *Our data fails to support Pateman's and Elden's hypothesis about (high) positive correlations between participation and efficacy in workplace democracy and participation and efficacy in the wider polity.*[14] It is possible, of course, that by

Table 7.8 Elden's hypothesis, Part 2. Correlation between participation and efficacy at workplace and political participation (membership of political party and participation in demonstration) (Pearson's r)

	Sweden		Norway		Denmark	
	Party member	*Part. in demonstration*	*Party member*	*Part. in demonstration*	*Party member*	*Part. in demonstration*
Own efficacy at workplace	.08	.06	—	—	.04	−.02*
Success with initiative	—	—	.003*	−.04	—	—
Efficacy in union	.07	.11	.06	.20	.13	.13
Taken own initiative	.05	.13	.003*	.14	.02*	.13
Been a union representative	.07	.08	−.01*	.10	.07*	.16

*Not significant at the 0.05 level.

Table 7.9 Elden's hypothesis Part 2. Correlation between participation and efficacy at workplace and political efficacy (difficult to understand politics) (Pearson's r)

	Sweden	Norway	Denmark
Own efficacy at workplace	−.03*	—	−.13
Success with initiative	—	.02	—
Efficacy in union	−.05	−.13	−.05*
Taken own initiative	−.002*	−.17	−.03*
Been a union representative	.03*	−.06	−.02*

* Not significant at the 0.05 level.

choosing other indicators, or by combining some indicators in indices we could have increased the correlations. However, a number of other dependent variables which have been tried do not yield substantially different results.[15]

Conclusion

In this chapter we have approached the question of workplace democracy in Scandinavia in an historical and empirical way. Through a short historical sketch we demonstrated that, starting in the beginning of the 1960s, a unique Scandinavian model of workplace democracy has developed. This model is based on a combination of institutions created by collective agreements, such as, for example, work councils, and institutions created by legislation, such as, for example, employee representation on company boards. The development of the model culminated at the end of the 1970s/beginning of the 1980s with the passing of the Act on Codetermination at Work, and the Act on Wage Earners' Funds in Sweden.

This development, backed by strong unions and strong social democratic parties, meant that the Scandinavian version of workplace democracy stood out as a 'role model' for the rest of the world. The purpose of this chapter has been to scrutinize critically this 'role model' in order to see whether the participatory institutions created have a correlate in the actions and perceptions of Scandinavian wage-earners.

In order to analyse this question we pursued a number of hypotheses concerning participation and efficacy at the level of the individual. We thus expected to see high levels of democratic participation at the workplace, high levels of job satisfaction and a positive correlation between participation and job satisfaction. We also expected to find high levels of both experienced and perceived efficacy at the workplace.

Generally speaking, all of these expectations were met – the hypotheses verified – except for the hypothesis on a positive correlation between participation and job satisfaction. Using four different measures of participation we found instead, concerning all four, negative correlations. This indicates that a causality between job dissatisfaction and participation, as analysed in, for example, the Swedish Citizenship Study (Petersson et al. 1989), is more likely than a causality running from participation to job satisfaction as postulated by, for example, Pateman (1970).

Concerning experienced efficacy we were surprised to see first, that the percentage of wage-earners who, within a given year, had taken an initiative to change conditions at their workplace was higher than 50 per cent in all Scandinavian countries. Secondly, we were even more surprised to see that of these around 50 per cent (44–48 per cent) had success with their initiative. Success rates were thus in the range 77–87 per cent. However, even more important in a democratic perspective, we found that apathy in all three countries was low. Thus, only 2–3 per cent of the wage-earners were dissatisfied and had not taken an initiative to change their work conditions.

The way wage-earners perceived their efficacy matched their experienced efficacy quite well. Thus, 54–87 per cent of wage-earners in Denmark and Sweden thought they had a 'high' or 'some' efficacy in influencing their general work conditions. However, given the Swedish institutional lead, we were surprised to see that Danish wage-earners had a somewhat more positive evaluation of their efficacy than their Swedish counterparts. Controlling for different background variables the difference was specified to be especially among manual employees, where as much as 40 per cent of Swedish manual employees said they had no possibility of influencing general working conditions at their workplace against only 4 per cent in Denmark. Why manual workers in Sweden hold such a negative perception of their own efficacy is not entirely clear, but it might have something to do with differences in the types of industry that employ manual labor in Denmark and Sweden.

One of the more interesting and much discussed aspects of workplace democracy is whether it has any effects on participation in other social arenas; that is, whether the workplace functions – as Pateman (1970: 66) puts it – as 'the primary classroom for transmitting patterns of political participation'. We investigated this hypothesis in two steps, as suggested by Elden (1981). The first part of the hypothesis postulates a positive correlation between self-determination in one's job and a high level of participation in workplace democracy, as well as a high level of job satisfaction and perception of efficacy. The second part postulates a positive correlation between these factors and wider political participation and efficacy.

The result of the empirical test was that whereas the first part of the hypothesis could be verified, this was not the case for the second part of the hypothesis. *Our data thus fails to support the 'classroom hypothesis'.* However, this does not mean that we did not find elements of learning related with participation at the workplace. We were thus able to show (Table 7.5) that persons who had participated (taken an initiative) and been successful, thought more highly of their workplace efficacy than either persons who had not taken an initiative or persons who had taken an initiative and failed. Generalizing from this result it might be the case that there is a process of 'political' learning going on within many different social arenas. However, the institutional frameworks may, in some areas, be so specific or intricate as to exclude a direct 'spill-over' to other areas. We shall follow up on this lead in the following chapter.

8
User Participation in Scandinavia – the 'Third Citizenship'?

Introduction

In this chapter we will take a closer look at user participation in Scandinavia from a citizenship perspective. Thus, the perspective is that of seeing the user role as constituting a set of rights to participate politically. These rights are, in our view, essentially comparable to the rights constituted by the system of political citizenship. In Marshall's terms, they might be seen as an essential part of a citizen's social rights, even though Marshall was more concerned with entitlements than participation in this area (Marshall 1950: 95ff). Proposing this point of departure means that the fundamental question becomes whether these rights in effect extend the rights connected with political citizenship, or whether they undermine or short-circuit traditional representative democracy? In other words, does the current extension of user rights bring us closer to the realization of Marshall's 'full citizenship', and could we therefore talk about the system of these rights as a 'third citizenship'; something which extends and is complementary to the 'first' (political rights), and 'second' (workplace democracy) citizenship?

This perspective is, if not completely new,[1] then at least not fully developed in the existing literature on political participation. What we shall try to do in the following is thus to pursue this perspective empirically,[2] as far as our data allows us.

There are a number of reasons why the user role has attracted increasing attention from politicians and researchers alike in the last decade. Firstly, the problems of financing the welfare state in especially Sweden and Denmark have led to an increased focus on the output side of the political system, and to a 'discovery' of the importance that users have for a successful implementation of policies in areas like for example education, health, social services, and so on. This has led to a range of implementation studies all stressing the limits of welfare state policies (Rothstein 1987, 1994,

1996; Rothstein and Bergström 1999). Secondly, statutory participatory rights have developed parallel to material rights in a number of institutional contexts. Hernes (1988: 203) has described this development as an attempt at a 'democratization of all areas of social life', and sees this development as a result of a conscious social democratic post-war policy.

However, there are reasons to be skeptical towards Hernes' interpretation of this historical development; especially in the area of user participation:

Firstly, the Scandinavian social democratic parties did not pay much attention to clients' and users' participatory rights until late in the 1980s.[3] Before that the pressure for such rights came mainly from two sources: (i) from organized clients' or users' groups. It is thus clearly the activity of such groups which lies behind, for example, the establishment of senior citizen councils in most Danish municipalities, and the establishment of complaint boards at Danish hospitals; (ii) from liberal political forces (parties) which have heavily criticized many public services for paternalism and lack of responsiveness. These parties have, especially when in government, through so-called 'modernization programs', worked to establish what they perceive to be a better accordance between citizens' preferences and public services. This has been done through such (by now well-known) measures as, for example, introducing citizens' 'free choice' between different public schools and different public hospitals, and by encouraging private alternatives to different public services through user fees, or by contracting-out. This attempt at strengthening 'exit' mechanisms has been supplemented by other attempts which have attempted to strengthen the 'voice' mechanism. In Denmark, for example, it is thus center-right coalition governments which have passed legislation establishing boards on all public schools and childcare institutions. These boards have a majority of user (parent) representatives, and have, at least formally, considerable decision-making powers. It is true that many of these measures have been combined with budget cuts, or are thought to have budget-saving effects, and that they have explicitly been seen as means to improve political steering capacity (Hoff and Sørensen 1989). None the less, these 'modernization reforms' have in a number of cases institutionalized users' participatory rights. Thus, it seems fair to conclude that what Hernes describes as an almost 'natural' evolution of social democratic policy is in fact a result of political pressure and struggle basically carried out by other political forces. The late social democratic 'usurpation' of the modernization ideas can thus be seen as an attempt to reestablish a threatened or unstable political hegemony. Thus, the originality in a report like for example the SAMAK report (see note 3) lies more in the way it breaks with traditional social democratic welfare state policies than in its policy proposals.

Secondly, it is doubtful whether there is a common Scandinavian development concerning users' participatory rights. In Sweden social democratic policies have been concentrated on improving the wage-earners' position on the market. This has manifested itself in the number of laws and reforms dealt with in chapter 7, and in laws improving the citizens' position as a consumer (establishing positions as a consumer ombudsman, municipal consumer advisors, and so on). However, concerning participatory rights for the users of public services Swedish social democracy has been more skeptical, fearing the manifestation of particularistic interests, and the possible inegalitarian consequences of such rights.[4] In Denmark it has more less been the other way around. Here social democracy, lacking the strength of its Swedish sister party, was unable to pass legislation concerning economic democracy. However, for historic reasons, there have been more self-organized and private alternatives to public services in Denmark, especially concerning schools and child care. Furthermore, the tradition for laymen participation in local administration seem to have been stronger in Denmark (Knudsen 1993). Both of these factors have made it easier to legislate on users' participatory rights in Denmark. The above-mentioned laws on user-dominated boards in schools and childcare institutions have thus been passed with solid parliamentary majorities. However, the development of users' participatory rights in Scandinavia now seem to be converging, as boards with user representation have now been established on a project basis in Swedish schools (as of 1996 – see Lindbom 1993, 1995; Duit and Möller 1997).[5]

The hypotheses

In this chapter we shall basically pursue the same hypotheses that have guided the analysis in some of the above chapters, allowing for some modifications made necessary by the special character of this area.

Firstly, we shall pursue the *welfare state, or stakeholder, hypothesis*. Thus, we expect the Scandinavians to have a high rate of participation as users of different public services, because they have much at stake due to the generous and encompassing public services and transfers. Also, we will expect participation to be especially vivid in the areas where formal channels for user participation have been established (schools and public day care). As a consequence of this argument, we expect the interest in private alternatives (insofar as these exist) to be low, as these are both costly, and prevent the individual from obtaining his/her 'rightful' share of public services. Following this line of thinking, we therefore also expect there to be a strong correlation between interest in private alternatives (exit) and dissatisfaction with a given public service. In testing this hypothesis we have chosen to rely on Hirschmann's (1970) well-known concepts of 'voice' and 'exit'. Thus, the citizen uses 'voice' when he/she tries to speak up, complain, or take other initiatives to change the service delivered to him/her. 'Exit', as we define it here, is when a citizen leaves an organization to obtain a wanted service elsewhere, or expresses a wish to do so. Both 'voice' and 'exit' can be seen as ways in which the citizen try to exercise or optimize his/her personal autonomy vis-à-vis a given (public) organization. Another way to express this is that, taken together, the two mechanisms expresses the character of *citizens' power* vis-à-vis the organization in question.[6]

Secondly, we shall pursue a *resource hypothesis* concerning citizens' perception of their own efficacy. Thus, apart from asking the respondents in our survey(s) about their use of voice (participation), and whether this use was successful or not, the respondents have also been asked about how they perceive their own possibilities for influencing a given public service.

There are many assumptions about the factors which determine users' efficacy, however none which have been analysed systematically on an empirical basis. One dominant assumption is that *resources decide*. It is thus assumed that the citizens' personal resources in terms of education, occupation, community network, leisure time, and so on, determine or are more important than other factors for a citizen's efficacy vis-à-vis a given public organization. This assumption is dominant in for example the influential theories on accessibility, which are preoccupied by the question of equal access, and by the possible socioeconomic bias created by different administrative barriers.[7] Also, the assumption underlies traditional social democratic thinking about the relationship between citizens/users and public services, creating on the one hand a reason to be cautious towards increased user participation, and on the other hand one more reason for a more equal distribution of resources in society.

In recent years this assumption has been challenged by so-called 'new institutionalists', who claim that institutional factors might be at least as important as the resources of external actors in determining policy outcomes.[8] Translated to our context this means that easy access, well-established channels of influence, a participatory culture in the organization in question, and so on, might well be more important for citizen efficacy than individual resources.

These two competing assumptions will be tested below in the form of a hypothesis stating that: *Individual resources are more important than institutional factors for citizens' perception of their possibility to influence a given public service.*[9] In addition, the new institutionalists direct our attention towards the processes of social learning that might be going on both inside and outside organizations (Martin 1994). Due to the lack of data we have no possibilities of analysing social learning inside public organizations. However, it is possible to investigate whether there is an element of social learning in citizens' interaction with different public organizations.

Thirdly, we shall pursue the *class mobilization hypothesis* applied to this area. The class mobilization hypothesis is concerned with the question of whether or not the type of participation under consideration is successful in bringing people with relatively small socioeconomic resources into politics. Thus, in the area of user participation one of the major concerns has been the question of whether or not the introduction or expansion of user participatory rights has had inegalitarian consequences. It is thus suspected (without much empirical evidence) that it will be first of all the well-educated, and the economically better off, who will take advantage of such rights. It is, however, unclear whether the fear of inegalitarian consequences is a fear which concerns political participation, policy outcomes or both. If political participation is considered to have a value in itself, as it is in most of the citizenship approaches touched upon in chapter 1, then one needs to be concerned with the equality in this participation along relevant parameters such as, for example, education, occupation, gender and age. Also, one should be concerned with the question about whether the possible social inequalities are *accumulated* when one moves from less to more demanding forms of participation. Thus, what we will test here is a hypothesis stating that: *Citizens who use voice or who are elected user representatives will deviate from the user group as such, because they will be better educated, have a higher occupational status, be men rather than women, and be middle-aged rather than young or old.* Strictly speaking, this is rather a class demobilization hypothesis, or at least a hypothesis assuming that the various forms of user participation will contribute to an *increased polarization* in political participation between different socioeconomic groups.

Finally, we shall test the so-called '*classroom hypothesis*'. As mentioned in chapter 7, the 'classroom hypothesis' assumes that participation in different types of 'small democracy' will have positive effects on participation in the 'big democracy'. We shall therefore test a hypothesis stating that: *There will be a positive correlation between active user participation and other forms of political participation.*

Choice of administrative areas

In our choice of administrative areas in which to empirically analyse the political aspect of the user role, we have also used the concept of 'voice' and 'exit' as points of departure.

In order to get an idea about the *variations* in the user role we have chosen a 'most different case' design. Thus, we have wanted to include areas with both good and bad possibilities for 'voice' and areas with both good and bad possibilities for 'exit'. In order to further extend the field of possible variations we have also used the crude distinction between service-providing and controlling administrative units. For Denmark, which is the country for which the most thorough analysis of the user role has been made, these three dimensions has led to the choice of six areas of analysis. For Sweden and Norway only three and two areas were selected. Firstly, we have chosen *public schools* (K-10 grade; all three countries have a comprehensive school system where 1–9 (10) grade is compulsory), *public child care for children aged 0–6 years* (crèches, day nurseries, public child-minders, subsidized day care, and so on), and the *health sector* (both general practitioners and hospitals) as areas in which the possibilities for 'voice' are relatively good; where 'exit' possibilities exist to some degree, and which can all be characterized as service providing.

Comprehensive (elementary) schools are an area where access to alternatives (=possibilities of exit) is possible. In Denmark and Norway this concerns both public and privately organized (but most often publicly subsidized) alternatives, whereas in Sweden access to (public) alternatives has only recently become easier. Also formalized voice mechanisms exists, albeit in a somewhat different form, in each of the three countries. In Denmark and Norway the users (parents/pupils) are represented on the school boards. In Sweden voice is, for various reasons (see Lindbom 1993), less formalized.

Child care is an area characterized by the existence of both wholly public, privately organized, but publicly subsidized, and private, unregulated alternatives in all three countries. However, the mix of these types is quite different between the countries. In Denmark and Norway authorities have traditionally welcomed private/voluntary initiatives in this area, resulting in around 40 per cent of childcare institutions being formally private. However, the great majority of these receive substantial public subsidies subject to prior approval by the municipality. In Sweden, 92 per cent of all day care centers were wholly public (Statistiska Centralbyrån 1985; Andersson 1994). However, this figure might have changed recently and today, 15 per cent of the children that attend preschool do so in private ones.[10] Furthermore, private, unregulated day care exists in all three countries on a considerable scale. This may include the services of relatives, neighbors, friends or unregistered child-minders, and may be either paid or unpaid. It is relatively more important in Norway than in Denmark and Sweden. Thus, it is estimated that the majority of day care for children aged 0–2 years in Norway has this form, as well as a considerable part of the day care for the 3–6-year-olds. Whether this mix of public, publicly subsidized, and private day care options correspond to parents' preferences is not known (Leira 1987: 14). However, it is know that in all three countries there is a considerable pressure – in the form of waiting lists and so on – towards creating more public day care. This indicates that for many parents the private solution they have, represents a 'no-choice' solution. Exit possibilities can therefore be said to exist in all three countries. However, they may in practice be more difficult to find than concerning for example schools, as well as more expensive. Also concerning child care formalized voice mechanisms exists. For Denmark, majority parental representation on boards has been mentioned above. In Norway, formal cooperation is organized through the board of directors and the parents council. The board of directors consist of parent, employee, and owner representatives.

The authority of the board is limited to the internal structure and functioning of the institution. The parents council is an advisory body only. In Sweden, parents are encouraged to participate in the activities of the day-care centers. However, they lack the formal voice mechanisms of the Danish and Norwegian parents. While this is true for the day-care centers run by the local communities covering 90 per cent of the Swedish children, roughly 6 per cent of the Swedish children, attend day-care centers run by parental cooperatives. In these parental influence is by definition considerable.

In discussing the health sector it is necessary to distinguish between general practitioners (GPs) and hospitals. In all three countries being a general practitioner is in principle an unrestricted trade. However, as health services are almost free in all three countries this means that the practitioners receive almost all their income from public sources. The trade is therefore heavily regulated, and so are the possibilities of exit. Concerning hospitals the possibilities of exit have until recently been very limited in all three countries. However, within the last couple of years it has become possible to choose between hospitals (within certain regional boundaries). Also, in Denmark, private hospitals have been started, constituting an exit possibility. Formal voice mechanisms exists in all three countries in the form of complaint procedures. However, both in Denmark and Norway these have only been developed recently.

Secondly, we have chosen *employment exchange offices* and *municipal social services departments* as areas in which there are no (viable) exit possibilities, and where the users are in a clear relation of dependency, because it is necessary to cooperate with these organizations in order to receive unemployment or social welfare benefits. Possibilities of voice exists in the form of formal complaint procedures.[11] The areas can be characterized as basically service-providing, but they also include a strong element of control.

Finally, we have chosen *municipal tax offices* as the tax offices clearly constitute controlling administrative units, even though they also have certain elements of service. Here the users have no (legal) exit possibilities. Formal voice mechanisms exists in the form of administrative recourse and independent administrative courts.[12]

Voice and exit

As discussed above, the Scandinavian welfare states are characterized by the great variety of user roles that they offer to the citizen. However, the relationship between citizen and administration is not only a question of the number of roles which the citizen can potentially enter, but also a question of *the intensity of the contact* in each of the roles. In the questionnaires we have therefore, as an introduction to the questions concerning each

Table 8.1 Different user roles. Percentage of population having established contact/sought treatment within last 12 months*

	Sweden	Denmark	Norway
Health sector	76	76	74
Child care	9	12	**
Schools	19	23	**
Employment exchange	**	5	**
Tax authorities	**	20	21
N	1989	1968	1773

*In this table, as well as in all of the following tables and figures, calculations are done on the basis of the population 18 years or more.
**Data are not available.

user role, asked whether the respondent have established contact/sought treatment within the last 12 months. The distribution of answers is found in Table 8.1.

Two things are noteworthy about Table 8.1. Most striking, perhaps, is the similarity between the countries in the areas in which comparison is possible. Secondly, the high percentage of actual users especially in the health sector and concerning the tax authorities. However, such features should not be very surprising, when one considers the similarities between the Scandinavian countries concerning the extent of welfare state institutions and sociodemographic structures.

Thus, in all three countries the (public) health sector consists of primary and secondary health services. The primary health services are delivered by general practitioners located in all parts of the countries according to state regulations. The secondary health services are delivered by the general and specialized hospitals. The high percentage of the population which have been in contact with the health sector within the last 12 month reflects first of all that the primary health services are widely used. In Sweden it is thus 87 per cent of the persons who have sought contact with the health sector, who have used the primary health services, while 'only' 13 per cent have used the hospitals. The similar figures for Denmark and Norway are 81 and 19 per cent and 86 and 14 per cent respectively.

Concerning child care, 12 per cent of the respondents in Denmark and 9 per cent in Sweden are users of public child care. Because 17 per cent of the population in Denmark have one or more children in the age 0–6 years these figures mean that *68 per cent of parents with pre-school children use public services in this area.* In Sweden 14 per cent of the population have pre-school children, and thus *64 per cent use public child care.* Furthermore, in Denmark 21 per cent of parents with pre-school children use different private forms of child care, while in Sweden this figure is 15 per cent. If these figures are added, we see that in Denmark no less than 89 per cent, and in Sweden no less than 79 per cent of parents with pre-school children use different forms of public or private child care.

The role as user of the school system is, like the role of user of public child care, connected with a certain phase in the life cycle, namely the period where one has small or school-age children. This is clearly reflected in the age distribution of the users – they are concentrated in the age group 20–49 years. In countries like the Nordic, where schooling is compulsory, and the school system almost a 100 per cent public or publicly financed, the number of users is determined almost purely by demographic factors. In 1990 (1987) it was 23 per cent of the Danish adult population and 19 per cent of the Swedish whose children attended comprehensive school (K-10 grade).

Employment exchange offices are difficult to place on the service/control axis, since they have both service and control functions. Thus, they both control whether the clients really are at the disposal of the labor market, as well as giving advice and help in connection with job applications and public employment programs. In Denmark it is 5 per cent of the population who have had contact with the employment exchange offices within the last year. Because roughly 50 per cent of the population are part of the active labor force, the figure equals 10 per cent of the active labor force – which is approximately what the unemployment figure was in Denmark in 1990. This means that almost all unemployed have contact with the labor exchange offices in one form or another.

Concerning the tax authorities the relation to the users is a clear control relation. What we have measured here is, however, the non-routine contact (not the annual reception or filling out of the tax assessment form, but other forms of written or verbal contact, which might or might not be related to the tax assessment form). This contact might be initiated by either the administration or the citizen. What we see from the figures is that as much as 20 per cent of the population in Denmark and 21 per cent in Norway have had this kind of contact. The magnitude of these figures is surprising, since both countries have pay-as-you-earn systems, where information concerning different kind of income, mortgages and so on is generated automatically by the tax authorities.

Voice

Table 8.2 shows first of all that there are considerable variations in the use of voice between the different sectors and between the countries. Three sectors stand out as having high percentages of users who use voice – namely child care, schools and tax authorities. In Denmark it is thus almost half the users within these sectors who have used voice within the last 12 months,[14] while in Sweden it is something less – around one-third.

Table 8.2 Voice. How many use it? Percentage of users. Absolute numbers in parenthesis[13]

	Sweden	Denmark	Norway
Health sector	18 (N = 271)	15 (N = 218)	27 (N = 339)
Child care	27 (N = 76)	46 (N = 104)	—
Schools	36 (N = 135)	44 (N = 196)	—
Employment exchange	—	19 (N = 17)	—
Tax authorities	—	49 (N = 174)	49 (N = 179)

In the health sector considerably fewer users have used voice – around one-sixth (in Norway, however, this figure is around one-quarter). A possible explanation of these differences is the long tradition for user involvement concerning schools and childcare institutions in Denmark. Such tradition is lacking in the health sector in both Denmark and Sweden, which might explain the lower and more similar figures. The high percentages concerning the tax authorities might be a result of a widespread dissatisfaction with the service/control activities of the tax administrations.[15] In the first book reporting on the Swedish Citizenship Survey data (Petersson et al. 1989) the dimensions: *satisfaction/dissatisfaction, initiative/no initiative, success/no success*, were combined in order to illustrate the 'power profiles' of the different user roles. As mentioned above, our conception of user power is somewhat broader; including also the exit dimension. We therefore think it more appropriate to say that these 'power profiles' illustrates only one – albeit important – dimension of 'user power'. The profiles of the different areas are shown in Figures 8.1 to 8.5.

There are several striking features about these profiles. Generally speaking, *the level of apathy is low.* In four out of the five areas it is only between 1 and 12 per cent of all users who are both dissatisfied, and have not taken an initiative to change the cause of their dissatisfaction. Only one area has a high level of apathy; the employment exchange offices in Denmark (no comparable data are available for Sweden and Norway). Apathy here is 20 per cent. This is in contrast to the other area also characterized as a 'controlling authority' – the tax offices. Here dissatisfaction is as high as with the employment exchange offices, but the propensity among the dissatisfied to take an initiative is markedly higher. One possible explanation of this difference is that formal voice mechanisms are well developed and well-known in the tax area, whereas they are less well-known in the context of the employment exchange offices. Another possible explanation is that the users of the employment exchange are less resourceful than the users of the tax offices. We shall examine this question further below.

Concerning the exertion of power, we notice that in general *the probability of using voice and being successful is quite high.* The rate of success is thus

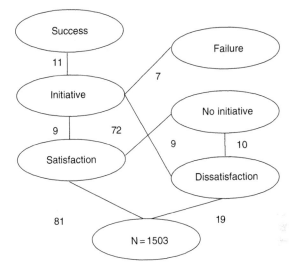

Figure 8.1a The power profile. Health sector. Sweden

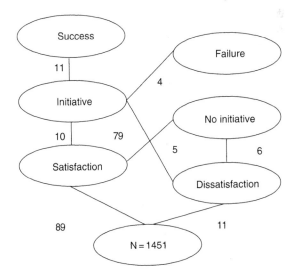

Figure 8.1b The power profile. Health sector. Denmark

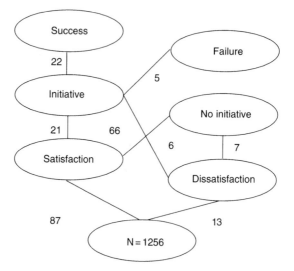

Figure 8.1c   The power profile. Health sector. Norway

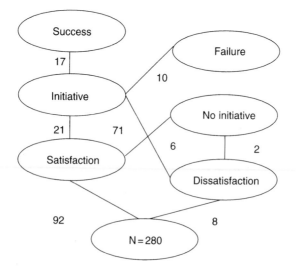

Figure 8.2a   The power profile. Child care. Sweden

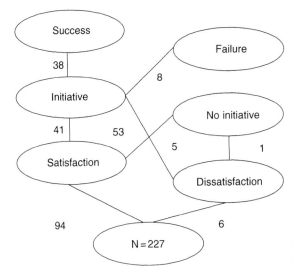

Figure 8.2b   The power profile. Child care. Denmark

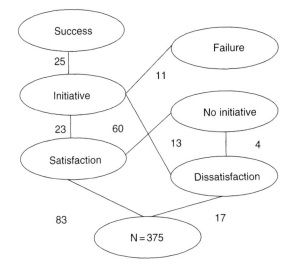

Figure 8.3a   The power profile. Schools. Sweden

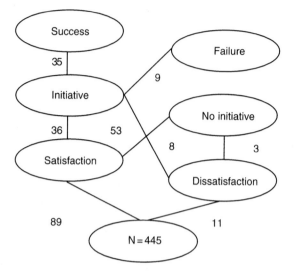

Figure 8.3b   The power profile. Schools. Denmark

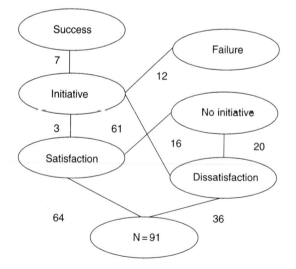

Figure 8.4 The power profile. Employment exchange offices. Denmark

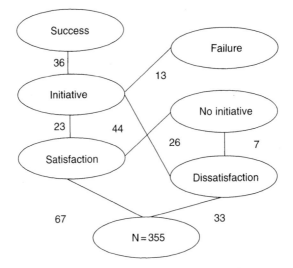

Figure 8.5a The power profile. Tax authorities. Denmark

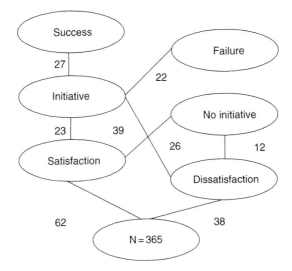

Figure 8.5b The power profile. Tax authorities. Norway

between 0.60 and 0.80 in most areas.[16] Thus, roughly speaking, *almost three-quarters of people using voice are successful*. Again a couple of areas deviate from this pattern. These are the employment exchange offices, where the rate of success is only 0.37, and the tax authorities in Norway, where the rate of success is 0.55. These figures could lead one to wonder whether there is a relationship between the possibility of success and the use of voice (the better the possibilities of success, the more users will use voice). However, the health sector seem to refute this hypotheses. Here the rate of success is quite high (Sweden: 0.61, Denmark: 0.73, Norway: 0.81), but the use of voice limited (between 15 and 27 per cent of the users). Also the tax sector in Norway runs counter to such hypotheses with a high rate of voice (49 per cent of users), and a moderate rate of success (0.55).

It is not very surprising that dissatisfied users take an initiative to change things. What is more surprising is that in areas such as schools, child care and tax, many satisfied users also take an initiative. The propensity to do so is between 0.23 and 0.44.[17] The combination of a high rate of initiative among both satisfied and dissatisfied users, and a high rate of success means that *a relatively large number of users – between 17 and 38 per cent – exert some measure of power*, as defined by Petersson et al. (1989). We note that there are some differences between the countries. Thus, the users in Denmark seem to be the most powerful in all three areas, whereas the users in Sweden fall some 10–20 percentage points behind. Norway falls in between. The reason for this difference might be the one already mentioned: that the tradition for and institutionalization of user participation in these areas is older in Denmark than in its neighboring Scandinavian countries, and the institutions thus apparently more receptive to user influence.

Exit

The question of exit has only been touched upon in the Danish citizenship survey. The analysis in this paragraph therefore refers to Denmark only.

Firstly, we have asked about the importance of *private alternatives* to public hospitals, schools, and child care. The distribution of these answers is found in Table 8.3.

The figures show that in all three areas *more than half of the respondents think that the existence of private alternatives is important*. The area with the

Table 8.3 The importance of private alternatives to public hospitals, schools and child care (percentages). *Denmark* only

	Important	Indifferent	Opposed to	N
Hospitals	52	24	24	1794
Child care	63	20	17	1687
Schools	72	15	8	1917

eldest and most established tradition for private alternatives, the school system, is also the area where most respondents think that private alternatives are important. In a welfare state such as the Danish, based heavily on universalism and publicly organized services in these areas, the figures are quite surprising. Unfortunately, the question of how many users of public schools have actually switched to private alternatives was not asked in the citizenship survey. Furthermore, the number of children attending private schools was not recorded. However, we know from other sources that around 3 per cent of all pupils in public schools will switch to private schools during their first seven years in school (Ministry of Finance 1995: 25–6),[18] and that 12 per cent of all children from kindergarten class until 10th grade attend private schools (Danmarks Statistik 1997: 19).

An obvious reason to stress the importance of private alternatives could be user dissatisfaction with the public services offered. Surprisingly, however, an analysis showed that satisfied and dissatisfied users have more less the same view about the importance of private alternatives. This was confirmed by a correlation analysis in which there was only a very weak correlation between user dissatisfaction and the value attributed to private alternatives (Pearson's r = .10). These results generated two other hypotheses that we also tested. Thus, we tested a hypothesis assuming that users with (perceived) little possibility for influence think that private alternatives are more important than users with good possibilities. Furthermore, we tested a hypothesis assuming that those who have used voice are less inclined to think that private alternatives are important, than those who have not. However, none of these hypotheses could be confirmed. *These results seem to point to the conclusion that possibilities for exit are not seen as an alternative to voice.* It is more likely that voice and exit are perceived as complementary, and that users wish to have *both* possibilities in their attempts at obtaining the desired 'service package'.

Finally, we have tested a hypothesis assuming that concrete experiences with private alternatives will have a positive effect on their evaluation. However, we were only able to test this hypothesis concerning hospitals and child care. In these areas the hypothesis was, not very surprisingly, confirmed (Hoff 1993). Generalizing from these results we will claim that concrete experiences are important for the evaluation of different kind of alternatives. For this reason we shall take a closer look at the importance of concrete user experiences below.

Resources and institutions

In this section we shall test the resource hypothesis which states that: *Individual resources are more important than institutional factors for citizens' perception of their possibility to influence a given public service.*

The regression model

In order to test the resource hypothesis we have constructed a simple multiple regression model with perception of own efficacy[19] as the dependent variable. We have chosen education, occupation and network to represent the essential personal resources of the users. Education and occupation are conventional variables which are not too difficult to operationalize.[20] However, the variables 'network' and 'institution' are in need of a definition. The reason why the network variable is entered here is because it is a common assumption that the 'strength' of a person's local community network is of importance for his/her perception of own efficacy in dealings with public authorities. The citizenship surveys have worked with two different measures of network: one, which we call *social network*, and another, which we call *knowledge network*. Social network is operationalized through questions about how much interaction the respondent has with neighbors, and how much support he/she can expect from them. Knowledge network is operationalized through questions about whether the respondent knows anybody who can help him/her with (free) medical, economical or juridical expertise.[21] In the regressions shown below the knowledge network variable is used, because we see this kind of support as most immediately relevant for a citizen in his/her dealings with public authorities.[22] 'Institution' can be operationalized in a number of ways. However, as an institutionalist approach was not a part of the original survey design, we have only been able to operationalize 'institution' in a very rudimentary fashion. 'Institution' is measured by whether the respondent has within the last 12 months had some interaction with a given public authority or not (been a user or not). On the basis of the answers a dummy variable has been created, where 1 = have had interaction, and 0 = no interaction. The results of the analyses are shown in Tables 8.4 to 8.6.[23]

Tables 8.4 to 8.6 show first of all that personal resources are of no or very little importance for citizens efficacy vis-à-vis the public institutions analysed here. Thus, the beta-coefficients are statistically insignificant in all

Table 8.4 Importance of personal resources and institutional factors for citizens' efficacy. *Health sector* (beta coefficients and r^2)

	Denmark	Norway
Institution	.01*	.04*
Education	.02*	.06*
Occupation	.01*	.01*
Network	.07*	.11*
r^2	.006	.015

*Not significant at the 95 per cent level (sign. of F > 0.05).

Table 8.5 Importance of personal resources
and institutional factors for citizens' efficacy.
Tax authorities (beta coefficients and r^2)

	Denmark	Norway
Institution	.01*	.13
Education	.04*	.01*
Occupation	.02*	.07*
Network	.07*	.02*
r^2	.006	.023

* Not significant at the 95 per cent level (sign. of
F > 0.05).

Table 8.6 Importance of personal
resources and institutional factors for
citizens' efficacy. *Child care and schools*
(beta coefficients and r^2). *Denmark only*

	Child care	Schools
Institution	.14	.25
Education	.02*	.06*
Occupation	.01*	.03*
Network	.10	.08*
r^2	.028	.069

*Not significant at the 95 per cent level (sign.
of F > 0.05).

cells in the tables except one. Similarly, institutional factors, operationalized in this rudimentary way, do not seem to have much explanatory power, and generally both the beta's and the r^2's are quite small. However, concerning childcare institutions and schools in Denmark (and tax authorities in Norway) institutional factors can be seen to have a small impact. Thus, for Denmark we have tried to reduce the regression model by omitting occupation. This increases the beta values for the institutional factor in these two areas to .27 and .38 respectively.

We can therefore conclude that neither individual resources nor institutional factors seem to be very important for citizens' perception of own efficacy. However, insofar any of these factors have an impact, institutional factors seem to be somewhat more important than individual resources. This is particularly true for public childcare institutions and schools in Denmark which stresses the special character of these institutions. It is likely that the high rates of initiative (voice) and efficacy found there is due to a unique combination of high user interest and strong organizational cultures stressing the values of participation and codetermination.

Table 8.7   Correlation between citizen's efficacy and experience from attempts at influencing services (percentage saying that possibilities at influencing are 'very good' or 'good'). *Health sector*

	Sweden	Denmark	Norway
No use of voice	30	41	37
Voice + success	39	55	67
Voice + uncertain	21	30	44
Voice + failure	12	25	19
Pearson's r	.34	.30	.48
N = (no voice/ voice)	1126/276	1072/207	839/334

Experience (user competence) as a personal resource

Apart from individual resources and institutional factors, another factor which might have a likely impact on a citizens' perception of efficacy is the experience of success/failure in his/her dealings with a given public organization. A likely hypothesis is that there will be a positive correlation between the experience of success when taking an initiative (using voice) and perception of efficacy. That this is indeed the case can be seen from Table 8.7.

The first row in the table shows the percentage saying that their possibilities to influence services are 'very good' or 'good', for the group of users who have not taken an initiative to change services within the last 12 months. The next three rows show the same percentage for the group of users who have taken an initiative and been (i) successful, (ii) for whom the outcome is not yet clear, and (iii) unsuccessful. Pearson's r shows the correlation between perception of efficacy (for those who have used voice), and the experience of success. As the figures show, this correlation is quite strong in all three countries. Similar, or even stronger correlations are found in the other selected areas.[24]

While this result is perfectly reasonable and logical it is also interesting because it shows that an element of social learning is probably involved here. More than being determined by individual resources or institutional factors the users' perception of their own efficacy seem to develop in an interplay with the institutions in question; an interplay in which experiences of success or failure are crucial.

Inequality

One of the most hotly debated issues concerning user participation and influence is the question about the possible inegalitarian consequences of such participation. Below we shall therefore pursue the so-called 'class mobilization hypothesis' described in the introduction. Furthermore, we shall consider whether there are certain socioeconomic characteristics connected with apathy, and the extent to which the 'powerful' (persons being success-ful in using voice) differs from the 'apathetic' (dissatisfied users, who have not used voice). Finally, we shall take a look at the 'classroom hypothesis' also described in the introduction.

Inequality in participation

Let us first take a look at the social characteristics of users who have used voice compared with the user group as such. Due to lack of space we have chosen to show the results for only two administrative areas. However, these areas are quite representative.[25]

Tables 8.8 and 8.9 show that concerning gender and age the differ-ences are not significant in most of the administrative areas. Looking at differences in education and occupation the pattern is clearer; at least concerning schools and public child care. In these areas there is a signifi-cant over-representation of persons with a long basic education, and of

Table 8.8 Health sector. Differences in sociodemo-graphic characteristics between users of voice and the user group as such (PDIs)

	Sweden	*Denmark*	*Norway*
Gender			*
Men	−8	−9	−5
Women	+8	+9	+5
Age (years)	*	*	*
18–29	+1	+1	−2
30–49	+5	+5	0
50+	−6	−6	−2
Education (years)		*	*
7–9	−9	−5	+1
10	+1	+3	+1
11+	+8	+2	−1
Occupation	*	*	*
Self-employed	+1	−4	−1
Non-manual	+6	+7	+2
Manual	−7	−3	−1
MCA-analysis:			
beta coefficients			
Gender	.08ns	.07ns	.06ns
Age	.06ns	.04ns	.05ns
Education	.06ns	.01ns	.01ns
Occupation	.06ns	.04ns	.01ns
R^2 (%)	2.0	0.8	7.9

*Differences between groups are not significant at the 0.05 level. ns not significant at the 0.05 level.

Table 8.9   Schools. Differences in sociodemographic characteristics between users of voice and the user group as such (PDIs)

	Sweden	Denmark
Gender	*	*
Men	−5	−3
Women	+5	+3
Age (years)	*	
18–29	0	0
30–49	+3	+6
50+	−3	−6
Education (years)		
7–9	−10	−10
10	−2	0
11+	+12	+10
Occupation	*	
Self-employed	−2	−7
Non-manual	+8	+12
Manual	−6	−5
MCA analysis: beta coefficients		
Gender	.05ns	.03ns
Age	.08ns	.07ns
Education	.16	.15
Occupation	.05ns	.14
R^2 (%)	4.9	5.2

*Differences between groups are not significant at the 0.05 level. ns = not significant at the 0.05 level.

non-manual employees. However, in Sweden the difference is only significant concerning education (Table 8.9). This over-representation is reflected in the MCA analyses which shows a small, but significant effect of education (and occupation) in both Sweden and Denmark.

If we look at the social characteristics of the persons who have been elected as user representatives in schools and public childcare institutions, the figures concerning childcare institutions seem to strengthen the conclusions drawn above (Tables 8.10 and 8.11). However, concerning schools, only gender seem to play a role. Thus, women are clearly over-represented among the user representatives, and even though we do find differences concerning education and occupation, especially in Sweden, these differences are not significant in the MCA analysis (that is, the differences seem to be a spurious effect of the gender composition of the representatives).

Summing up, the statistical evidence suggests that the class (de)mobilization hypothesis cannot be confirmed in this area; or at least, that it can only be

Table 8.10 Child care. Differences in socio demographic characteristics between elected user representatives and the user group as such (PDIs)

	Sweden	Denmark
Gender		*
Men	−18	−3
Women	+18	+3
Age (years)	*	*
18–29	−4	−6
30–49	+5	+7
50+	−1	−1
Education (years)		
7–9	−2	0
10	+13	−11
11+	−11	+11
Occupation	*	
Self-employed	−8	−5
Non-manual	+6	+19
Manual	+2	−14
MCA-analysis:		
beta coefficients		
Gender	.10ns	.05ns
Age	.14	.05ns
Education	.12	.18
Occupation	.08	.22
R^2 (%)	4.9	5.4

*Differences between groups are not significant at the 0.05 level. ns = not significant at the 0.05 level.

confirmed with big modifications. *Concerning age, the assumption of the hypothesis was not confirmed. The same goes for gender, where the differences run counter to the hypotheses (women are in fact over-represented vis-à-vis men). Concerning education and occupation the hypothesis is confirmed in the school and childcare areas.*[26] *However, this is not the case for the health sector or the tax authorities.* Altogether these results *do not* seem to support the fears of persons and groups concerned with the possible social bias of user participation. Differences in the sociodemographic composition between the user group as such, and active participants (users of voice and representatives) are small. Only childcare institutions, and to some extent schools, seem to deviate from this pattern, participation here being more socially biased.

We shall pursue the question of social bias in user participation further by focusing on the group of apathetic users. Thus, it is often assumed, that the expression of apathy is connected with certain sociodemographic

Table 8.11 Schools. Differences in socio-demographic characteristics between elected user representatives and the user group as such (PDIs)

	Sweden	Denmark
Gender		
Men	−16	−15
Women	+16	+15
Age (years)	*	*
18–29	−3	0
30–49	+7	+6
50+	−4	−6
Education (years)		*
7–9 .	−11	−4
10	+5	0
11+	+6	+4
Occupation		*
Self-employed	−5	0
Non-manual	+12	+10
Manual	−7	−11
MCA analysis:		
beta-coefficients		
Gender	.18	.18
Age	.15ns	.06ns
Education	.07ns	.05ns
Occupation	.10ns	.02ns
R^2 (%)	8.8	3.6

*Differences between groups are not significant at the 0.05 level. ns = not significant at the 0.05 level.

characteristics such as low education, low occupational status, and so on. However, the question is seldom analysed empirically. Below we have therefore compared the sociodemographic composition of the apathetic and the powerful users (Table 8.12).

In Table 8.12 we do find some significant differences between the groups of powerful and apathetic users. For Sweden the educational composition of the two groups is quite different: persons with a lower basic education are considerably over-represented among the apathetic users. For Denmark significant differences are found in the occupational and gender composition of the two groups. Concerning occupation, there is a considerable over-representation of the high and middle white-collar groups among the powerful users. Concerning gender, it turns out that women are over-represented among the powerful users; the only result that runs counter to

Table 8.12 *The apathetic versus the powerful.* Differences in sociodemographic characteristics between the groups of apathetic and powerful users (health sector + public child care + schools)

	Sweden powerful users (1)	Sweden apathetic users (2)	(1−2)	Denmark powerful users (3)	Denmark apathetic users (4)	(3−4)
Gender			*			
Men	47	50	−3	42	54	−12
Women	53	50	+3	58	46	+12
Age (years)						*
18–29	20	27	−7	14	22	−8
30–39	38	26	+12	40	30	+10
40–49	23	19	+4	29	20	+9
50–59	9	13	−4	7	13	−6
60–69	7	7	0	6	9	−3
70+	9	9	−5	4	6	−2
Education (years)						*
7–9	42	55	−13	35	41	−6
10	17	17	0	38	36	+2
11+	42	28	+14	27	22	+5
Occupation			*			
Self-employed1	0	3	−3	3	3	0
Self-employed2	8	6	+2	4	12	−8
Non-manual1	16	10	+6	16	9	+7
Non-manual2	27	19	+8	20	9	+11
Non-manual3	21	26	−5	28	31	−3
Skill. work.	10	15	−5	12	9	+3
Unskill. work.	19	20	−1	17	28	−11
N	212	217		277	103	

*Differences between groups are not significant at the 0.05 level.

the expectations of the class (de)mobilization hypothesis. However, one must remember that here we are looking at extremes in an attempt to maximize the possible social differences. *In that perspective the most important result is actually how small most of the differences are.* Thus, instead of paying attention to the differences one might as well note, for example, that in Sweden there are almost no differences in the occupational composition of powerful and apathetic users. In Denmark, this is the case for education.

The 'classroom hypothesis'

It is a classical assumption in participatory democratic theory that participation in different forms of local or 'small' democracy has a kind of 'spill-over'

Table 8.13 Correlation between user participation and other types of political participation (Pearson's r)

	Political interest	Electoral participation	Party membership	'Grass-roots' activities
Denmark	.06	.01ns	−.01ns	.14
Sweden	.07	—	.04ns	.16

ns = not significant at the 0.05 level. — = missing data.

effect – that it will provide citizens with the political knowledge and participatory experiences necessary to participate in the 'big' democracy.

In chapter 7 the existence of such a relationship was tested concerning participation at the workplace. The result was basically negative. However, this does not exclude the possible existence of such relationships in other areas – such as, for example, user participation. We have therefore also tested this so-called 'classroom hypothesis' in the area of user participation. The result of the analysis is found in Table 8.13.

The tables show the correlation between user participation[27] and political interest, electoral participation, party membership, membership of (other) voluntary organizations and 'grass-roots' activities. As we can see from the table correlations between user participation and participation in the 'big' democracy are weak or insignificant. The strongest correlation is found between user participation and 'grass-roots' activities which is a reasonable result because these activities have a number of similarities.

This result is in line with the result concerning participation at the workplace discussed in chapter 7. We can therefore conclude that the 'classroom hypothesis' set forth by Pateman and others is disconfirmed also when it comes to user participation.

Does this result mean that there is no positive correlation at all between user participation and citizens' competencies and ability to participate politically? Judging from the results produced in this section, the answer to this question seem to be yes: there is apparently no 'spill-over' between the part of 'small democracy' analysed here and different dimensions of the 'bigger' democracy. However, we think that to make such a statement would be jumping to conclusions, because, as we showed above, users seem to develop a kind of 'administrative' or 'participatory' competence through (successful) participation. However, this competence seem to be limited to the administrative area in question, and it is therefore a competence of a rather specific and non-generalizable character.[28]

Conclusion

The analysis above has shown that the fundamental question asked in the introduction to this chapter can be answered in the affirmative. Thus, we think it fair to conclude that no matter whether users' participatory rights are formalized or not, users seem to perceive participation as an important channel into politics; a fact which is demonstrated by a widespread – and in some areas vivid – participation. Users therefore de facto seem to perceive their user role(s) as complementary to the system of political and workplace right; as a kind of 'third citizenship'. Furthermore, since user participation does not seem to introduce any serious new social biases into the practices of participation it is difficult to see it as undermining or short-circuiting the traditional forms of representative democracy.

The details in this argumentation were brought forward through the test of the three hypotheses set forth. Testing the welfare state or stakeholder hypothesis we were able to show, firstly, that a considerable number of users participate; that is: take an initiative through formal or informal channels to change the content of the service directed towards themselves or their children (use 'voice'). In particular, schools, public childcare institutions and tax administrations have a vivid participation with somewhere between 27 and 49 per cent of users taking an initiative within a given year. Secondly, we found that quite a few users – between 17 and 38 per cent – experience themselves as powerful, when power is defined as taking an initiative and being successful with it. However, here we noted some differences between the countries. Danish users in the three mentioned areas are the most powerful, whereas the Swedish users fall some 10–20 percentage points behind. The Norwegian users fall in between. This difference might have to do with the historical-institutional factor: that the tradition for and institutionalization of user participation in these areas is older in Denmark than in its neighboring Scandinavian countries, and the organizational culture(s) therefore more supportive of user participation and influence.

However, the last part of the welfare state hypothesis, which predicts a low level of interest in private alternatives to public services, was falsified. Being able to test this part of the hypothesis in Denmark only, we found that more than half of the respondents (between 52 and 72 per cent) believed that private alternatives were important concerning hospitals, child care and schools. Testing different assumptions about these surprisingly high percentages – among these an assumption about a positive correlation between dissatisfaction with the public services offered and a positive view on private alternatives (which was falsified) – made us conclude that private alternatives ('exit') were not seen as an alternative to voice. Rather, users seem to perceive voice and exit as complementary, and wish to have both possibilities at their disposal when they try to obtain the desired 'service package'.

The next step in our analysis was to take a look at the factors which effect citizens' perception of their own efficacy as users. In doing so we pursued the so-called 'resource hypothesis', which assumes that it is citizens' personal resources in terms of education, occupation and knowledge network which determines citizens efficacy vis-à-vis a given public organization. We contrasted this view with an idea inspired by the 'new institutionalists'; namely that institutional factors might be at least as important as personal resources for citizens' perception of their own efficacy. We then entered all of these variables in a multiple regression model, even though we were only able to operationalize the institutional factors in a very rudimentary way. Looking at the different policy areas the results were basically the same: that neither individual resources nor institutional factors are of much importance for citizens' perception of their own efficacy. However, insofar as any of the variables had a (small) impact, the institutional factor was more important than individual resources; a result particularly true for public childcare institutions and schools in Denmark.

In our further search for factors of importance in accounting for citizens' perception of efficacy, we found that experiences of success or failure as a user were of great importance. Thus, we found a strong positive correlation between the experience of success when taking an initiative (using voice) and perception of efficacy. This led us to the conclusion that rather than being determined by individual resources or institutional factors, users' perception of their own efficacy seem to develop in an interplay with the institution in question. Experiences of success strengthen the feeling of efficacy, which can then be seen as a resource in its own right; a sort of 'administrative' or 'participatory' competence.

The third step in our analysis was to deal with the question of the possible inegalitarian character of this type of participation. Departing from the class mobilization hypothesis, which predicted a considerable social, age and gender bias in this type of participation, the differences in the composition of the user groups, the initiators (the users of voice), and elected representatives along the mentioned sociodemographic dimensions were analysed. The result was that sociodemographic differences between the three groups are small. Only concerning schools and child care did we find some differences in the educational and occupational composition of the different groups in the predicted direction (that is, that users of voice and elected representatives will be better educated and have a higher occupational status than the average user). However, even though they were significant, differences were found to be small; a result confirmed by a number of multiple regression analyses showing that in general the sociodemographic variables did not have much explanatory power in explaining the variations in neither participation nor representation.

Finally, we dealt with the question about whether there are any positive effects of user participation on other types of political participation through a test of the so-called 'classroom hypothesis'. What we found was that there were small or insignificant correlations between user participation and different dimensions of the 'big' democracy (electoral participation, party membership, and so on). Only concerning 'grass-roots' activities did we find a noteworthy correlation, but we are, of course, unable to say anything about the direction of causality. We therefore concluded that there is no 'spill-over' from user participation to the different dimensions of 'big' democracy. Even though this means a falsification of the 'classroom hypothesis', we still think there is a positive effect of user participation as successful users seem to develop the above-mentioned 'participatory' competence. However, one has to realize that this competence is of a limited character: bound to the administrative area in question, and therefore of a non-generalizable character.[29]

9
Political Action and Political Distrust

Introduction: political distrust and political protest in Scandinavia

Mobilization of citizens in political parties and voluntary associations in Scandinavia, as well as the welfare state, have contributed to a tradition of consensual democracies with high political trust and low levels of unconventional protest. Since the 1970s, however, this consensual style would seem to have deteriorated. In this chapter, we examine political protest behavior (or, more precisely, participation in political actions), its sources and consequences, and the relationship between protest and political distrust. As a point of departure, an overview with a few cross-national data and time series are presented below.

With some qualifications, the picture of consensual politics in Scandinavia still applies. Ironically, Denmark and Norway, where protest parties have been most successful (see chapter 4), reveal the highest levels of *satisfaction with democracy*. As emerges from Table 9.1, Danes are the EU citizens that express the most satisfaction with the way their democracy works. Furthermore, satisfaction with democracy has been increasing since the 1970s (Goul Andersen 1994b: 60). Norway used to have even higher figures (Aardal and Valen 1989: 277), fell a little behind in the 1990s (Aardal and Valen 1995: 225–6), and then came on par with Denmark in 1995 when the proportion who were satisfied was 82 per cent (Aardal 1999: 177). In Sweden, the figures are above the European average, but not by much.[1]

Political trust seems to range from average to high as compared to other countries. As measured by 'confidence in parliament' from the World Values Survey in 1990 (Listhaug and Wiberg 1995: 304–5), Norwegians had the highest level of trust in Europe, and in Sweden, it was around average. In Denmark, it was even a bit lower in that particular measurement but this is atypical. In Denmark, trust has been fluctuating considerably, whereas in Sweden, it has declined almost monotonously since 1968 (Gilljam and Holmberg 1995: 85; Holmberg 2000: 34). Thus, the average

Table 9.1 Satisfaction with the way democracy works in respondent's country, 1998 (percentages)

	Satisfied	Not satisfied	Don't know	PDI 1995	PDI 1998
Denmark	83	16	1	65	67
Luxembourg	78	18	4	68	60
Ireland	75	17	8	42	58
Netherlands	75	23	2	30	52
UK	61	30	9	5	31
Austria	60	35	5	—	25
Sweden	56	41	3	—	15
Spain	50	44	6	−28	6
Finland	50	46	4	—	4
Germany	50	48	2	22	2
France	39	56	5	18	−17
Portugal	35	59	6	−2	−24
Greece	33	65	2	−36	−32
Belgium	29	66	5	22	−37
Italy	28	68	4	−47	−40
EU15	47	47	4	1	0

Source: Eurobarometer 42/1995 and 49/1998.

proportion that agreed with the two distrust items increased from 41 per cent in 1968 to 75 per cent in 2000 (Figure 9.1). Comparable data also indicate that Swedes are the least trustful (Table 9.2). The high trust among Norwegians, on the other hand, is confirmed by all comparable measures (Aardal 1999: 170).

For example, in 1991, 70 per cent of Swedes surveyed agreed that 'Those people that are in Parliament and run things don't pay much attention to what ordinary people think'; in the Norwegian citizenship survey, the figure was only 54 per cent. In the 1987 election survey, 14 per cent of the Norwegians answered that 'only a few [politicians] are trustworthy'; in the Danish 1991 political trust survey of the Rockwool Foundation, the figure was 39 per cent (Goul Andersen 1992b: 33; Aardal and Valen 1989: 279). Behind the surface of an apparently stable political system, political trust in Sweden has deteriorated; in Norway, trust is fluctuating but at a higher level, with Denmark falling in between (see also Borre and Goul Andersen 1997: ch. 11).[2]

Whereas we have encountered a relatively 'activist' Scandinavian profile on all previous forms of participation, the trends and levels of *political protest* (defined here as participation in actions, see below) seem close to the European average (Table 9.3). The highest ranks are observed on the most 'conventional' forms such as signing petitions (Norway/Sweden)

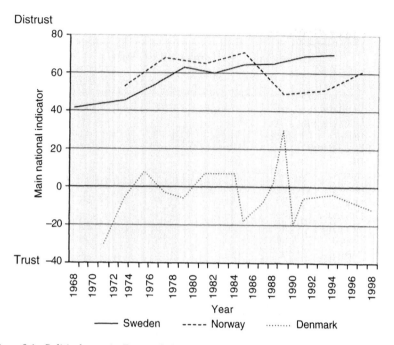

Figure 9.1   Political trust in Denmark, Norway and Sweden, 1968–1994. Main national indicators

Wording:
Sweden: Average proportion who agree on the following two items:
1. 'The parties are only interested in people's votes, not in their opinions.'
2. 'Those people that are in the Riksdagen and run things don't pay much attention to what ordinary people think.'
   Norway: Composite index of three questions (graph indicating proportion with index values 4–6):
1. 'Do you think that people in government waste a lot of money we pay in taxes, do they waste some of it, or they don't waste very much of it?'
2. 'Do you think that almost all the politicians are smart people who usually know what they are doing, or do you think that quite a few of them don't know what they are doing?'
3. 'Do you think that most of our politicians can be trusted, that politicians by and large can be trusted, or that only a few Norwegian politicians can be trusted.'
   Denmark: PDI: Percentage disagree minus percentage agree on the following item:
'In general, one can trust that our political leaders make the right decisions for the country.'
Sources: Gilljam and Holmberg (1995: 85); Holmberg (2000: 34) Aardal and Valen (1995: 201); Goul Andersen (1992b: 72).

and legal demonstrations (Denmark);[3] participation in action groups in Scandinavia appears to be low; and participation in violent or illegal actions is negligible (Topf 1995b: 86–90). The only measure with a high score in Scandinavia is unofficial strikes. However, even if the level of protest is moderate by comparative standards, it has increased over the last decades, whereas conventional political participation seems to have declined. The questions are what explains such change, and how it affects citizenship.

Table 9.2 Political trust in Denmark and Sweden, 1988–1994 (percentages)

	Sweden				Denmark						Local government 1990
	1988	1991	1994	1998	1990	1991	1992	1993	1994	1998	
Very high	3	2	1	1	1	2	5	3	3	4	5
Fairly high	41	36	35	30	27	38	52	32	50	55	39
Fairly low	44	50	50	51	46	35	31	38	35	30	33
Very low	11	11	13	17	20	10	10	22	10	9	13
Don't know	1	1	1	1	6	14	3	6	2	2	10
PDI	−11	−23	−27	−37	−38	−5	+16	−25	+8	+20	−2

Wording: 'In general, how much trust do you have in Swedish (Danish) politicians?'

Sources: Gilljam and Holmberg 1995: 86; Holmberg 2000: 34; Siune et al. 1992: 34; 108; Goul Anderse 1992, 1993; Danish Election Survey 1994 and 1998.

Table 9.3 Political protest participation in various countries (Percentages)

	Ever signed petition		Ever joined demonstration		Action group
	1981	1990	1981	1990	1989
Denmark	44	51	19	27	14
Norway	56	61	20	20	—
Sweden	54	72	15	23	—
Finland	30	−41	14	−14	—
UK	63	75	10	14	11
Germany	47	57	15	21	14
Netherlands	35	51	13	25	17
Belgium	24	47	14	23	26
France	45	56	27	33	26
Italy	42	48	27	36	29
Spain	24	23	25	23	20
Austria	−39	48	−7	10	—

Source: European/World Values Survey 1981/1990, and Eurobarometer 31/1989, quoted from Topf (1995b: 86–90).

Theories and conceptualizations of political protest

Few political phenomena have attracted as much interest as protest and new social movements. We shall begin by introducing a few clarifying distinctions. In the first place, it is important to distinguish between three levels of analysis: *the level of (social) movements*; *the level of organizations or groups*; and *the level of actions* (Goul Andersen 1981b). Secondly, following Petersson et al. (1989), we distinguish between the '*large*' democracy and the '*small*' democracy, depending on the aim of the groups or actions: Local or national.

Many theories in the field have focussed at the level of movements and conceptualized the study object as 'new social movements'. Measurement of political participation, on the other hand, usually focus on participation in actions or action groups, often conceptualized as 'unconventional' or 'protest' behavior. The correspondence between these levels is not straight-forward. '*Social movement*' is a more abstract concept that embraces not only actions and organizations but also formation of common identities; *action groups* may be studied at the collective level or in terms of membership (which is difficult to distinguish from voluntary associations).[4] *Participation in actions* is most straightforward to define and to measure but although actions are typically organized by action groups or some other 'alternative' forms of organizations, even political parties or voluntary associations may organize actions. Unions and left-wing parties have a long tradition of doing so (Rasmussen 1997), and even the Swedish Employers' Federation once arranged a protest march against economic democracy. Further, 'actions' not only includes activities of 'new social movements' but also actions at the 'small democracy' level with a very narrow scope.

The basic contention here is that there is not so much 'unconventional' about protest behavior if this is defined as participation in actions. By 'protest behavior' we mean *any sort of participation, which seeks to influence decision-makers through direct manifestations (i.e., actions), rather than through representative channels (associations and parties).* Such participation may range from signing a petition to more unconventional behavior. An impor-tant element often is to attract the attention of the media and to put pres-sure on decision-makers through the mobilization of public opinion. We suggest that this is a 'natural' extension of the standard repertoire of political participation, appropriate for a 'postmodern' society in which people have larger political resources, except time; where conflicts are too crosscutting or issues are too short-lived to be represented by parties and associations; where media and public opinion play an important role; and where the outcome side (or implementation stage) is increasingly recognized as important. Actions may be used wherever considerations of costs and benefits makes it appropriate: (i) because there are no obvious alternatives (especially at the level of 'small democracy'); (ii) because it gives 'political losers' an extra opportunity (especially at the level of 'large democracy'); or (iii) simply as a supplement. We do not by definition imply anything about issue content or political leaning: just as the modern mass party was 'invented' by the socialists but copied by other political forces, actions may be copied by all sorts of social and political forces. All that is involved is a process of *learn-ing* the particular organizational skills.

This 'postmodernity' hypothesis contrasts with many competing theories. Theories about 'new social movements' tend to assume that they comprise a relatively coherent phenomenon. Thus Alain Touraine (1981) argued that 'new social movements' were 'really' fighting for 'autonomy' in a 'programmed society', and Jürgen Habermas (1981) saw 'new social movements' as representing the values of the 'life world' against the 'colonization of the system world'. We think this implies assumptions about issue content that are generalized much too far. The same applies to *discourse analyses* which criticize the idea of structural determination (as implied by Habermas and Touraine) but claim that common identities may be discursively constituted: there is a possibility that 'new social movements' may converge on the issue of 'radical democracy' (Laclau and Mouffe 1985; Mouffe 1992). Considering the variety of movements, this appears to us to be wishful thinking. Our hypothesis has the very opposite implication: that participants are less and less characterized by any 'common identities'.

A *value perspective* (Gundelach 1995: 418–19) suggests that postmaterialist values embodied both in the organizational form and the objectives of protesting give coherence to the phenomenon. As far as issue content is concerned, the counter-arguments are the same as above. As to organizational form, it is argued that participation in action groups is based on expressive gratifications rather than on instrumental benefits. We think, however, that these motivational assumptions apply equally well to 'conventional' participation: As all associations work for collective goals (Olsen 1965), either selective incentives are needed, or else participation must be rooted in some 'wertrationel' or 'expressive' logic. Gratifications can rarely be purely 'instrumental'[5] (Panebianco 1988). Thus, postmaterialism is likely to affect all forms of political participation.

Yet another perspective is found in *class mobilization* theories which associate the emergence of new social movements with the mobilization of the 'new middle class', or particular segments of this class (Svensson and Togeby 1986). We expect this to be a historically contingent phenomenon, however – in other words, we expect this particular form of political organization to spread to other social groups as it turns out to be efficient, and as organizational skills are learned. The same argument applies to the suggestion that 'unconventional participation' is related to *legitimacy problems*. We believe, on the contrary, that such behavior is becoming increasingly 'conventional', as a natural extension of participation opportunities. The acid test of these propositions is to examine the association between protesting and political distrust over time.

From an institutionalist perspective, it has been suggested that political protest is linked to the *lack of institutionalization* of conflict. New issues cut across 'routine politics' where conflicts are institutionalized (Olsen and Sætren 1980), and protest may even be a precursor of institutionalization. This is in accordance with our own suggestions but with the addition that political actions may in principle be a supplement in all areas. Finally, a *'grass-roots hypothesis'* claims that protesting brings new and powerless groups into politics (Olsen and Sætren 1980). This hypothesis has served mainly as a 'straw man', however: considering what we know about political behavior, this hypothesis is highly unlikely. However, it may contain a core of truth: protesting may provide a 'second opportunity' for the losers in routine parliamentary politics, or for groups that challenge the power of established groups.

Measurement of political protest

Before testing the hypotheses, we need to discuss operationalization problems. Our measure of political protest is *participation in actions,* which means that some activities in 'grass-roots movements' are omitted. This may be a little bit too narrow but it does free us from the difficult task of distinguishing between voluntary associations and grass-roots movements. The next question is what should count as actions. As indicated, we apply a broad definition stretching from signing a petition, wearing badges and contributing money, to working in action groups and participating in illegal activities. Although there were substantial country differences in question wordings, response categories and in reference periods (see Figure 9.2), it is possible to obtain roughly equivalent measures.[6] The main problem is to match the Norwegian response categories – that is, signing a petition,

	Norway	Denmark	Sweden
Reference period	3 years	3 years	1 year
Reference situation	Political action	Political activity	Seek to obtain improvements or counteract deteriorations
Showcard	No	Yes	Yes
Wording	Now, we'd like to know if you have done anything of the following in relation to a political action. Have you ...	This card shows various forms of activities that can be applied in relation to a political action. Have you ...	There are various ways to seek to obtain improvements or counteract deteriorations in society. Have you done anything of the following within the last year*
Specification of issue areas	General	None	For each type of activity

Figure 9.2   Measurement of political protest in the Scandinavian Citizenship Surveys

*For some purpose which is not only of concern to yourself and your family.

donating money, participating in demonstrations and meetings, political strikes, and 'other ways'. To match the last category in the two other countries, we have collapsed the remaining categories – excluding boycotts (which we assume people forget unless they are reminded): wearing badges, participating in action groups, participating in illegal actions, and other activities.[7]

As the Swedish question referred to 'obtaining improvements' or 'counteracting deteriorations' in society, some response categories are too broad.[8] In particular, the category 'contribution of money' is likely to include money for charity and aid to developing countries. This is confirmed by very high frequencies for this category. To make figures more commensurable, we have singled out respondents who have participated in no other ways than contributing with money *and* who have participated in no other areas than 'health and care', or 'problems in other countries'. 15.9 per cent of the Swedish respondents satisfied the first criterion and 9.2 per cent satisfied

Table 9.4 Participation in protest actions, and contacting, 1987 and 1990 (percentages)

	Norway	Denmark	Sweden
Reference period	3 years	3 years	1 year
Sign petition	31	38	36
Economic contribution	20	23	30
Demonstration	19[1]	16[1]	5
Strike	8[2]	9	2
Badges	—	6	10
Action group	—	2	2
Illegal actions	—	0.6	0.3
Other actions	7[3]	2	2
At least one of these	7	8	13
At least one of the above mentioned (actions, total)	45	50	48
Boycott	—	22	14
Contacts with ...			
– politicians	—	—[4]	8
– organizations	—	12	19
– public officials	—	15[5]	21
– media	—	6	9
– lawyer	—	6	8

Notes:
1. 'Meetings or demonstrations'.
2. 'Political strike'.
3. 'Other ways'.
4. For technical reasons, this question had to be deleted from the Danish file.
5. 'Contacted public employee'.

Table 9.5   Factor analysis of political action variables (Varimax rotation)

	Denmark (single factor)	Norway (single factor)	Sweden	
			(Factor 1)	(Factor 2)
Sign petition	0.65	0.67	0.77	0.01
Econ. contribution	0.63	0.69	0.82	0.02
Demonstration/				
meeting	0.77	0.77	0.23	0.63
Strike	0.52	0.46	−0.10	0.81
Other action	0.66	0.55	0.57	0.37
Eigen value	2.12	2.04	1.79	1.04
Percentage of				
variation	42.5	40.8	35.7	20.9

both. These have been recoded to 'no participation' on the category of economic contributions.[9]

Table 9.4 presents the proportion of participants in the different activities in the three countries, including the categories of contacting in the Swedish and Danish surveys.[10] It turns out that by far the most frequent activity is signing a petition, followed by making economic contributions. In Denmark and Norway, demonstrations (and meetings) and strikes were also mentioned quite frequently, and much more frequently than in Sweden. Finally, there remains the question of deciding whether or not these activities form a common dimension. Beginning with the five categories in the Norwegian survey, Table 9.5 reveals that the Danish and Norwegian data fit nicely with the assumption of unidimensionality whereas the Swedish data produce a two-dimensional solution. However, it is only participation in strikes that disturbs the unidimensionality, and this is a very infrequent phenomenon in Sweden.

It turns out that 45 per cent of the Norwegians and 50 per cent of the Danes had participated in one way or another within the last three years. In Sweden, 48 per cent had participated within the last year. We also find roughly the same country difference on the single most important form of protest – signing a petition. As the Swedish reference period is shorter, we may safely conclude that the Swedes are the most active in protesting, followed by the Danes and finally the Norwegians. In most other studies, Norwegians come out as slightly more active than the Danes do whereas the high activity among Swedes is a general finding (Topf 1995b; Togeby 1991).

Social and political variations

Social and political variations in protest participation in Scandinavia are described in Table 9.6. In the Danish case, we have also presented a slightly modified variable which is comparable with the 1979 participation survey in order to examine whether the social and political basis of protest has changed, that is if protesting has been dispersed to new groups.[11] Generally speaking, social variations in the three countries are quite similar: protesting is positively affected by education, youth, and non-manual employment. However, it is remarkable that participation is lower among higher-level non manuals than among middle-level non manuals;[12] even in the 1990s, the social elite to some degree abstains from protesting. A significant country difference is found with respect to gender. As in other fields, Denmark is a 'laggard' at this point: women are less active than men in Denmark by 1990 whereas we find the inverse relationship in Sweden and a zero association in Norway. But the most remarkable finding is that social variations are small. Even if we use the total index (rather than the dichotomous variable) as dependent, the variance explained by social factors remain below 11 per cent in Norway and even less in the two other countries. Even unskilled workers participate quite frequently in protest actions, and apart from the low participation among elderly citizens, even age effects are quite small. As indicated by the Danish data, the age effect has declined very markedly (see also, for example, Gundelach 1995): In 1979, there was a sharp drop-off in participation at the age of 40 years (even more precisely, at 35 years – see Goul Andersen 1980: 120). In 1990, there is no longer a significant difference between the young and the 30–49 years category. This is in accordance with a generational interpretation: The generations born after the Second World War have a higher level of participation which is maintained over the life cycle. However, as there is not an equivalent decline at the age of 50 in 1990, more than generational replacement is involved. It seems that new patterns of behavior also spread across neighboring generations – that is, that learning has taken place among the pre-war generations. And overall it emerges that social variations have declined. Since 1979, the proportion of participants has nearly doubled among the lower educated whereas it has remained nearly constant among the better educated. The same holds for social class. According to a MCA analysis, total variance explained by gender, age and education has declined from 11 to 6 per cent. If class is added, the explained variance is even lower as the age effect largely hinges upon those aged 60–69 years. This confirms earlier findings of a study of the young (Svensson and Togeby 1991). In short, both a generational hypothesis and a ('new') class mobilization hypothesis are increasingly disconfirmed by the data. The same holds for the assumption of common identity formation. Although adherents of left-libertarian parties remain the most active, participants are not very distinct politically, and far less so than in the 1970s. In short, our data confirm the alternative 'postmodernity' hypothesis that protesting is a 'new' mode of political articulation that is gradually dispersed to the entire society.

Table 9.6   Social variations in protest participation. Participants in percentages, and beta values (MCA analysis)

	Denmark time series		Denmark	Norway	Sweden
	1979	1990	1990	1990	1987
Total	28	47	50	45	48
Men	30	49	52	45	46
Women	25	45	47	44	51
18–29 years	40	57	59	49	56
30–39 years	36	58	61	57	59
40–49 years	23	51	54	46	51
50–59 years	19	50	53	42	41
60–69 years	11	34	37	32	39
70+ years	—	19	20	21	27
Low education	19	37	40	33	41
Medium	35	50	52	45	56
High	62	65	66	64	59
Unskilled worker	20	44	49	36	48
Skilled worker	33	55	60	41	47
Lower-level nonmanual	39	62	58	47	55
Medium-level nonmanual			72	67	60
Higher-level nonmanual	38	52	55	56	57
Farmer	12	37	39	47	44
Self-employed	23	45	45	47	51
Left wing	68	73	74	68	66
Social Democrats	23	42	46	43	48
Center Parties	27	52	55	49	55
Conservative/Liberal	21	42	44	47	49
Progress Party	20	36	37	38	—
Beta values	*Dichotomous var.*			*Index*	
Gender	.04	.03	.06	.00	.09
Age	.17	.11	.20	.14	.16
Education	.24	.19	.17	.27	.16
R^2 (%)	11.2	5.9	9.2	10.8	7.4
Gender	.04	.02	.04	.00	.09
Age	.10	.06	.06	.10	.12
Education	.22	.18	.15	.21	.11
Social class	.12	.11	.16	.17	.12
R^2 (%)[1]	9.1	4.9	6.1	11	6.5

Note:
1. Includes only the economically active population. This explains why R^2 is lower even if one more explanatory variable is added.

Sources: 1979 participation survey (Denmark) and citizenship surveys.

Table 9.7 Political protest among voters and adherents of center parties, 1987 and 1990 (percentages)

	Norway	Denmark	Sweden
Social Democrats	43	46	48
Center Party (No./Sw.), Liberals (Dk)	41	46	45
Liberals (No.)/Rad. Lib. (Dk)/People's Party (Sw.)	54	60	59
Christian People's Party	52	63	65
Center Democrats (Dk)		44	
Conservatives	47	42	49

Finally, we may test the expectation that protesting is an especially attractive option to 'political losers'. If this is the case, we should expect to find variations between the center parties as the Christian parties have certainly been losers in the question of cultural change. As revealed by Table 9.7, this is in fact confirmed in all three countries. Voters/adherents of Christian parties (who are neither strong in terms of socioeconomic resources nor 'postmaterialist' in any conventional sense) are among the most frequent protesters. This finding also lends support to the contention that protests occur mainly outside the realm of routine politics. Finally, the data cast serious doubt on the assumption that political protesting is a very coherent phenomenon. This is also disconfirmed in the next section when we look at the concrete issues involved.

What is protest about?

As emerges from Table 9.8, it is difficult to find any common denominator for the issues that are involved in protesting. A major distinction is between the 'large' (national) democracy and the 'small' democracy (local issues). Policy issues about women, immigration, nuclear power, defense and peace, foreign relations, solidarity with foreign countries, and freedom belong to the former. The environment can be classified as either. Taken together, national issues account for about one-half of all participation in protest actions in Norway and Sweden (the question was not posed in Denmark). Most of these national issues are related to 'new social movements' or to 'postmaterialism'; most of the rest are not. Only a few issues may be summarized under such headlines as demands for 'autonomy', 'life world values' or 'radical democracy'. And the specification of price/wage/taxation policies as target for actions in Norway illustrates that protesting may proceed far into 'routine politics'.

At the local level, major issues are welfare services (health care, schools, leisure facilities and so on) and local environmental or traffic problems. Country differences are a bit uncertain, as the question format is different.

Table 9.8 Protesting about various issues. Norway and Sweden (percent of population)

Norway[1]		Sweden[1]	
Issue	*Relative frequency*	*Issue*	*Relative frequency*
		Dwelling	3
Local issues (traffic, child care, school and so on)	14	Local environment, traffic	8
		Leisure, sport facilities	8
		Health care	11
		Schools	5
Regional policy	9	Child care	3
		Work-related issues	5
Price/wage/taxation policies	8	Consumer policy	1
Women's policy	3	Women's policy	1
Immigration	3	Immigration	5
Environmental issues	14	Environment, nuclear power	9
Foreign countries	3	Foreign countries	17
		Peace and defense	7
		Freedom for Swedish citizens	2
Other issues	12	Other issues	9

Note:
1. In Norway, respondents were asked only once; in Sweden, they were asked for each type of activity (only issues related to protest are included, not contacting).

Norwegians seem to be preoccupied with the environment whereas the Swedes were more concerned with foreign policy and peace. However, this may also reflect changes in the political agenda and the declining importance of the peace movement from 1987 to 1990.

From our hypotheses we would expect a marked difference between the participants at the local and national levels. At the local level, protest actions are mainly concerned with local interests, which are frequently difficult to articulate in other ways. At the national level, on the other hand, actions probably serve more as an alternative or as a supplement to influence via political parties or promotional groups. Consequently, we would expect the 'losers' at the parliamentary level to be particularly active here. Because the center parties are generally very influential in the Scandinavian multiparty systems, it is mainly among the adherents of left-wing/left-libertarian parties that we would expect to find high participation at the national level.

The results in Table 9.9 largely confirm these assumptions. In Norway, left-wing voters are over-represented everywhere, but at the local level, the over-representation is small. This holds also for issues concerning prices,

Table 9.9 Political composition of participants in various actions. Sweden 1987 and Norway 1990

	Left Wing	Social Dem.	Center Parties	Conservatives	Progress Party	Others	N
I. Norway							
All voters	11	2	20	26	10	1	1445
Local actions	17	27	21	26	7	2	211
Regional policy	10	27	29	22	11	1	147
Prices, wages, taxes	18	30	19	24	7	2	129
Women's policy	32	18	18	21	11	—	44
Immigration	37	17	19	20	5	2	41
Environment	22	22	23	25	6	—	202
Foreign countries	41	21	16	14	4	4	56
Other issues	16	31	19	23	9	2	194
II. Sweden							
All voters	9	48	25	17	—	1	1557
Dwelling	15	44	20	22	—	—	46
Local environment	11	41	31	16	—	1	130
Leisure, sport fac.	10	46	24	20	—	—	128
Health care	8	46	31	14	—	1	191
Schools	8	34	41	16	—	1	74
Child care	29	38	25	8	—	—	52
Work-related	9	56	21	14	—	—	86
Consumer policy	15	27	46	12	—	—	26
Women's policy	−36	−21	−36	−7	—	—	14
Immigration	26	46	18	7	—	3	96
Environment, nuclear power	24	36	28	10	—	2	164
Foreign countries	14	43	28	14	—	1	289
Peace and defense	22	42	22	12	—	2	120
Freedom for Swedish citizens	12	33	21	35	—	—	43
Other issues	6	45	26	22	—	1	148

wages and taxes. But among those who participate in protesting on 'new politics issues', the proportion of left-wing voters varies between 22 and 41 per cent – that is, two to four times their proportions among Norwegian voters in general.

Basically, the same pattern is found in Sweden, but with two exceptions. At the local level, left-wing voters are significantly over-represented among those who protest against insufficient childcare facilities. And at the national level, left-libertarians are only slightly over-represented among participants in the foreign country issues.[13] Finally, we may observe that the Social Democrats are over-represented in the area of 'work-related issues', and even the Swedish Conservatives are over-represented on one particular issue – 'Freedom for Swedish citizens'.

To sum up, in social as well as in political terms, political protesting is not a coherent phenomenon. People with different backgrounds participate in different areas, and, more generally, political protest has changed from being a 'new left' and 'new middle-class' phenomenon to becoming a standard form of political articulation, used by various social and political groups when it is considered to be appropriate. This also means that participation has become less dependent on socioeconomic resources.

Political protest and political distrust

Although it has become less common to speak of legitimacy problems, let alone legitimacy crises, political protest is usually associated with some notion of political distrust, and previous empirical studies have also demonstrated a significant correlation between protesting and distrust (see, for example, Goul Andersen, Buksti and Eliassen 1980: 242). However, at this point, things have also changed quite dramatically. Thus it emerges from Table 9.10 that in Denmark, there is no longer any association

Table 9.10   Protesting and political trust (average index scores)

Political protest: Number of types of action	Norway (scale 0–6)		Denmark (scale 0–4)		Sweden (scale 0–10)	
	Index	N	Index	N	Index	N
No action	2.27	977	1.61	994	5.17	1026
1	2.64	370	1.64	477	5.14	432
2	2.61	218	1.65	267	5.30	377
3 or more	2.8	208	1.57	230	5.41	152
II. MCA analysis	*eta*	*beta*	*eta*	*beta*	*eta*	*beta*
gender	0.04	0.04	0	0	0.04	0.01
age (18–69)	0.04	0.03	0.11	0.10*	0.11	0.13***
education	0.15	0.13***	0.02	0.01	0.02	0.01
class	0.13	0.09	0.10	0.09	0.1	0.10*
protesting	0.13	0.10*	0.03	0.03	0.06	0.07

Significance: * < 0.05, ** < 0.01, *** < 0.001.
Scales:
Norway: An additive index of three issues:
1. 'Those people that are in the Riksdagen and run things don't pay much attention to what ordinary people think.'
2. 'Do you think that people in government waste a lot of money we pay in taxes, do they waste some of it, or they don't waste very much of it?'
3. 'Do you think that almost all the politicians are smart people who usually know what they are doing, or do you think that quite a few of them don't know what they are doing?'
Sweden: Average of 'trust in Parliament' and 'trust in political parties', measured on a scale 0–10.
Denmark: 'In general, how much trust do you have in Danish politicians? (4 = 'Very high'; 3 = 'fairly high'; 2 = 'don't know'; 1 = 'fairly low'; 0 = 'very low').

between political protest and political trust, and in Norway and Sweden, participation in political protest is even *positively* related to political trust. Now, this might be a spurious effect of background variables related both to distrust and to political protest behavior. However, an MCA analysis reveals that in Norway, the effect remains statistically significant even after such controls (p=0.011), and in Sweden, the association is strengthened and approaches statistical significance (p=0.072). Further controls for party choice reveals that even in Denmark, there is a positive association between protest and political trust among supporters of left-wing and center parties. In short, protesting is no longer related to political distrust; rather, the Norwegian data indicate that it may even lead to increasing political trust – in other words, it may have some of the same integrative effects as conventional participation. These findings confirm that political protest is increasingly becoming a 'conventional' form of participation and a part of the standard repertoire of political behavior in Scandinavia.[14]

Postmaterialism and political protest

So far, the results confirm the postmodernity hypothesis. But even though we found that protesting is dispersed to issues that cannot be considered postmaterialist, this does not rule out the possibility that at the individual level, there may still be a positive relationship between postmaterialism and protesting. Indeed, there is such a relationship: in a comparative Nordic study from 1987, Lise Togeby (1991) found strong associations between postmaterialism and 'grass-roots participation', and the effect remained strong even when controlled for spurious effects of gender, age, education, class and urbanization (Table 9.11). Thus, there is clear evidence

Table 9.11 Postmaterialism and grass-roots participation in the Scandinavian countries, 1987. Proportions with high levels of grass-roots participation (percentages)

	Norway	Denmark	Sweden
1. Most materialist	5	4	9
2	5	8	9
3	5	8	19
4	11	14	17
5. Most postmaterialist	42	43	43
Eta	0.37	0.34	0.29
Beta[1]	0.26	0.26	0.25

Note:
1. MCA analysis. Controlled for gender, age, education, class and urbanization.

Source: Togeby (1991: 91–2, 105).

of a non-spurious relationship between postmaterialism and political protest. There remains, however, a problem of interpretation. As mentioned above, protesting is not restricted to postmaterialist *issues*. The question is, then, whether it is a preference for this particular *form* of participation that explains the correlation.

Unfortunately, only the Danish citizenship survey asked about postmaterialism. Thus, we are unable to differentiate between participation at the national and local levels, because these questions were not asked in Denmark. But we may nevertheless refine the analysis somewhat, and the data in Table 9.12 give any reason to believe that our results may be generalized.

From three standard batteries (Inglehart 1990), a materialism/postmaterialism index was constructed by adding the number of postmaterialist first choices (weight = 2) and the number of postmaterialist second choices (weight = 1).[15] The association with protesting was almost the same as in the 1987 survey. The main findings from a series of MCA analyses are presented in Table 9.12.[16] Now, the theory of postmaterialism suggests that postmaterialism explains a major share of the effect of social background factors (especially age but to some degree also gender, education and social class). This implies that the effect of social background factors should decline sharply when we control for postmaterialism, and that the effect of postmaterialism is almost unaffected by control for social background variables. As in Togeby's analysis, this is confirmed by our data (equation 1): The effect of postmaterialism (among the 18–69-year-old category) only declines from eta = 0.31 to beta = 0.28 whereas the effects of the background variables are seriously diminished.

Alternatively, however, one might imagine that political interest was the decisive mediating variable between background variables and political protest. Political interest is in fact an even stronger determinant of protest behavior (equation 2), but it does not to the same degree act as an intervening variable – that is, control for political interest does not reduce the effect

Table 9.12 Effects of postmaterialism and other factors on political protesting. Denmark 1990 (MCA analyses and beta coefficients)

18–69 years old	Bivariate (eta)	Equation (1)	Equation (2)	Equation (3)	Equation (4)	Equation (5)	Equation (6)
Gender	0.04	0.05	0.02	0	0.06	0.01	0.02
Age	0.17***	0.06	0.09*	0.08*	0.07	0.08	0.09
Education	0.21***	0.08*	0.10**	0.04	0.08	0.08	0.05
Class	0.20***	0.12**	0.14***	0.12**	0.10	0.10	0.09
Political interest	0.32***	—	0.32***	0.29***	—	0.29***	0.27***
Party choice	0.31***	—	—	—	0.22***	0.28***	0.21***
Post-materialism	0.31***	0.28***	—	0.24***	0.22***	—	0.18***
R² (%)	—	13.0	15.1	20.1	18.1	21.8	24.3

of background variables to the same degree as control for postmaterialism. This brings us to equation (3): postmaterialist theory predicts that the effect of postmaterialism is a value effect rather than a political engagement effect, and that postmaterialism is not a spurious effect of political interest. Clearly, the theory even passes this test. Both the effects of political interest and postmaterialism are slightly reduced by mutual controls but the effect of postmaterialism remains as high as beta = 0.24.

There is yet another possibility that the effect of postmaterialism may be spurious: Postmaterialists frequently vote for left-wing parties, and, being political losers, left-wing voters are more likely to protest, according to our explanation above. Equations (4 and 5) confirms that the effect of social background variables is really mediated mainly through political interest and party choice. However, the prediction that the effect of postmaterialism is a spurious effect of party choice is not confirmed. As revealed by equation (6), the effect of postmaterialism remains strong and significant even after controls for party choice and political interest.[17]

So far, the theory of postmaterialism resists any attempt at falsification. The theory also suggests, however, that postmaterialists *prefer* participation in actions *at the expense* of other forms of participation because of the less instrumental and more expressive gratifications associated with this form of political behavior. Against this suggestion, we have argued that expressive gratifications are not special to participation in actions or action groups but characterize nearly all sorts of participation for collective ends. And at this point, the data fail to confirm the theory (see Table 9.13). Postmaterialism is positively related not only to protesting but also to participation in promotional groups and even to participation in political parties. Effects are higher on protest (beta = 0.18) but significant also on membership of organizations (beta = 0.13) and party activity (beta = 0.11). This shows that postmaterialists *do* like to protest, but first and foremost, *they like to participate*; most of the extraordinarily strong effect on protesting is likely to derive from the issues involved in protesting rather than from that particular form of protesting.[18] In fact, this is not very surprising as there is a strong positive association between party activity and protesting (r = 0.22), as well as between voluntary association membership and protesting (r = 0.27). Even in 1979, positive associations were recorded. But at that time, the associations were much weaker (Goul Andersen 1980).

Some other interesting information is found in Table 9.13. It is sometimes argued against petitioning that people may be persuaded to give a signature without really knowing what they are doing. However, this is strongly contradicted by the finding that protesting is even more strongly correlated with political interest than participation in political parties (regardless of controls for social background variables). This indicates that protesting is a very politically *conscious* form of participation. At the same time it emerges that participation in political parties is more class-determined than protesting.

Table 9.13   Effects of postmaterialism and other factors on political participation (MCA analyses and Beta coefficients)

	Entire population: eta coefficients			Controlled effects: beta coefficients[1]		
	Protest	Voluntary associations[2]	Political Party[3]	Protest	Voluntary associations[2]	Political party[3]
Gender	0.06	0.06	0.11	0.02	0.02	0.05
Age	0.25	0.25	0.12	0.09	0.16***	0.09*
Education	0.23	0.21	0.05	0.05	0.12**	0.05
Class	0.2	0.22	0.22	0.09	0.1	0.20***
Political interest	0.31	0.23	0.3	0.27***	0.10*	0.26***
Party choice	0.32	0.14	0.11	0.21***	0.08	0.06
Postmaterialism	0.31	0.19	0.09	0.18***	0.13*	0.11*
				24.3	10.9	16.1

Notes:
1. Labor force only (only respondents with information about party choice).
2. Number of memberships of voluntary associations
3. Scale 0–3: Not member, passive member, active member, office holder.

This gives the opportunity to examine another argument frequently launched against actions and action groups – namely that those who protest are not very representative, socially or politically.

Representativeness of protestors

We have already seen that protesting is less strongly related to social background factors than previously. But we get a more precise impression of the social representativeness by comparing the social composition with the population at large. When we speak of representativeness, it is unimportant whether effects are spurious or not (Schlozman and Verba 1979). As above, we compare on the basis of signing a petition, contributing economically, and participating in meetings and demonstrations. But as with our discussion of voluntary associations in chapter 5, when we speak of representativeness, we speak of aggregates rather than individuals (that is, we speak of 'positions'). This means that participants must be weighted by their frequency of participation. As a proxy, we have weighted by the number of *acts* of participation. The results are presented in Table 9.14.

It emerges that major changes have taken place since 1979. Among the 18–70-year old-category, gender inequality has evaporated. The proportion of participants who are 40 years old or more has increased from 27 to 46 per cent. The educational bias of participants in actions is halved. And turning to social class, inequality is nearly eliminated. What remains is a moderate under-representation of unskilled workers and an equivalent over-representation of lower- and medium-level non manual employees.

Table 9.14 Social and political composition of protestors (18–70 years old) in Denmark, 1979 and 1990 (percentages)

	Proportion of participants		Proportion of sample		Deviance	
	1979	1990	1979	1990	1979	1990
Men	57	50	50	49	7	1
Women	43	50	50	51	−7	−1
18–29	40	25	24	22	16	3
30–39	31	29	25	24	6	5
40–49	14	23	19	23	−5	0
50–59	10	14	16	15	−6	−1
60–69	5	9	16	16	−11	−7
Low educ.	39	32	63	42	−24	−10
Medium	34	37	28	36	6	1
High	27	31	9	22	18	9
Unskilled workers	17	17	27	22	−10	−5
Skilled workers	15	11	14	11	1	0
Lower/med. nonmanuals	49	51	38	44	11	7
Higher nonmanuals	10	11	7	11	3	0
Farmer	2	4	6	5	−4	−1
Other self-employed	7	6	8	7	−1	−1
Left wing	43	33	13	20	30	13
Social Democrats	29	28	41	32	−12	−4
Center parties	7	11	10	12	−3	−1
Other bourgeois parties	21	28	36	36	−15	−8
Public employees	46	42	33	35	13	7
Publ. empl. new middle class	38	33	23	26	15	7

As mentioned previously, higher-level non manuals are not over-represented; this is perfectly understandable from a notion of protest as opposition to the elites but difficult to explain from a postmaterialist point of view.

As far as class mobilization is concerned, it was a bit of an exaggeration to speak of class mobilization even in 1979 because at this time 'only' 38 per cent of the (weighted) participants belonged to the 'new middle class of public employees'. By 1990, the proportion had declined to 33 per cent in spite of a simultaneous increase in the proportion of public employees. The same holds if we look at public employees at large. Finally, protesters have become more politically representative of the population at large. Even though general votes support for the left-wing parties had increased from 13 to 20 per cent in the two samples, the proportion of participants who adhered to the left wing declined from 43 to 33 per cent. At the same time, the under-representation of social democrats and supporters of the center parties has nearly disappeared; what remains is a certain under-representation of the right-wing parties. If we compare with the composition of party members in Table 4.11, we observe that protesters have become more socially and politically representative on most dimensions than party members.

Conclusion: from protest to single-issue participation

Not least in the Scandinavian context, the increasing levels of political protest for a long time provoked interpretations which were both too dramatic and too wide-ranging. Today, there is little left to legitimize any sharp distinction between protesting or 'unconventional' political participation on the one hand and other forms of political participation on the other. Protesting has become routine politics, although perhaps with a slightly anti-elitist flavor. *Protesting has become single-issue campaigning.* As such, any notion of 'new social movements' seems unwarranted – at least if it is conflated with protest participation as defined here. And if protesting is defined more narrowly, including only more unconventional forms of participation, it becomes a rare phenomenon in a Scandinavian context. Protesting is not a very coherent phenomenon. It is positively related to other forms of participation, and it is not even related to political distrust – rather the opposite.

Neither structural theories of societal change, theories of radical democracy, nor class mobilization theories can account for this diversity. The only sociological theory that may be relevant is the theory of postmaterialist value change. However, postmaterialism seems to affect nearly all forms of political behavior, not only participation in actions and action groups. What remains is that participation in actions (most usually at the lowest levels of inclusion, by signing a petition or the like) has become a standard way of acting politically, in accordance with the theory of postmodernity outlined above. It is a way of participation that is not very demanding, especially as regards long-term commitment and increasingly provides an opportunity for people who are politically interested but otherwise assume the role of spectators to try to influence political decisions, at a low level of costs. However, contrary to the prejudices often found among political elites, our data indicate that signatures are by no means given at random but should be taken seriously as a conscious attempt to influence politics. From an instrumental perspective on citizenship, protesting – or what should perhaps rather be termed single-issue participation – is not distinguished from other, more traditional forms of participation; and even the reservations as to the impact of changing forms of political participation on political equality (Goul Andersen, Buksti and Eliassen 1980) no longer seems warranted. What remains is not least to examine the effects of changing forms of political participation on political identities and on 'social and political capital formation'. However, this is outside the scope of this book.

Part II
Challenges to Citizenship

10
Marginalization and Citizenship

Marginalization, polarization and the welfare state

Until the 1980s, discussions about citizenship were usually conducted within the framework of an optimistic vision of the future which saw the continued development of the welfare state as the way to increasing fulfillment of citizenship. By contrast, recent discussions have been more concerned with the challenges which might lead to other, less promising paths – in particular, the dangers of loss of citizenship as a consequence of globalization and post-industrial change (Roche 1992). These challenges are the subject of the next three chapters. In the first place, the classical visions were implicitly based on the assumption of autonomous nation-states; but what happens when nation-states become increasingly interdependent and, in particular, when supranational European integration creates new rights, new opportunities for participation, and new conditions of identity formation? Next, the classical visions were based on the assumption of relatively homogeneous populations with equal civil, political and social rights; but what happens when such societies experience massive immigration and increasing cultural heterogeneity? These questions are discussed in chapters 11 and 12, respectively.

The present chapter deals with another major challenge to citizenship: marginalization in the labor market which is often seen as a consequence of globalization and post-industrial change. The classical visions of citizenship were based on the assumption of full employment; but what happens if this goal is no longer attainable? Even though 'conventional' inequality may not be increasing, do we face a more serious division between the majority population of employed persons and a new group of underprivileged or even an 'underclass' who enjoy little more than purely formal citizenship and become 'second-class citizens, or less' (Roche 1992: 55; Lister 1990)?[1]

Although research on unemployment and labor markets abounds, solid empirical knowledge is limited, even about causal effects of unemployment on psychological distress (Björklund and Eriksson 1998; Halvorsen 1999b) and much less about consequences for social integration and participation (but see Gallie and Panugam 2000). Also comparative research on the Nordic countries is quite limited (see, for example, Tema Nord 1996: 575; Carle and Julkunen 1997; Torp 1999). Indeed, when it comes to the implications of unemployment and labor market marginalization for democratic citizenship, research interest has been largely absent (Svensson and Togeby 1991; Andersen et al. 1993: 126–8; Goul Andersen et al. 1998). The reasons are obvious: Throughout the 1980s, the time of interviewing, unemployment was virtually unknown in Sweden and not very widespread in Norway. Until the Swedish and Finnish economic crisis in the 1990s, Denmark was the only Scandinavian society with an experience of enduring mass unemployment. Our data for this project are not very adequate as far as the number of cases is concerned but on the other hand, they contain variables that are usually not included in studies of unemployment but which are indispensable from a democratic citizenship point of view.

First, however, we have to consider the arguments and the concepts in more detail. Our proposition here is that labor market marginalization is indeed a serious threat but that the Scandinavian welfare states are quite well-equipped to counteract this challenge; not only to combat unemployment[2] but, in particular, to alleviate the consequences for citizenship.

In general terms, we may define marginalization as an intermediary state between full inclusion and full exclusion (Halvorsen 1995; Johannessen 1995). Below, we concentrate on the unemployed and ignore pensioners, the early retired and the disabled.[3] However, we have to distinguish between different kinds of marginalization which are not necessarily connected. At least we must distinguish between *labor market* marginalization, *economic* marginalization, *social* marginalization and *political* marginalization. Although integration in all these fields are traditionally considered as aspects of full citizenship, it is now becoming clearer that people may be marginalized in some respects without being marginalized in others.

Labor market marginalization means long-term or recurring unemployment (or under-employment). Traditionally, the right to work has been considered to be a very important aspect of citizenship. However, full citizenship is imaginable without having a job in the formal economy. Employment is a resource for participation in social and political life as witnessed by the closing of the gender gap. But depending on the rights and the opportunities for people without work, and on the cultural values and practices (such as the stigmatizing effects of unemployment), this relationship may be strong, weak or entirely absent (Goul Andersen 1996a; Halvorsen 1999b).

By *economic marginalization* we mean a loss of integration in the standards and way of life of a society – the impossibility of maintaining a proper standard of living and being able to live like the majority because of poverty. To what extent labor market marginalization leads to economic marginalization, depends, in turn, on welfare arrangements which are, in all the Nordic countries but particularly in Denmark, relatively generous in the sense that minimum levels are relatively high and duration, in practice, is relatively long (NOSOSKO 1999: 11). By *social marginalization* we mean a loss of social integration and social participation. This may depend to a large extent on economic resources, or it may depend on social psychological mechanisms linked more directly to labor market participation – loss of identity, of structure in daily life, and so on (Jahoda 1982); whether the one or the other mechanism is decisive – and for which groups – is a politically contested issue about which very little is known (Halvorsen 1999b).

Political marginalization means that people are not integrated in political life – that is, that they lose interest, participate very little and lose a sense of efficacy. The behavioral consequences of such isolation may be passivity, or it may occasionally lead to unrest. This sort of participation among people who were unable to organize was described already in Marx's comments about the behavior of the 'lumpenproletariat'.

Finally, *political polarization* between the fully integrated and the marginalized may take two different forms: A couple of decades ago, social scientists were concerned about legitimacy and the development of distrust and hostility towards the surrounding society among the marginalized. More recently – as the marginalized have usually proved to be 'politically harmless', to quote Dahrendorf (1994) – more attention has been directed towards the maintenance of solidarity among the integrated – first and foremost their willingness to pay for the public support of the marginalized.

These variables are often assumed to be related in a deterministic way (Figure 10.1): Enduring unemployment leads to a marginalization in the labor market which in the long run leads to social and political marginalization (Møller 1995; Pixley 1993; White 1990). As a consequence of this segregation, which tends to be transferred from generation to generation, mutual solidarity, and finally even mutual understanding, between the fully integrated and the marginalized breaks down. This may even involve a number of reinforcing 'vicious circles': labor market marginalization may often be tantamount to structural unemployment, loss of qualifications and bottlenecks among the highly qualified which makes it difficult to fight unemployment without deteriorating consequences for inflation. Social marginalization reinforces labor market marginalization because socially marginalized persons are unlikely to return to be fully reintegrated into the labor market. And finally, political marginalization means lack of influence opportunities which may lead to a worsening of the social conditions of the marginalized.

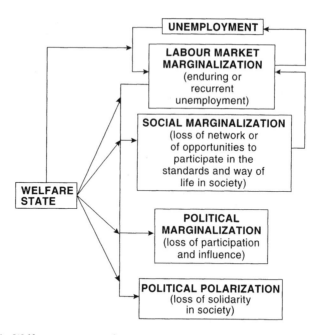

Figure 10.1   Welfare state, unemployment, marginalization and political polarization: contingent associations and 'vicious circles'

However, the very purpose of the welfare state is – as far as possible – to break or at least to modify all these associations and vicious circles:

- To fight unemployment through general economic policies or employment programs.
- To prevent labor market marginalization (for example, through active labor market policies).
- To prevent economic and social marginalization (by providing economic resources).
- To prevent political marginalization by providing resources and opportunities for participation.
- To prevent political polarization (for example, by avoiding stigmatization and, more generally, by avoiding sharp divisions between the marginalized and the integrated).

In short, the effects sketched in Figure 10.1 are contingent on appropriate welfare state action which, in turn, depends on the welfare system (Esping-Andersen 1990, 1999). However, some institutional differences cannot be subsumed under the headlines of welfare state models. Even the Scandinavian systems differ: in Denmark, Sweden and Finland, the Ghent system of employment insurance means that most of the unemployed are unionized (see chapter 6). This may force unions to assign higher priorities to the interests of the unemployed and thus contribute to reduce 'insider'/'outsider' divisions. The systems also differ in their relative priority of active labor market policies (with Sweden as a vanguard), as well as in compensation levels which are higher in Denmark and Sweden than in Norway, especially for low-income groups (NOSOSKO 1999: 11).

The purpose here is not to identify and test all steps in the model but only to provide a few indications about to what extent social and political marginalization and polarization has been avoided. Because of small samples in the citizenship surveys we only make a simple distinction between the employed and the unemployed (even though some of the unemployed are not marginalized, the relationship with dependent variables will be equivalent). As a supplement to this data, we include the Danish and Swedish 1998 Election Surveys, some data from a Danish survey of long-term unemployed from 1994,[4] and a few findings based on secondary literature.

Economic and social marginalization

Although the proportion of long-term unemployed in the Scandinavian countries is low, partly because of flexible labor markets, partly because of activation programs (OECD 1998, 2000: 220–2), these countries have been unable to avoid marginalization in the labor market where unemployment concentrates on a minority of the labor force whereas the majority never experience any unemployment.[5] However, taking into account that most people live in families, the experience unemployment at the family level is much more common (Goul Andersen 1999).

In Denmark, *average* compensation rates declined from 75 to 65 per cent from 1975 to 1995 (Pedersen, Pedersen and Smith 1995). But compensation remained 90 per cent for low-income groups, and this combines with the predominance of double-earner families and a relatively low level of 'unemployment homogamy' (in Denmark, it was 14 per cent in 1994, see Goul Andersen 1995; see also Halvorsen 1999d). Taken together, this means that the majority of the unemployed enjoy a tolerable standard of living. By 1988, according to the European Commission (1995: 140–1), only some 3 per cent of the Danish households where the head of household was unemployed fell below the relative poverty line. The EU average was close to 40 per cent (from as high as 48 per cent in the UK to around 22 per cent in the Netherlands). Another indicator of economic integration, closer to way of life factors, is homeownership: Being a tenant is certainly not an indicator of economic marginalization but remaining a homeowner may be seen as an indicator of economic integration. As singles are typically tenants regardless of employment status, and as singles are over-represented among the unemployed, we control for marital status. As shown in Table 10.1, the difference in homeownership among married/cohabiting is modest: 83 per cent of the employed were homeowners; 70 per cent of the unemployed; and 61 per cent among the long-term unemployed. Among those who had been without ordinary employment for nine years or more, the proportion was still 55 per cent. Even though conditions have since then been tightened in terms of duration of benefits (lowered from eight to four years), even long-term unemployment remains, generally speaking, less of an economic disaster than it is in many other countries. In Sweden, this is even less so: compensation is only 80 per cent but in practice runs infinitely provided that the unemployed accept activation.

However, marginalization is also a matter of identity and well-being. An indicator of this is found in a battery of questions concerning the respondents' well-being during unemployment, compared with previously when they were employed. The results in Table 10.2 are quite surprising: 34 per cent reported a decline in general well-being, but 28 per cent reported an improvement, and only 12 per cent reported experiencing less contact with friends and acquaintances. Now, these answers should certainly not be over-interpreted. They show, first and foremost, that the unemployed are able to *cope* with their problems (Halvorsen 1994). Besides, average measures are a bit misleading as very serious problems for some of the unemployed cannot be balanced by improved well-being of others. The data do not contradict numerous findings (for example, Mørkebjerg 1985; Thaulow 1988; Nygaard Christoffersen 1995; Björklund and Eriksson 1998)

Table 10.1 Proportion of homeowners among married/cohabiting couples. By termination of last ordinary employment. Denmark 1994 (percentages)

Last ordinary employment	Man	Woman	Total		N	
1985 or earlier	—	(58)	(55)	1	18	19
1986–88	(45)	57	55	10	39	49
1989–90	(66)	62	63	19	60	79
1991	(53)	77	70	26	52	78
1992	49	73	64	60	100	160
1993	55	66	62	91	150	241
1994	72	69	70	42	75	117
Total (incl. NA)	53	65	61	266	516	782
Election survey 1994:						
All unemployed	59	76	70	64	120	184
Employed	83	83	83	846	788	1634

Source: Unemployment Survey 1994.

Table 10.2 Well-being of the long-term unemployed, compared with the period before unemployment. Percentages and PDI (Denmark 1994)

	General well-being	Contacts with friends and acquaintances	Consumption of beer, wine and liquor (−)	Tobacco consumption (−)	Physical exercise
Much better	11	8	3	2	13
Somewhat better	17	20	5	4	29
No difference, DK	38	60	63	35	41
Not relevant	—	—	19	40	9
Somewhat worse	23	9	7	12	6
Much worse	11	3	3	7	2
PDI: Better minus worse well-being	6	+16	−2	−13	+34

Note: Sign has been changed so that positive sign means relative overweight improved well-being. Drinking more and smoking more has been counted as worse well-being.

Source: Unemployment Survey 1994.

that unemployment is associated with nearly all types of social problems as well as with a deterioration in health.

On the other hand, there are well-known causality problems in cross-sectional studies, and it would be equally misleading to generalize from such studies to the majority of the unemployed. Social marginalization seems to be a minority phenomenon even among those who are marginalized in the labor market. The majority are to a large degree able to maintain their former way of life, to maintain social contacts, and to cope with an unpleasant situation.

This assumption is confirmed when the respondents were asked if they would like to remain unemployed if it was possible to maintain unemployment benefits for an infinite period. 44 per cent answered they 'would welcome it', and 29 per cent indicated that they 'could make the best out of it'. Once again, one should be careful not to overinterpret such figures, – people in employment would most likely give the same answers – but they do indicate that economic security is a key factor in preventing social marginalization among the unemployed. This finding is confirmed by country variations among the young unemployed where the Danes appear less negatively affected by unemployment than the Swedes, the Norwegians and the Finns (Hammer 1997; see also Halvorsen 1999b). From an economic perspective, one could be concerned about disincentives and poverty traps from these data; however, employment commitments, according to the ISSP (International Social Survey Programme), appear to be higher in Denmark (and in Scandinavia) than in other countries (Svallfors, Halvorsen and Goul Andersen, 2001), and on the whole, Scandinavian labor markets are considered to be highly flexible (OECD 1998).

Unemployed and trade unions: unemployed as 'insiders'

As mentioned in chapter 6, an important side-effect of the Ghent system is the unionization of the unemployed. This means that the unemployed have a possibility of influencing union policies. Many unions also have activities directed specifically to their unemployed members. But do the unemployed participate? Do they identify with the labor movement? Do they feel efficacious, or do they feel alienated and powerless? In the Danish case, we have enough respondents to attempt to answer such questions. In Sweden, there were only 22 unemployed union members, and the extremely low unemployment furthermore makes it questionable whether anything can be inferred about the behavior of the unemployed under conditions of mass unemployment; as is well known, selection problems increase with decreasing unemployment.

But allowing for these reservations about the Swedish data, we may notice from Table 10.3 that, at least in Denmark, unemployed members are almost as engaged as the employed but somewhat less active (this seems also to be the case in Sweden). One could also imagine that the unemployed would feel distrust towards the established labor movement. Yet in Denmark, there is no association between unemployment and feeling of affinity with the labor movement, and in Sweden and Norway, the unemployed in our samples actually feel a little *more* affinity with the labor movement than the employed, although the difference is not statistically significant (Table 10.4). In the Danish case, we are also able to test the proposition derived from economic theories of 'insider'/ 'outsider' relations that interest conflicts are deepening as the insiders seek to safeguard their

Table 10.3 Trade union activity interest and participation, by employment status (percentages of members)

	Denmark		Sweden	N	
	Interest	Participation	Participation	Denmark	Sweden
Employed	58	22	27	874	1038
Unemployed[1]	52	14	(5)	90	22
MCA Analysis					
Effects of unemployment[2]					
Eta	0.03	0.06			
Beta	0.01	0.04			

Notes:
1. Only unemployed who have indicated some occupational position (for example, manual worker).
2. Controlled for age, education and class.
Source: Scandinavian Citizenship Surveys.

Table 10.4 Employment status, trade union activity and affinity with labor movement. (percentages feeling 'much' or 'some' affinity)

				N		
	Denmark	*Sweden*	*Norway*	*Denmark*	*Sweden*	*Norway*
Employed	49	43	49	1013	1266	988
Unemployed	49	54	57	106	26	44
MCA Eff. unemployment						
Eta	0.00	0.03	0.02			
Beta[1]	0.02	0.05	0.01			

Note: 1. Controlled for age, education and class.

Source: Scandinavian citizenship surveys.

Table 10.5 Union power at workplace and influence upon trade unions, by employment status. Denmark. Trade union members only (PDI)

	Influence on union	*Union power*	N
Employed	−25	14	849
Unemployed	−15	17	84
MCA analysis			
Eta	0.02	0.02	
Beta	0.03	0.00	

Notes: PDI Influence on union: 'Much' or 'some' minus 'little' or 'none'. PDI Union power: 'Much' minus 'none'.

Source: Scandinavian Citizenship Surveys.

own interests by means of the trade unions. However, as it turns out from Table 10.5, the unemployed in Denmark feel that they have at least as much influence upon their unions as the unemployed.

These findings confirm that the unemployed feel that unions are doing something for them, which they in fact are (this is also strengthened by the links between unions and unemployment insurance funds).[6] To sum up, the unemployed in Denmark and Sweden are not only unionized; they also identify at least as much with the labor movement as the employed, and they are at least as satisfied with their influence on the unions. This indicates that the trade unions play an important role for the integration of the unemployed in society by providing a channel of real influence. Conflicts between 'insiders' and 'outsiders', on the other hand, are not observable.

Political marginalization

The next task is to examine, more generally, political participation and political efficacy among the unemployed. Two questions are equally relevant (Schlozman and Verba 1979): Do the unemployed participate less, and if so, is it because of unemployment as such or is it, statistically speaking, a spurious effect of the social composition of the unemployed? Even if the effect is spurious, low participation still means that the interests and experiences of the unemployed are not effectively communicated to the political elites, but it would be misleading to speak about political marginalization.

Table 10.6 presents the results from the Scandinavian citizenship surveys. As mentioned, the numbers of unemployed in the Norwegian and particularly in the Swedish surveys are small which, other things being equal, produces smaller, and less significant, associations than in Denmark. But with a single exception, it turns out that in all three countries, and across the various forms of participation, the unemployed are less active than the employed. The exception is the high level of political interest among the unemployed in Sweden but even in this case the difference is not significant. In Denmark, on the other hand, we find a highly significant difference in political interest – 66 per cent of the employed are interested in politics, as compared to only 40 per cent among the unemployed. However, most of this association is spurious; when we control for gender, age, education and class, there remains a significant but weak effect (beta = 0.06). In short, the unemployed are not much involved in politics, but this is mainly because of a higher incidence of unemployment among less politically interested groups.

Electoral participation is also lower among the unemployed. In Denmark, the effect seems largely spurious – that is, an effect of age and class – whereas it appears to be genuine in the two other countries where the estimations of nonvoting are more reliable. In all three countries, but especially in Denmark and Norway, we also find a clear difference in party membership. As a rule of thumb, abstention rates are about twice as high among the unemployed; in Denmark and Norway, rates of party membership are at least three times as high among the employed as among the unemployed. This also means that there are very few party members who are unemployed. Thus, political decisions in this field are likely to be made on the basis of second-hand or third-hand experiences, not to say myths, about the unemployed. Even though the *interests* of the unemployed may be defended by trade unions, there is certainly a risk of extraordinarily *poor* decision-making in this field, because the possibilities for political communication and feedback are very small.

Political protest is also remarkable in being the only form of political participation where we do not encounter significant differences between employed and unemployed in *any* of the three countries. This confirms the

Table 10.6 Political participation, by employment status, 1987/1990 (percentages, eta, and beta-coefficients (Multiple Classification Analysis)[1]

	Denmark	Norway	Sweden
Interested in politics (per cent)			
Employed	66	61	48
Unemployed	40	52	63
Eta (four-point scale)[2]	0.13***	0.04	0.03
Beta	0.06*	0.02	0.02
Vote in last election			
(per cent, unweighted)			
Employed	94	91	86[3]
Unemployed	88	74	71[3]
Eta	0.06*	0.12***	
Beta	0.02	0.10***	
Party Membership (per cent)			
Employed	11	13	15
Unemployed	4	2	11
Eta (three-point scale)[2]	0.07*	0.06*	0.01
Beta	0.02	0.04	0.01
Political protest (per cent)			
Employed	57	49	53
Unemployed	54	37	41
Eta (five-point scale)[2]	0.05	0.05	0.02
Beta	0.04	0.02	0.03
Voluntary associations			
(no. of memberships)			
Employed	3.6	1.6[3]	3.5
Unemployed	2.6	0.6	2.2
Eta	0.12***	0.13***	0.09***
Beta	0.06*	0.10***	0.06*

Notes:
1. Controlled for gender, age, education and occupational class.
2. In the MCA analyses, scales were, as far as possible, used as dependent variables: four-point political interest scale (much/some/little/none); four-point party scale (nonmember/passive member/active member/office holder), except in Norway (member/nonmember); 6-point political protest scale (number of activities).
3. 1998 election (see Statistika Centralbyrån Allmänna valen 1998. Del 4. 1998 års valundersøkning. Statsvetenskapliga Institutionen, Göteborgs Universitet). In 1994, the figures were 90 and 79 per cent, respectively.
*** p < 0.001.
** p < 0.01.
* p < 0.05.

observation in previous chapters that the social biases in participation between various institutional channels are being definitively changed.

As far as voluntary associations are concerned, we have used number of memberships as our dependent variable because it produces the highest correlations with social background variables. Unemployment is no exception: in all three countries, we observe highly significant differences between the employed and the unemployed, and although the association is partly spurious, there remains a significant causal effect in all countries. It should be mentioned, though, that membership may reflect economic capacity and that social differences in *participation* tend to be less outspoken. Still, regardless of which measure we choose, there is a significant association, as is also shown in other studies (Fridberg 1994).

To sum up so far, unemployment is related to political participation but the causal effects are small. Furthermore, in analysing the effects of unemployment, there are well-known selectivity problems which means that it is virtually impossible to make all relevant controls.[7] However, strictly speaking, the arguments about marginalization applies only to long-term unemployed, and it is furthermore possible to imagine that some very marginalized group is hiding behind the average figures. To take account of this, the test can be refined in two ways: Firstly, we may examine, on the basis of other material, whether there is more marginalization among the long-term unemployed. And next, we may examine whether there is a group of almost entirely passive people among the unemployed. Because of small sample sizes and a lack of comparable measures of participation, we rely only on Danish data in the following tables.

To begin with the question of distribution, we have combined the measures from the citizenship surveys into an overall index. Each measure was assigned values from 0 to 3 – that is, we achieve a composite index ranging from 0 to 15. The distribution among employed and unemployed is presented in Table 10.7. It emerges that there is a large group among the unemployed with very low participation – 25 per cent score an index value below 6. Among the employed, the comparable figure is only 9 per cent. Still, there are only 2 per cent at the most extreme values (0–2), and it also turns out that the distribution of the unemployed comes close to that of unskilled workers. In Table 10.8, we have compared the effect of unemployment with the effect of other background variables. It emerges that the effect of unemployment is significant but at the same time, it is smaller than the effect of any other background variable. Thus unemployed people *are*, on average, less active, and to some degree, this *is* explained by unemployment, but the effect seems far too small for us to describe it in terms of political marginalization.

As to the first question about difference between short-term and long-term unemployed, we can only use data from the Danish 1994 election survey. Table 10.9 confirms that there is a clear difference between the short-term and the long-term unemployed as far as political interest is concerned. Among people without unemployment experience within the last two years, 66 per cent were interested in politics; among short-term unemployed and among the presently employed with recent unemployment experience, the figures were 52–59 per cent; and among the long-term

Table 10.7 The distribution of employed and unemployed on a composite index of political participation, Denmark 1990 (percentages)

	By employment		Comparison
Index value	*Employed*	*Unemployed*	*Unskilled worker*
0–5	9	25	18
6–7	27	32	32
8–9	36	27	33
10–11	18	13	13
12–15	9	3	4
Mean	8.3	7.1	

Note: Composite index of the following:
Vote: 0 = nonvoter 3 = voter.
Political interest: 0 = none 1 = little 2 = some 3 = much.
Party member: 0 = not member 1 = passive 2 = active 3 = office holder.
Action: Number of actions; 3 = 3 or more.
Voluntary associations: As action.

Table 10.8 Effect of various background variables on a composite index of political participation. MCA analysis. Denmark 1990

	Eta	*Beta*	*p*
Gender	0.10	0.10	0.000
Age	0.17	0.16	0.000
Education	0.18	0.13	0.000
Class	0.28	0.20	0.000
Unemployment	0.14	0.08	0.004
R^2 (%)		12.5	0.000

Note: See Table 10.7.

Table 10.9 Political interest and discussions with friends, by unemployment experience. Denmark 1994 (percentages)

Present employment status and unemployment experience within the last two years	*Political interest*	*Discussion with friends*	*Discussion with family*	*N*
Employed; no unemployment experience	66	65	72	913
Employed; have been unemployed <6 months	52	62	66	104
Employed; have been unemployed at least 6 months	56	59	69	61
Unemployed <6 months	59	68	63	41
Unemployed 6 months or more	46	59	66	106

Source: Danish 1994 Election Survey.

unemployed, it was only 46 per cent. However, this is a smaller difference than was recorded in the citizenship survey, and the election survey further revealed that the differences in political discussion with friends or with family are negligible.[8] Thus, we may conclude that unemployment is an important factor but by no means any new dominant cleavage that over-shadows more conventional lines of division; at least as long as we speak of a situation of massive unemployment.[9]

Political polarization

Finally, the concept of a 'two-thirds' society also involves the notion of political polarization. Originally, scholars were most concerned with maintenance of trust among the unemployed but increasingly, it has been formulated as a question of solidarity and willingness to pay for the unem-ployed among the employed majority. One might even imagine that the employed would become distrustful of a political system which taxed the employed heavily in order to provide for the unemployed and groups entirely outside the labor market.

Such predictions are not confirmed, however. As emerges from Table 10.10, there are no significant associations between unemployment and distrust in the citizenship surveys, not even in Denmark, where structural unemploy-ment is widespread. However, at this point, the Danish citizenship survey is atypical, probably because of widespread distrust at the time of interviewing; in most other studies, including the 1994 election survey, we find a small but significant effect (see also Goul Andersen 1992b; Bild and Hoff 1988).

Still, slightly higher levels of political distrust among the unemployed in Denmark do not amount to any political polarization, nor are there any events at the level of collective action that could point in this direction. A more plausible danger is the risk of a decline in solidarity among the employed majority. To explore this, we use the data from the Danish 1990 citizenship survey, and the 1994 election survey, respectively.

Table 10.11 shows the proportion agreeing that 'Social reforms have gone too far in this country. More than now, people should manage without social security and support from the public' (1990 and 1994), and that gov-ernment 'uses too much money' for unemployment benefits (1994 only).

Unlike in 1990, the 1994 survey indicates a significant effect of unem-ployment on both items. Still, the association is weak when controlled for spurious effects. Even more importantly, only 28 per cent of the employed agreed that social reforms had gone too far, and only 13 per cent wanted to cut unemployment benefits. Similar patterns are recorded on nearly all types of questions concerning the unemployed, with the single modifica-tion that most people think that the unemployed should accept almost any kind of job that is offered to them (Goul Andersen 1996b).

Table 10.10 Unemployment and political distrust. Average index values, eta and beta coefficients (MCA analysis)

	Denmark 1990	Denmark 1994	Norway 1990	Sweden 1987
Employed	1.10	1.50	2.55	5.14
Unemployed	1.07	1.27	2.02	4.96
Eta	0.01	0.10	0.06	0.01
Beta[1]	0.01	0.07	0.05	0.01
Sig.[1]	0.806	0.019	0.072	0.762

Scales:
Norway: An additive index of three issues:
'Those people who are in Parliament and run things don't pay much attention to what ordinary people think.'
'Do you think that people in government waste a lot of money we pay in taxes, do they waste some of it, or they don't waste very much of it?'
'Do you think that almost all the politicians are smart people who usually know what they are doing, or do you think that quite a few of them don't know what they are doing?'
Sweden: Average of 'trust in Parliament' and 'trust in political parties', measured on a scale 0–10.
Denmark: 'In general, how much trust do you have in Danish politicians? (4 = 'Very high'; 3 = 'fairly high'; 2 = 'don't know'; 1 = 'fairly low'; 0 = 'very low').
1. MCA analysis. Controlled for gender, age, education and class.

Table 10.11 Unemployment and attitudes to welfare in general and to size of unemployment benefits. Percentages favoring cutbacks, and eta and beta coefficients (MCA analysis). Denmark 1990 and 1994

	1990: Social reforms gone too far	1994: Social reforms gone too far	1994: Unemployment benefits too high
Employed	34	28	13
Unemployed	21	15	3
Eta	0.08	0.09	0.10
Beta[1]	0.03	0.06	0.08
Sig.[1]	0.222	0.034	0.006

Note:
1. MCA analysis. Controlled for gender, age, education and class.

Wording:
1. 'First we have a question about social expenses.
A says: Social reforms have gone too far in this country. More than now, people should manage without social security and support from the public.
B says: Those social reforms that have been made in our country should be maintained at least to the same extent as now.' (percentage agreeing mostly with A).
2. 'I now want to ask about your view on public expenditures for different purposes. I shall read some public tasks to you, and I ask you for each of these tasks to say whether you think the public uses too much money, a suitable amount, or too little money on these tasks.... Unemployment benefits (amount going to the individual)?'

Table 10.12   Unemployment experience and attitudes to welfare in general.[1] Denmark 1994. (PDI)

Pro-welfare PDIs	No unemployment experience	Only unemployment experience in family[1]	Respondent has unemployment experience[1]	Total
Total	+33	+42	+61	+41
Private sector	+24	+29	+59	+30
Public sector	+47	+56	+66	+51
Unemployed	—	—	+63	+63
N	709	266	310	1285
	391	149	87	627
	285	106	53	444
	—	—	151	151

Note: 1. More than one month within last two years.

Wording: See Table 10.11 (question 1). Entries are proportion agreeing mostly with B minus proportion agreeing mostly with A, in percentage points.

So far, the results indicate few signs of a breakdown of solidarity. It might be objected, however, that the effect is blurred by the fact that some of the employed have unemployment experience themselves or are public employees. It even turns out that only one-third of the labor force is totally unaffected by unemployment in their family and at the same time work in the private sector. Therefore we have performed an even stronger test in Table 10.12 in order to contrast two minorities: the unemployed and privately employed without employment experience. However, the difference in attitudes is modest, and even in the last-mentioned group there is a large majority against retrenchment.

Conclusions

We have not been able to establish exactly to what extent the Scandinavian welfare states are responsible for the tendencies – and lack of tendencies – we have observed, nor can we judge on the effects of intra-Scandinavian differences in the welfare states. But at least it emerges that *within* the Scandinavian welfare states, social marginalization and political polarization because of unemployment has remained fairly limited. So far, there are few signs of a 'two-thirds' society that could undermine citizenship for some 'new underclass'.

The most relevant test case at the time of interviewing is Denmark which has had a long experience of mass unemployment and labor market marginalization. Even marginalization in the labor market, however, seems less dramatic than one could expect: The proportion of long-term unemployed is relatively low, and during periods of prosperity, quite large numbers of long-term unemployed, with the exception of the elderly, tend to return to the labor market. More importantly, however, the social consequences of unemployment are more ambiguous than often described. To be sure, unemployment is an extremely bad experience for most people. But a majority seem able to cope with this situation and even to a large degree to maintain their former way of life. Poverty is rare among the unemployed, and the majority seem quite well-integrated in social life.

This holds also for political participation, where the unemployed often do have a slightly lower than average participation rate – sometimes attributable to their other social characteristics, sometimes attributable to unemployment. However, in all instances, the effects of unemployment are weak, and lower than the effects of age, education and class.

Under these conditions, it is perhaps not so surprising that the unemployed remain quite confident in the political system. A potentially more worrying problem is the maintenance of solidarity among the employed. Within reasonable limits of taxation, however, a breakdown of solidarity is not very likely: in the first place, people live in families, and even those who are not personally affected may often have a close relative with unemployment experience. Next, there is a large public labor force who tend to identify with the welfare state. And thirdly, even those privately employed and without any sort of unemployment experience (about one-third of the labor force, and about 20 per cent of the entire adult population) have so far not exhibited any signs of declining support for the welfare state. If a backlash should occur, then, it is not likely to be a rebellion of 'contributors to the welfare state'; rather, it could be a response of the entire population to economic pressures. However, in spite of aging populations and increasing demands, it does not seem that Scandinavian welfare states will face insurmountable budgetary pressures in the near future. And in this situation, there seem to be no serious threats to social solidarity.

11

'Reluctant Europeans': The Scandinavians and the Challenge of the European Union

Introduction

Democracy and citizenship in the Scandinavian countries cannot be seen in isolation from the European Union of which Denmark achieved membership from 1973 and Sweden and Finland from 1995. Norway has remained outside, but as a member of the European Economic Area (EEA), it is just as much affected by many EU decisions as the other countries. Since the 1990s, this has become an increasingly important challenge to citizenship and democracy in the Scandinavian countries.[1] Along with the aim to liberate (and increasingly also to regulate) markets, the need for Western Europe to redefine its role in world politics after the German reunification and the end of the Cold War gave a strong impetus to the acceleration of the European integration process in the 1990s. For the political elites of Western Europe the development of the European Union has presented itself as the obvious answer to the major challenges of the time. Thus, at the elite level in Denmark, Sweden, Finland, and even in Norway there has been relatively little disagreement about the positive value of European integration. But in Scandinavia, more than elsewhere, the general population has been reluctant to accept the elites' visions of the European future.

Even though the European Union may not be moving towards a genuine federation, important steps have been taken that challenge citizenship and democracy at the national level without providing very convincing alternatives at the European level. In many debates in the 1990s, this question was addressed under the heading of 'the democratic deficit' of the EU. However, this concept has typically connoted mainly the questions of the formal democratic rules within the EU system, the balance between the different institutions, and similar issues. Sometimes the concept of 'democratic deficit' has nearly become synonymous with the unobtrusive role of the European Parliament (until recently), and solutions to the problem discussed mainly in terms of expanding the influence of the Parliament. More recently, however, research interest has also been directed towards discussing the potentials for development of a new citizenship or even of a 'deliberative democracy' at the European level (Eriksen 2000). Indeed, a convincing case can be made that citizenship is not necessary limited to the nation-state (Habermas 1992); in formal terms, 'European citizenship' and the development of social rights at the European level indeed means that citizenship has already expanded far beyond the confines of nation-states. Also, in purely institutional terms, the European Parliament has increasingly come to resemble a national parliament, especially when it comes to democratic controls with the executive, the European Commission. However, the European Union is not simply (becoming) a federal state which can be assessed as such, and the problems of democracy and citizenship are not only matters of institutions, that is, of rules, procedures and norms; they are also a matter of political culture. The European Parliament and European elections is a case in point: many steps has been taken towards expanding the democratic influence of the European Parliament, and in 1999 when the European Commission was forced to resign, this was almost tantamount to the introduction of parliamentarism at the European level. Also, the European Parliament has since 1979 been directly elected, and by proportional representation, in all member countries. Thus, rules can certainly be changed to make European institutions more democratic. But what can be done to improve the poor participation in European elections, and what can be made to ensure that citizens vote for the European policies they want to be adopted and not out of for example dissatisfaction with their national governments?

Before turning to the empirical evidence below, we shall begin with a few conceptual clarifications. In discussing the democratic challenges of the European Union, we find it useful to introduce two distinctions. The first one, alluded to above, is the distinction between democratic institutions (rules, procedures and norms) that ensure democratic representation and accountability on the one hand, and citizenship (rights and political culture) on the other. The other is the distinction between the national level and the supranational level. Before turning to the problems of citizenship rights and political culture which is our main interest here, we briefly comment on the institutional aspects.

As indicated, the discussion about 'democratic deficit' has mainly been concerned with the institutional dimension, and with the problems of democratic representation and democratic accountability – that is, the control of executive powers by the people or by their democratically elected representatives. On the supranational level, this is not least a matter of the democratic control of the Commission by the European Parliament, and of openness of decision-making at the European level. These problems have been debated intensely and are also fields where a lot of reforms have taken place since the early 1990s, not least those resulting from the Maastricht

Treaty and the Amsterdam Treaty. The other main institutional problem is the problem of accountability at the national level. In most respects, the European Union remains so far more like a confederation of states than a federation. From this national/confederative perspective, a major democratic problem is how national governments and their civil servants can represent and are held responsible to national parliaments for their actions in the decision-making bodies of the EU and in the preparation of common rules with the European Commission. In the Scandinavian countries, governments are quite strongly controlled by European Committees in Parliament. Denmark was a forerunner in this respect (for instance, the government must always have its mandate of negotiation approved by the European Committee) but the new member countries in 1995 have all established similar or even more far-reaching rules. However, due to overload problems, lack of transparency, and insufficient information at the preparatory stages, effective influence and control may be less than one could assume on the basis of formal rules only.[2]

Turning from representation and accountability to citizenship, we may take our point of departure in the distinction between the three dimensions of rights, participation and identities referred to in chapter 1. These dimensions largely coincide with the distinction between formal rules (rights) and political culture (participation and identities). With regard to formal rights, it is well-known that European citizens have achieved far-reaching civil, political and social rights; however, we know less about the political culture side – that is, about participation and identities in a broad sense. From a citizenship perspective, this is what is most important when making a judgement on the democratic quality of the European Union. It has often been assumed, explicitly or implicitly, that when democratic procedures were established and when democratically elected bodies at the European level were given sufficient influence, citizens' participation and identities would adjust to this situation. The low and declining participation rates in European elections is a clear illustration that this is not the case.

Unfortunately, we do not have any data to cover the national aspect – that is, the ability of ordinary people to understand and influence the process of European decision-making at the national level. However, it is probably safe to conclude that this capacity is very low – and much lower than when issues to be decided on a national level are on the agenda. Except for the indirect influence rooted in the ultimate power to veto the government's decisions concerning delegation of authority to the EU (which is secured only by the Danish constitution), democratic citizenship remains very under-developed in this respect; most people have virtually no ideas even about how decisions are de facto made. But it should be underlined that we have no data on this, nor do we have any clear empirical indications about how the new and more complex, multi-level governance structure has affected citizens' sense of efficacy vis-à-vis politics in general at the national level (see Figure 11.1).

What level?	What is the problem?	
	Institutions: Representation and democratic accountability to the people /democratically elected bodies	Citizenship and political culture
National level	1. Rules, norms and procedures that ensure popular and/or parliamentary influence on and control with the government's actions in the EU (e.g. parliamentary committees)	3. Citizens' opportunities to understand and to participate in national government's decision-making in relation to EU decisions
Supranational level	2. Rules, norms and procedures that ensure popular and/or parliamentary influence on and control with decision-making at the European level, especially with the European Commission (e.g. European Parliament, Ombudsman, and so on	Rights (formal rules) / Participation and identities
		4. European citizenship, social rights, and formal democratic rights at the European level / 5. Citizens' opportunities to understand and participate in decision-making at the European level. Citizens' identities: Orientation to the political community and the political regime in the EU.

Figure 11.1 Dimensions of the 'democratic deficit' in the EU: four aspects

Having underlined that the problems of citizenship are only one dimension of the democratic challenge, and having stressed that this citizenship discussion also has a national dimension to it, we may now move to the analysis of the conditions of European-level democratic citizenship in the Scandinavian countries. This discussion which is mainly about *European orientations* has received far less attention than the discussion about *attitudes to Europe* which has dominated research interest in the Scandinavian countries. However, on the basis of scattered evidence, we are nevertheless able to provide a quite clear picture of the conditions of European-level citizenship in the Scandinavian countries. Even though one cannot immediately translate the problems of citizenship at the national level to European-level counterparts, we are able to draw quite a few analogies. Unlike the preceding chapters, we shall concentrate not on the participation dimension, except for the question of powerlessness or lack of efficacy. A main emphasis will be on the question of whether the Scandinavians have a feeling of European identity and solidarity, and whether they support EU as a political system. One might suggest that the EU, at least as far as its Scandinavian member countries are concerned, is characterized not by any 'civic culture', let alone 'participant culture', and not even by a 'spectator democracy' but rather by a 'subject political culture' (cf. Almond and Verba 1963) where ordinary citizens feel subject to the rules of the European political system but do not identify much with the system and feel unable to have any influence on its decisions. Along with more specific interests, this may also be a core reason why Scandinavians have been characterized as 'reluctant Europeans'.

Nordic referenda on the European Union

Even though attitudes for or against EU is basically out of the scope of this article (but see, for example, Jenssen, Pesonen and Gilljam (eds) 1998; Borre and Goul Andersen 1997), we begin by presenting the results of the Nordic referenda on the European Union. As can be seen from Table 11.1, in the two referenda in 1972 and 1994 the Norwegians decided by small margins to remain outside the EU whereas the Swedes and Finns decided to join in 1994, but again by small margins. Denmark is unique in having had six referenda between 1972 and 2000: The Danes voted yes to membership in 1972 and to the Single European Act in 1986. In the political debates both referenda were defined mainly as issues of economic cooperation. However, the Danes defeated the Maastricht Treaty of the European Union

Table 11.1 Nordic referenda on the European Community, 1972–2000

Country/subject	Date	Percentage 'yes'	Result	Turnout
Denmark				
Membership of EC	2 October 1972	63.3	Yes	90.1
Single European Act	27 February 1986	56.2	Yes	75.4
European Union (Maastricht Treaty)	2 June, 1992	49.3	No	83.1
European Union (with reservations)	18 May, 1993	56.7	Yes	86.5
Amsterdam Treaty	28 May 1993	55.1	Yes	76.2
Single Currency	28 September 2000	46.9	No	87.5
Norway				
Membership of EC	25 September 1972	46.5	No	79.2
Membership of EU	28 November 1994	47.7	No	89.0
Sweden				
Membership of EU	13 November 1994	52.3*	Yes	83.3
Finland				
Membership of EU	16 October 1994	56.9	Yes	74.0

Note:
* A third alternative was blank (0.9 per cent).

Sources: Jenssen, Pesonen and Gilljam (1998: 16–17); Statistical Yearbook (Denmark).

in 1992. The Maastricht Treaty was subsequently approved with Danish reservations in 1993 (Edinburgh Agreement), and the Amsterdam Treaty was passed with the consent of the people in 1998. In 2000, the referendum was about abolishing the Danish exemption from the third phase of the Economic and Monetary Union: The common currency.

Thus, except for the Danish referendum in 1972, which was held at a time when the label was still EEC (European Economic Community) before it changed to EC (European Communities) in 1973 and to EU (European Union) in 1994, there has been an almost equal division between adherents and opponents in all referenda, and in four instances (Norway 1972 and 1994; Denmark 1992 and 2000), a large majority in Parliament was defeated by the voters. Returning later to the question of who is for and who against, we shall go on by establishing, however, that European orientations are not simply a matter of for or against but also encompass dimensions of efficacy and European identity.

Elections to the European Parliament

Before turning to the questions of (European) identity, solidarity and efficacy vis-à-vis the EU system we will take a look at the turnout for elections for the European Parliament. As the powers of the Parliament has gradually grown, especially during the 1990s, one would expect 'rational voters' to vote in increasing numbers at these elections. However, as we see from Table 11.2, this is by no means the case. For the EU as a whole turnout has decreased from 63 per cent in 1979 to around 50 per cent in 1999. To make matters even worse the sharpest decrease have taken place between 1994 and 1999. Countries with a particularly low turnout are Finland, Holland, Portugal and the UK – that is, both 'old' and 'new' member countries. The 'good democrats' of Europe are the populations of Belgium,[3] Greece and Luxembourg, which exhibit a high and relatively stable turnout. As mentioned above, this development paints a rather bleak picture of the possibilities of establishing a 'true' representative democracy at the EU level. Apart from a few noteworthy exceptions the populations of the EU countries seem to be discounting the type of representative democracy which the European Parliament constitutes, and in that sense there seem to be some truth to the claim that the EU is mainly a 'community of elites'. In the following paragraphs we shall dig more into the possible causes of this situation.

Dimensions of attitudes

Most Scandinavian surveys of attitudes to the EU have been concerned with the single dimension of attitudes to EU membership and European integration. From a citizenship perspective, one would expect attitudes to

Table 11.2 Participation in elections to the European Parliament in Denmark, Sweden and other countries in the EU (percentages)

	1979	1984	1989	1994	1999
Denmark	47.8	52.3	46.2	52.9	50.5
Sweden	—	—	—	41.6[3]	38.8
Finland	—	—	—	57.6[4]	30.1
Holland	58.1	50.5	47.2	35.6	30.0
Austria	—	—	—	67.7[4]	49.4
Belgium	91.4	92.2	90.7	90.7	91.0
Greece	78.6	77.2	79.9	71.7	75.3
Portugal	—	72.6[5]	51.2	35.5	40.0
Luxembourg	88.9	88.8	87.4	88.5	87.3
Eire	63.3	47.6	68.3	44.0	50.2
Germany	65.7[1]	56.8[1]	62.3	60.0	45.2
France	60.6	56.7	48.8	52.7	46.8
Spain	—	68.9[2]	54.6	59.1	63.0
UK	31.6	32.6	36.2	36.4	24.0
EU	63	61	58.5	56.7	49.8

Notes:
1. West Germany.
2. Election in 1987. *Source:* European Parliament.
3. Election in 1995.
4. Election in 1996.
5. Election in 1987.

be multidimensional, including also feeling of efficacy or powerlessness, and European identity and solidarity, as well as trust in European political institutions. Unfortunately, only the first three sets of questions were covered by the Danish citizenship survey and the Danish 1990 election survey; on the basis of the results from these surveys, a subset of these questions were replicated in two small Norwegian and Swedish surveys by 1991. By now, these surveys are mainly of a historical interest; however, apart from revealing the same basic dimensionality as in Denmark, they also revealed that at that time, the Norwegians had the strongest feeling of solidarity with Southern Europeans, whereas the Swedes were most favorable in terms of economic expectations to the EU. A factor analysis on basis of the Danish election survey 1990 is presented in Table 11.3. It reveals three factors with eigenvalues above the standard criterion of 1.0. Together, they explain 50 per cent of the variance. After oblique rotation, the items fall clearly into three categories.

The first dimension, which is by far the strongest, must be interpreted as an overall for/against European integration dimension. Six items have strong factor loadings mainly on this dimension: perception of economic advantages; attitude towards fiscal harmonization; confidence in the decisions of

Table 11.3 Dimensions of EC attitudes, Denmark 1991. Factor loadings in final solution after oblique rotation

	Factor 1: for/against European integration	Factor 2: powerlessness	Factor 3: European identity
1. Economic advantage of inner market	.65	−.23	.01
2. Too slow adaptation of taxes	.65	.24	.14
3. Good decisions in the EC	.61	−.24	−.02
4. Economic and Monetary Union	.64	−.09	−.24
5. EC role in world politics	.66	.08	−.15
6. Binding cooperation in the EC	.59	−.07	−.02
7. EC dictates Danish politics	−.28	.57	−.27
8. Impossible to maintain the welfare state	−.38	.55	−.17
9. Know so little about inner market	.20	.63	.08
10. EC too lavish	−.06	.62	.25
11. Economic solidarity between EC countries	−.09	−.04	−.71
12. More powers to the European Parliament	.39	.09	−.43
13. Feel as a European	.16	−.06	−.58
Eigenvalue	4.56	1.35	1.13
Explained variance (%)	32.5	9.6	8.1

Exact question wording:
1. The Common Market in the EU will be an economic advantage for Denmark.
2. Denmark's adaptation of taxes to the Internal Market proceeds too slowly.
3. Normally, one can be confident that the EC makes the right decisions.
4. Cooperation in the EC should lead to the establishment of an economic and monetary union.
5. The EC should play a role in world politics that corresponds with its economic importance.
6. Considering the economic interdependence between EC countries, it is in fact through more binding cooperation that the Danes will have the most influence on the development of Denmark.
7. No matter which parties are in office, the EC will decide what will happen in this country.
8. As the EC integration proceeds, it will be impossible to maintain the Danish welfare state in the long run.
9. I know so little about the Internal Market in the EC that I have given up trying to find out what is going on.
10. EC is too lavish with the taxpayers' money.
11. There should be a thorough redistribution of wealth in the EC so that the rich countries pay to improve the conditions of the poorer countries.
12. The European Parliament should be endowed with more powers.
13. I feel myself to be just as much an European as a Dane.

the EC; attitudes towards establishing an economic and monetary union; towards strengthening the role of the EC in world politics; and achievement of influence via binding cooperation in the EC.

It is interesting to note that the items on increasing the influence of the European Parliament and on the perception that it will be impossible to maintain the welfare state also score on this dimension, although they score higher on other dimensions. This multidimensionality is not at all difficult to explain: Increasing the power of the European Parliament is not only a matter of European identity but also a recurrent theme in discussions for and against European integration. By the same token, the perception that the EU will make it impossible to maintain the Danish welfare state does not only tap a feeling of powerlessness but is also one of the arguments that has frequently been launched against EU.

The second dimension must be interpreted as a dimension of powerlessness, and it is quite interesting that it combines items that would at first glance appear highly different. The strongest loading is found on an efficacy item ('I know so little about the Internal Market in the EC that I have given up trying to find out what is going on') but the factor also includes an item stating that Danish politics will, in the future, largely be dictated by the EC (which does not load very much on the first dimension above), the perception that the EC integration will make it impossible to maintain the Danish welfare state, and, finally, the perception that the EC is too lavish.

The third dimension measures European identity or European orientations: Attitudes towards a redistribution between the rich and the poor EC countries, feeling as a European, and (this item is multidimensional) attitude towards assigning more powers to the European Parliament. This dimension might also be labeled a 'European citizenship' dimension or perhaps a 'cosmopolitanism'/'parochialism' dimension. People scoring high on this dimension are perhaps the 'good citizens' of a true European Union – but they include both adherents of and opponents of the Danish membership.

Factors 1 and 2 show only a modest correlation of 0.25, whereas factor 3 is almost unrelated to the other two dimensions (correlations of 0.08 and 0.11, respectively). Thus, the data confirm that it makes sense to analyze EU attitudes as something that goes beyond the question of being for or against. From a citizenship perspective, it is the other two dimensions that are the most interesting: Does the decline of the nation-state imply an increase in the feeling of powerlessness and a loss of identity, or are the losses counter-weighted by a growth in attention, efficacy and identity formation at a higher level?

Below, we shall deal first with the question of European identity and solidarity, and thereafter with the questions of general support for the political dimension of the EU, efficacy and powerlessness.

European identity and solidarity

As the European Union is basically a *political* community, the development of some quasi-nationalist sense of community is not a necessary (nor a desirable) precondition of the development of a democratic political culture; but a political community nevertheless presupposes a certain level of *political* identity as a European, and a certain feeling of solidarity with citizens of other EU countries. We have only a few Danish time series on this; besides, the Eurobarometer surveys provide some information on attitudes towards the political community in the European Union (cf. Niedermayer and Sinnott (eds), 1995).

As far as solidarity is concerned, there seems to be little improvement, rather the contrary. But the feeling of a European identity reveals a silent revolution during the second half of the 1990s. Until 1994, about three-quarters of respondents disagreed with the item 'I feel myself to be just as much an European as a Dane'. But by 2000, little more than one half give

Table 11.4 European identity and solidarity, Denmark 1990/91–2000 (percentages and Percentage Difference Index (PDI))

		Agree	Neutral, I, don't know	Disagree	PDI: European minus National
There should be a thorough	1991	41	26	33	8
redistribution of wealth in the	1993	45	23	32	13
EC so that the rich countries	1994	41	22	37	4
pay to improve the conditions of the poorer countries	1998	35	28	37	−2
The Northern European EU countries should sacrifice some of their wealth to the benefit of the Southern European EU countries	1990	27	27	46	−19
Even though the Southern Europeans have joined the EU, I feel no solidarity with them	1990	52	24	24	−28
I feel myself to be just as much	1991	17	8	75	−58
a European as a Dane	1993	19	9	72	−53
	1994	19	5	76	−59
	1998	23	12	65	−42
	2000	33	13	54	−21

Source: Election surveys 1990–1998; citizenship survey 1990; survey of EU Referendum 1993; and Survey of welfare values 2000 (AIM Nielsen/Mandag Morgen/Strategisk Forum). 1990 election survey conducted in January 1991.

Table 11.5   Attachment to Europe and to own country
(percentages feeling 'very attached')

	Europe	Own country	Difference
Luxembourg	33	53	20
Denmark	31	81	50
Sweden	31	57	26
Austria	29	60	31
UK	9	58	49
EU-15	18	52	34

Question: 'People may feel different degrees of attachment to
Europe/to their country. Please tell me how attached you feel.'

Source: Eurobarometer 51 (Spring 1999), B10–12.

this answer while the proportion that agree has doubled from 1991. Not
surprisingly, the feeling of European identity is strongest among the better-
educated. It may be added that according to Eurobarometer (51/1999, B:
11–12), Danes are the nationality in Europe, who (next to the people of
Luxembourg) feel the strongest attachment to Europe – together with the
Swedes, that is, the two nationalities in Europe that are usually considered
the most skeptic towards European integration (see Table 11.5). At the
same time, however, the Danes (but not the Swedes) feel a much stronger
attachment to the nation-state than most other European nationalities
(whereas the attachment to regions or local community is roughly the
same in most countries).

Furthermore, orientation towards the political community of the
European Union has changed. With Easton (1965), we can distinguish
between specific and diffuse support to the European political community.
Although the Eurobarometer questions are far from perfect operationalizations of either, they are usually interpreted as questions located at various
points on a dimension between the two poles. Traditionally, the picture of
the Danes was that they reluctantly supported the European Union only
on economic grounds (diffuse support); however, this has changed quite
a lot. Followed by the Swedes, the Danes remain the strongest 'Euro-
skeptics' when it comes to questions about joint decision-making in
concrete policy areas (for example, Eurobarometer 51, 1999: B 36–7).[4] But
general and diffuse support for European cooperation has improved
markedly (see Table 11.6). In the 1990s, a large majority of Danes have
regarded membership as a 'good thing', and have been favorable to the
idea of uniting Western Europe. The figures here remain a little lower than
among the 'old' EU countries, whereas the Danes are a little more inclined
to regard EU membership as beneficial for the country.

Table 11.6 General orientation to the EU (specific and diffuse support), 1996. PDI: Positive minus negative evaluations (percentage points)

	Unite Western Europe	EU member-ship a 'good thing'	Membership is a benefit for country	Average of three items
Six 'old' EU countries	52	52	20	41
Four 'poor' EU countries	65	52	43	53
Denmark	31	32	34	32
UK	20	20	−13	9
Sweden	25	−4	−33	−4
Average for three new EU countries	24	10	−17	5
Change 1982–1996:				
Six 'old' EU countries	−15	−4	−30	−16
Four 'poor' EU countries	+8	+8	+30	+15
Denmark	+29	+27	+14	+23
UK	−3	+37	+12	+15

Notes:
Simple, unweighted averages. Four (formerly) 'poor' countries include Ireland, Portugal, Spain and Greece; three new EU countries include Sweden, Finland and Austria.

Source: Eurobarometer 45 (June 1996); Eurobarometer Trends 1974–1993.

But Danish attitudes have changed dramatically, and most of the difference between Denmark and the 'old' member countries has disappeared, due to a simultaneous deterioration of support in these countries. Whether one should emphasize the last-mentioned observation, or the improvements in Denmark, or interpret both as a sign of convergence, is uncertain. But at any rate, the Danes are no longer motivated simply by the economic advantages of belonging to the EU. By the same token, what distinguish the fears of the Danes and the Swedes is not fear of losing national culture or national identity, but the fears of losing influence for small countries, and the fears of 'importing trouble' in terms of more drugs and crime (Table 11.7). Allied to this are fears of losing jobs to low-wage countries, but this is a fear shared by all EU countries (at this point, however, the Swedes differ significantly from the Danes). Finally, we observe that the Danes and the Swedes are significantly *less* worried by the possible costs of solidarity with the (would-be) poorer EU countries than the citizens of other member countries.

In short, European identity and solidarity, at least in relative terms, seem strong in the Scandinavian countries, and at least on the aggregate level, the widespread skepticism towards the European project in these countries does not express parochialism, nostalgia for the past, or self-sufficiency. But the fear of being overruled is quite strong. Diffuse support for the European Union and for European unification is improving in Denmark, but the

Table 11.7 Citizens' fears of European integration, 1999. PDIs: 'Fear' minus 'no fear' (percentage points)

	Denmark	Sweden	EU15	Difference DK/S – EU15
Loss of power for small member states	22	21	−14	36
More drugs and crime	38	56	22	25
Transfer of jobs to countries with lower prod.costs	36	60	34	14
Our language being used less and less	−17	−28	−15	−7
Loss of our national identity and culture	−3	−2	0	−3
The end of national currency	5	1	9	−6
The loss of social benefits	11	24	17	0
Enlargement expensive	1	5	14	−11
Less subsidies from the EU	−2	3	15	−15
More difficulties for country's farmers	5	26	25	−10
Richer countries paying more for the others	−29	−24	−1	−26

Q: 'Some people may have fears about the building of Europe, the European Union. Here is a list of things which some people say they are afraid of. For each one, please tell me if you – personally – are currently afraid of it, or not?'

Source: Eurobarometer 51 (Spring 1999), pp. 30–1.

Swedes remain more 'reluctant Europeans' than the Danes. However, when it comes to concrete transfers of powers to decision-making at the European level, the Danes remain the largest skeptics.

Efficacy

As shown above, the main problem of citizenship does not seem to be one of national versus European identity but rather one of (lack of) efficacy and powerlessness. Regardless of whether we speak of internal efficacy (political competence) or external efficacy (responsiveness), the feeling of being able to influence is decisive for whether we may speak of a participant (or civic) culture, or of a subject political culture. Unfortunately, evidence points mainly towards the latter model, and there are few signs of improvements. This feeling of lack of efficacy is not much greater in Scandinavia than elsewhere; what distinguishes them mostly is the *difference* between such feelings on the national and on the supranational level. The Danes are also more inclined to think they can make a difference on the national level than citizens of most other member countries. Thus, even though one should not

Table 11.8 Influence of citizens at national level and EU level. 1996. PDI: 'A great deal' or 'some', minus 'not very much' or 'no influence at all' (percentage points)

	Influence on EU	Influence on national government	Difference in PDI: National minus European influence
Denmark	−74	−38	+36
Sweden	−78	−45	+33
Netherlands	−66	−44	+22
Finland	−75	−54	+21
Luxembourg	−32	−13	+19
Austria	−65	−51	+14
Ireland	−58	−45	+13
Portugal	−34	−22	+12
France	−62	−51	+11
Germany	−48	−40	+8
EU – 15	−59	−53	+6
UK	−75	−69	+6
Greece	−58	−54	+4
Spain	−56	−54	+2
Belgium	−62	−62	0
Italy	−55	62	−7

Q: 'How much influence, if any, do you think the opinion of people like yourself have on the decisions taken by the national government/ by the EU?'

Source: Eurobarometer 45 (December 1996), p. 95.

in the discussion about the 'democratic deficit' of the EU forget that a similar deficit may exist at the national level, it turns out that exactly the perceived *difference* in efficacy (in this case: responsiveness) is larger in the Scandinavian countries than elsewhere.

The most striking observation from Table 11.8 is perhaps that in many member states people feel almost as inefficacious towards the national political system as towards the European political system; the Italians even feel that it would be easier to influence European politics than national politics[5]. In all of the larger countries, the difference is perceived as quite marginal whereas we find examples of both trends among the small countries: the Belgians and the Greeks seem to have few illusions about their ability to influence politics at the national level, due to low responsiveness, whereas the Dutch citizens resemble the Scandinavians.

Table 11.9 also include Danish time series and data on internal efficacy, as well as the questions on EU influence on Danish politics referred to in the factor analysis above. To begin with the last-mentioned indicators of powerlessness, it was a widespread feeling in the early 1990s that the EU

Table 11.9   Efficacy and powerlessness towards the EU. Denmark, 1990–2000.
Percentages and PDI (percentage points)

		Agree	Neutral, don't know	Disagree	PDI: efficacy minus powerlessness
As the EC integration proceeds,	1991	45	26	29	−16
it will in the long run be	1993	43	22	35	−8
impossible (1993–1994:	1994	41	22	37	−4
difficult) to maintain the	2000	38	28	34	−4
(2000: present) Danish welfare state					
I know so little about the EU	1991	43	17	40	−3
that I have almost given up	1993	30	15	55	25
finding out what is going on[1]	1994	51	13	36	−15
	1998	41	18	41	0
	2000	45	14	41	−4
No matter which parties	1991	53	19	33	−20
are in office, the EC will	1993	39	16	45	6
decide what will happen in this country					
When politicians discuss economic policy, I only understand very little of what they are talking about	1998	37	17	46	9

Note: 1. In 1991: 'Know so little about EC Internal Market...'
Source: As Table 11.3.

would come to dictate Danish politics, and throughout the decade, a majority agreed that EU would threaten the maintenance of the Danish welfare state. Even though these answers should not be interpreted too literally, there does seem to exist a strong fear of being overruled, as it emerged also from the questions about fear in Table 11.7 above. As far as internal efficacy is concerned, it is noteworthy that around one-half of the respondents, according to their own statements, have more or less given up on understanding European politics. In its high degree of complexity, it is at least as difficult for citizens to understand as economic policies (at the national level).

It seems, however, that, at least in the short run, referenda may contribute to increasing efficacy. All time series reveal a reduced feeling of powerlessness in 1993, after the two subsequent referenda.

Concerning political self-confidence or internal efficacy we only have a single time series and no data that are comparative across countries. Instead we have, in Table 11.10, made a systematic comparison for Denmark between political self-confidence on the local (municipal), national and EU

Table 11.10 Political self-confidence: local, national and European level. Denmark 1998. Unweighted data (N = 2032)

	How easy or how difficult is it for you to follow what is going on ...		
	In local politics in your municipality	*In Parliament (Folketinget)*	*In the EU*
Very easy	17	14	5
Rather easy	44	43	19
Rather difficult	28	31	37
Very difficult	6	10	37
Don't know	5	2	2
PDI	+ 27	+ 16	− 50

	In general, would you say that you have enough knowledge to be able to deal with what's going on, or would you say that you have too little knowledge concerning what's going on ...		
	In local politics in your municipality	*In Parliament (Folketinget)*	*In the EU*
1. Enough knowledge	22	16	5
2.	22	24	9
3.	21	24	20
4. Too little knowledge	32	34	63
Don't know	2	2	3
PDI	− 10	− 18	− 58

Source: Data from the 'Democracy from Below' project; one out of five projects under the Danish Social Science Research Councils program 'Democracy and Institutional Development'.

level based on data from the 'Democracy from Below' project (1998). Not surprisingly, it turns out that, as in Sweden (Petersson et al. 1997: 121), self-confidence is highest at the local and national levels. However, the notable thing about the figures are *how big* the differences actually are. Thus, only 24 per cent think it is easy to follow what is going on in politics at the EU level, and only 14 per cent feel that they have the adequate knowledge to do this. And, as we saw above, around half of the voters have totally given up on trying to understand European politics.

Concluding this section we found something like a 'silent revolution' in the EU orientation of the Danes, even though general attitudes for and against seem to be quite stable, at least at the aggregate level. Whether this is also the case in Sweden and Finland is impossible to say due to the lack of time-series data. We found signs of a strongly growing European identity, and a much more positive attitude towards the EU as a political community and a political system than earlier. The Danes are skeptical towards EU regulation across a wide range of concrete policy areas, but it is no longer possible to characterize the Danes as 'bad Europeans'. Furthermore, the time is past when it seemed to be solely the question of economic advantages which governed the Danish attitude towards the EU. However, the citizens' lack of efficacy is high when it concerns the EU. It is of little comfort that this is a general EU problem, and the data are certainly not very encouraging from a democratic perspective. The contrast between the European and the national level is particularly striking in Scandinavia where citizens' internal and external efficacy at the local and national level has traditionally been high.

The elite and the people: social polarization in attitudes towards the EU?

In this paragraph we shall look at whether social differences are bigger when it comes to EU politics than in local or national politics. Thus, it might seem obvious to assume that the increased importance of the EU contributes to the undermining of the relative equality which has traditionally characterized political participation as well as efficacy in the Scandinavian countries. A popular hypothesis is that we are witnessing a polarization in attitudes towards the EU between an internationally oriented and self-confident elite on the one hand and a majority of apathetic citizens on the other.

In order to test this hypothesis we have constructed three additive indices on the basis of the questions in Table 11.10. The results in Table 11.11 shows that it is important to distinguish between efficacy at different levels. The patterns are different. Among other things we see that at the local level it is the young who feel least politically self-confident, while the young are the most self-confident when it comes to EU politics. However, concerning other social differences these seem to be equally strong at both the national and the EU level; the only difference being that lack of self-confidence is at a much higher level concerning the EU.

It is an open question how these results shall be interpreted. A simple interpretation would be to conclude that the social bias at the EU level does not differ much from the bias at the national level, and that the EU is therefore not contributing to an increased polarization. An alternative interpretation is that the development of 'multi-level governance' complicates politics also at the national level, making it more difficult for especially socially disadvantaged groups to deal with politics in general. It is

Table 11.11 Political self-consciousness at the local, the national and the EU level. Index values, eta and beta coefficients (MCA analysis). Denmark 1998

	Local level (municipality)	National level ('Folketing')	EU level	Unweighted N
Total	2	−5	−54	2032
Men	11	10	−46	992
Women	−6	−19	−61	1041
18–29 years	−20	−1	−46	468
30–39 years	2	−5	−57	390
40–49 years	10	−3	−60	362
50–59 years	10	−5	−53	329
60–69 years	12	−9	−59	228
70+ years	15	−11	−54	255
Comprehensive school, 7–9 years	−2	−22	−63	702
Same, 10 years	1	−8	−60	740
High School, 12 years	9	−19	−36	583
Unskilled	−20	−28	−66	274
Skilled	−9	−18	−61	225
Lower salaried	3	−3	−60	395
Higher salaried	24	26	−4	273
Self-employed	20	6	−46	142
Eta coefficients				
Gender	.13	.23	.14	
Age	.21	.05	.10	
Education	.07	.27	.21	
Occupation	.26	.30	.17	
Beta coefficients (MCA; only employed)				
Gender				.16
Age				.08
Education				.17
Occupation				.10
R^2 (%)				8

impossible to say which interpretation is the correct one on the basis of the available data. However, it should be mentioned that during the 1980s and 1990s a general trend concerning political efficacy seemed to a rather marked polarization between the better- and the less-educated (Goul Andersen; work done in relation to the Danish Power Study). This trend might have many causes, but it is likely that the EU is one of them.

Anyway, what is beyond doubt is that the lack of efficacy at the EU level is very big; except for the groups on top of the social ladder.

Another way to shed light on the question of social polarization is to consider the social differences between the proponents and the opponents of the EU. The interesting question here is whether or not we see long-term changes in the dividing lines in the direction of isolating the EU opponents among the socially disadvantaged groups.

The empirical data presented in Table 11.12 do not seem to confirm such a trend. In the five referenda on EU issues held in Denmark there are both stable and changing patterns. One of the stable patterns is that enthusiasm

Table 11.12   Who voted for the EF (1972), the Common Market (1986) and the Union (1992, 1993, 1998)? (percentages)

	1972	1986	1992	1993	1998	N (1998)
Election result (percentage of valid votes)	63.3	56.2	49.3	56.8	55.0	
Men	68	60	53	62	59	2794
Women	67	54	46	52	51	2708
18–29 years	66	42	48	54	50	1128
30–49 years	66	52[1]	45	51	51	2138
50–59 years	72	67[1]	51	60	59	925
60+ years	70	68	56	66	63	1311
Comprehensive school 7–9 years	64	—	44	57	52	2067
Same, 10 years	76	—	51	57	53	1921
High school, 12 years	79	—	53	56	61	1512
Worker	58	45	36	52	46	1704
Salaried employee	74	51	53	55	60	1677
Self-employed	88	86	64	74	71	284
Student, pupil, etc.	—	—	51	51	51	503
Pensioner (no employment)	61	—	51	60	59	1279

Note:
The figures from 1992, 1993 and 1998 are weighted so that the distribution of votes in the sample corresponds to that of the actual election result.
1. 30–44 years and 45–59 years.
Sources:
1972: Nikolaj Pedersen (1975).
1986: Ole Borre (1986).
1992: Hans Jørgen Nielsen (1992).
1993: Survey conducted by Torben Worre, Hans Jørgen Nielsen, Steen Sauerberg, Jens Hoff and Jørgen Goul Andersen. Around 2000 respondents.
1998: Survey by ACNielsen AIM for the weekly *Mandag Morgen*.

concerning the EU is lower among women than among men. Another stable pattern is the higher 'Yes' vote among the older generations. Even though it is often claimed that the younger generations are the most enthusiastic concerning the EU, the 'Yes' vote has been highest among voters over 50 at all EU polls since 1972. Thus, the higher lack of self-confidence among the older generations must not be mistaken for a general dissociation with the EU. None the less the figures seem to indicate a weak shift in a positive direction in attitudes towards the EU among the young after 1992. Whether this tendency will stabilize after the 2000 referendum on the Euro remains to be seen.

What we do not see, however, is a clear polarization in general attitude towards the EU between an 'upper' and a 'lower' Denmark. The well educated and the politically interested have always had the most positive attitude towards the EU. However, in 1993 educational and occupational differences almost disappeared as many skeptical social democrats followed the line of the newly elected social democratic government. In 1998 the pendulum swung in the opposite direction marking an increased polarization both concerning education and occupation; especially among the young voters. However, whether this is a long-term trend is uncertain. If it is, it will run counter to the tendency in other EU countries where the long-term trend has been towards a decreasing social polarization (Wessels 1995).

Ideological changes

We are not going to enter into the question of how attitudes towards the EU are related to sympathy for different political parties. Suffice it here to say that in both Denmark and Sweden attitudes towards EU have traditionally been related to a left–right polarization; the left wing being traditionally against and the right wing traditionally in favor of the EU[6] (Listhaug, Holmberg and Sänkiaho 1998; Aardal et al. 1998). However, at least in Denmark and Finland the political profile of both proponents and opponents seem to be rapidly changing these years. Danish data from the election surveys (1990, 1994, 1998) show that there is no longer a clear correlation between general attitude towards the EU and left-wing orientation, orientation towards economic equality, and environmental consciousness. Rather, the attitude towards the EU is now correlating with hostility towards immigrants, and also with isolationism (which is nothing new, however). One way to illuminate these changes is by parting the electorate into four ideological 'characters' based on their attitude towards economic equality and attitude towards immigrants (as in Borre and Goul Andersen 1997). The four 'characters' are:

- 'old socialists', who are in favor of economic equality, but skeptical towards immigrants.

Table 11.13   General attitude towards the EU after ideological 'character'. PDI: (positive − negative attitude) (percentage points)

	1990		1998	
	For economic equality	*Against economic equality*	*For economic equality*	*Against economic equality*
Immigrants as a threat	'old socialist' 3	'right wing' 34	'old socialist' −4	'right wing' 11
Immigrants not a threat	'new left' −13	'non-socialist green' 47	'new left' 27	'non-socialist green' 31

Source: Danish election surveys.

Remark: in 1990, but not in 1998, it was possible to answer 'neither agree nor disagree'. However, it seems unlikely that this difference in wording will affect the distribution of answers very much. It might give a bit more variation on the economic equality dimension in 1990, and thereby lead to bigger changes.

- 'new left', who are for economic equality, and positive towards immigrants.
- 'non-socialist greens', who do not support economic equality, but are positive towards immigrants.
- 'right-wingers', who are negative towards both economic equality and immigrants.

Table 11.13 shows, for Denmark, how the general attitude towards the EU was distributed among these 'characters' in 1990 and in 1998 respectively. While 'the new left' was the 'ideological center' in the fight against the EU in 1990 this picture has now changed radically. In 1998 this group was almost the group most positive towards the EU; nearly as positive as 'the non-socialist greens'. Conversely, sympathy for the EU has cooled off markedly among right wing parties. However, the overall effect of these changes has until now first of all led to an evening out of the differences between the groups, giving the opponents of EU a less clear ideological profile than before. Thus, where the main dividing line in 1990 was the left–right axis, it had in 1998 become the so-called 'new politics' axis, even though the differences are smaller than they used to be.

Conclusion

EU's so-called 'democratic deficit' has many dimensions, as illustrated in Figure 11.1. However, while it is normally institutional problems which are discussed under this heading, our analysis has emphasized the dimension which could be termed political culture. Thus, we have looked in particular at the orientations of the Scandinavians towards the EU as a political community and a political system, and their perception of their own role in this system. As Denmark is the Scandinavian country with the longest membership of the EU (having joined in 1973), while Sweden and Finland have only been members since 1995, most of the time-series data in this chapter are based on different Danish surveys, while most of the comparative data are derived from the Eurobarometer studies. Our most important findings are:

- In both Denmark and Sweden an European identity seems to be gaining ground. Next to the population in Luxembourg, the Danes and the Swedes are the nationalities in the EU who feel the strongest attachment to Europe. For the Danes this shows a remarkable shift in attitudes since 1994.
- Traditionally, the picture of the Danes (and the Swedes) was that they reluctantly supported the EU only for economic reasons. This picture has also changed considerably. Thus, general support for European (EU) cooperation has improved markedly, especially in Denmark, even though the Swedes and the Danes still remain the strongest 'Euro-skeptics' when it comes to questions of joint decision-making in concrete policy areas. At the time of writing, the Danes, and to a lesser extent the Swedes, are therefore just as 'good Europeans' as the citizens in the 'old' EU member countries.
- In Denmark and Sweden the feeling of lack of power (efficacy) in relation to the EU is widespread and deep. However, this situation is very similar in most other EU countries. What distinguishes the Danes and the Swedes in this respect is that they have a much higher feeling of efficacy towards their national or local political system. Thus, what is remarkable is not the lack of efficacy in itself, but rather the difference between such feelings on the national and the supranational level. This situation led us to talk of the existence of a 'subject (political) culture' rather than a 'participatory (political) culture' as characterizing citizenship at the EU level.
- Concerning the possible social polarization in attitudes towards the EU we tried to test a popular hypothesis stating that a polarization is taking place between an internationally oriented and self-confident elite on the one hand, and a majority of apathetic citizens on the other. What we found were that the social bias at the EU level differs little from the bias at the national level, even though the lack of efficacy is certainly much higher at the EU level. We were at odds on how to interpret this finding, but it seems likely that the development of 'multi-level governance' is also complicating politics at the national level, thereby making it even more difficult for socially disadvantaged groups to get a grip on politics in general.

- Even though we did not find a clear polarization between an internationally oriented and self-confident elite and a mass of apathetic citizens, it is clear that the well-educated and politically interested have always been more positive towards the EU. However, in 1993 the educational and occupational differences did almost disappear, but in 1998 the pendulum swung back. What the long-term trend will be is therefore uncertain. We only know that in most other EU countries the long-term trend has been towards a diminishing social polarization.
- In Denmark, Sweden and Finland attitudes towards the EU have traditionally been strongly correlated with a left–right axis. However, this correlation has dissolved during the 1990s. Thus, the group of voters which we called 'the new left' had almost become the most positive group towards the EU by 1998. Conversely, the sympathy for the EU has cooled off markedly on the right wing. The overall effect of these changes has been an evening out of the differences between the different political groupings giving both proponents and opponents of EU a broad political profile.

In a citizen perspective, however, the most important factors are the failing participation in the political system in the EU, the lack of efficacy, and the danger that the EU might contribute to an increased polarization in efficacy between different social groups. Focusing on these factors the notion of citizenship in an EU context does not look good. Democratically speaking, the EU figures as an 'elite project' with a 'subject (political) culture'. This is, of course, a European, and not specifically a Scandinavian problem, and what could be done to tackle it is difficult to say. However, it was interesting to note that the lack of efficacy seemed to diminish in relation to the different referenda. Thus, the Danes have certainly benefited from their many referenda, and seem to be better informed about the EU system than citizens in many other EU countries. The same seems to be the case in other EU countries where referenda on EU matters have been held. We might therefore hypothesize that one way to remedy the 'democratic deficit' in the EU could be common European referenda. Another possible solution could be common European election campaigns for the European Parliament, or at least a common election day. At any rate it is clear that the alternative to such initiatives seems to be that the EU continues to be a 'democratic monster' in a citizenship perspective. Up till now, at least, the steps to 'democratize' the EU institutions have been unable to change this situation.

12
Immigrants, Refugees and Citizenship in Scandinavia

Introduction

Until about 10–15 years ago the question of immigration was not an important political issue in the Scandinavian countries. Heated political discussions about the topic, as well as xenophobia and racist incidents, were regarded as problems for other countries. Insofar as the issue was brought up, it was contained within a labor market discourse – something that had to do with the demand for labor power, and the conditions of the labor market (Baldwin-Edwards and Schain 1994: 14; Hammar 1991: 183–4).

In the last decade this situation has changed dramatically. In all three Scandinavian countries groups or political parties with anti-immigrant platforms have formed, and existing parties, especially but not only on the right, have adopted anti-immigrant rhetoric. For both the media and politicians the questions of immigration, asylum and citizenship have become important issues. The policy area has moved from 'low' to 'high' politics.

This in itself is not enough to warrant treatment of the issue in this book, since there are many other important policy issues we do not treat here. However, what does warrant special treatment of the subject is that it constitutes one of the major problems of increased 'globalization', and as such is something which has also forced the Scandinavian countries to re-think their particular version of citizenship.

More specifically, immigration raises a number of questions which illuminates both the type and inclusiveness of a national citizenship particularly well. For example: Which civil, political and social rights are conferred upon (different types of) immigrants? To what extent are these rights used? What does this tell us about the democratic character of the host country?

A normative yardstick for such an analysis could be Brubaker's (1989: 3) remarks on citizenship in liberal democracies. Thus, he states that citizenship in all liberal democracies is based on the idea of an egalitarian (nation) state-membership. The idea is basically one of *full membership*, and gradations of membership are therefore inadmissible except in special, transitional cases: in principle *there shall be no second-class citizens*. Furthermore, state-membership should be *democratic*. Enjoying the rights and carrying out the duties of citizenship is premised on the idea that all citizens can in principle affect these rights and duties through their political participation. Therefore a population of long-term resident nonmembers violates the democratic conception of membership. There must be some ways for resident nonmembers to become members, and *in the long run, residence and membership must coincide* (Brubaker 1989: 4).

In order to scrutinize how well the Scandinavian countries match this (republican) citizenship ideal, it is necessary to look at how arriving immigrants, asylum seekers and refugees are treated, how existing procedures for naturalization work, and what civil, political and social rights are conferred upon the different groups. However, this way of looking at immigrants is still, as some observers have noted (for example, Withol de Wenden 1994: 105), a way of treating them mainly as 'objects' of different state policies. Increasingly immigrants, especially second-generation immigrants, leave the 'object-role', and become active in reshaping the dominant form of citizenship, frequently arguing for a 'new citizenship', based more on the ideas of participation, and a multicultural society than on nationality and descent.[1] To get a coherent idea about the relationship between citizenship and immigration it is therefore also necessary to look at the different political activities of immigrants: their turnout in local elections, their participation in different types of associations, and so on.

Finally, this chapter will also consider the attitudes of the resident Scandinavian populations towards immigrants. To what extent are Scandinavians willing to grant civil, political and social rights to resident nonmembers of their societies? How widespread is tolerance and xenophobia, and have such attitudes changed over time? And to what extent are such attitudes related to groups that could feel 'threatened' by immigration – such as, for example, the unskilled or unemployed?

Historical background

In contrast to countries such as France and the UK, it is only relatively recently that the Scandinavian countries have become countries of immigration. This development is primarily related to the economic boom in the late 1950s and 1960s, where the demand for labor power in the Scandinavian economies increased dramatically. In Sweden, labor immigration reached its absolute peak in 1969 and 1970, where two years net immigration amounted to some 100 000 persons. In Scandinavia, or rather among the Nordic countries, a considerable part of labor immigration has always been Nordic. As a result of Nordic cooperation, Nordic immigrants were early given full economic and social rights, and from 1954 employees have enjoyed a right to free movement within the Nordic labor market. This Nordic agreement facilitated a relatively large interchange of labor, and in the 1970s more than half of all labor immigration to Sweden was Nordic, with most persons coming from Finland. However, as differences between the Nordic countries in terms of wages and working conditions have become less conspicuous the special emigration from Finland has decreased, and been partly replaced by inter-Nordic immigration moving in all directions, for short-term employment, family reunion, studies, and so on.

Following the economic recession and the oil crises in 1973 most Western European countries restricted immigration from non-European Community countries. In Sweden labor recruitment was halted in 1972, and in Denmark in 1973. This, of course, did not halt all immigration, because family reunification was still allowed. Free Nordic migration also continued. Furthermore, in the Scandinavian countries, asylum seekers have always been entitled to a thorough investigation of their cases, and can stay but not work, while waiting for a decision.

Thus, since the early 1970s, the immigration of workers from non-Nordic countries has been of little significance in Scandinavia. However, what has grown is the number of immigrants being close relatives to either Scandinavians or to immigrants already residing in Scandinavia, as well as the number of refugees and asylum seekers. This last factor has resulted in important changes in both the geographic origin and the weight of different groups of immigrants. Thus, the number of asylum seekers increased dramatically in the late 1980s. This was primarily due to the collapse of the communist regimes in the Soviet Union and Eastern Europe, and the expansion of the war in former Yugoslavia. The dramatic increase was felt especially in Germany, but only in Germany and Sweden did the number continue to increase through 1992. In France, the number of asylum seekers declined after 1989, in Spain after 1990, and in the UK, Italy and Austria after 1991 (Baldwin-Edwards and Schain 1994: 3). In general, this decrease in the number of asylum seekers can be seen as a result of legal and administrative changes which have made it more difficult for asylum seekers to enter the West European countries, and to gain refugee status. At the national level, these changes have included: carrier or airline sanctions, strict visa requirements, penalization of undocumented asylum seekers, the notion of 'safe countries' of first asylum, accelerated asylum procedures, which limit the rights to a full hearing for the applicant, and so on.

At the European transnational level, the Schengen Treaty (1985), the Dublin Convention (1990) and the External Frontiers Convention (1991) incorporated many of the restrictions mentioned above, and also addressed the issue of multiple refugee applications.[2] Even though the recognition rates vary widely in Europe (from 28 per cent in France to 3.2 per cent in UK), these rates have in all cases been declining. Thus, the trend across Europe has been to award more to certain inferior categories of recognition – humanitarian status, category B, etc., which confer considerably fewer rights than full refugee status (Baldwin-Edwards and Schain 1994: 4).

To sum up, the concept of 'foreign citizens' or 'resident non-members of society'[3] covers a very heterogeneous group of persons, with widely different motives for staying in the Scandinavian countries more than the three months it normally takes to be registered as a 'foreign citizen'. According to a standard practice 'foreign citizens' can be divided into three groups according to their country of origin. Firstly, there is a group of foreign citizens from the (other) Nordic countries, (other) EU countries and North America. These are people who typically take residence in the Scandinavian countries due to their education, work, or marriage. It is also persons from countries not subject to very restrictive immigration policies. Secondly, there is a group of persons who are normally (in the media, political debates) referred to as 'immigrants'. These are persons immigrated since the late 1960s primarily to work, but after the restrictive immigration policies started, especially to be reunited with their family. Thirdly, there is the group of refugees. These can be either 'quota refugees', that is refugees selected from international camps or spontaneously arriving refugees. Upon entry they are given either asylum or a residence permit. The percentage of foreign citizens in the Scandinavian countries is shown in Table 12.1.

As we can see from the table, Sweden, and increasingly Denmark, together with France, occupies an intermediate position among the OECD countries in terms of its percentage of foreign citizens. Norway on the other hand occupy a bottom position, and can be said to have relatively few resident foreign citizens as compared to other European OECD countries. However, these figures must be read with caution. Thus, they do not necessarily reflect the actual number of foreigners residing in each of the countries as naturalization rights and practices differ widely among the European countries (see below). Traditionally France has had a high

Table 12.1 Foreign citizens in Scandinavia as a percentage of total population compared with selected OECD countries

Country	1987	1997
Denmark	2.7	4.7
Norway	2.9	3.6
Sweden	4.8	6.0
Austria	4.3	9.1
France	6.8	6.3
Germany	6.9	9.0
Netherlands	4.0	4.4
UK	3.2	3.6

Source: SOPEMI (OECD 2000).

naturalization rate, while Germany has had a very low rate (except for *Aussiedler*; that is, ethnic Germans from especially Eastern Europe). The difference between France and Germany might therefore reflect this fact rather than indicate a real difference in percentage of foreigners.

Between a third and a half of the foreign citizens residing in the Scandinavian countries come from either other Nordic countries, (other) EU countries or North America. These are countries from where immigration is not considered a problem; indeed the term 'immigrant' is not normally used to described such people. Thus, foreign citizens who come from countries whose political, cultural and religious traditions differ widely from the Scandinavian traditions, and whose presence are therefore by some perceived as a threat or challenge to these traditions, can be seen to constitute only around 2 to 4 per cent of the population. However, especially in Denmark and Norway these foreign citizens are concentrated in a few municipalities in and around the capitals of Copenhagen and Oslo where they constitute up to 10 or 20 per cent of the population.

Political rights and electoral participation

With naturalization a right to some amount of political participation is normally acquired. The extent of these rights has itself been a political issue. A good example is the German case, where the CDU/CSU has vigorously supported an ethnic model of citizenship including a quasi-automatic naturalization of ethnic Germans from Eastern Europe (*Aussiedler*). This not the least because this group has been a potential base of electoral support for the CDU/CSU, which the parties have successfully mobilized. The SPD on the other hand has (unsuccessfully) tried to advance a republican model, not least because all evidence seem to suggest that if naturalized most guestworkers from for example Turkey would constitute an electoral clientele for the SPD (Faist 1994: 54ff). The same type of considerations have to some extent guided the Socialist Party platform in France, as well as the British Labour Party's endorsement of the continued full voting rights for Irish citizens in Britain even following Ireland's withdrawal from the Commonwealth in 1947 (Miller 1989: 130ff).

In the cases mentioned above, especially in Germany with its high proportion of resident non-citizens, the question of naturalization and voting rights is of considerable importance for determining the political majority.[4] In Scandinavia, where the relevant group of foreign citizens is relatively small, such considerations have been less salient. The drive for an increased rate of naturalization and voting rights for foreign citizens have been determined more by a belief in the importance of these measures for a successful (political) integration, than by considerations on the possible gain and losses by any political parties. Even so, it is relatively clear that the social democratic and left-wing parties have been more in favor of such measures than the right-wing parties, also because analyses shows that immigrant voting tend to support left-of-center political parties (Rath 1988).[5]

As a result of the increased belief in a multicultural model of integration, the right to vote and to run for office in local and regional elections was given to foreign citizens in 1975 in Sweden, 1980 in Denmark and 1982 in Norway. In order to participate in these activities all three countries demand that the foreign citizen has been a permanent resident for at least three years. None of the countries allow foreign citizens to vote or run for office in national elections.[6] Also, none of the countries put any limitations on the possibilities of foreign citizens for organizing in associations, clubs, and so on. On the contrary, and in line with a multicultural citizenship model, subsidies have been given to immigrant associations and churches, as well as to the immigrant press and to cultural activities, etc. (Hammer and Bruun 1992; see below). The electoral turnout of foreign citizens in Scandinavia is shown in Figure 12.1. As can be seen from the figure, the electoral turnout of foreign citizens in Sweden has declined steadily – from 60 per cent in 1976 to over 40 per cent in 1994 and as low as 35 per cent in 1999 (SCB 1995: 4 and 1998: 75). In Norway turnout declined from 46 per cent in 1982 to 40 per cent in 1987. It has since then stabilized around this level.

Thus, the turnout of foreign citizens is considerably lower than for national citizens, and has furthermore declined more. Thus, in Sweden the

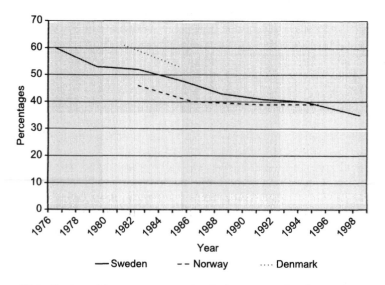

Figure 12.1 Foreign citizens turnout at local elections in Sweden, Norway, and Denmark. Percentages

turnout for foreign citizens was 30 per cent lower than for national citizens in 1976, 40 per cent lower in 1985 and 44 per cent lower in 1994. In Norway it was 27 per cent lower in 1982 and 28 per cent lower in 1991. In Denmark it was 12 per cent lower in 1981 and 17 per cent lower in 1985.[7] Two things are in need of explanation here. Firstly, the higher Danish turnout (at least till 1985), and secondly, the declining tendency of the turnout in all three countries.

The first question is the easiest to answer. Thus, in Denmark it is possible to vote not only for political parties but simultaneously also for individual candidates. It has therefore been possible for a foreign citizen to vote directly for a candidate from for example his/her own country; a possibility which did not exist in Sweden and Norway, where the votes were cast for party tickets. Analyses shows that this difference matters. Thus, the turnout was consistently higher in the municipalities where one or more immigrants/ foreign citizens ran for office. In some of these municipalities the turnout was even higher than the turnout of national citizens. A study of the number of immigrants[8] running for office at the elections for municipal and regional councils in Denmark in 1981, 1985 and 1989 shows a steady increase from 9 in 1981, to 45 in 1985, and 77 in 1989. Of these, four were elected in 1981, and eight in 1985, whereas we have no information on elected immigrants in 1989 or in 1993. Immigrants have ran on both (Danish) party tickets as well as on independent immigrants tickets. In 1981, 1985 and 1989 there were 2, 8 and 7 such independent immigrant tickets (Andersen and Nielsen 1989). In Norway one such ticket is know to have played a role in the local elections in Oslo in 1995.

The second question is harder to answer, as there seem to be a number of reasons for the decline in turnout. A Norwegian survey made among foreign citizens in connection with the municipal elections in 1991 points towards a number of factors related with low turnout. Thus, linguistic difficulties as well as social isolation, and a low level of knowledge about the political parties, all seem to contribute to a low turnout rate. A similar study made in relation to the municipal elections in 1985 points towards the importance of such factors as length of residence, marital status and gender. Thus, the longer the period of residence the higher turnout. Also married persons were more inclined to vote than unmarried, and women more than men (Bjørklund 1999: 160).

However, this does not explain the *declining* turnout rate. A possible explanation here might be the changed geographic composition of the group of foreign citizens, with non-Europeans now constituting a bigger share of the group. Finally, a third explanation might be, that foreign citizens who are politically engaged put more emphasis on other types of political participation; for example, direct political action (demonstrations, political contacts, and so on), and participation through associations and/or consultative boards (see below).

In Sweden electoral turnout for each foreign nationality has been systematically studied since 1976. We are not going to go into details with these numbers, but a few facts are worth mentioning. Chilean citizens in Sweden had the highest turnout among all foreign nationalities in 1994 (59 per cent). Also citizens from the other Nordic countries and USA have a turnout above average. Groups with a low turnout are Asians (Chinese, Vietnamese), persons from ex-Yugoslavia and Africans. The data also – as in Norway – show a correlation between naturalization and voting turnout. Thus, at the 1994 local elections in Sweden the turnout for naturalized foreigners was 77 per cent. This is still somewhat lower than the turnout average which was 84 per cent, but considerably more than the average of 40 per cent for foreign citizens (cf. Figure 12.1).[9] Furthermore, there seems to be a correlation between length of naturalization and voting turnout. Thus the group of foreign citizens naturalized before 1970 had an even higher turnout than the population average (SCB 1995: 4). What is important for political integration in Scandinavian political culture thus seems to be *naturalization* and *length of residence*.

In Norway surveys analyzing the party preferences of foreign citizens have been made in both 1987, 1991 and 1995. They show that left-of-center parties were receiving 60 to 80 per cent of the votes of so-called 'non-western' foreign citizens,[10] while the right-of-center parties were receiving only between 10 and 30 per cent of the votes (Bjørklund 1999: 163). These findings are similar to findings in studies from France (Withol de Wenden 1994), Britain, Sweden and the Netherlands (Rath 1988).

Our own analysis of Swedish data[11] confirm the preference for left-of-center parties among foreign citizens, and also show that foreign citizens are more left-leaning than the 'indigenous' Swedish population in general – both when it comes to party preferences as well as actual party choice. Also, and in line with the considerations on political integration above, second generation immigrants seem to move closer to the Swedish population concerning political attitudes. These results are seen in Table 12.2.

In the Norwegian 1995 election survey the most left-leaning group was found to be 'non-Western' male immigrants where as much as 77 per cent voted for left-of-center parties. The same was true for only 33 per cent of male Norwegian citizens (Bjørklund 1999: 164).

Other types of political participation

As discussed in chapter 1 there are many other types of political participation apart from electoral turnout which are relevant for the understanding of the role of immigrants and refugees in the Scandinavian democracies.

Table 12.2 Party sympathy and party choice among foreign citizens in Sweden. Percentage preferring working-class parties*

	1987	1994
Party sympathy		
Swedes	57 (2424)	52 (1621)
Immigrants**	61 (176)	63 (75)
Second gen. immigrants	56 (127)	—
Party choice, local elections		
Swedes	—	46 (1621)
Foreign citizens	—	57 (75)

*Here the Socialdemocratic Party, the Left Party ('Vänsterpartiet') and the Environmental Party has been considered working-class parties.
**The 1987 figure does not distinguish between naturalized and non-naturalized immigrants. The 1994 figure is 'foreign citizens' only. The numbers in parentheses are absolute numbers of valid answers/votes. Thus the 'don't know'/no vote categories have been omitted in the calculations.

The two most important types seem to be participation in various types of voluntary associations and so-called 'direct political action' (demonstrations, petitions, and so on.). We shall take a closer look at both below.

Political, religious and civic organizations

As mentioned in chapter 5 voluntary associations of various kinds have played a central role as 'intermediaries' between the people and the elite. They have, as workplace democracy (chapter 7) and the user boards in the public sector (chapter 8), been regarded as a 'school of democracy'; traditionally even as the very backbone of everyday political life or the political culture. For this reason an important indicator of how well immigrants and refugees are integrated in the political culture in the Scandinavian countries must be to what extent these groups are members of, and participate in the activities of different voluntary association.

Since the middle of the 1960s the number of immigrant or refugee associations has been constantly growing. It is estimated that there are somewhere between 2000 and 2500 such associations in Scandinavia today (Hammer and Bruun 1992). More than 1500 of these are located in Sweden, some 400 in Denmark, while at least 450 are known to exist in Norway. The number of members in these associations is not known. However, Layton-Henry (1990) has estimated that by 1985 there were at least 170000 members in the by then 1200 associations in Sweden.[12]

Most of these associations have a national or an ethnic character and are thus basically oriented towards the immigrants' country of origin. However, a substantial part is also formed around specific purposes or activities. Compared with Denmark and Norway. the Swedish immigrant organizations have the best nationwide coverage. In Sweden there are thus 39 so-called 'national associations' ('Riksförbund'). Many of these associations solve important tasks for their members, and are by ministries and others seen as important partners in the process of integration and the development of a multicultural society. None the less the immigrant associations do not, despite their growing numbers, play the same role in society as 'indigenous' Danish/Swedish/Norwegian voluntary associations. Thus, *in general they are not very visible in the public debate*. This is probably due to both a conscious policy by some associations to concentrate on the contact between immigrants themselves, and between immigrants and their home country, and to the difficulties many immigrants find in adjusting to Scandinavian ideas of what voluntary associations should be.

Immigrant and refugee associations have been very 'successful' in recent years in the sense that their cooperation is increasingly sought by both central and local authorities and by private organizations and institutions. They are also contacted by an increasing number of individuals for a variety of reasons. However, most associations are badly suited for this role. Most of them have no or few regular employees, and the personnel most often have no professional training in running either organizations, multicultural cooperation or conflict resolution. Furthermore, they very often have limited economic resources. Thus, many immigrant associations are undergoing a change from being traditionally *meeting places*, for fellow citizens – often from the same village or region – to being *interest organizations* more along Scandinavian lines. This metamorphosis puts political demands on the associations, which in turn generates demand for representation and influence.

There is a very big variation in the types of immigrant voluntary associations, and many associations take on a number of different activities. This makes it rather difficult to make a sharp distinction between, for example political, religious and cultural or social types of associations. In recent years especially religious congregations and cultural associations as well as 'narrow' interest organizations have been targeted by public authorities, because they have been able to solve a number of social problems connected with immigration. The broader immigrant interest organizations on the other hand seem to have lost in importance. Table 12.3 shows immigrant activity in immigrant associations. As can be seen from Table 12.3 immigrants in Sweden and Denmark seem to be considerably better organized than immigrants in Norway. However, the figures from both Sweden and Norway should be read with some caution because the sample sizes are so small.

Table 12.3 Immigrant* participation in activities in immigrant organizations (percentages)

	Sweden	Denmark	Norway
Member of immigrant organization	15	15	3
Active in organization	9		2
Charge in organization	3		2
N	176	1132	89

*Both naturalized and non-naturalized immigrants. The Norwegian figures include both first- and second-generation immigrants. Figures regarding Denmark are taken from L. Togeby (1998) 'Et demokrati, som omfatter alle, der bor i Danmark?' p. 143.

For Denmark, we also have some data on membership and participation in trade unions and sport clubs for different ethnic groups, as well as data on how well different ethic groups are organized in immigrant organizations (Togeby 2000). As we can from Table 12.4 the ethnic groups shown in the table are in general not very well organized in neither trade unions nor sports clubs compared to the population in general (see chapter 5). Only the Turkish group (the men) stand out here with a membership and a participation in trade unions at almost the same level as wage-earners in Denmark in general. This probably has to do with the fact that many members of the Turkish groups were among the first 'guest workers' to arrive in the 1960s and early 1970s. At that time they got jobs, and were expected to adjust to Danish workplace culture, which in most workplaces includes being a union member.

Table 12.4 Participation in trade unions and sports clubs. Different ethnic groups (percentages)

	Bosnia		Somalia		Lebanon/Palestine		Turkey	
	Men	Women	Men	Women	Men	Women	Men	Women
Member of trade union[1]	36*	16	28*	12	28*	10	60*	47
Participated in trade union meetings	12*	3	11*	2	9*	4	30	29
Member of sports club with Danes	22*	4	20*	9	14*	5	19*	7

Note: Percentages are calculated on the basis of all respondents; not only wage-earners.
*means that the difference between men and women is significant at the .05 level.

Source: Togeby 2000.

The data (not shown here) on how well different ethnic groups are organized and participate in immigrant (ethnic) associations shows that only
the Somali group seem to participate in such activities to a relatively high
extent. Some 30 per cent of the Somali men are members of such associations and participate in their differerent activities.

These figures demonstrate two things: firstly, that some of the major
ethnic (immigrant) groups (in Denmark) participate relatively little in
major voluntary associations compared to the average population (with a
few exceptions), and secondly, that the reason for this is not that they are
especially oriented towards their 'own' (ethnic) associations. Rather, they
participate relatively little in the life of voluntary associations in general.

Direct political action

Activities like demonstrations, petitions, and so on are political instruments traditionally used by minorities or underprivileged groups. The only
data we have concerning these types of political activities are from the
1995 Norwegian election survey, where questions were asked about whether
'non-Western' foreign citizens had signed petitions, taken part in political
actions or demonstrations, taken action in parties or trade unions or contacted politicians or bureaucrats. These data are shown in Table 12.5.

Interestingly, these data show that even though foreign citizens participate
less than the average population in all of these activities except for participation in political actions and demonstrations, their participation in these
activities is significant, and compares better with that of the average population than their electoral turnout. A possible explanation might be that this
kind of single-issue involvement is less demanding in terms of overall

Table 12.5 Percentage of all voters and of 'non-western' immigrants who have tried
to make an impact on local or regional government during the last four years
(1991–95)

	Signed a petition	Participated in political action, demonstration or protest meeting	Taken action in political parties, trade unions or similar	Contacted local or regional adminis- tration	Contacted local politicians	N
All voters	26	11	14	13	20	303
Non-Western immigrants	17	17	9	9	10	95

Source: Bjørklund 1999: 167.

knowledge of the political system, and that the threshold for participating in these type of activities is therefore lower than when it comes to voting.

Attitudes towards immigrants and refugees

The attitudes of the 'indigenous' Scandinavian populations towards immigrants and refugees are extremely important. Firstly, because one must expect these attitudes to be or become reflected in public policies vis-à-vis asylum seekers and refugees, and secondly because these attitudes mirror essential traits of Scandinavian political culture – how well do the Scandinavians live up to their ideals about a full (participatory and egalitarian) citizenship for everyone?

However, before we dwelve deeper into the question of attitudes towards immigrants and refugees a note of caution is warranted. Thus, Gaasholt and Togeby (1995) make a strong case for the idea that especially in this area attitudes are quite volatile. This has to do with the fact that the question is relatively new on the political agenda, that few people have personal experiences related to immigrants and refugees, and that the public at large – as we shall see below – exhibit quite ambiguous attitudes of both hostility and tolerance. What the politicians hear when they 'listen' to the public opinion in this area might therefore be nothing more than the echo of their own ideas and prejudices presented to the public by media often searching for problems and sensations.[13] However, even though these observations question traditional assumptions about the causality between attitudes, politicians and politics, and even though they make us sensitive towards the way in which 'popular attitudes' are socially constructed, attitudes are still efficacious in politics – no matter what their originating source and real or symbolic content is. Below, we shall therefore analyse the structure of attitudes towards immigrants and refugees in Scandinavia. As the Citizenship Surveys contained very few questions on this issue our data have been supplemented by data from the Swedish SOM survey in 1994, from Gaasholt and Togeby (1995) and Togeby (1998) as well as from other Danish surveys.

If we take a look first at the extent to which the Scandinavians (here the Danes) are willing to grant resident refugees social, civil and political rights – that is, to allow them full membership of their societies – we find at first glance attitudes which seems to reflect the Scandinavian self-understanding: that the Scandinavians are tolerant and open-minded, and have a humanitarian approach to refugees.

As we can see from Table 12.6 around three-quarters of the adult Danish population is ready to give refugees who have been granted asylum the

Table 12.6 'Do you think that refugees who have been granted asylum, should have the same rights as everybody else to seek work, get an education and receive social benefits?' (percentages)

	1985	1993	1998
Yes, same rights	76	70	87
No	16	27	
Don't know	8	3	
Sum	100	100	
N	1482	1675	*

*Survey data. N not reported.

Source: SFI (Danish National Institute of Social Research) (1985), Gaasholt and Togeby (1995: 111). Togeby (1998: 149).

same social rights as everybody else in society. Furthermore, this distribution has not changed much between 1985 and 1993. The same positive attitude is found if asking about other types of social rights. Thus, the Scandinavians (Danes) seem quite willing to grant refugees (and immigrants) full social citizenship. However, when the questions focus on naturalization (the right to Danish citizenship), and political participation the tolerance is considerable more limited: a majority think that it is too early for immigrants to vote at local elections after three years' residence (*which is current law!*), and almost 50 per cent agree with a statement saying that 'immigrants should only be allowed to get a Danish citizenship when they have learned to behave like Danes' (Gaasholt and Togeby 1995: 43).

This ambiguity in attitudes is studied more in detail by Gaasholt and Togeby (1995). They show that there is both a widespread reservation or hostility towards immigrants and refugees, but also a considerable amount of tolerance towards these groups. Gaasholt and Togeby explain this apparent paradox by suggesting that hostility and fear can be seen as a sort of 'natural' reaction among the population in a society exposed to recent immigration of a certain magnitude (Gaasholt and Togeby 1995: 13). In order for this hostility and fear not to develop into xenophobia, it is important that it is counterbalanced or held in check by a certain level of tolerance. For this reason measures of hostility, and of tolerance are well-suited to illustrate the character of the attitudes of the Scandinavian populations towards immigrants and refugees.

As both the Danish and Swedish data show (Tables 12.7 and 12.8) there is on the one hand a widespread hostility towards immigrants, but on the other also a considerable amount of tolerance. It is worth mentioning that the number of people in Table 12.7 who believe that 'immigrants should be free to exercise their religion in Denmark' has increased during the last couple of years (Togeby 1998: 149; 1999: 448). However, as also the Swedish data shows, this tolerance stops short of granting (in this case) Muslim

Table 12.7 Hostility and tolerance towards immigrants and refugees in *Denmark* (percentages)

	Pro-immigrant answers
Hostility: 'Immigrants are a serious threat to Danish culture' (no)	45
'Do you think there should be further restrictions upon the entry of refugees to Denmark?' (no)*	27
Tolerance: 'Different people have different attitudes towards what constitutes a 'good citizen': to be a 'good citizen' is it important to be tolerant towards immigrants?' (somewhat/very important)**	78
'Society should create possibilities for immigrants to maintain their own language and culture' (yes)*	42
'Immigrants should be free to exercise their religion in Denmark' (yes)*	54

* data are from Gaasholt and Togeby (1995); other data are from the Citizenship survey.
** a scale from 1 to 10 was used; where 1 = not at all important, and 10 = very important. The scale has been recoded the following way: 1–4 = not important, 5–7 = somewhat important, 8–10 = very important.

groups full *political rights*. Thus, the Scandinavians are neither very tolerant nor very intolerant, but seem to exist in an ambiguous 'grey zone'. It is exactly this ambiguity which makes 'popular opinion' in this area very open to 'social construction' by politicians and the media. More detailed analysis show that attitudes changes quite a lot depending on the exact wording of questions, and depending on how prominent certain issues concerning immigrant and refugees figure on the political agenda. However, such analysis also shows (Gaasholt and Togeby 1995: 68ff) that the group expressing very negative or directly racist attitudes is rather small; consisting of about 5–8 per cent of the adult population. In the other end of the scale the group expressing very tolerant attitudes consists of some 10–25 per cent of the population (measured by an index of tolerance; Gaasholt and Togeby 1995: 45).

Part of the Scandinavian self-perception is also that Scandinavians are on the average more tolerant than most other European peoples. Table 12.9,

Table 12.8   Hostility and tolerance towards immigrants and refugees in *Sweden*. (Percentages)

	Pro-immigrant answers
Hostility:	
'Considering how the world looks today what do you think is most worrying about the future: that there will be more refugees in Sweden?'	
(not very worrying/not worrying at all)	28
'Sweden should accept more refugees' (good/very good proposal)	13
'Sweden should accept fewer refugees' (bad/very bad proposal)	20
Tolerance:	
'Immigrant policies should help immigrants preserve their national traditions and culture' (good/very good proposal)	23
'Should the following groups in society be entitled to their own:	
– Muslim cultural associations? (yes)	76
– (Muslims) to build mosques? (yes)	52
– Muslim newspapers? (yes)	74
– Muslim schools? (yes)	20
– Muslim representatives in political assemblies? (yes)	46
– Muslim political parties? (yes)	30

All data from 1994 SOM survey. Own computations.

which compares Denmark with some of the major EU countries, show that this is a truth with some modifications. Concerning the first question (about the number of non-nationals) the attitude of the Danes does not differ much from the average in the EU. Concerning the second question (about the presence of people of another nationality, and so on), the Danes are the most hostile here on all items.

Concerning the third question (restrictions on political refugees) the Danes are, on the other hand, among the most tolerant. Seen together, the distribution of answers to the three questions indicates that the Danes do not differ substantially from the European average on either hostility or tolerance towards immigrants and refugees.

In a search for factors which can explain these attitudes it is of considerable interest to take a closer look at the possible structural sources of hostility and tolerance. Concerning such structural sources especially a hypothesis

Table 12.9 Hostility and tolerance towards immigrants and refugees in the EU*. Percentage pro-immigrant answers

		Hostility: 'Generally speaking, how do you feel about people living in (our country) who are not nationals of the EC countries. Are there too many, a lot but not too many, or not many?' (a lot but not too many/ not many)	Hostility: 'Some people are disturbed by the opinions, customs and ways of life of people different from themselves. Do you personally find the presence of people of another nationality, race or religion disturbing in your daily life?' (no) nat. race rel.*			Tolerance: 'Some people, suffering from human rights violations in their country are seeking political asylum. For this type of immigration what do you think should be done in the EC: accept them without restrictions, accept them with some restrictions or not accept them?' (without restrictions)
Denmark	52		73	68	58	36
Germany	43		79	76	80	22
France	47		85	78	77	21
Spain	70		93	91	88	43
Sweden	60		89	89	**	18
UK	52		86	86	86	18

*Eurobarometer 39, 1993.
**Sweden was not included in the Eurobarometer surveys at that time.
Source: Eurobarometer 48, 1997.

which could be called the 'competition hypothesis' has figured prominently in the debate. The 'competition hypothesis' states that groups who compete directly with immigrants and refugees about in particular jobs, will be more hostile and less tolerant than other groups. Such groups will normally be unskilled workers and/or unemployed. Below, we shall therefore take a look at the attitudes of these groups as compared to other groups in the population in both Denmark and Sweden. Tables 12.10 and 12.11 shows a sociodemographic profile of attitudes towards immigrants and refugees in Denmark and Sweden.

These tables, which are representative for the hostility and tolerance questions shown in Tables 12.8 and 12.9, at a first glance seem to confirm the 'competition hypothesis'. Thus, especially unskilled workers as well as the groups outside the labor market – among these unemployed – seem to be more hostile and less tolerant than other groups.[14] However, what we also see from the tables, especially Table 12.11, is that age and education also seem to be important for attitudes towards immigrants.[15] In fact, in

Table 12.10   Hostility and tolerance towards immigrants and refugees in *Denmark*. Sociodemographic profile of attitudes (percentage pro-immigrant answers)

	1 Hostility: 'Immigrants are a serious threat to Danish culture' (no)		2 Tolerance:' ... to be a "good citizen" it is necessary to be tolerant towards immigrants' (somewhat/very important)	
Gender				
Men	45	−.001ns	76	.05
Women	45		80	
Age				
18–29	50	−.17	82	−.15
30–39	52		82	
40–49	51		82	
50–59	42		76	
60–69	36		74	
70+	28		66	
Education				
7–9 years	31	.33	70	.26
10 years	47		81	
11+ years	73		90	
Occupation				
Unskilled worker	35	−.13	68	−.15
Skilled worker	52		79	
Lower nonmanual	52		83	
Medium nonmanual	64		92	
Higher nonmanual	67		87	
Self-employed	40		81	
Employment status				
Gainfully employed	51	−.19	82	−.17
Unemployed	38		76	
Disabled (<60)	33		65	
Early retired (60–66)	27		78	
Old age pens. (67+)	30		67	
Housewives	37		87	
*Party choice**				
Socialist	50	−.06	81	−.09
Rightwing	31		74	
N	1877		1877	

*Party choice is respondents answer to a question about what the respondent voted at the last national election (1988). The following parties are placed under the 'socialist' heading: the Social Democracy, People's Socialist Party, The Communists, The Green Party and the Radical Liberal Party. The following parties are regarded as 'right-wing' parties: the Center Democrats, Christian People's Party, the Liberal Party, Conservative Party and the Progress Party. ns = not significant at the 0.05 level.

Table 12.11 Hostility and tolerance towards immigrants and refugees in Sweden. Sociodemographic profile of attitudes. Percentage pro-immigrant answers

	1 Hostility:* '...worrying with more refugees in Sweden' (not worrying)		2 Tolerance: 'Immigrant policies should help immigrants preserve their culture' (good proposal)		3 Tolerance: 'Right to own Muslim cultural associations' (yes)		4 Tolerance: 'Right to Muslim representatives in political assemblies' (yes)	
Gender								
Men	29	.008 ns	18	−.14	74	.03 ns	44	.006 ns
Women	26		28		78		46	
Age								
18–29	33	−.11	22	−.06	73		49	.09
30–39	34		20			.03 ns	47	
40–49	28		24		79		50	
50–59	25		22		80		42	
60–69	22		26		80		41	
70+	20		26		72		32	
					68			
Education								
7–9 years	23	.11	22		63	.24	38	.13
10–11 years	25			.03 ns	79		46	
12+ years	34		24		87		52	
			24					
Occupation								
Worker	26	−.03 ns	24		69	.08	42	.04 ns
Nonmanual	30			.04 ns	85		46	
Self-employed	28		22		69		46	
			20					
Party choice**								
Socialist	28	−.01 ns	29	.15	76	−.02 ns	48	.06
Rightwing	27		16		78		43	
N	1508		1508		1508		1508	

*The full wording of the questions used here is found in Table 12.8.

**Party choice is respondent's answer to a question about what party he/she prefers. The following parties are placed under the 'Socialist' heading: the Social Democracy, 'Vänsterpartiet' (former Communist party), the Green Party. Under the 'right-wing' heading we find: the Center Party, The Liberal Party ('Folkpartiet'), The Conservative Party ('Moderata Samlingspartiet'), The Christian Democratic Party, and New Democracy ('Ny Demokrati').

Table 12.12   Relation between hostility/tolerance and occupation, employment status and party choice controlled for age and education. *Denmark*. Beta coefficients and r².

	Q1	Q1	Q1	Q2	Q2	Q2
Age	.09ns	.06ns	.10	.06ns	.04ns	.05ns
Education	.24	.30	.29	.06ns	.05ns	.03ns
Occupation	.13			.09ns		
Empl. Status		.05ns			.00ns	
Party choice			.10			.01ns
r²(%)	9.6	9.2	11.1	1.5	0.4	0.3

ns = significance of F > .05.
Q1 = question 1 in Table 12.10.
Q2 = question 2 in Table 12.10.

both the Danish and the Swedish cases the strongest correlations are found between education and hostility/tolerance.[16] This warns us that there might be considerable interaction effects between the independent variables. What we have done is therefore to control the relationship between hostility/tolerance and occupation, employment status, and party choice for age and education. The result of these controls are found in Table 12.12.[17]

Table 12.12 shows that concerning hostility in Denmark the effect of occupation and employment status are spurious. In all three regression models *education* has by far the most explanatory power. Formulated differently this means that unskilled workers and persons outside the labor market (unemployed) are more hostile mainly because they have a lower level of education than other groups in society, and not *because* they are either unskilled or unemployed. Concerning tolerance none of the regression models have much explanatory power, but at least we can say that none of the other independent variables seem to be more important than education.

These results means that the competition hypothesis cannot be confirmed. The correlations we found between occupation and employment status and hostility turned out to be spurious, and explained by the low level of education among (unskilled) workers and groups outside the labor market; among them the unemployed.

Summing up, these results show that even though a number of different factors might have some importance in explaining attitudes towards immigrants and refugees the level of education is by far the most important single factor in explaining these attitudes. This result is consistent with other results found in both Scandinavian and international literature (Hoskin 1991; Eurobarometer Opinion Poll no. 47 1997.1: 4; Togeby 1998: 113; Aardal and Valen 1995: 173). It is therefore often concluded that what should be done in order to limit hostility and expand tolerance is to make sure that tolerance (liberal values) is taught at all levels of the educational system (see, for example, Hoskin 1991). However, it is doubtful whether it is exactly the knowledge component of education which makes education important for attitudes. Thus, in an interesting analysis of the importance of different elements of education on ethnic tolerance, Gaasholt and Togeby (1995: 95ff) shows that only a minor part of the explanatory value of education has to do with concrete knowledge about immigrants and refugees. General aspects of a higher level of education seem to be of more importance, such as for example increased ability to handle complexity, and more resistance towards messages by politicians and the media.

Conclusion

Even though the number of foreign citizens residing in the Scandinavian countries is still relatively small, these countries – especially Sweden and Denmark – have, over the last decade, approached the European average more and more. This has forced the Scandinavian countries, like most other European countries, to rethink the in- and exclusiveness of their national citizenship, as well as its social, civil and political dimensions.

In order to understand this development we have in this chapter: (i) analysed the ways in which the presence of immigrants and refugees have challenged these dimensions of citizenship; (ii) looked at how well the Scandinavian countries have lived up to their own ideals of an egalitarian and participatory citizenship for all groups in society; and (iii) looked at how well the Scandinavian countries live up to their official ideals of developing multicultural societies. This has meant looking at the way in which the authorities relate to different ethnic groups. Also, it has meant investigating the popular seedbed for this policy: the extent of tolerance towards persons of other ethnic origin, and with other cultural and religious traditions, as well as the extent of hostility and xenophobia.

The focus of this chapter has been the extent to which political, civil and social rights are conferred upon the group of immigrants and refugees, and how these rights are used. The question of the ex- or inclusiveness of citizenship in Scandinavia has therefore only received scant attention, even though it could clearly merit a more thorough analysis. Suffice it here to say that what we have witnessed is a more and more restrictive practice towards immigrants and refugees. This, of course, is also due to the fact that Sweden and Denmark, as EU members, are part of the institutional framework (the Trevi Group, the Dublin Convention and the External Frontiers Convention) being developed in order to regulate the flow of asylum seekers and refugees into the EU.

Having gone through the arduous process of being an arriving refugee or asylum seeker, and having one's case tested by an autonomous board, the asylum seeker or immigrant, if successful, is granted either asylum or a residence permit. Having obtained this status in Scandinavia also means, in principle, having obtained the same social and civil rights as the 'indigenous' population; that is, the same right to social benefits, health care, school and childcare facilities, and so on, as well as rights to organize, publish, practice religion, and so on, freely. Concerning political rights these are limited to the right to vote and run for office at local and regional elections. This right was given to foreign citizens in 1975 in Sweden, in 1980 in Denmark and in 1982 in Norway. All three countries demand that the foreign citizen has been a permanent resident for at least three years in order to participate in these activities.

After a much publicized start, with voting turnout rates around 50–60 per cent, turnout has declined quite dramatically, with current rates around 40 per cent. However, the decline has been markedly bigger in Norway and Sweden than in Denmark. This seems due to the fact that in Denmark it is possible to vote simultaneously for a political party or list, and an individual candidate; a possibility which did not exist in Norway and Sweden until recently. Analysis has shown that this difference matters, and that turnout was consistently higher in municipalities where one or more immigrants/foreign citizens ran for office.

Concerning the party choice of foreign citizens our analysis of Swedish data, as well as the Norwegian data referred, show that on average foreign citizens are somewhat more left-leaning than nationals; especially male 'non-Western' foreign citizens.

Voting is not the only, and definitely not the most important political activity of immigrants and refugees in Scandinavia. Of more importance seem to be the growing number of civic/political/religious associations and various types of direct political action. Thus it is estimated that there are now somewhere between 2000 and 2500 such associations in Scandinavia today (Hammer and Bruun 1992) covering a very big variety of activities. Immigrants in Sweden and Denmark are the best organized with a substantial number of national associations, and with membership rates around 15 per cent of the total immigrant population. Concerning different types of direct political action such as signing petitions, participating in demonstrations, contacting local politicians or bureaucrats, and so on, a Norwegian study showed that the participation in these types of activities for foreign citizens is considerable. Except for participation in demonstrations and other types of political actions foreign citizens participate less than the average population, but the participation along this dimension compares much better with that of the average population than election turnout.

Finally, we looked at the attitudes towards immigrants and refugees held by the Scandinavian citizenry. These attitudes are quite ambiguous showing both a widespread hostility, but also a considerable amount of tolerance. However, such ambiguity is not unique in a European context, and actually the Scandinavian countries (Denmark) do not seem to differ substantially from the EU average on a number of questions concerning immigrants and refugees. The analysis also showed (for Denmark) that the group expressing very negative attitudes is rather small, amounting to around 5–8 per cent of the adult population, while 10–25 per cent of the population express very tolerant attitudes. More concretely, there is a widespread support for granting refugees with a residence permit full social and civil (cultural) rights. However, the tolerance stops short of granting refugees and immigrants full political rights. Furthermore, the Scandinavians have restrictive attitudes towards access to their countries, and a rather solid majority (Denmark) thinks that access for political refugees should be restricted more than it is now.

Summing up, what we see are Scandinavian countries being quite restrictive as to whom they let into their territory. However, once let in, foreign citizens are – in principle at least – granted full social and civil rights. Concerning civil rights the associational activities of refugees and immigrants are even encouraged and subsidized. This policy seem to have widespread support among the Scandinavian populations. Thus, part of the promise of a multi-ethnic policy seem to be redeemed – most firmly in Sweden, with Norway and Denmark lagging somewhat behind. However, both official policies as well as popular attitudes stops short of wanting to grant resident foreign citizens full or even useful political rights. Voting turnout in local and regional elections is not encouraged and is declining. Also, governments are very reluctant towards developing real cooperative ties with immigrant associations. Thus, when it comes to the nuts and bolts of democracy in Scandinavia – the creation and implementation of policies – immigrants and refugees find themselves in a clearly marginalized position.

13
Conclusion: The End of Scandinavian Exceptionalism?

Scandinavian exceptionalism?

Even though Norway was once described as a 'distant democracy' (Martinussen 1977) when held up against participatory democratic ideals, it is probably no exaggeration to speak of the Scandinavian democracies at that time as coming close to 'ideal democracies' if we take comparative analyses of democratic systems in the real world as our standard of evaluation. The Scandinavian countries have been stable democracies with consensual politics and social peace, and they have been affluent countries characterized by strong egalitarianism embodied in generous welfare states (heralded as the 'Scandinavian welfare model'). And if we use comparative figures as standard, the Scandinavian countries could also qualify as 'participatory' democracies in the sense that social and political participation has been high and quite evenly distributed between major social groups – in particular, due to the high mobilization of people with few socioeconomic resources in political parties, in trade unions and farmers' associations, and in elections.

Probably, some of the major reasons are to be found in the fact that these countries have been small, homogeneous nation-states, prototypical in terms of class mobilization and class-based politics – not because such class conflicts were particularly strong (except in Finland, which is outside the scope of this book) but rather because there were few other significant cleavages (with the exception of Norwegian center–periphery conflicts). As to the legacy of class mobilization, one should also take into account the strong political mobilization of farmers which, especially in Denmark and Norway, preceded the mobilization of the urban working class.

Even if it may be an exaggeration to speak of Scandinavian exceptionalism, these countries have been unusually successful in terms of democratic governance and democratic participation. Since the heydays of industrial society and the nation-state, however, quite profound changes have taken place, sometimes classified as a post-industrial and a post-national revolution, or given some equivalent umbrella labels. The question is how these changes have affected the traditional picture of Scandinavian democracies – and whether the picture given above is any longer correct.

These were some of the main questions which we set out to examine in this book which concentrates on democracy 'from below'. Although this includes, first and foremost, political participation, our focus has been on the quality of democracy, rather than on explanations of individual political behavior. For this reason, we chose the concept of citizenship as the core perspective of the analysis. Citizenship concerns not only participation but also (civil, political and social) rights, and identities – two aspects that have mainly been addressed in the second part of the book which has analysed major challenges to citizenship in an increasingly post-industrial and post-national society. The concept of citizenship also serves to point out what are the major challenges to the ideal of 'full citizenship' – that is, equal access of citizens to participate in all areas of social and political life. In the second part of the book, we have analysed some of the effects of labor market marginalization, Europeanization, and immigration which are all related to current processes of globalization and post-national change.

The notion of post-industrial change is central to the first part of the book, especially to the question of what happens to class-based politics and political institutions, and what the consequences of any changes will be. This part of the book focuses on the dimension of participation and is structured around the various channels of participation: elections, political parties, voluntary associations and political protest or single-issue participation. However, a major aim of Scandinavian welfare policies has also been described as the 'democratization of all areas of social life' (Hernes 1988), including the workplace and welfare institutions. Decentralization ('bringing decisions as close to the people as possible') and providing people with more control over their own daily life situation has been the standard formula for democratization of society – and for remedying whatever linkage problems there may be in traditional channels of participation. Along with the question as to whether Scandinavian citizenship may be characterized as 'activist, participatory, and egalitarian' (Hernes 1988), these are the major questions addressed in the first part of the book. From a citizenship perspective, political engagement and political competence also become a central interest. In particular, we have been concerned with the notion of a 'spectator democracy' characterized by high political interest but low active participation and low commitment.

The legacy of class mobilization

The Scandinavian countries have been seen as ideal-typical examples of a thorough mobilization along the basic cleavages of the industrial nation-state; in particular, class cleavages. Few other countries have seen such high levels of political mobilization in mass parties, in trade unions and farmers' associations, and in leisure, cultural and religious associations. Class mobilization has contributed not only to a high level of political participation but also to a high degree of social equality in participation, because collective resources could compensate for inequality in individual resources. As traditional class cleavages are melting, the question is to what extent class-based institutions are eroding; how this affect the overall pattern of political participation and the social equality in participation; and whether alternative channels of political influence have developed that can compensate for such a decline.

Beginning with *political engagement*, it was demonstrated in chapter 2 that political interest has certainly not declined in the Scandinavian countries. On the contrary, the Danish data in particular revealed signs of a long-term increase; furthermore, we found high levels of political discussion, not least among the young. The legacy of class mobilization (and gender mobilization) in the Scandinavian countries is especially clear at one particular point: we found unusually low levels of political apathy. When it comes to optimistic predictions of a cognitive mobilization, due to increasing levels of education, on the other hand, our findings were negative: with increasing levels of education, political interest within all education groups, especially among the better-educated, seems to decline, indicating that it is mainly the relative rather than the absolute level of education that is important here.

But in spite of relatively high and slightly increasing levels of political interest, we found signs of declining participation in all conventional forms of politics such as elections, political parties, voluntary associations and trade unions. As to *electoral turnout* we found a long-term decline from the 1980s or the 1990s in all Scandinavian countries. Looking at each individual country, this trend appears somewhat uncertain, due to strong fluctuations from one election to another, but when we compare across countries, we feel much more confident in speaking of a general trend. In all Scandinavian countries, average participation rates in the 1990s were lower than in the previous decade. Low participation has also been encountered in local elections in Denmark and Norway, and the discrepancy in participation in local and national elections has widened, even though widespread decentralization has taken place in the same period. Sweden has maintained a high turnout in local elections, probably because they are held concurrently with national elections. Testing for a large number of alternative explanations, we found the long-term decline in electoral participation to be mainly explainable by class demobilization and the decline in civic virtues – less people feel that it is 'their duty to vote'. Even though class differences in turnout seem to be slightly widening, however, this remains the most egalitarian channel of political participation.

Membership of political parties (chapter 4) used to be exceptionally high in the Scandinavian countries, with a Danish peak value of 27 per cent of the electorate in 1947. In Denmark, the figure has dropped to 5 per cent in 1999. We hypothesized that this was mainly due to class demobilization and to other factors which parties have very little chance to influence. This implies that declining membership should be a general trend, not limited to Denmark, which for a long time seemed to be the deviant case in Scandinavia. However, by the end of the 1990s, membership figures have declined to (almost) equally low levels in Norway and Sweden (both around 7 per cent). However, the data revealed less decline in party activity than in membership. Apparently, the declining membership reflects a disproportional exit of passive supporters, and crude membership figures seem to give an exaggerated picture of the decline in activity; on the other hand, this means that party membership is increasingly changing from being a mass phenomenon to being an elite phenomenon.

Not surprisingly, the decline of parties also pertains to political identities: Comparative data on electoral volatility and party identification indicate that the development in all the Scandinavian countries is converging towards a situation of lower party attachment. Like voting, the pattern of convergence becomes much more clear when we compile information from all the Scandinavian countries rather than considering each one individually. Our data indicate that most political change tends to appear at an earlier time in Denmark than in Sweden, but that similar changes have taken place in all Scandinavian countries. Contrary to our general preference for institutional and contingent explanations, rather than social structural and deterministic ones, our findings seem to reject institutional explanations of the destiny of political parties and speak in favor of a more deterministic convergence hypothesis about effects of anonymous processes of structural change. The parties seem to be victims of such processes, with little chance of influencing their position. Even though the demobilization of the working class in political parties so far remains more visible in Denmark than in Sweden, it appears that the era of Scandinavian exceptionalism with regard to class mobilization in political parties is now coming to an end.

Turning to *voluntary associations* (chapter 5), it is generally recognized that the Scandinavian countries are countries of voluntary associations par excellence. Even though nearly all existing survey measurements of voluntary association membership have been notoriously flawed, this assumption is also supported by comparative measures which underestimate levels but are more reliable when it comes to country differences. Thus, Sweden has the highest ranking among the countries in the World Values Survey, and Denmark has the highest ranking in the Eurobarometer surveys. However, if we exclude trade unions, the Netherlands, USA and Germany reveal equally high rates of membership, and when it comes to 'working memberships' (defined as doing unpaid work for the association) national differences are even smaller. Thus, membership and activity in non-union associations is high in Scandinavia but probably not unique. Based on data from the

Scandinavian Citizenship Surveys we showed that, on average, Danes and Swedes hold membership in just over three (types of) associations, and only some 6–7 per cent of the adult population are classified as members of no association. Norwegian figures on membership are unreliable due to inadequate measurement but data on active membership can be made comparable and these indicate that Norway is probably the Scandinavian country with the strongest voluntary associations, apart from trade unions. Danish data on active membership indicate that higher membership is not followed by higher activity, rather the contrary. Recent Swedish data point in the same direction. Thus, also as far as associations are concerned, data increasingly cast doubt about Scandinavian exceptionalism.

This trend also holds for the most visible Scandinavian exceptionalism, namely *trade union membership* (chapter 6). Due to the particular unemployment benefit system (the Ghent system), which is largely controlled by the trade unions, Denmark, Sweden and Finland have avoided the decline in unionization which has been a general trend in nearly all other countries. On the contrary, union membership continued to increase (to some 85 per cent) until 1990. However, there are strong signs of 'institutional sclerosis': at least as *movements*, trade unions seem to face severe problems. Thus, in Denmark and Sweden, we found declining levels of active participation, a low level of identification with the unions, low levels of efficacy vis-à-vis the unions, and low evaluations of union influence. Norwegian union members scored higher, and although membership is much lower, Norwegian unions seem healthier as movements than unions in Sweden and Denmark. Thus, what is gained in membership in these two countries seems to be lost in participation. Before painting too bleak a picture of unions in Scandinavia, however, it must be acknowledged that interest in union politics has remained relatively high, that their sheer size means that many people are actively involved, and that there remains a basic support for unions among their members. Thus, unions will probably continue to play an important role in mass political mobilization, but they are weakened, and even membership may be more vulnerable than it appears, especially in the light of institutional change such as changes in the unemployment benefit system.

Political protest – that is, direct political action through such measures as signing petitions, participating in demonstrations, joining action groups, and so on – has not normally been considered a conventional form of politics in a Scandinavian context. However, as demonstrated in chapter 9, political protest has increasingly changed from a 'new left' and 'new middle-class' phenomenon to a standard form of political articulation, used by various groups depending on their situations. And protesting is no longer related to political distrust; on the contrary, the sign of association may even have reversed so that this form of participation may have some of the same politically integrative effects as conventional participation. Political protest is therefore best seen as single-issue participation – that is, as an alternative way of participating politically when there are no other opportunities or when the chances of success through the more 'established' channels are low. Furthermore, it provides an outlet for participation on an ad hoc basis rather than making a long-term commitment. Even though the level of political protest or single-issue participation has increased in all Scandinavian countries, comparative data do not indicate any Scandinavian exceptionalism at this point – in accordance with the fact that this is not linked to any tradition of class-based politics.

Equality and participation

A major question is how these changes in patterns of political participation have affected social equality in participation, once a hallmark of Scandinavian citizenship. As mentioned, strong class mobilization in parties, unions (and farmers' associations) and elections meant not only high levels of participation but also high equality. Generally speaking, social inequality in participation does not seem to have deteriorated much, however, and at the same time, it is a general trend that the gender gap is closed or even reversed, most notably when we speak of electoral participation, trade union membership, and political protest.

However, this general observation conceals important differences and countervailing tendencies. Thus, the demobilization of the working class is very noticeable as far as party membership is concerned, especially in Denmark and Norway, but much less so (so far, at least) in Sweden. For example, in 1971 party membership was at least as widespread among manual workers as among other social groups in Denmark, but in 1990 party membership was about twice as high among non manuals. More specifically, workers are also strongly under-represented among Social Democratic party members, as compared to their share of the parties' voters. This represents a dramatic decline, as compared to the situation around 1970 when workers were over-represented among Social Democratic party members. In Denmark, workers' share of party members declined from around 70 per cent to only one-third between 1970 and 1990. However, in Sweden workers have remained slightly over-represented among party members in general, and even among party activists, 38 per cent were manual workers by 1987. In short, as to party membership and party activity, there were no clear signs of class demobilization in Sweden around 1990 – apart from the abolition of collective party membership. Finally, it is an important observation that Scandinavian political parties stand out as the only channels of political participation that have remained strongly male-dominated, and dominated by the middle-aged and old.

In *voluntary associations* (and somewhat surprisingly this holds also for trade unions), we found some of the same socioeconomic and demographic biases as are usually found in political participation in general. However, generally speaking, these biases were not very strong, and in non-union voluntary associations there were even signs that participatory equality had been increasing. As to the gender gap in participation, a remarkable difference was found between Norway, where the gender gap was nearly closed, and Denmark, where little seems to have changed; especially at the level of office holders. This proves to be a general trend across all sorts of participation where Denmark – at least among the Scandinavian countries – stands out as a laggard in gender equality, just as has been the case with representation of women in Parliament. At the same time, it is a remarkable change that women now have higher rates of unionization than men; this is easily explainable from their occupational positions but nevertheless an important break with the past.

One could expect that the change in patterns of participation from parties and trade unions towards single-issue participation would contribute to a higher level of social inequality in participation; however, the social inequality in single-issue participation has changed very significantly, and if we take into account all sorts of social background variables, political protest or single-issue participation has in fact become one of the most socially representative forms of participation; definitely more representative than party membership.

It was also asked whether those who are active in politics are politically representative of all citizens, or whether they have political biases that give advantages or disadvantages to particular political ideas. At this point, there seems to be surprisingly little difference between the activists and the 'silent majority'. Thus, we found very little political bias in the voluntary association system; the political distribution of citizens, members, activists and office holders was nearly identical; a result which was similar in all three Scandinavian countries. Even in trade unions, where there has traditionally been a close cooperation and much overlapping membership with the Social Democratic party, office holders are politically representative of the active members. Not surprisingly, passive members are somewhat less socialist than the activists, but the main discrepancy is between members and nonmembers. However, because activists and office holders are fairly representative of the members, this suggests that the trade unions are increasingly becoming simple interest associations rather than movements: they do not give much of a socialist interpretation to members' experiences, and besides, as noted above, along with white-collar unionization, they no longer contribute much to political equality. Thus, despite high rates of membership, the Scandinavian trade unions fit quite well into the picture of class demobilization.

As for *political parties*, we also looked quite closely at the attitudes of party members towards a number of policy issues as compared to the attitudes of nonmembers. Most notably, we found that party members, at least in

Denmark, exhibit significantly more ethnic and political tolerance than nonmembers. Not surprisingly, we also found that party members scored significantly higher than nonmembers on measures of efficacy and political trust. This difference in civic attitudes between members and nonmembers may be interpreted as a sign that parties contribute to the promotion of civic values, and that the strongly declining membership of political parties, other things being equal, can to some extent be seen as a threat towards the reproduction of civic attitudes. It also means, however, that politicians nowadays do not have many opportunities to get in contact with people having 'deviant' attitudes via the political parties. This might very well be one of the explanations of the problems of communication between the political elite(s) and the electorate which has become very visible in Scandinavia in recent years, not only over immigration policy, but also over such issues as the EU where the linkage between elite and mass orientations is very weak.

Summing up on the conventional forms of politics in Scandinavia – electoral participation, political parties, voluntary associations and trade unions – there are now quite a few signs of an 'institutional sclerosis'. Participation and/or membership show signs of decline, there are signs of low and/or declining identification with parties and unions, and the class-mobilizing nature of these institutions has vanished. They are no longer vehicles for an increased social equality in political participation, compensating the lower classes for their lack of individual resources. Now, these tendencies should not be exaggerated, and in particular one cannot conclude that the ideals of 'full citizenship' are eroded because there is no *general* decline in political participation, nor a general increase in social inequality in political participation. Furthermore, and very relevant from a citizenship perspective, the gender gap is closing in all fields, except for the membership of political parties.

Among other things, there has been a certain increase in single-issue participation, and in particular, the social biases of such participation has been significantly reduced. Further, other forms of political participation (some of which are commented on below) have developed. And it is an important finding that political apathy is rare and that political engagement is increasing rather than decreasing. But long-term political commitments, in particular active commitments, seem to be declining, and participation is tending to become more particularized, more individualized, or not at all directly related to the input side of the political system. Without any pejorative connotations, the scenario of a 'spectator democracy' with engaged and conscious spectators who, however, feel little opportunity or few incentives to engage actively in the 'big democracy', may catch quite a few of the tendencies described – even though the argument should not be pushed too far because it is an attempt of a 'post hoc' interpretation rather than a carefully specified and tested proposition.

'Small' democracy

However this may be, an analysis of conventional and 'quasi-conventional' forms of political participation cannot stand alone. As mentioned, strong political forces have worked to broaden citizenship or to 'democratize all areas of social life', and the efforts to 'bring decisions closer to the people' or to those who are affected has also been seen as a remedy for problems of representation and participation in the 'big democracy'. In chapters 7 and 8 we have looked at two such areas where democratic participation has become institutionalized during the last 25 years: the workplace and public sector service institutions. Apart from simply describing this 'small-scale democracy', we have of course also been interested in analysing whether participation in these areas compensates to some extent for declining participation in the conventional forms of politics, perhaps even contributing to the mobilization of people with low levels of individual resources, or whether such institutions may unintendedly contribute to aggravating resource-determined differences in political participation.

In both the workplace, where workplace democracy in the form of employee representatives on company boards and different forms of codetermination was formally established in the mid-1970s, and in some public sector service institutions (such as schools and day care centers), where parent-dominated boards were established during the 1990s, we found high levels of participation. However, far too much emphasis have been given to these formal institutions, which may act as a vehicle for more informal participation but which have not as such made much of a difference. Thus, participation was particularly high when it came to the more individual and informal ways of seeking influence; for example, by contacting management or teachers directly. Furthermore, efficacy in these areas was high: between 60 and 87 per cent of persons who took an initiative to change things in these areas reported that they were successful. These results seems to indicate that political participation has indeed found new channels. This is very important as such: Many people participate; participation is quite evenly distributed; and people feel that they possess a considerable control over salient aspects of their own life situation.

However, exaggerated claims have sometimes been made as to the further implications of such participation. Thus, we have tested the so-called 'school of democracy' hypothesis. This hypothesis, formulated among others by Pateman (1970), states that participation at, for example, the workplace has a positive effect on participation in other political arenas; most notably on more conventional forms of politics. However, we could not detect much 'spill-over' between the aspects of 'small democracy' we have analysed, and the analysed dimensions of the 'big democracy'. In this sense, the hypothesis was disconfirmed. We found, however, elements of learning in the sense that active employees or users did seem to develop a kind of 'participatory' competence through (successful) participation. However, this competence seemed to be limited to the area in question, and is therefore a competence of a specific and non-generalizable character. Concerning social equality in participation this was only analysed concerning activists in the different public sector service institutions. Here we found surprisingly small sociodemographic differences between actives and the user groups as such, especially in the light of the significant social biases in the recruitment of, for example, school board members.

Thus, together with political protest/single-issue participation, the workplace and the public sector service institutions do indeed seem to be the places were many of the politically active citizens of today use their participatory energy. Also, these areas seem to some degree to compensate for the 'class demobilization' in the conventional forms of politics, as participation here is less socially biased than in the conventional forms. However, this 'small democracy' seems to be largely decoupled from the 'big democracy'. The 'small democracy' is mainly concerned with its own internal matters, and participation here does therefore not seem to be able to compensate for the declining participation in the conventional forms of politics. Thus, the dialogue between politicians, other decision-makers and the people does not seem to have improved much as a result of these institutional innovations.

The post-national challenge

In this book we have looked at three of the effects of post-nationalism which could seriously challenge the notion of 'full citizenship' in a Scandinavian context; namely the political consequences of labor market marginalization (which is typically explained by globalization), the citizenship effects of EU membership, and the effect of the increasing number of immigrants and refugees.

As to labor market marginalization, we have relied mainly on Danish figures as our data are from a period where only Denmark had a record of long-term mass unemployment. It came as no surprise to find that the unemployed are less politically active, and show less political interest than other citizens. However, even though unemployment plays a role in social and political participation, it is less important than factors like education or social class. Further, unemployment does not seem to be strongly related to political identities – that is, to constitute anything resembling a new political cleavage. Important factors contributing to avoid such marginalization are the unions and the welfare state. Due to the particular unemployment system, nearly all unemployed are union members, and they in fact appear less dissatisfied with their influence on the unions than the employed. In this sense, there is little 'insider'/'outsider' division in the labor market. Furthermore, the Scandinavian labor markets are much more flexible than their Continental European counterparts, due to a long tradition of active labor market policies and – in the Danish case – very low levels of job protection. Last, but most importantly, the provision of generous levels of unemployment benefit, especially high minimum levels, has been efficient in maintaining the unemployed as 'part of society'. This holds even more for the early retired, and by and large also for disablement pensioners. Thus, the Scandinavian countries are far from the threats of a 'two-thirds society' that could undermine citizenship, even though this remains as a (distant) latent danger.

The challenge of EU membership to citizenship in the Scandinavian countries is often discussed under the heading of 'democratic deficit'. We have concentrated on the citizenship aspects of this problem. Thus, we have looked at the turnout in elections to the European Parliament, European identity and solidarity, and efficacy towards the political system in the EU. Looking at the turnout in the elections for the European Parliament we found this to be very low compared to the turnout at the national elections, and in Sweden even with a declining tendency. Concerning the question of European identity we found a remarkable shift in attitudes; at least in Denmark. Thus, in 1990 there was no sign of a European identity, but in 1999 the Danes (and the Swedes) had the strongest European identities among the people in the EU countries. Also, concerning the general orientation towards the EU most of the difference between Danes and the populations in, for example, the six 'old' EU member states has disappeared. Looking at the feeling of efficacy towards the political system in the EU we found a very low level of efficacy. This, however, is not unique in a European context. None the less the contrast between efficacy at the EU and the national level is particularly striking in Scandinavia, where citizens' feeling of efficacy concerning national and local politics has normally been high. Finally, we also looked at the possible social bias in efficacy and attitudes towards EU policies in order to see whether these questions are creating a polarization between, on the one hand, an internationally oriented and self-confident elite, and, on the other hand, a big group of disempowered and apathetic citizens. Even though there is certainly a social bias in efficacy, this was not found to be bigger concerning the EU than concerning the national level. In addition, we did not find a very marked polarization in attitudes towards EU policies, even though the well educated and the politically interested have always been the most pro-EU. Drawing the threads together we can say that in a citizenship perspective the EU membership represents a real challenge for the Scandinavian member countries because it seems to represent a 'subject culture' rather than a 'participatory culture'. Compared to citizenship at the national level, citizenship at the European level is underdeveloped; in particular the low level of participation and the lack of efficacy represents a problem. Another way to state this is to say that for the

Scandinavian countries (as well as for all other member countries) the EU represents a *democratic paradox*: thus, on the one hand it seems necessary to increasingly make citizenship more and more European, in order to adequately handle the challenges of post-industrialism and post-nationalism. However, if this course is followed it seems to increase the democratic problems discussed above – at least in the short run.

From being countries with very homogeneous populations the Scandinavian countries have changed within the last 10–15 years. As a result of the arrival of different waves of immigrants and refugees Sweden and Denmark now have a proportion of foreign citizens permanently living within their territory which exceeds that of, for example, the Netherlands, and competes with that of France. The presence of such large numbers of foreign citizens puts the Scandinavian ideal of a universal 'full citizenship' to the test. This is precisely because the ideal of 'full citizenship' or the 'Scandinavian citizenship' is based not only on formal civil, political and social rights but also on the idea that everyone has resources enough, and feel confident enough to take advantage of these possibilities, and that citizenship is therefore both 'participatory and egalitarian'. In order to test whether this is also the case for immigrants and refugees, we have looked at the political participation of these groups, and also at the attitudes of the 'native' Scandinavian populations towards such participation. Concerning political participation, immigrants and refugees have the right to vote at local elections (but not at national elections) in all three Scandinavian countries after three years of residence. However, since this right was given to foreign citizens (in 1975 in Sweden, and in 1980 and 1982 in Denmark and Norway respectively) turnout has been lower than for 'natives' and steadily declining. Thus, in Sweden for example turnout was 60 per cent in 1976, 40 per cent in 1994 and 35 per cent in 1999. The reasons for this decline are nor entirely clear, but the two most likely explanations are a changed geographic composition of the group of foreign citizens with non-Europeans now constituting a bigger share of the group, and/or that foreign citizens follow the pattern of the 'natives', and chose to use their political energy in other types of political participation.

Looking at such other types of political participation we found that around 15 per cent of all immigrants are members of immigrant organizations, whereas we have no data for their participation in other types of voluntary associations. Concerning political protest behavior (signing a petition, participating in a demonstration, and so on) a 1995 Norwegian survey showed that even though immigrant participation in such activities was below the population average (except for demonstrations) immigrants were using this form of political participation to a significant degree, and performing relatively much better than concerning election turnout. We found attitudes towards immigrants and refugees to be quite ambiguous, showing both widespread hostility but also a considerable amount of tolerance. However, this is the normal situation in a European context, and the Scandinavian countries do not seem to differ much from the European pattern. Concretely, there is a widespread support for granting refugees with a residence permit full social and civil rights. However, the tolerance stops short of granting refugees and immigrants full political rights. The lack of the right to run for, and vote at national elections for immigrants and refugees with residence permits might seem like a minor flaw in the picture of 'Scandinavian citizenship'. However, when we add to this the fact that voting turnout at local elections is declining and not encouraged officially, that immigrants and refugees very rarely become members of political parties or candidates for established parties, and that governments are very reluctant towards developing real cooperative ties with immigrant associations, it is difficult to escape the conclusion that immigrants and refugees in Scandinavia are politically marginalized – far removed from the political decision-making centers.

Answering the initial question, we can say that citizenship and democracy in the Scandinavian welfare states is still exceptional but increasingly less so. There is no doubt that post-industrialism and post-nationalism have left their marks, and placed the Scandinavian countries more in the 'mainstream' of contemporary social, economic and political changes. Exceptionalism is preserved as far as the 'small democracy' is concerned, and as far as these countries are welfare states with a strong public support. Thus, they have been able to avoid social and political marginalization, except may be for immigrants and refugees, and have generally produced citizens who are politically interested and knowledgeable. However, participation in conventional forms of politics has been declining, and conventional forms of politics have lost their class-mobilizing character. Post-nationalism, especially the 'Europeanization' of politics and the increasing numbers of immigrants and refugees, has challenged the unitary character of 'Scandinavian citizenship', and the ability of the Scandinavian welfare states to adequately address these challenges. However, the Scandinavian countries are not alone in having to address these challenges, and what remains to be seen is what effects it will have on 'Scandinavian citizenship' that these challenges are increasingly discussed and solved at a European or international level.

Notes

1 Introduction

1. The tension between capitalism and democracy is a classical theme in the socialist tradition. Unlike Marx, who explicitly rejected the idea as an illusion, Marshall believed in the possibility of a 'true' (and not just formal) citizenship in a capitalist society. In the nineteenth century, the idea of citizenship as an 'unnatural practice' (Oldfield 1990a) was also reflected in the widely shared belief that even formal political citizenship – that is, the right to vote – should be restricted to the wealthy and independent citizens.

2. Alongside these traditions, a 'radical democratic' tradition (see, for example, Mouffe 1992) is sometimes described as a fifth tradition; however, this tradition may best be characterized as a mixture of liberalism and republicanism.

3. There is a considerable overlap between the discussions about citizenship in the context of welfare state theory and in the context of political participation and political culture. In welfare state theory, welfare state regimes and specific policies are often evaluated from a citizenship perspective: In particular on the basis of the social *rights* they provide (treating receivers as equal and autonomous citizens), and on the basis of their ability to provide for 'full participation' in all spheres of social life in accordance with the ways and standards of life in that society. Esping-Andersen (1990) equates 'full citizenship' with 'decommodification', that is, a situation where citizens enjoy the same status and the same opportunities to act in economic, social and political life, irrespective of their market position. However, in this book we are concerned with participation in political and public life.

4. This holds also for Easton's (1965) category of 'political support' (defined as affective orientations towards the system). And as pointed out by Almond and Verba (1963) themselves, their concepts were to a large degree derived from the notions of 'civic virtues' in the citizenship tradition. Instead of 'orientations', some modern theories of citizenship (Mouffe 1992) prefer to speak of 'identities'. But the two concepts are largely synonymous.

5. The concepts of political participation, political culture and citizenship are closely related and linked as follows: Political participation may be seen as the *fulfillment* of rights and as *practicing* the 'civic virtues'. And theories of political culture may be seen as a *specification* of some of the aspects of 'identities' and 'civic virtues' of the citizenship theories.

6. In Denmark and Norway, the mobilization of the peasantry began even before the mobilization of the working class, and unlike most Western democracies, all Nordic countries still have farmers' parties. To illustrate, at the time that Marx characterized the French peasantry as a 'sack of potatoes' unable to organize, Danish farmers began building strong political, economic and cultural institutions of their own, including (from the 1880s) the farmers' cooperative movements which gained control over manufacturing of agricultural products (and later on over much sales of materials and machines to farmers as well). By the First World War, almost all Danish farmers were organized in farmers' associations (or smallholder associations), and around one-half of the workers were organized

in trade unions which continued to grow alongside the membership rates of the political parties. In all the Scandinavian countries, the building of the welfare state from the 1930s rested on a class compromise between these two major social movements (Esping-Andersen 1990), and the very origins of the welfare system, not least the tax-financed universalism, must be traced back to reforms that rested on agrarian interests, such as the social reforms introduced in Denmark in 1891 (Baldwin 1990).

7. Tocqueville was also the first to point out how such problems could be solved; namely by creating political institutions aiming at enhancing the active participation of citizens in government, and by the formation of voluntary associations.

8. Furthermore, these studies included membership and participation in trade unions and employers' associations. In a study of youth participation, Svensson and Togeby (1986) did not include citizen contacting on purely individual issues but on the other hand extended the definition of protest activities to include such mobilizing activities as (political) rock festivals. In addition, they included political discussion and media attention, as well as trusted positions in nonpolitical interest associations.

9. In their book *Medborgarnes makt* [*Power of Citizens*] (1989) they even included the distribution of labor within the family and control over life situation as consumers. This may be going too far but it remains clear that political consumerism at least should in principle be included in a definition of political participation.

2 Political Engagement

1. Another 'issue voting' tradition, inspired by Downs (1957), has stressed the importance of economic issues in politics. On such 'valence issues', ideological disagreement is small: what matters is policy effects, and therefore operationalizations of voter rationality as 'attitude consistency' become misleading. In line with classics such as Key (1966) and Fiorina (1981), a large number of studies conclude that voters *at least* react retrospectively in a quite rational manner on such issues (Lewin 1991 surveys some of the studies).

2. This also challenges the proposition that the participation predicted by social differences in political engagement can serve as a baseline against which the effect of class-mobilizing and other institutions can be measured (Verba, Nie and Kim 1978).

3. In Scandinavia, it is an explicitly formulated goal of the basic educational system to provide children with a sense of civic competence that enables them to become active citizens. Furthermore, it is worth noting that the Scandinavian countries assign higher economic priorities to basic education than other welfare systems (Goul Andersen and Christiansen 1991).

4. There may be validity problems in the question of subjective political interest (van Deth 1989). A plausible objection is that expressing political interest may be seen as more prestigious in some social groups than in others. However, since similar social variations are found on all dimensions of political involvement, there is little reason to believe that this is any serious validity problem. The question of cross-national comparability is somewhat more difficult but there are no immediate indications that the meaning of the questions is different across countries.

5. The figure of politically uninterested declines during an election campaign. Thus, in the Swedish 1988 election survey, only 7 per cent were 'not at all' interested in politics. But the proportions of 'highly' or 'rather' interested did not exceed the figures from the 1987 citizenship survey.

6. Van Deth (1989: 283) reports standard deviations between 0.93 and 0.99 for Germany and the Netherlands, as compared to 0.71 for Norway, 0.85 for Sweden and 0.89 for Denmark. Despite the residual welfare state in the USA, however, the American figure for 1981 was lower than in Denmark: 0.87.

7. Exactly the same weak association, close to zero, was found in the 1998 Danish election survey.

8. Additional inclusion of income or vocational training as independent variables do not add to the explanation; controlled effects are typically not significant at the 5 per cent level. Basically, they lead only to a more detailed differentiation of the class variable.

9. There is a strong political interest among strong working-class identifiers, but this holds also for workers who identify with the middle class. The least politically interested are those who have weak identification with the working class or only lean towards the working class without identifying with this class.

10. From Danish data it also seems that the mobilization of political interest among workers is quite dependent on industrial conflict that links politics to the concrete material interests of workers. Further, it emerges from the 1994 election survey that workers are more guided by perceived personal economic interests in their choice of party than other classes (Borre and Goul Andersen 1997).

11. Apart from capacity problems, this is also due to the fact that profound changes in the educational system makes comparisons over time very complicated in the Swedish case.

12. Norwegian data are insufficient, and Norway furthermore lags behind in the provision of public child care.

3 Electoral Participation

1. In Denmark, Høgh (1972) and Elklit (1988) have studied electoral mobilization in the nineteenth century but apart from ecological estimates in Thomsen (1987), Jeppesen and Meyer (1964) was the only detailed study of nonvoting in the twentieth century. In Norway, nonvoting was analysed in Campbell and Rokkan (1960), SSB (1969), Martinussen (1973), Listhaug and Kindseth (1979), Valen and Aardal (1983) and Pettersen (1988, 1989). A collection of older data is found in Heidar (1983). Paradoxically, Sweden, with its very high turnout rates, has the longest research tradition on electoral participation, including classic and recent analyses such as Tingsten (1937), Korpi (1981), Holmberg (1990), SCB (1993), and Gilljam and Holmberg (1993: 62–69). Sweden has also detailed statistical information about participation in elections during most of the century (since 1960 based on survey data), some of which is reanalysed below.

2. Non-voters are typically under-represented in samples, and many non-voters report that they have voted. According to Holmberg (1984: 24; 1990: 189), some 20–30 per cent of the non-voters in the Swedish samples report that they have voted; as response rates are often only 50 to 60 per cent among non-voters as compared to some 80 per cent among voters, the proportion of non-voters in survey samples is frequently little more than one-half of the true proportions in Sweden. The Danish experience is even worse, whereas the Norwegian election surveys seem more representative at this point (Aardal 1999: 204). In the Swedish citizenship surveys, implicitly excusing nonvoting in the question wording about voting seems to have improved representativity substantially (Teorell and Westholm 1999: 141).

3. The same holds for yet another possibility: declining party identification. As we shall see in the following chapter, there is clear evidence of declining party identification in Sweden and Norway but in Denmark, party identification was very low already in 1971 when it was measured for the first time. This means that if there has also been a decline in Denmark, this took place at least a decade before the decline in turnout. A similar argument pertains to political trust (see below).

4. In Denmark, the corresponding years were 1849 and 1901; Sweden achieved a democratic constitution (but with a highly restricted franchise) in 1866 and/parliamentary rule (definitively) in 1917.

5. The Danish time series falsify an assumption that electoral participation is negatively related to the frequency of elections. This is also disconfirmed by country comparisons (figure below): In Norway, the ordinary election period is four years (since 1945), and the government does not have the right to dissolve parliament. In Sweden, the right has not been used in practice, as the ordinary election period in the period 1970–95 was only three years. In Denmark, parliament is frequently dissolved, and the average election period from 1945 to 1998 was only 2.6 years. Nevertheless, from 1960 to 1998, Norway invariably had the lowest turnout rates among the three countries.

National Elections in Norway, Sweden and Denmark

	Norway	Sweden	Denmark
Normal election period	4 years	3 years (1970–1995)	4 years
Right of government to dissolve parliament	no	yes	yes
Average election period	4 years	3 years (1970–1995)	2.6 years (1945–1998)

6. This involves the assumption that after 1960, gender differences are zero, and that farm and forest workers constitute a negligible proportion of the working class (besides, they do not differ much in participation).

7. As the Norwegian sample was confined to the 18–79 years old category, this may imply a slight exaggeration of the proportion of non-voters; however, even though people aged 80 years or more are substantially less likely to vote, their numbers are few that is, the degree of overestimation is small.

8. Especially among the younger age groups, the gender gap in Norway has become considerable. Thus in the 1997 parliamentary election, electoral participation was apparently more than 10 percentage points higher among women than among men in the age group 18–29 years (calculations from Aardal and Narud 1999: 219).

9. This changing pattern was also confirmed by a more comprehensive analysis of age variations in electoral participation in all Swedish elections in the period 1968–91 (Oscarsson 1994: 363). Compared to all previous elections, the decline in electoral participation among this age group in both the 1988 and the 1991 elections was considerably larger than the decline among those aged 35–74 years.

10. Valen, Aardal and Berglund (1996) reported increasing differences between education groups in the 1995 local election in Norway, however.

11. There could be sampling problems, however, so that the most marginalized among the unemployed do not appear in our sample; still, we may safely conclude that unemployment has negligible causal effects on the declining level of electoral participation.
12. The Swedish citizenship survey is not included because it only measured participation in municipal elections.
13. A further differentiation between age groups, or between various types of single people, does not contribute any significant and consistent patterns.
14. Simple additive index of four dichotomous or dichotomized questions which form a common factor in factor analysis. The questions were:

1. How often does it happen that you and your neighbors borrow things like food, tools, utensils etc. from each other? (often/sometimes)
   Do you have some relatives, friends or neighbors who could help you in the following:
2. In building or skilled craftsmanship.
3. To lend you a small sum of money such as 500 Kr. (70 Euro)
4. To take care of children or other family member in the event of illness.

15. The premise of increasing distrust is only fully confirmed in Sweden, however (Gilljam and Holmberg 1995: 85–7), whereas the Norwegian and Danish data are ambiguous at best (Aardal 1999: 170–3; Goul Andersen 1992b, 1993d; Borre and Goul Andersen 1997: 303; Nielsen 1999b).
16. Party identification is not included; as mentioned, it reveals a strong long-term decline in Sweden and more recently also in Norway (chapter 4); in Denmark, there was no significant change from 1971 to 1994. Thus it is not so plausible as an explanation of the common trend.
17. It may be added that in the Danish questionnaire, the value question and the question on voting were separated, appearing in the early part and towards the end of the questionnaire, respectively.
18. Taking Denmark as an example, the most important local taxes are proportional income taxes which at the county level typically amount to some 10 per cent of all income subject to tax, and at the commune level to some 20 per cent. The communes are typically refunded some 20–25 per cent of their expenses by the state (Albæk 1996). Excepting unemployment benefits and interest on the national debt, more than one-half of all public expenditure in Denmark are spent at the local level.

4 Political Parties

1. The press was typically affiliated with the political parties, and news broadcasting was largely subordinated to the press. Party control evaporated in the 1960s and the 1970s, however, partly because of new norms of journalism (Thomsen 1992; Westerståhl 1992; Søllinge 1992).
2. In Sweden and Norway, the links between the unitary trade union movement and the social democratic parties even included collective membership. In Sweden, membership declined by 75 per cent when collective membership was abandoned in 1990. In Norway, collective members constituted about one-half of the members in 1950 but had become insignificant when it was finally abandoned by 1997.

3. In Denmark, the farmers' cooperative movement controlled a very large share of the country's economy, including, for example, most manufacturing of agricultural products.

4. More or less explicitly, most attempts to classify the functions or activities of political parties refer to such a trilogy of levels or perspectives (for example, King 1969; Easton 1965).

5. The superior organizational strength of Danish parties also meant that they were able to politicize local elections earlier than in the other Nordic countries (Sundberg 1989: 290).

6. The Social Democratic Party in Finland is an exception. In the first place, because its membership increased until 1980. And secondly, because it has never been a mass movement like its Scandinavian sister parties. It has always had fewer members than any other social democratic party in Scandinavia.

7. The assumption of equivalence is confirmed by Table 4.5, which yields similar results. The Swedish data are from 1987, however, and it is unclear to what degree collective members of the SAP have perceived themselves as members. As some collective members probably have, and as party membership in Sweden declined from 1987 to 1990, the country difference may be slightly exaggerated.

8. In Denmark, the 'true' figure in 1990 was 6.5 per cent, as compared to the survey estimate of 10.6 per cent. This deviance is unaffected by weighting. In Finland, a similar discrepancy is encountered (Sundberg 1987: 34). In Sweden, overclaiming amounts to only 1–2 percentage points (Petersson et al. 1998: 58), and also the Norwegian deviation is much smaller than in Denmark (Listhaug 1989; Heidar 1983; Svåsand 1992). The deviation may be explained by (i) self-selection: the politically active are over-represented among those who accept to participate in the survey; (ii) prestige: there may be some prestige in claiming to be politically active; (iii) bad memory: people may 'forget' that they didn't pay their fees and have been excluded from the party (in Denmark typically after only one year).

9. The unorthodox implication is that if parties want more members, they should not seek to attract support among the most politically interested (for instance, by offering influence); rather, they should try to attract relative passive support members, for example, by providing cheap membership (and perhaps *some* influence).

10. The main differences are: (i) Finland always had an additional sixth party (the Swedish People's Party); (ii) apart from Finland, the Communists were only influential immediately after the Second World War; (iii) the Norwegian Liberal Party, which once gained an absolute majority of votes, was more of a counter-cultural alliance which gradually decomposed as urban liberals joined the Conservatives, while farmers and Christians formed their own parties; (iv) in Denmark, the party of the farmers is a (rightist) Liberal party whereas smallholders and urban intelligentsia joined in the centrist 'Radical Liberals'; (v) in Denmark, a small 'Justice Party' (building on the ideas of Henry George) was represented in the periods 1924–57, 1973–75 and 1977–79. In Sweden, these five parties were unchallenged until 1988 whereas other minor parties occasionally surfaced in the other countries.

11. Two Norwegian parties and three Finnish parties were represented by only one seat each.

12. In Norway and Finland, the liberals became fringe parties with only occasional representation. In Norway, 'Venstre' broke over the EC Referendum (it was reunited by 1988) and survived as a liberal green party, winning a single seat

from time to time. In Finland, 'Folkpartiet' united with the Centre Party 1982–1986. It won a single seat in 1991 but dropped out in 1995.

13. The problems of the Swedish environmentalists derive from the partial transformation of the Swedish Communists Party to a 'left-libertarian' party from the 1960s. However, as this was a gradual change from within, and as the label 'communist' was maintained until 1990, this left space for the environmentalists.

14. Bartolini and Mair (1990: 29) report that for 34 elections covered by reliable data, the correlation between net and gross volatility is r = 0.60 (if Canada is excluded, it increases to r = 0.73).

15. There are several explanations for this deviation. In the first place, 'volatility' is operationalized somewhat differently, as we have not corrected for party splits, which, we think, precisely indicate volatility of the party system. But the most important explanation is the different periodization (we have used 1950 to 1969 rather than 1945 to 1964 in order to avoid disturbing effects of the Second World War) and the inclusion of the latest figures.

16. At this point, Danish figures are probably underestimated. According to recall information, bloc volatility was only some 7–8 per cent in 1990 and 1994. Still, this is about twice the level reported in 1971.

17. By and large, this corresponds with figures from other national election studies: In countries where party identification used to be high (the USA, the UK, Scandinavia), it has declined; in countries with a tradition of low party identification (Germany, the Netherlands), it has remained low (Schmitt and Holmberg 1995: 128; Wattenberg 1990; Kolodny and Katz 1992: 883–4; Koole and van der Velde 1992: 633) – with the possible exception of Austria where party identification appears rather oscillating (Müller 1992: 39; Plasser and Ulram 1992, quoted in Müller 1993: 443).

18. The Nowegian series is based on the format used by CSES (Comparative Study of Electoral Systems) whereas The Danish and Swedish series is based on a translation and adaptation of the old Michigan question about these identities. However, in 1998 both these countries also applied the CSES format which provided a figure of 49 per cent in Denmark and 52 per cent in Sweden, as compared to 53 per cent in Norway (Holmberg 2000: 40).

19. There may be a number of other explanations as well (not the least the changes in the media structure and practices, which we have only hinted at here).

20. The effects were small but as party members are much older than the electorate at large (except in a few Mediterranean countries, see Widfeldt 1995: 152–3), the effects would be larger if associations were controlled for age (as the young are generally better educated than the old).

21. The Danish 1971 survey indicates that there used to be an even stronger negative association. However, this rests on only some 50 observations among the better-educated, and a Scandinavian survey conducted by Ingemar Glans in 1969 fails to confirm such an association. Besides, the 1994 Swedish election survey reveal a stronger *negative* association with education than the 1987 citizenship survey (Gilljam and Holmberg 1995: 182; see also Widfeldt 1995: 159 who present data from Swedish, Norwegian and Finnish election surveys 1988, 1989, and 1991 respectively).

22. If we include the 1991 distrust survey, the proportions of workers among social democratic voters and party members become 47 and 37 per cent, respectively. Equivalent findings are found in all Danish surveys. However, the Eurobarometer surveys present strongly deviating figures, both for members and for voters

(Widfeldt 1995: 157). From the marginals, it is obvious that the Eurobarometer results are wrong; but it is unclear what has produced the biased results.

23. The 1971 election survey and a comparative Scandinavian survey from 1969, conducted by Ingemar Glans.

24. We furthermore observe a movement to the right among the politically interested, among party activists and among office holders, reflecting a movement to the right among the political elite in Denmark in the 1980s and 1990s.

5   Participation in Voluntary Associations

1. The term 'voluntary associations' is used here as an umbrella for 'interest groups' and 'promotional groups', including leisure groups. Voluntary associations distinguish from political parties by not putting up candidates in elections whereas the distinction between voluntary associations and action or single-issue groups is blurred but must be defined from organizational characteristics (Gundelach 1980; see also chapter 9). However, for an individual-level analysis, we need only distinguish between *membership and participation in associations* and participation in actions. In practice, this combination does not give much overlap and does not leave out much voluntary activity.

2. Unlike most of the literature, we do *not* address the question of impact of associations on individual political participation in a narrow sense; a citizenship perspective is not about explaining variance in some dependent variable at the individual level but about the status of democracy. Nor do we examine the impact on efficacy, political trust and civic attitudes (but see, for example, Gundelach and Torpe 1997; Torpe 2000); this would be in line with a citizenship perspective our but data are rather inadequate for this.

3. Baumgartner and Walker (1988) report higher figures for the USA, but they have counted memberships rather than *types* of memberships. The assumption that the Scandinavian figures are deflated is also confirmed by the few aggregate accounts (Baumgartner and Walker 1988: 909; Petersson et al. 1989: 107).

4. Our surveys do not include questions concerning members' awareness of the interest-articulating activities of the associations (in the USA, between one-fifth and one-third of the members of cultural, local, fraternal and charity associations are aware of such activities; see Baumgartner and Walker 1988: 922).

5. In principle, it is easy to distinguish, but there are problems in deciding on the operational boundaries. Thus, we have classified housewives' associations as interest groups and women's groups as promotional groups (although, strictly speaking, they violate the openness of membership criterion). By the same token, we have classified car owners' associations as interest groups but cyclists' associations as promotional groups (this is in accordance with the openness criterion, since nearly everyone owns a bicycle but not everyone a car).

6. Some humanitarian associations are 'altruistic' charity organizations. Others are more like interest groups – for example, associations who not only raise funds to fight particular diseases but also represent the interests of patients with such diseases. Associations for fighting heart diseases or cancer lean toward the altruistic pole whereas some associations are also a sort of interest associations for chronically disabled (such as muscular atrophy associations and so on). Our Danish and Swedish data are sufficiently detailed to permit a distinction but in the present analysis this has been left out.

7. The classification of moral and religious associations as 'political' is highly problematical when we move outside Scandinavia. However, in Scandinavia, such membership usually does not denote membership of an alternative religious community, nor of charity associations, but rather membership of some association fighting for the political goals of religious people (for example, in relation to the content of public broadcasting).

8. Members and contributors of political associations are clearly aware of the political activities of such associations (Baumgartner and Walker 1988: 922).

9. A Swedish report, 'Folkrörelsesutredningen' (Ju mer vi är tilsammans, SOU 1987: 33) estimated that total membership in associations attached to some countrywide association was above 31 million. This indicates that even our survey estimates here are underestimated by nearly one-third. Even though the report included political parties among the associations and children among the members, this does not explain the discrepancy. There are three possible explanations: (i) multiple memberships: even though our lists of types of association are detailed, some persons will still be members of more than one association within each category; (ii) unreliable respondents: even though the lists are detailed, people may not recall all their memberships; and (iii) unreliable associations: the official records of the associations may be exaggerated (see also Petersson et al. 1989: 122–3).

10. The question wording, the format, the showcard and the instruction of interviewers were identical in 1979 and 1990 but with the single exception that 'general meeting' was mentioned as an example of 'meetings'. This small addition seems to have given more narrow associations for respondents.

11. The Scandinavian countries, and in particular Denmark, have had their own 'third way' version of capitalism. Cooperative movements of farmers, controlling most of the production of food as well as large sections of wholesale trade related to agriculture; the consumers' cooperative movement controlling a large section of retail trade; and the credit associations which were formerly democratic, non-profit institutions financing most long-term loans in the country. Increasingly, however, these institutions have lost their character of popular movements and have turned into 'normal' capitalist companies – de facto or even de jure as joint-stock companies.

6 Participation in Trade Unions

1. Due to the opposite effects of class structural change and LO expansion, the Danish figure has remained almost constant in the 1990s. The main difference between Denmark and Sweden is that clerical staff (and from 1994 low- and medium-level technicians and computer programmers) are affiliated with the LO in Denmark, whereas in Sweden, they typically belong to the main white-collar confederation (TCO). In Norway, the borders are more fluid, because there is more competition; white-collar confederations even organize some groups of manual workers. Another difference is that the formation of industrial unions has lagged behind in Denmark.

2. Other institutional factors include centralized bargaining and corporatism (Griffin et al. 1991), union structure (Visser 1990: 93–191), labor legislation (Troy 1986: 97–9), closed shop arrangements, and so on.

3. The question is based on false premises, because it is possible to be a member of an unemployment insurance fund without being member of a trade union. But in the minds of most people, the two are connected.

4. However, even in American public opinion, unions are recognized as necessary to protect workers' interests (Lipset 1986) so this is clearly insufficient to maintain unionization.

5. It should be noted that the Norwegian citizenship survey underestimates the proportion of trade union members in Norway by some 10 percentage points. The data are analysed under the assumption that this only has a minor impact on the associations observed. We cannot entirely rule out the possibility, however, that the under-reporting is a little stronger among the less-educated strata.

6. This had already been confirmed by the Danish 1979 survey, which revealed that the gender difference had almost disappeared among employees aged less than 40 years. But among female part-time employees aged 40 years or more, only 52 per cent were organized by 1979 (Goul Andersen 1984a: 204).

7. This is confirmed also by other sources (see the evidence compiled in Goul Andersen 1993c: 61–2).

8. The questions about affinity were not identical. In Denmark and Sweden, the feeling of affinity with various movements was measured on a scale from 0 to 10. In Norway, respondents were asked if they felt 'much', 'some' or 'no' affinity. From a *logical* point of view, all values 0–5 (5 is the center) express negative or neutral feelings i.e. 'no' affinity, whereas values 6–10 express 'some' or 'much' affinity. However, *empirical* criteria indicate that the category 5 should count as 'some' affinity: If we assume that the countries are alike in most respects but differ in a few, we should choose the solution which, *across a number of movements*, minimize the difference. Counting 5 as 'some' affinity fits this assumption. But at the same time, it is a conservative assumption as our hypotheses predict higher affinity with the labor movement in Norway than in the two other countries.

9. The question formats are not entirely identical. But from logical criteria, modified by the (conservative) assumption that Denmark and Sweden are much alike, we have recoded the two Swedish 0–10 scales to four, respectively three, categories that are commensurable with the Danish and the Norwegian surveys.

7 Workplace Democracy in Scandinavia

1. See Figure 7.1 for a definition of these concepts.

2. There are many ways to measure working-class strength. Here we will see it as especially related to membership of unions and of socialist or social democratic parties, and to participation in working-class political activity such as strikes and demonstrations. It must be remembered also that 'strength' is relative; depending also upon the strength of adversaries (here primarily the organizations of big business and agriculture).

3. The Aspengreen Committee was set up by the Norwegian LO as a response to an increased interest in worker participation from both employers and the bourgeois parties (expecting increased productivity), and from the Socialist People's Party, which had successfully made industrial democracy part of its 1961 electoral platform.

4. And to be used for educational and research purposes.

5. Such a correlation has been found in a study of industrial democracy in 11 European countries (Stymne 1982). In the same study positive correlations were also found between institutional arrangements for influence (organizational structure and norms), and actual influence.

6. The exact wording of the question can be translated as something like: 'How great do you think your possibilities are for influencing decisions about your general work conditions?' (There is a slight difference between the exact wording of the question in the Swedish and the Danish questionnaires.)
7. This question has not been asked in the Norwegian survey.
8. Here a 'natural' distinction can be made between workplaces with more and with less than 50 employees, because employees are only guaranteed representation on company boards in the latter case.
9. An obvious and easily managed distinction is between manual and non-manual employees.
10. In his excellent 1981 APSR article; see references.
11. Since both parts of the hypothesis have already been tested empirically, and verified, it might seem futile to do it once again. However, our data are very different from the data used by Elden and Greenberg. Datawise, they both have their strength in the first part of the hypothesis. Our data have their strength in the second part of the hypothesis.
12. The correlation between autonomy in job and efficacy at workplace could look like a tautology. However, we will insist on the different realities the two items represent. Thus, the first item is concerned with the degree to which wage-earners can plan and regulate their own work, while the second is concerned with how they see their influence on their workplace in general.
13. Elden finds a correlation of 0.65 between a measure (index) of self-determination at work and a measure (index) of efficacy at the workplace.
14. The correlation Elden finds between the two is 0.28; again not a very impressive correlation.
15. However, some recent analysis has shown that the 'classroom hypothesis' can be verified, with some modifications: Thus, on the basis of survey data on LO members Madsen (1997) found a strong correlation between participation in the workplace democracy and the 'big' democracy among the more collectivistically orientated members but not among those who were more individualistic. (Madsen 1997: 247).

8 User Participation in Scandinavia – the 'Third Citizenship'?

1. The breakthrough for such analysis in Scandinavia came with the Swedish Power and Citizenship Study (Maktutredningen) carried out in the period 1985–1990. The following analysis is thus much indebted to especially O. Petersson, A. Westholm, G. Blomberg (1989). See also SOU (1990: 44).
2. The first version of this chapter had a lengthy paragraph about the different theoretical perspectives on the user role, which has been excluded here. To get an idea of these perspectives see Hoff (1993), or Hoff and Stormgaard (1991).
3. The so-called SAMAK report which came in 1988 represented a swing in this direction. The SAMAK report was a joint report from the Scandinavian Social Democratic Parties on public sector reforms.
4. Lindbom (1993: 23) thus concludes, drawing especially on the experiences from the Swedish school system, that: 'During the 1970's it seems to have been much easier to further legislation concerning wage-earners and unions participatory rights than users participatory rights.'
5. 170 schools are participating in the project, which was initiated by the Swedish Social Democratic Party. The Swedish parliament (*Riksdagen*) passed a law in

1996 which constituted the legal foundation for the user boards in schools. The user boards can decide questions concerning economy, how the teachers work, the allocation of their work hours, and pedagogical instruments (Jarl 1999: 66).

6. There are other ways to conceptualize citizens' power vis-à-vis (public) organizations. However, we shall only touch briefly on these in this chapter (for an extended discussion; see Hoff 1993).

7. The theory of accessibility is originally developed by Bernard Schaffer and colleagues at the Institute of Development Studies, University of Sussex, at the beginning of the 1970s (Schaffer and Huang 1975). In the 1980s it has been used in studies of public organizations – especially in Norway (see, for example, Jensen 1986; Bleiklie et al. 1987).

8. Some have also tried to show this empirically. Especially interesting in a Scandinavian perspective is Rothstein (1987, 1990).

9. As this hypothesis was not part of the original research design, we are only able to operationalize the institutional factors in a very simple way; see below.

10. Skolverket 2000/the National Agency for Education (www.skolverket.se).

11. We have had to skip the users of the social services departments in the empirical analysis, as too many of the users did not answer the crucial questions properly. The data on employment exchange offices and social services departments are only available for Denmark.

12. We only have data from Norway and Denmark concerning this area.

13. The question we have asked in order to measure voice is whether the respondent has done anything (within the organization) to improve the treatment/ service he/she has received within the last twelve months. This way of operationalizing voice might be criticized for not distinguishing between different features of the service in question. Thus, some attempts at improving a service might be directed towards rather peripheral aspects of the service, while others will touch upon the core of the service production. We will defend ourselves by pointing out that if a user takes an initiative to improve a certain aspect of a given treatment/service this is probably because he/she sees this aspect as important. If it is true that users attach different importance to different aspects of the service, the researcher should not a priori define the importance of the different aspects.

14. We shall remind the reader, that within the tax sector users are defined as persons who have had a non-routine contact with the authorities.

15. A correlation analysis show that the correlation between dissatisfaction and voice concerning tax administrations is 0.39 and 0.29 (Pearson's r) in Denmark and Norway respectively.

16. Measured by 'per cent succeeded'/ 'per cent initiative'.

17. Measured by 'percent satisfied taking an initiative'/ 'percent satisfied'.

18. Of course some pupils also switch from private to public schools. However, the 2.9 per cent is the net loss of pupils from public to private schools. This loss seem to have been increasing from 1978 and onward.

19. In Denmark and Norway the users were asked about their general perception of their possibility to influence the services in question. In Sweden, the questionnaire was more detailed in this respect, and questions were asked about the possibility to influence various aspects of the service. However, some of the questions were almost similar to the questions asked in Denmark and Norway. We have therefore felt that it was legitimate to compare the three countries anyway. Only concerning schools were the questions too dissimilar. Here the solution has been to create an index for Sweden based on three questions.

However, it is clear that comparisons between Sweden and the two other countries must be done cautiously here in this area.

20. We are well aware that education and occupation are not normally considered as ratio or interval variables. However, in operationalizing them we have tried to construct scales moving from what is normally considered low to high education, and low to high occupational status (education: 1 = compulsory comprehensive school (7–9/10th grade), 2 = additional one year to comprehensive school, 3 = additional 3 or more years to comprehensive school)(occupation: 1 = manual worker (skilled or unskilled), 2 = non-manual employee, 3 = self-employed). For details; see Asbjørnsen, Hoff and Goul Andersen 1995, appendices 1 and 2. A test for multicollinearity shows that there is virtually no multicollinearity between the two variables in Denmark, whereas there is some for Norway and Sweden. We therefore ran the regressions also without either one or the other of the two variables. However, this did not change the results very much. The method used is the MCA analysis in SPSS; a method which is quite robust to breaches in the test assumptions.

21. The variable is constructed as a simple index, where 'yes' is given the value + 1 and 'no' the value − 1. The index thus represents a scale ranging from − 3 to + 3.

22. However, we have also tried to use the social network variable in the regression; both alone, and with the knowledge network variable. This does not alter the results very much.

23. It has not been possible to include Sweden in these analyses, because the Swedish survey did not ask the non-users of the different services about their opinions on the users' possibilities for influence.

24. The correlations have also been controlled for effects of age, gender, education and occupation (successful/unsuccessful use of voice entered in multiple regression models with these variables). This does not alter the strength of the correlations. Beta coefficients are thus between 0.21 and 0.50; all significant.

25. For a complete overview of all the areas, see tables in Hoff (1995).

26. The occupational group which is over-represented both among users of voice, and among user representatives is non-manual employees. It is debatable, of course, whether this group has a 'higher occupational status' than the self-employed. As both occupational groups are quite heterogeneous insofar as they consist of both persons with relatively low and very high incomes (and organizational power) it is not possible to settle the question without a further subdivision of both groups. Because of small numbers such subdivision is only statistically feasible concerning non-manual employees. A breakdown of the figures has been done in the case of Denmark (Hoff 1993), and show that it is especially the higher echelons of non-manual employees which are over-represented.

27. In Table 8.14 user participation is measured by an index covering the areas of health, child care and schools.

28. This result is confirmed by the correlations between participation at the different administrative areas analysed here, which were found to be small or insignificant.

29. As mentioned, the analyses in this chapter are based on the Scandinavian Citizenship Survey's conducted research between 1987 and 1990. A later Danish survey, carried out in 1998 and reported in Goul Andersen, Torpe and Andersen (2000), has replicated and even extended the questions asked in 1990. However the results from the two surveys are strikingly similar, and the 1998 results thus adds further validity to the hypotheses confirmed above (see Goul Andersen et al. 2000: 47–77).

9   Political Action and Political Distrust

1. Such figures should, of course, not be taken too literally. In the first place, it is not entirely clear what the question measures, and secondly, comparability may be less than perfect. However, the obvious reservation that there may be serious differences in meaning and interpretation of the question is contradicted by the fact that Danish figures were quite low in the 1970s, and by the similarities between the Scandinavian rankings produced by different measures.

2. However, political trust in Denmark has never returned to the 1971 level; besides, it may have declined prior to the first measurements (Listhaug 1995: 277). This is confirmed by Gallup surveys on the perceived intelligence and morals of politicians (1960–1982); surveys on government competence (conducted since 1946) also indicate that somewhat more negative evaluations have become the rule (Goul Andersen 1992b: 27, 74–5). General analyses of political distrust in Denmark are found in Svensson (1989, 1996); Goul Andersen (1992a); Nielsen (1992); Borre and Goul Andersen (1997: ch. 11); Nielsen 1999b. For the odd pattern in relation to the EU referenda in 1992 and 1993 (high trust and 'No' majority in 1992; low trust and 'Yes' majority in 1993), see Goul Andersen (1993d, 1994a) and Siune et al. (1992).

3. Gundelach (1995) presents a somewhat higher rank for Denmark, partly because his measure 'proportion with at least two forms of participation' in practice comes close to the proportion having participated in demonstrations.

4. The distinction between political parties and grass-roots organizations is more straightforward, because the latter do not run for elections. There is no sharp distinction between 'conventional' voluntary associations and grass-roots movements but one may construct ideal types that distinguish on four dimensions: (i) Organization (formal-hierarchical vs. informal-network); (ii) influence strategy (direct access to decision-makers/co-optation vs. indirect pressures via public opinion, (iii) time perspective (permanent vs. ad hoc); and (iv) scope of interest (broad vs. single-issue). Corresponding with this, we find different terms for individual participation: (i) grass-roots participation (cf. Gundelach 1995); (ii) participation in actions; (iii) participation in ad hoc groups; and (iv) participation in single issue groups.

5. One could imagine a few exceptions: Corrupt associations, or a few associations, which are able to offer (perceived) career opportunities for nearly all members.

6. The Norwegian question referred to 'political action' rather than 'political activities' in the Danish survey. This could give slightly narrower connotations but does not seem to constitute a problem in practice. In an equivalent measurement in the 1970s, the word 'action' was also used in a Norwegian survey whereas the Danish survey used the phrase 'action or activities'. Nevertheless, the figures on participation were highest in Norway (Olsen and Sætren 1980; Goul Andersen 1980). Furthermore, the Norwegian protesters turn out to be the least 'aggressive', as compared with the Swedes and the Danes (see below).

7. One might fear that including the wearing of political badges would be going too far but from the figures, it seems reasonable. In Norway, the category 'other activities' added 0.7 per cent to the total number of participants (according to the four previous activities). In Denmark, the figure was 0.6 per cent (of which wearing badges accounted for 0.3 per cent). Thus there is no reason to fear that the Danish and Swedish figures have been greately 'inflated' by the inclusion of too many categories under the heading 'other activities'.

8. In accordance with the question wording, the response categories even included ordinary party or voluntary association activity, which are entirely omitted here.
9. The Swedish questionnaire referred to 'demonstrations' instead of 'demonstrations and meetings' in Denmark and Norway. This might inflate the figures in Denmark and Norway. Indeed, one-third of the Danish respondents having participated in 'meetings and demonstrations' (that is, 5.4 per cent of all respondents) indicated in another question that they had never participated in a demonstration. However, only 1.3 per cent of all respondents were counted as participants solely because of participation in meetings and demonstrations, and among these, only 0.8 per cent had never participated in a demonstration. Thus, the aggregate figures on the proportion of participants are not inflated very much. Moreover, 7 per cent of the Swedish respondents who answered that they had participated in a demonstration answered to a later question on 'action willingness' that they would not be willing to demonstrate!
10. The category 'contact with politicians' was deleted because of technical problems with the Danish data set.
11. Based on signing a petition, economic contributions, and participation in meetings and demonstrations.
12. Because some very activist groups of public employees (such as school teachers) are placed in the 'middle group', we have also controlled for sector; however, the same relationship is found among both public and private sector employees.
13. This may reflect the more active and less Western-oriented foreign policy tradition in Sweden, but may also reflect the measurement problems referred to above: economic contributions remain a particularly widespread way of participation in this area, and our solution above may not have been radical enough.
14. Gundelach (1995), on the basis of the World Values Survey data, found a positive correlation between 'grass-roots participation' and political distrust in most countries, including Denmark. But the correlations were very low and thus basically confirm the tendency described here.
15. A number of alternative indexes were also operationalized but these turned out to produce slightly lower correlations with protest. 67 cases (out of 1968) were deleted because of incomplete answers.
16. As may be inferred from the R^2's, there are some interaction effects (which are neglected here) but the assumption of additivity is not seriously violated.
17. There seems to be a small interaction with age but this only confirms the theory of postmaterialism since the (controlled) effect of postmaterialism is largest among the younger generations.
18. Even if we control for party activity and voluntary association membership, a positive effect of postmaterialism (beta = 0.15) remains, but this is lower than the effects of all other variables except social background variables. Finally, if we include all respondents, irrespective of age and employment (coding economically inactives as inactives or students), all effects except gender effects become significant and the explained variance increases to 30 per cent.

10 Marginalization and Citizenship

1. The new underclass may appear in different guises: (i) as 'the working poor' in those countries that accept dramatic increases in social inequality; (ii) as groups with 'precarious jobs'; or (iii) as structurally unemployed in countries that maintain social protection and high minimum wages above the market values of the

labor power of the lower-qualified. In this context, we shall only address the last mentioned (see, however, Halvorsen 1999a).

2. It is noteworthy that without accepting any dramatic increase in inequality, the Nordic countries have managed to reduce unemployment very significantly (OECD 2000): by 2000, Norway has nearly full employment (about 3 per cent), Denmark has the lowest unemployment for 25 years (about 5 per cent), Sweden is recovering rapidly (5–6 per cent) and Finland more slowly from the shocks of the early 1990s (but still with unemployment close to 10 per cent).

3. Unlike disability, early retirement is usually not a matter of marginalization. At least in Denmark, where a favorable early retirement allowance was introduced in 1979 in order to fight unemployment, more and more people have chosen an early exit in order to enjoy an active retirement (Nørregaard 1996). The long-term effects of early retirement on unemployment have been estimated as small; as a welfare reform, on the other hand, it is very popular.

4. The Danish election survey included about 4000 respondents on social background variables; the Swedish election survey counted 2400 respondents; and the unemployment survey included about 1250 unemployed with at least six months of unemployment in 1994 before the interviewing took place. All surveys interviewed nationwide, representative samples.

5. From 1984 to 1991, 54 per cent of the Danish labor force was not affected by unemployment at all whereas almost 60 per cent of total unemployment was concentrated among the 10 per cent with the highest unemployment rate. 90 per cent of total unemployment was concentrated among less than one-quarter of the labor force (Husted and Baadsgaard 1995, quoted in Hummelgaard 1995: 59).

6. More generally, the modeling of interests of the unemployed in economic theory bears no resemblance to the way the unemployed themselves conceive their own interests: According to 'insider/outsider theory', outsiders should prefer to keep minimum wages and wage increases low in order to generate more jobs and in order to be able to compete for jobs with insiders. In Denmark, however, the unemployed are more interested in defending minimum wages and high wage increases than the employed (Goul Andersen 1994b). This is understandable under the institutional conditions of the unemployed in the welfare system but it means that the theory has no relevance for the understanding of the behavior of real economic actors.

7. On the other hand, there may also be some biases in the representativeness of the sample because the most socially marginalized among the unemployed may not have been reached.

8. The Danish 1994 unemployment survey, on the other hand, failed to confirm an association between duration of unemployment and participation. Unfortunately, only unpaid social work in voluntary associations was measured. Among people who had been without ordinary employment for five years, the proportion was 25 per cent; among those who had been without employment for 3–4 years, it was 22 per cent, the same proportion as among those who had become unemployed within the last one or two years (Goul Andersen 1995: 106).

9. In a situation where unemployment declines, it is possible that long-term unemployment will increasingly be concentrated among people with small resources so that we may find a stronger association; however, this is likely to reflect the selection effect: people with small personal resources participate less and are less likely to get a job.

11 'Reluctant Europeans': the Scandinavians and the Challenge of the European Union

1. Jacques Delors, the earlier chairman of the EU Commission, predicted that by 1998, 80 per cent of all national legal acts in the economic and social areas would derive from the EU system. This prediction has now been confirmed. Also, by 1993 the French Constitutional Board stated that already only around 20–25 per cent of all French legal acts were completely independent of the EU legal acts (see Majone 1994).
2. For further readings on the subject of the institutional dimensions of EU's 'democratic deficit' we suggest Weiler 1999; Andersen and Burns 1996; Schmidt 1997; Bellamy, Bufacchi and Castiglione 1995; and Joerges and Vos 1999.
3. Belgium should probably be excluded from the analysis because of its law on compulsory turnout at elections.
4. This pertains even to environmental policy and (un)employment policy, in spite of the fact that the Danish government has been very active in trying to promote joint decision-making in these fields. Less surprisingly, the Danes, the Swedes, and the Finns are also opposed to giving the EU influence over social policy.
5. Another Eurobarometer question concerning satisfaction with democracy at the European and at the national level reveals a similar pattern. As political distrust has been at a peak in Sweden in the 1990s, it comes as no surprise that the Swedes are currently less satisfied with democracy and feel less efficacious at the national level than the Danes. However, it is probably reasonable to regard Denmark as the prototypical Nordic country in this respect: As indicated in earlier chapters, the apparent stability of the Swedish political system during the 1970s and 1980s served only to conceal a legitimacy crisis which did not find an outlet as in Denmark and to some extent in Norway, and which therefore has tended to accumulate more than in the other countries.
6. With the exception of some of the very nationalistic parties on the extreme right (Denmark: Fremskridtspartiet, Dansk Folkeparti, Sweden: Ny Demokrati), which are strongly opposed to the EU.

12 Immigrants, Refugees and Citizenship in Scandinavia

1. This discussion has been especially vivid in France in connection with the reform of the Nationality Code in 1986, but is also in various forms found in the Scandinavian countries.
2. In a very interesting article Alan Butt Philip (1994) describes the immigration policy of the European Union. The jurisdiction of the Union in matters of immigration is very unclear, and most member states, especially Denmark and the UK, have been reluctant to endorse any Union regulation in this field. However, due to the urgent need of regulating immigration especially since the passing of the Single European Act in 1986, the question has become increasingly central in the EU. In the first period after 1986 it was dealt with in an ad hoc group consisting of the member countries. With the event of the Maastricht Treaty questions of asylum and immigration became a part of the Treaty in the so-called 'third pillar'; still to be regulated on an intergovernmental basis. However, with the Amsterdam Treaty these questions were moved to the 'first pillar', which means

that they are in principle regulated on a supranational level; a move which gives the EU Commission and the EU Parliament a much stronger role in the regulation of these matters. Even though a five-year 'transitory period' was agreed upon, this development will undoubtly bring about a more uniform regulation of immigration policies in the EU; signs of which it has been possible to observe since 1999.

3. Both Hammar (1990) and Layton-Henry (1990) use the term 'denizens' about the group of resident immigrants. By using this term they want to point to the fact that this group of persons is characterized by a special citizenship status; typically with rather substantial civil and social rights but with limited political rights.

4. For example in Frankfurt, the city with the highest proportion of immigrants in Germany, giving voting rights to settled foreigners is estimated to increase the electorate by more than 15 per cent (Koch-Arzberger 1992).

5. A saying goes that it was only after having read a study concluding that many immigrants were sympathetic towards social democracy (SAP), that Oluf Palme came out strongly in favor of voting rights for immigrants at local elections in Sweden (Bjørklund 1999: 155).

6. This is the normal state of affairs in all European countries. However, Britain is a case apart as it grants full voting rights (in both national and local elections) to all immigrants who are citizens of Commonwealth countries or Ireland (Miller 1989).

7. In Denmark there is no data on electoral participation by foreign citizens after 1985. The Danish Statistical Bureau have told us, that this is because 'it is not profitable to produce this kind of data'(!).

8. The study makes no distinction between naturalized and non-naturalized citizens.

9. One would expect such correlation to be clearer in Sweden than in Denmark and Norway since in Sweden elections for Parliament, and regional and municipal councils are held simultaneously.

10. 'Non-western' foreign citizens are defined as persons from Third World countries (Africa, Asia, South and Central America), Turkey and ex-Yugoslavia.

11. The data referred to are data from both the Swedish Citizenship Survey (1987), and data from the so-called 'SOM surveys' (1994). The latter have kindly been made available for us by the Swedish Social Science Data Archive on behalf of the researchers involved in the surveys.

12. Compared with data from the Citizenship Survey this figure seem somewhat exaggerated (see Table 12.4 below).

13. The same point, maybe with an even more critical edge, is made by Marco Martiniello in his review of Hoskin (1991). He writes: 'More precisely, could not opinion polls...be considered a means of constructing the public opinion which it is precisely supposed to study?' (Martiniello 1993: 205).

14. The Swedish data do not allow us to distinguish between skilled and unskilled workers.

15. Gender, on the other hand, has no importance for attitudes towards immigrants. In five out of six questions shown in Tables 12.10 and 12.11 differences between the sexes are insignificant. Party choice also does not seem very important for these attitudes, even though there are significant differences between those preferring socialist parties and those preferring right-wing parties in four out of six questions. The tendency is for those preferring socialist parties to be somewhat less hostile, and somewhat more tolerant than those preferring the rightwing parties.

16. Correlation coefficients (Pearson's r) are shown in the upper right-hand corner of the cells in Tables 12.10 and 12.11.

17. An MCA analysis in SPSS is used for these controls. Due to an error in the data file such table has been impossible to construct for Sweden.

Bibliography

Aardal, Bernt (1999) *Velgere i 90–årene*. Oslo: NKS-Forlaget (in cooperation with Henry Valen, Hanne Marthe Narud and Frode Berglund).

Aardal, Bernd and Valen, Henry (1989) *Velgere, partier og politisk avstand*. Oslo: Statistisk Sentralbyrå.

Aardal, Bernt and Valen, Henry (1995) *Konflikt og opinion*. Oslo: NKS-forlaget.

Aardal, B., Jenssen, A.T., Oscarsson, H., Sänkiaho, R. and Säynässalo, E. (1998) 'Can Ideology Explain the EU Vote?', in A.T. Jenssen, P. Pesonen and M. Gilljam (eds), *To Join or Not to Join? Three Nordic Referendums on Membership in the European Union*. Oslo: Scandinavian University Press, pp. 235–65.

Aardal, Bernt and Narud, Hanne Marthe (1999) 'Går kvinner og menn hver sin vei', in Bernt Aardal, *Velgere i 90–årene*. Oslo: NKS-Forlaget, pp. 214–35.

Aarts, Kees (1995) 'Intermediate Organizations and Interest Representation', in Hans-Dieter Klingemann and Dieter Fuchs (eds), *Citizens and the State*, Beliefs in Government, vol. 1. Oxford: Oxford University Press, pp. 227–57.

Abramson, Paul R. and Aldrich, John H. (1982) 'The Decline of Electoral Participation in America', *American Political Science Review* (hereafter *APSR*), vol. 76, pp. 227–57.

Ahlen, Kristina (1989) 'Swedish Collective Bargaining Under Pressure: Inter-Union Rivalry and Incomes Policy', *British Journal of Industrial Relations*, vol. 27, pp. 330–46.

Albæk, Erik (1996) 'Denmark', in Erik Albaek, Lawrence Rose, Lars Strömberg and Krister Stahlberg (eds), *Nordic Local Government*. Helsinki: The Association of Finnish Local Authorities, pp. 17–86.

Albeda, W. (1977) 'Between Harmony and Conflict: Industrial Democracy in the Netherlands', *Annals*, *AAPSS*, 431, May 1977.

Almond, Gabriel and Verba, Sidney (1963) *The Civic Culture. Political Attitudes and Democracy in Five Nations*. Princeton: Princeton University Press.

Andersen, Johannes (1980) 'De politiske partiers krise', *Politica*, vol. 13 no. 2, pp. 87–102.

Andersen, Johannes, Christensen, Ann-Dorte, Siim, Birte and Torpe, Lars (1993) *Medborgerskab. Demokrati og politisk deltagelse*. Herning: Systime.

Andersen, Ole Stig and Nielsen, Torben (1989) *Stem sort – Indvandrene og kommunalvalget*. Præstø: Kitab.

Andersen, S.S. and Burns, T. (1996) 'The European Union and the Erosion of Parliamentarian Democracy', in S.S. Andersen and K.A. Eliassen (eds), *The European Union: How Democratic Is It?* London: Sage.

Arter, David (1984) *The Nordic Parliaments: a Comparative Analysis*. London: Hurst.

Åsard, E. (1986): 'Industrial and Economic Democracy in Sweden: from Consensus to Confrontation', *European Journal of Political Research*, vol. 14, pp. 207–19.

Asbjørnsen, N., Hoff, J. and Goul Andersen, J. (1995) *Nordiske medborgerskabsundersøgelser*. Project on Democratic Citizenship in the Nordic Countries. Project Paper no. 3. Department of Political Science. Working Paper 1995/19. Copenhagen.

Ashenfelter, Orley and Pencavel, John E. (1969) 'American Trade Union Growth: 1900–1960', *Quarterly Journal of Economics*, vol. 83 (August), pp. 434–48.

Avey, Michael J. (1989) *The Demobilization of American Voters: a Comprehensive Theory of Voter Turnout*. New York: Greenwood.

Back, P.-E. (undated) *Sammenslutningarnas roll i politikken 1870–1919*.

Bain, George S. and Elsheikh, Farouk (1979) 'An Inter-Industry Analysis of unionisation in Berlin', *British Journal of Industrial Relations*, vol. 17, pp. 137–57.

Bain, George Sayers and Price, Robert (1980) *Profiles of Union Growth: a Comparative Statistical Portrait of Eight Countries*, Warwick Studies in Industrial Relations. Oxford: Blackwell.

Baldwin, Peter (1990) *The Politics of Social Solidarity: Class Bases of the European Welfare State 1875–1975*. Cambridge: Cambridge University Press.

Baldwin-Edwards, Martin and Schain, Martin A. (1994) 'The Politics of Immigration: Introduction', *West European Politics*, vol. 17, no. 2, pp. 1–16.

Barber, Benjamin J. (1984) *Strong Democracy: Participatory Democracy for a New Age*. Berkeley: University of California Press.

Barnes, Samuel, Kaase, Max et al. (1979) *Political Action: Mass Participation in Five Western Democracies*. Beverly Hills: Sage.

Bartolini, Stefano and Mair, Peter (1990) *Identity, Competition, and Electoral Availability: the Stabilisation of Europe Electorates 1886–1985*. Cambridge: Cambridge University Press.

Bauböck, Rainer (1994) *Transnational Citizenship: Membership and Rights in International Migration*. Aldershot: Edward Elgar.

Baumgartner, F.R. and Walker, J.L. (1988) 'Survey Research and Membership in Voluntary Associations', *American Journal of Political Science*, vol. 32, no. 4, pp. 908–28.

Beaumont, P.D. and Harris, R.I.D. (1991) 'Trade Union Recognition and Employment Contraction, Britain, 1980–1984', *British Journal of Industrial Relations*, vol. 28, pp. 267–70.

Beck Jørgensen, T. (1992) 'Brugere og organisationer', in Torben Beck Jørgensen and Preben Melander (eds), *Livet i offentlige organisationer*. Copenhagen: Jurist- og Økonomforbundets Forlag.

Bellamy, R., Bufacchi, V. and Castiglione, D. (eds) (1995) *Democracy and Constitutional Culture in Union of Europe*. London: Lothian Foundation.

Bennulf, Martin and Hedberg, Per (1999) 'Utanför demokratin. Om det minskade valdeltagandets sociala och poliska rötter', in Erik Amnå (ed.), *Valdeltakande i förändring*. Demokratiutredningens forskarvolym XII, SOU 1999:132. Stockholm: SOU/Fakta Info Direkt, pp. 75–136.

Bergqvist, Christina et al. (eds) (1999) *Likestilte demokratier? Kjønn og politikk i Norden*. Oslo: Universitetsforlaget.

Bertl, W., Rudak, R. and Schneider, R. (1988) *Arbeitnehmerbewusstsein im Zeichen des technischen und sozialen Wandels*. Düsseldorf: Hans Böckler Stiftung.

Bild, T., Christensen, B. and Hoff, J. (1992) *Blæksprutterne, stjernerne og de stille eksistenser*. Copenhagen: HK-forlag.

Bild, Tage and Hoff, Jens (1988) 'Party System and State Dependents'. Working paper. Department of Political Science, University of Copenhagen.

Bild, Tage, Jørgensen, Henning; Lassen, Morten and Madsen, Morten (1993) *Fællesskab og forskelle. Sammenfatningsrapport fra APL-Projektet*. Aalborg: CARMA and LO.

Bille, Lars (1992) *Party Organizations: a Data Handbook on Party Organizations in Western democracies*, edited by Richard S. Katz and Peter Mair. London: Sage.

Bille, Lars (1997) *Partier i forandring. En analyse af danske partiorganisationers udvikling 1960–1995*. Odense: Odense University Press.

Björklund, Anders and T. Eriksson (1998) 'Unemployment and Mental Health: Evidence from Research in the Nordic Countries', *Scandinavian Journal of Social Welfare*, vol. 7, pp. 219–35.

Bjørklund, Tor (1999) *Et lokalvalg i perspektiv. Valget 1995 i lys av sosiale og politiske endringer.* Oslo: Tano Aschehoug.

Bleiklie, I. et al. (1987) 'Forvaltningen og den enkelte', in Leif Skare (ed.), *Forvaltningen i samfundet.* Oslo: Tano.

Bogason, P. (1990/91) 'Danish Local Government', in Joachim Jens Hesse (ed.), *Local Government and Urban Affairs in International Perspective.* Baden-Baden: Nomos Verlagsgesellschaft, pp. 261–90.

Borchorst, A. (1993) 'Working Lives and Family Lives in Western Europe', in S. Carlsen, and J.E. Larsen (eds), *The Equality Dilemma.* Ligestillingsrådet. Copenhagen.

Børn og Unge (1993), vol. 24, no. 20.

Borre, Ole (1980) 'Electoral Instability in Four Nordic Countries, 1950–1977', *Comparative Political Studies*, vol. 13, no. 2, pp. 141–71.

Borre, Ole (1986) 'The Danish referendum on the EC Common Act', *Electoral Studies*, vol. 5, pp. 189–93.

Borre, Ole and Goul Andersen, Jørgen (1997) *Voting and Political Attitudes in Denmark.* Aarhus: Aarhus University Press.

Boyd, Richard W. (1981) 'Decline of US Voter Turnout: Structural Explanations', *American Politics Quarterly*, vol. 9(2), pp. 133–59.

Brubaker, William R. (1989) 'Introduction', in William R. Brubaker (ed.), *Immigration and the Politics of Citizenship in Europe and North America.* Lanham, MD: University Press of America.

Bruun, Inger (1995) *Statistik om indvandrere og flygtninge 1995.* København: Mellemfolkeligt Samvirke.

Büchner, Bernd (1993) *Die Europäische Gemeinschaft in der öffentlichen Meinung. Dänemark, Grossbritannien, Italien und die Bundesrepublik Deutschland im Ländervergleich.* Firenze: European University Institute.

Buksti, Jacob (1989) 'Partiapparaternes rolle og udvikling', *Politica*, vol. 21, pp. 279–87.

Buksti, Jacob A. and Johansen, Lars Nørby (1978) *Organisationernes Hvem – Hvad – Hvor.* Copenhagen: Politikens Forlag.

Burnham, Walter Dean (1980) 'The Appearance and Disappearance of the American Voter', in Richard Rose, *Electoral Participation.* Beverly Hills: Sage, pp. 35–73.

Campbell, Angus, Converse, Philip E., Miller, Warren E. and Stokes, Donald E. (1960) *The American Voter.* New York: Wiley.

Campbell, Angus and Rokkan, Stein (1960) 'Citizen Participation in Political Life: Norway and the United States', *International Science Journal*, vol. 12(1), pp. 69–99.

Carle, Jan and Julkunen, Ilse (eds) (1997) *Arbetslöshetens villkor – om ungdom, arbetslöshet och marginalisering i 1990-talets Norden.* Copenhagen: Nordiska Ministerrådet.

Castles, Stephen and Miller, Mark (1993) *The Age of Migration.* London: Macmillan.

Converse, Philip E. (1964) 'The Nature of Belief Systems in Mass Publics', in David E. Apter (ed.), *Ideology and Discontent.* Glencoe, IL: The Free Press, pp. 206–61.

Copenhagen Statistical Office (1993) *Orientering fra Københavns Statistiske Kontor. Valget til Københavns borgerrepræsentation den 16.november 1993.* København.

Crouch, Colin (1990) 'The Future Prospects for Trade Unions in Western Europe', *Political Quarterly*, vol. 57, no. 1, pp. 5–17.

Curtis, James E., Grabb, Edward G. and Baer, Douglas E. (1992) 'Voluntary Association Membership in Fifteen Countries: a Comparative Analysis', *American Sociological Review*, vol. 57, pp. 139–52.

Dahl, R.A. (1985) *A Preface To Economic Democracy*. Berkeley: Quantum Books.

Dahl, R.A. (1986) *Democracy, Liberty and Equality*. Oslo.

Dahl, Robert A. (1989) *Democracy and its Critics*. New Haven: Yale University Press.

Dahrendorf, Ralf (1994) 'The Changing Quality of Citizenship', in Bart van Stenbergen (ed.), *The Condition of Citizenship*. London: Sage, pp. 10–19.

Dalgaard, N. (1992) *Den industrielle parlamentarisme. Arbejdslivets demokratisering som teoretisk og politisk problem*. Ph.D. thesis. Institute of Political Science. University of Aarhus, Denmark.

Dalgaard, N. (1993) 'Debatten om økonomisk demokrati i Danmark og Sverige', *Politica*, vol. 25, no. 3.

Dalton, Russell J. (1988) *Citizen Politics in Western Democracies: Public Opinion and Political Parties in the United States, West Germany, and France*. Chatham, NJ: Chatham House.

Damgaard, Erik (1974) 'Stability and Change in the Danish Party System over Half a Century', *Scandinavian Political Studies*, vol. 9, pp. 103–25.

Damgaard, Erik (ed.) (1980) *Folkets veje i dansk politik*. Copenhagen: Schultz.

Danish Ministry of Finance (1990) *Borgernes og virksomhedernes vurdering af den offentlige sektor*.

Danish Ministry of Finance (1992) *Borgernes frie valg*.

Danmarks Statistik (1997) *Statistiske efterretning 1997: 7*

Danmarks Statistik (1992) *Levekår i Danmark 1992*. Copenhagen: Danmarks Statistik.

Delamotte, Y. (1977) 'The "Reform of the Enterprise" in France' *Annals, AAPSS*, no. 431, May 1977.

Derber, M. (1977) 'Collective Bargaining: the American Approach to Industrial Democracy', *Annals, AAPSS*, no. 431, May 1977.

Djupsund, Göran and Svåsand, Lars (eds) (1990) *Partiorganisasjoner: Strukturer och processer i finske, norske og svenske partier*. Åbo: Åbo Academy Press.

Dokras, U. (1990) *Act on Codetermination at Work – an Efficacy Study*. Stockholm: Almqvist & Wiksell International.

Downs, Anthony (1957) *An Economic Theory of Democracy*. New York: Harper & Row.

Duit, A. and T. Möller (1997) *Demokrati på prov. Erfarenheter av försöksverksamhet med föräldrastyrdastyrda skolor*. Rapport to Skolverket.

Duverger, Maurice (1954) *Political Parties*. London: Methuen.

Dworkin, R. (1981a) 'What is Equality? Part 1. Equality of Welfare', *Philosophy and Public Affairs*, vol. 10, no. 3, pp. 185–216.

Dworkin, R. (1981b) 'What is Equality? Part 2. Equality of Resources', *Philosophy and Public Affairs*, vol. 10.

Easton, David (1965) *The Political System*. New York: Alfred A. Knopf.

Elden, J.M. (1979) 'Three Generations of Work Democracy Experiments in Norway: Beyond Classical Socio-Technical Systems Analysis', in Gary Cooper and Enid Mumford (eds), *The Quality of Working Life: the European Experiment*. London. Associated Business Press.

Elden, J.M. (1981) 'Political Efficacy at Work: the Connection Between More Autonomous Forms of Workplace Organization and a More Participatory Politics', *The American Political Science Review*, vol. 75, pp. 43–58.

Elklit, Jørgen (1988) *Fra åben til hemmelig afstemning. Aspekter af et partisystems udvikling*. Aarhus: Forlaget Politica.

Elklit, Jørgen (1991) 'Faldet i medlemstal i danske politiske partier', *Politica*, vol. 23, pp. 60–83.

Epstein, Leon D. (1975) 'Political Parties', in F.I. Geenstein and N.W. Polsby (eds), *Non-governmental Politics*, Handbook of Political Science, vol. 4. London: Addison-Wesley, pp. 229–77.

Eriksen, E.O. (2000) 'Deliberative supranationalism in the EU', in E.O. Eriksen and J.E. Fossum (eds), *Democracy in the European Union. Integration through Deliberation?* London: Routledge, pp. 42–64.

Esping-Andersen, Gösta (1990) *The Three Worlds of Welfare Capitalism*. Cambridge: Polity Press.

Esping-Andersen, Gøsta (1999) *Social Foundations of Postindustrial Economies*. Oxford: Oxford University Press.

Eurobarometer 37 (1992). Published by Commission of the European Communities.

Eurobarometer 39 (1993). Published by Commission of the European Communities.

Eurobarometer Opinion Poll no. 47.1 (1997) published by Commission of the European Communities.

European Commission (1995) *Employment in Europe 1994*. Brussels: European Commission.

Even, William E. and Macpherson, David A. (1990) 'Plant Size and the Decline of Unionism', *Economic Letters*, vol. 32, pp. 393–8.

Faist, Thomas (1994) 'How to Define a Foreigner? The Symbolic Politics of Immigration in German Partisan Discourse, 1978–92', *West European Politics*, vol. 17, no. 2, pp. 50–71.

Fiorina, Morris (1981) Retrospective Voting in American National Elections. New Haven: Yale University Press.

Flyvbjerg, Bent (1991) *Rationalitet og magt*. Odense: Akademisk Forlag.

Franklin, Mark N. (1996) 'Electoral Participation' in Lawrence LeDuc, Richard G. Niemi and Pippa Norris (eds), *Comparing Democracies: Elections and Voting in Global Perspective*. Thousand Oaks: Sage, pp. 216–35.

Freeman, Richard B. (1988) 'Contraction and Expansion: the Divergence of Private Sector and Public Sector Unionism in the United States', *Journal of Economic Perspectives*, vol. 2 (spring), pp. 63–88.

Freeman, Richard B. (1989) *On the Divergence in Unionism Among Developed Countries*, Working Paper no. 2817, National Bureau of Economic Research, January 1989.

Fridberg, Torben (1994) *Kultur- of fritidsaktiviteter 1993*, Report 94:6. Copenhagen: The Danish National Institute of Social Research.

Fridberg, Torben (2000) *Kultur- og fritidsaktiviteter 1999*. Copenhagen: Socialforskningsinstituttet.

Fürstenberg, F. (1977) 'West German Experience with Industrial Democracy', *Annals*, AAPSS, no. 431, May 1977.

Gaasholt, Øystein and Lise Togeby (1995) *I syv sind – Danskernes holdninger til flygtninge og indvandrere*. Aarhus: Politica.

Galenson, William (1952) *The Danish System of Labour Relations*. Cambridge, Mass: Westheim Fellowship Publications.

Gallagher, Michael, Laver, Michael and Mair, Peter (1992) *Representative Government in Western Europe*. New York: McGraw-Hill.

Gallie, Duncan and Paugam, Serge (eds) (2000) *Welfare Regimes and the Experience of Unemployment in Europe*. Oxford: Oxford University Press.

Gilljam, Mikael and Holmberg, Sören (1993) *Väljarna inför 90-talet*. Stockholm: Norstedts Juridik.

Gilljam, Mikael and Holmberg, Sören (1995) *Väljarnas val*. Stockholm: Norstedts Juridik/Fritzes.

Glans, Ingemar (1993) *Det stabila klassröstandet. Utvecklingen i Danmark och Sverige.* Aarhus: Institut for Statskundskab, Aarhus Universitet. Paper presented to the Nordisk Statskundskabskonference, Oslo, August 1993.

Goul Andersen, Jørgen (1979) *Mellemlagene i Denmark*. Aarhus: Forlaet Polg.

Goul Andersen, Jørgen (1980) 'Deltagelse i græsrodsaktioner', in Erik Damgaard (ed.), *Folkets veje i dansk politik*. Copenhagen: Schultz, pp. 102–40.

Goul Andersen, Jørgen (1981a) *Teknisk Rapport. Forenings- og samfundslivet i Danmark*. Aarhus: Department of Political Science, Aarhus University.

Goul Andersen, Jørgen (1981b) 'Græsrodsbevægelser – en indkredsning'. *Grus*, no. 3, 1981, pp. 7–37.

Goul Andersen, Jørgen (1984a). *Kvinder og politik*. Aarhus: Forlaget Politica.

Goul Andersen, Jørgen (1984b) 'Udviklingen i sociale modsætningsforhold frem mod år 2000', in J. Goul Andersen, Finn Kenneth Hansen and Ole Borre, *Konflikt og tilpasning*. Egmont Fondens Fremtidsstudie no. 3, Copenhagen: Aschehoug, pp. 13–89.

Goul Andersen, Jørgen (1984c) 'Aspekter af den politishe kultur i Danmark efter 1970', in E. Damgaard (ed.), *Dansk demokrati under forandring*. Copenhagen: Schultz, pp. 17–49.

Goul Andersen, Jørgen (1992a) 'The Decline of Class Voting Revisited', in Peter Gundelach and Karen Siune (eds), *From Voters to Participants: Essays in Honour of Ole Borre*. Aarhus: Politica, pp. 91–107.

Goul Andersen, Jørgen (1992b) *Politisk mistillid i Danmark*. Aarhus: Department of Political Science/The Rockwool Foundation Research Unit.

Goul Andersen, Jørgen (1992c) 'Årsager til mistilid', in Jørgen Goul Andersen, Hans Jørgen Nielsen, Niels Thomsen and Jørgen Westerståhl, *Vi og Vore politikere*. Copenhagen: Spektrum: The Rockwool Foundation, pp. 161–202.

Goul Andersen, Jørgen (1993a) 'Samfundssind og egennytte'. *Politica*, vol. 25, no. 2, pp. 163–88.

Goul Andersen, Jørgen (1993b) *Politik og samfund i forandring*. Copenhagen: Columbus.

Goul Andersen, Jørgen (1993c) 'Politisk deltagelse i 1990 sammenlignet med 1979', in Johannes Andersen, Ann-Dorte Christensen, Kamma Langberg, Birte Siim and Lars Torpe, *Medborgerskab. Demokrati og politisk deltagelse*. Herning: Systime, pp. 45–74.

Goul Andersen, Jørgen (1993d) 'Udviklingen i den politiske tillid, 1991–1993'. Working Paper, The Rockwool Foundation Research Unit/Department of Political Science, University of Aarhus.

Goul Andersen, Jørgen (1994a) 'Danskerne og Europa: Skillelinjer, motiver og politisk kultur', in Jon Bingen and Rutger Lindahl (eds), *Nordiske skjebnevalg?* Oslo: Europa-programmet, pp. 143–69.

Goul Andersen, Jørgen (1994b) 'Samfundsøkonomi, interesser og politisk adfærd', in Eggert Petersen et al., *Livskvalitet og holdninger i det variable nichesamfund*. Aarhus: Department of Psychology, Aarhus University/Aarhus University Press, pp. 15–136.

Goul Andersen, Jørgen (1994c) 'Skal ledigheden bekaempes ved at satse på sevicesektoren', *FA/Årsberetning* 1993–94, pp. 12–17.

Goul Andersen, Jørgen (1995) *De ledige ressourcer*. Copenhagen: Mandag Morgen.

Goul Andersen, Jørgen (1996a) 'Marginalisation, Citizenship and the Economy: the Capacity of the Universalist Welfare State in Denmark', in Erik Oddvar Eriksen and Jørn Loftager (eds), *The Rationality of the Welfare State*. Oslo: Universitetsforlaget, pp. 155–202.

Goul Andersen, Jørgen (1996b) 'Hvordan skal arbejdsløsheden bekæmpes?', in Eggert Petersen et al., *Danskernes trivsel, holdninger og selvansvarlighed under 'opsvinget'. Træk af den politisk-psykologiske udvikling 1982–86–88–90–94*. Aarhus: Department of Psychology, Aarhus University/Aarhus University Press, pp. 169–258.

Goul Andersen, Jørgen (1998) *Borgerne og Lovene*. Aarhus: Aarhus University Press and the Rockwool Foundation Research Unit (chap. 2).

Goul Andersen, Jørgen (1999) 'Changing Labour Markets, New Social Divisions and Welfare State Support: Denmark in the 1990s', in Stefan Svallfors and Peter Taylor-Gooby (eds), *The End of the Welfare State? Responses to state retrenchment*. London: Routledge, pp. 13–33.

Goul Andersen, Jørgen (2000) *Work and Citizenship. Unemployment and Unemployment Politics in a Social Democratic Welfare State*. Paper presented at COST A13 Working group on Unemployment seminar, University of Munich, 31 March–1 April 2000. Aalborg: Centre for Comparative Welfare State Studies, Aalborg University.

Goul Andersen, Jørgen and Bjørklund, Tor (1990) 'Structural Changes and New Cleavages: The Progress Parties in Norway and Denmark', *Acta Sociologica*, vol. 33, no. 3, pp. 195–217.

Goul Andersen, Jørgen and Bjørklund, Tor (2000) 'Radical right-wing populism in Scandinavia: From tax revolt to neo-liberalism and xenophobia', in Paul Hainsworth (ed), *The Politics of the Extreme Right: From the Margins to the Mainstream*. London and New York: Pinter, pp. 193–223.

Goul Andersen, Jørgen, Buksti, Jacob A. and Eliassen, Kjell (1980) 'Deltagelsesmønstre og politisk mistillid', in Erik Damgaard (ed.), *Folkets veje i dansk politik*. Copenhagen: Schultz, 208–53.

Goul Andersen, Jørgen and Christiansen, Peter Munk (1991): *Skatter uden velfærd. De offentlige udgifter i international belysning*. Copenhagen: Jurist-og Økonomforbundets Forlag.

Goul Andersen, Jørgen and Hoff, J. (1992) '"Reluctant Europeans" and the European Union: Citizenship and Democratic Deficit'. Working Paper 1992/4. Institute of Political Science, University of Copenhagen.

Goul Andersen, Jørgen and Hoff, J. (1995) 'Lighed i den politiske deltagelse', in M. Madsen, H.J. Nielsen and G. Sjöblom (eds), *Demokratiets mangfoldighed: Tendenser i danskpolitik*. Copanhagen: Politiske Studier, pp. 30–76.

Goul Andersen, Jørgen, Hans Jørgen Nielsen, Niels Thomsen and Jörgen Westerståhl (1992) *Vi og vore politikere*. Copenhagen: Spektrum/The Rockwool Foundation.

Goul Andersen, Jørgen et al. (1998) *Unemployment, early retirement and citizenship: Marginalisation and integration in the Nordic Countries*. CCWS Working Paper.

Goul Andersen, Jørgen, Torpe, Lars and Andersen, J. (2000) *Hvad folket Magter. Demokrati, magt og of magt*. Copenhagen: Jurist-og Økanomforbundets forlag.

Goul Andersen, Jørgen, Munk, Martin and Clement, Sanne Lund (forthcoming) *Ulighed, polarisering, demokrati* (working title). Copenhagen: Magtudredningen/Hans Reitzels Forlag.

Gramsci A. (1971) *Selections from the Prison Notebooks of Antonio Gramsci*. London: Lawrence & Wishart.

Granberg, Donald and Holmberg, Sören (1991) 'Election Campaign Volatility in Sweden and the United States', *Electoral Studies*, vol. 10, pp. 208–30.

Green, Francis (1992) 'Recent Trends in British Trade Union Density: How Much of a Compositional Effect?', *British Journal of Industrial Relations*, vol. 30, no. 3 pp. 445–58.

Greenberg, E.S. (1981) 'Industrial Democracy and the Democratic Citizen', *The Journal of Politics*, vol. 43, pp. 964–81.

Greve, A. (1976) *Trade unions and industrial democracy*. Institute for Work Psychology and Personnel Relations, Working and Discussion Papers no. 7. The Norwegian School of Economics and Business Administration. Bergen. Norway.

Griffin, Larry J. Botsho, Christopher, Wahl, Ana-Maria and Isaarc, Larry W. (1991) 'Theoretical Generality, Case Peculiarity: Qualitative Comparative Analysis of Trade Union Growth and Decline, *International Journal of Comparative Sociology*, vol. 32 (1–2), pp. 110–36.

Griffin, Larry J., McCammon, Holly J. and Botsko, Christopher (1990) 'The "Unmaking" of a Movement? The Crisis of U.S. Trade Unions in Comparative Perspective', in Maureen T. Halinan, David M. Klein and Jennifer Glass (eds), *Change in Societal Institutions*. New York: Plenum Press, pp. 169–94.

Grønnegård Christensen, J. (1992) *Den usynlige stat*. Copenhagen: Gyldendal.

Gundelach, Peter (1980) Grœsrødder er seje. Aarhus: Forlaget Politica.

Gundelach, Peter (1995) 'Grass-Roots Activity', in Jan W. van Deth and Elinor Scarbrough (eds), *The Impact of Values*, Beliefs in Government, vol. 4. Oxford: Oxford University Press, pp. 412–40.

Gundelach, Peter and Riis, Ole (1992) *Danskernes værdier*. Copenhagen: Forlaget Sociologi.

Gundelach, Peter and Torpe, Lars (1997) 'Social Reflexivity, Democracy and New Types of Citizen Involvement in Denmark,' in Jan W. van Deth (ed.), *Private Groups and Public Life* London: Routledge.

Gustafsson, G. (1990/91) 'Swedish Local Government', in Joachim Jens Hesse (ed.), *Local Government and Urban Affairs in International Perspective*. Baden-Baden: Nomos Verlagsgesellschaft, pp. 241–60.

Gustavsen, B. and Hunnius, G. (1981) *New Patterns of Work Reform. The Case of Norway*. Oslo: Universitetsforlaget.

Habermas, Jürgen (1962) *Strukturwandel der Öffentlichkeit*. Danish transl. *Borgerlig offentlighet* (1980). Copenhagen: Fremad/Norsk Gyldendal.

Habermas, Jürgen (1981) *Theorie des Kommunikativen Handelns*, 1–2. English transl. *The Theory of Communicative Action* (1987). Cambridge: Polity Press.

Habermas, Jürgen (1992) 'Citizenship and National Identity', *Praxis International*, vol. 12, no. 1, pp. 1–19.

Habermas, Jürgen (1994) 'Citizenship and National Identity', in Bart van Stenbergen (ed.), *The Condition of Citizenship*. London: Sage, pp. 20–35.

Halvorsen, Knut (1994) *Arbeidsløshet og arbeidsmarginalisering – levekår og mestring*. Oslo: Universitetsforlaget.

Halvorsen, Knut (1995) *Virker velferdsstaten? Arbeidsmarginalisering og levekår. Sluttrapport*, HiÖ-rapport 1995:5. Oslo: Oslo College.

Halvorsen, Knut (1999a) *Unemployment in Disguise: The case of Norway*, CCWS Working Paper 1999:2, Department of Economics, Politics and Public Administration, Aalborg University.

Halvorsen, Knut (1999b) 'Impact of very long-term unemployment on self-esteem and psychological distress: Suffering depends on society attitude', in Knut Halvorsen, *Arbeidsløshet som sosialt problem*, HiO-rapport 1999:13. Oslo: Oslo College.

Halvorsen, Knut (1999c) *Labour force status of married/cohabiting couples in Norway: Associations and explanations of (un)employment homogamy*, CCWS Working Paper 1999:3, Department of Economics, Politics and Public Administration, Aalborg University.

Hammar, Tomas (1979) *Det första invandrarvalet*. Stockholm: Publica.

Hammar, Tomas (1990) *Democracy and the Nation State*, Research in Ethnic Relations Series. Aldershot: Avebury.

Hammar, Thomas (1991) '"Cradle of Freedom on Earth": Refugee Immigration and Ethnic Pluralism', *West European Politics*, vol. 14, no. 3, pp. 182–97.

Hammar, Tomas and Kerstin Lindby (1979) *Swedish Immigration Research – Introductory Survey and Annotated Bibliography*. Stockholm: The Swedish Commission on Immigration Research.

Hammer, Ole and Inger Bruun (1992) *Grænser for indflydelse*. En undersøgelse af indvandrernes politisk indflydelseskanaler i de nordiske lande udført for Nordisk Ministerråd (projekt 41.06.16.00). Copenhagen: Mellemfolkeligt Samvirke.

Hammer, Torild (1997) 'De arbeidslediges økonomi', in Jan Carle and Ilse Julkunen (eds) (1997) *Arbetslöshetens villkor – om ungdom, arbetslöshet och marginalisering i 1990-talets Norden*. Copenhagen: Nordiska Ministerrådet, pp. 155–72.

Hancke, Bob (1991) 'The Crisis of National Unions: Belgian Labor in Decline', *Politics and Society*, vol. 19, no. 4, pp. 463–87.

Hansen, T. (1990/91) 'Norwegian Local Government: Stability Through Change', in Joachim Jens Hesse (ed.), *Local Government and Urban Affairs in International Perspective*. Baden-Baden: Nomos Verlagsgesellschaft, pp. 211–70.

Heckscher, G. (1984) *The Welfare State and Beyond*. Minneapolis: University of Minnesota Press.

Heidar, Knut (1983) *Norske politiske fakta 1884–1992*. Oslo: Universitetsforlaget.

Hernes, Helga (1988) 'Scandinavian Citizenship', *Acta Sociologica*, vol. 31, no. 3, pp. 199–215.

Hernes, Gudmund and Martinussen, Willy (1980) *Demokrati og politiske ressurser*. NOU 1980:7. Oslo: Statens Trykningskontor/Universitetsforlaget.

Hine, Davis (1986) 'Leaders and Followers: Democracy and Manageability in the Social Democratic Parties of Western Europe', in William E. Paterson and Alistair H. Thomas (eds) (1986) *The Future of Social Democracy*. Oxford: Clarendon Press, pp. 261–90.

Hirsch, Barry T. and Addison, John T. (1986) *The Economic Analysis of Unions: New Approaches and Evidence*. Boston: Allen & Unwin.

Hirschmann, A.O. (1970) *Exit, Voice and Loyalty: Responses to Decline in Firms, Organizations and States*. Oxford: Oxford University Press.

Høgh, Erik (1997) *Vaelgeradfrerd i Danmarh 1849–1901*. Copenhagen: Jørgen Paludans Forlag.

Hoff, J. (1993) 'Medborgerskab, brugerrolle og magt' in Johannes Andersen et al., *Medborgerskab – demokrati og politisk deltagelse*. Systime: Herning, pp. 75–106.

Hoff, J. (1994) 'EC's Regional Policy in Denmark: The Implementation of a Policy', Unpublished paper, Institute of Political Science, Copenhagen.

Hoff, J. (1995) 'Micropower: the Politics of Welfare State Roles – User Participation in Scandinavia', *Institut for Statskundskab Arbejdspapir, 1995/17*.

Hoff, J. and Sørensen, E. (1989) 'Moderniseringen af den offentlige sektor – magt, demokrati og diskurs', *GRUS*, no. 29, pp. 81–104.

Hoff, J. and Stormgaard, K. (1991) 'Information Technology Between Citizen and Administration', *Informatization and the Public Sector*, vol. 1, no. 3, pp. 213–35.

Hofstede, G. (1984) *Culture's Consequences: International Differences in Work-Related Values*. Beverly Hills, London and New Delhi: Sage.

Holmberg, Sören (1974) 'Riksdagen representerar svenska folket'. *Empiriska studier i representativ demokrati*. Lund: Studentlitteratur.

Holmberg, Sören (1984) *Väljare i förändring*. Stockholm: Liber.

Holmberg, Sören (1990) *Rött, Blått, Grönt. En bok om 1988-års riksdagsval*. Stockholm: Bonniers.

Holmberg, Sören (1990) 'Att rösta eller inte rösta', i Mikael Gilljam and Sören Holmberg, *Rött, Blått, Grout, En bat om 1988 års rihsdagsval*. Stockholm: Bonniers, pp. 186–215.

Holmberg, Sören (1992) 'The Undermining of a Stable Party System', in Peter Gundelach and Karen Siune (eds), *From Voters to Participants: Essays in Honour of Ole Borre*. Aarhus: Politica, pp. 22–36.

Holmberg, Sören (1998) 'The Extent of European Integration', in Anders Todal Jenssen, Pertti Pesonen and Mikael Gilljam (eds), *To Join or Not to Join?: Three Nordic Referendums on Membership of the European Union*. Oslo: Scandinavian University Press, pp. 269–83.

Holmberg, Sören (2000). *Välja parti*. Stockholm: Norstedts Juridik.

Horvat, B. (1977) 'Debate on the Transition to Workers Management in the Advanced Capitalist Countries', *Economic Analysis and Workers Management*, vol. 11, no. 3/4.

Hoskin, Marilyn (1991) *New Immigrants and Democratic Society: Minority Integration in Western Democracies*. New York: Praeger.

Hummelgaard, Hans (1995) 'Polarisering af velfærdssamfundet', in *Social Forskning. temanummer om velfærdsstatens fremtid*. Copenhagen: Socialforskningsinstituttet, pp. 55–60.

Husted, Leif and Baadsgaard, Mikkel (1995) *Uddannelse og ledighed*, AKF Memo. Copenhagen: AKF.

Hyman, Richard (1991) 'European Unions: Towards 2000', *Work, Employment & Society*, vol. 5, no. 4, pp. 621–39.

IDEA (1997) *Voter Turnout from 1945 to 1997: a Global Report on Political Participation*. Stockholm: International IDEA.

Inglehart, Ronald (1990) *Culture Shift in Advanced Industrial Societies*. Princeton, NJ: Princeton University Press.

Jackman, Robert W. (1987) 'Political Institutions and Voter Turnout in the Industrial Democracies', *APSR*, vol. 81(2), pp. 405–23.

Jahoda, M. (1982) *Employment and Unemployment: a Social-Psychological Analysis*. Cambridge: Cambridge University Press.

Jarl, Maria (1999) *Det unga folkstyret*. Statens Offentliga Utredningar.

Jensen, T.Ø. (1986) 'Publikumserfaringer med forvaltningen', *Norsk Statsvitenskabeligt Tidsskrift*, vol. 2, no. 2, pp. 7–29.

Jenssen, A.T. (1993) *Verdivalg. Ny massepolitik i Norge*. Oslo: ad Notam Gylendal.

Jenssen, A.T., Pesonen, P., and Gilljam, M. (eds) (1998) *To Join or Not to Join?: Three Nordic Referendums on Membership in the European Union*. Oslo: Scandinavian University Press.

Jeppesen, Jens and Meyer, Poul (1964) *Sofavælgerne*. Aarhus: Institut for Statskundskab/Nyt Nordisk Forlag Arnold Busck.

Joerges, C. and Vos, E. (1999) *EU Committees: Social Regulation, Law and Politics*. Oxford: Hart Publishing.

Johansen, Lars Nørby (1980) 'Organisationsdeltagelse', in Erik Damgaard (ed.), *Folkets veje i dansk politik*. Copenhagen: Schultz, pp. 62–101.

Johannessen, Asbjørn (1995) 'Arbeidsmarginalisering og levekår', HiO-rapport 1995:4. Oslo: Oslo College.

Jones, Ethel B. (1992) 'Private Sector Union Decline and Structural Employment Change, 1970–1988', *Journal of Labor Research*, vol. 13, no. 3 (summer), pp. 257–72.

Jørgensen, Henning, Lassen, Morten, Lind, Jens and Madsen, Morten (1992) *Medlemmer og meninger*. Copenhagen: LO and Carma.

Jørgensen, Henning, Lassen, Morten, Lind, Jens, and Madsen, Morten (1993) *Medlemmer og meninger. Rapport over en spørgeskemaundersøgelse blandt medlemmer af LO-forbundene*. Aalborg: CARMA/LO.

Kaase, Max and Marsh, Alan (1979) 'Political Action Repertory: Changes over Time and a New Typology', in Samuel H. Barnes, Max Kaase et al., *Political Action: Mass Participation in Five Western Democracies*. Beverly Hills: Sage.

Kaase, Max and Barnes, Samuel H. (1979) 'Conclusion: The Future of Political Protest in Western Democracies', in S.M. Barnes, M. Kaase et al. (eds), *Political Action: Mass Participation in Five Western Democracies*. Beverly Hills: Sage.

Karasek, R. (1978) *Job Socialization: a Longitudinal Study of Work, Political and Leisure Activity*. Working Paper no. 59. Institute for Social Research, Stockholm.

Karronen, Lauri and Selle, Per (eds) (1995) *Women in Nordic Countries: Closing the Gap*. Aldershot: Dartmouth.

Katz, Richard S. et al. (1992) 'The Membership of Political Parties in European Democracies, 1960–1990', *European Journal of Political Research*, vol. 22, pp. 329–45.

Katz, Richard S. and Mair, Peter (eds) (1992a) *Party Organizations. A Data Handbook*. London: Sage.

Katz, Richard S. and Mair, Peter (1992b) 'Introduction: the Cross-National Study of Party Organizations', in Richard S. Katz and Peter Mair (eds), *Party Organizations*. London: Sage, pp. 1–20.

Katz, Richard S. and Mair, Peter (1995) 'Changing Models of Party Organization and Party Democracy: The Emergence of the Cartel Party' *Party Politics*, vol. 1(1), pp. 5–28.

Key. V. O. (1966) *The Responsible Electorate*. New York: Vintage.

King, Anthony (1969) 'Politics Parties in Western Democracies: Some Sceptical Reflections', *Polity*, vol. 2(2), pp. 111–41.

Kitschelt, Herbest (1988), 'Left-Libertarian Parties: Explaining Innovation in Competitive Party Systems', *World Politics*, vol. 40(2), pp. 194–234.

Kirchheimer, Otto (1966) 'The Transformation of Western European Party Systems', in Joseph LaPalombara and Myron Weiner (eds), *Political Parties and Political Development*. Princeton, NJ: Princeton University Press.

Kjellberg, Anders (1983) *Facklig organisering i tolv länder*. Lund: Arkiv.

Kjellberg Pedersen, L. and Weber, J. (1983) 'Stabilitet og politisk involvering', in Ole Borre (ed.), *Efter vælgerskredet*. Aarhus: Forlaget Politica, pp. 84–103.

Klausen, Kurt Klaudi and Selle, Per (eds) (1995) *Frivillig organisering i Norden*. Oslo: Tano.

Knudsen, T. (1993) *Den danske stat i Europa*. København: Samfundslitteratur.

Koch-Arzberger, Claudia (1992) 'Wahlverhalten von Ausländern – Chance oder Gefährdung der Demokratie', in Karl Starzacher et al. (eds), *Protestwähler und Wahlverweigerer. Krise der Demokratie?* Cologne: Bund Verlag, pp. 113–30.

Kolodny, Robin and Katz, Richard (1992) 'The United States', in Richard S. Katz and Peter Mair (eds), *Party Organizations: a Data Handbook*. London: Sage, pp. 871–930.

Koole, Ruud and van de Velde, Hella (1992) 'The Netherlands', in Richard S. Katz and Peter Mair (eds), *Party Organizations: a Data Handbook*. London: Sage, pp. 619–731.

Kornhauser, W. (1960) *The Politics of Mass Society*. New York: The Free Press.

Korpi, Walter (1981) *Den demokratiska klasskampen*. Stockholm: Tidens Förlag.

Kristensen, Ole P. (1980) 'Deltagelse i partipolitiske aktiviteter', in Erik Damgaard et al., *Folkets veje i dansk politik*. Copenhagen: Schultz, pp. 31–61.

Kugelberg, C. (1984) 'Flexiblare regler öppnar barnomsorgen för flera', *Plan*, 1984/3.

Laclau, Ernesto and Mouffe, Chantal (1985) *Hegemony and Socialist Strategy*. London: Verso.

Lafferty, W. (1986) 'Den sosialdemokratiske stat', *Nytt Norsk Tidsskrift, no. 3*.

Lane, Jan-Erik and Ersson, Svante (1991) *Politics in Western Europe*. London: Sage.

Layton-Henry, Zig (ed.) (1990): *The Political Rights of Migrant Workers in Western Europe*, Modern Politics Series, vol. 25, London: Sage.

Leira, A. (1987) *Day Care for Children in Denmark, Norway and Sweden*, Report 87: 5. Oslo: Institute of Social Research.

Lewin, Leif (1970) *Folket och eliterna*. Stockholm: Almqvist & Wiksell.

Lewin, Leif (1991) *Self-Interest and Public Interest in Western Politics*. Oxford: Oxford University Press.

Lewin, Leif (1993) 'Economic Man, Political Man', *Politica*, vol. 25, no. 2, pp. 133–42.

Lijphart, Arend (2000) 'Turnout', in Richard Rose (ed.), *International Encyclopedia of Elections*. Wasington, DC: CQ Press, pp. 314–22.

Lindbom, A. (1993) *Närdemokrati i Norden*. Självforvaltning och skolförvaltningsreformer. Paper presented at the meeting of the Nordic Political Science Association, Oslo, 19–21 August.

Lindbom A. (1995) *Medborgarskabet i välfärdsstaten. Föräldrainflytande i skandinavisk grundskola*. Uppsala: Acta Universitatis Upsaliensis.

Lindholm, B. (1985) *Barnen i välfärden. Barnomsorgens utveckling och framtid*. Borås.

Lipset, Seymour Martin (1986) 'Labor Unions in the Public Mind', in S.M. Lipset (ed.), *Unions in Transition. Entering the Second Century*. San Francisco: ICS Press, pp. 287–322.

Lipsky, Martin (1980) *Street-Level Bureaucracy*. New York: Russell Sage.

Lister, Ruth (1990) *The Exclusive Society: Citizenship and the Poor*. London: Child Poverty Action Group.

Listhaug, Ola (1989) *Citizens, Parties and Norwegian Electoral Politics 1957–1985:* an Empirical Study. Flataasen: Tapir.

Listhaug, Ola (1995) 'The Dynamics of Trust in Politicians', in Hans-Dieter Klingemann and Dieter Fuchs (eds), *Citizens and the State. Beliefs in Government*, vol. 1. Oxford: Oxford University Press, pp. 261–97.

Listhaug, O. and Kindseth, O. (1979) 'Sex, resources and political participation', SPS vol. 2.

Listhaug, Ola and Wiberg, Matti (1995) 'Confidence in Political and Private Institutions', in Hans-Dieter Klingemann and Dieter Fuchs (eds), *Citizens and the State*, Beliefs in Government, vol. 1. Oxford: Oxford University Press, pp. 298–322.

Listhaug, O., Holmberg, S. and Sänkiaho, R. (1998) 'Partisanship and EU Choice''', in Jenssen, et al. (eds), *To Join or not to Join? Three Nordic Referendums on Membership in the European Union*. Olso: Scandinavian University Press, pp. 215–34.

Locke, John (1959) *An Essay Concerning Human Understanding*. New York: Dover Publications.

MacIntyre, Alisdair (1981) *After Virtue*. London: Duckworth.

MacIntyre, Alisdair (1988) *Whose Justice? Which Rationality?* London: Duckworth.

Macpherson, C.B. (1977) *The Life and Times of Liberal Democracy*. Oxford: Oxford University Press.

Macpherson, C.B. (1985) *The Rise and Fall of Economic Justice and Other Papers*. Oxford.

Madsen, Morten (1997) *Democracy and Individualization*, Licentiatserien 1997 no. 5, Institute of Political Science, Copenhagen.

Mair, Peter (1994) 'Party Organizations: From Civil Society to the State', in Richard S. Katz and Peter Mair (eds), *How Parties Organize: Change and Adaptation in Party Organizations in Western Democracies*. London: Sage, pp. 1–22.

Majone, G. (1994) 'The Rise of the Regulatory State in Europe', *West European Politics*, vol. 17, no. 3, pp. 77–101.

March, J. and Olsen, J.P. (1989) *Rediscovering Institutions: the Organizational Basis of Politics*. New York: The Free Press.

March, James G. and Olsen, Johan P. (1995) *Democratic Governance*. New York: The Free Press.

Marcuse, Herbert (1964) *One-Dimensional Man*. Danish transl. (1968) *Det endimensionale menneske*. Copenhagen: Gyldendals uglebøger.

Markovic, M. (1982) *Democratic Socialism – Theory and Practice*. Brighton, Sussex: The Harvester Press.

Marshall, Thomas H. (1950) 'Citizenship and Social Class', in T.H. Marshall *Class, Citizenship and Social Development: Essays*. Cambridge: Cambridge University Press.

Martin, C. (1994): 'Basic Instincts? Sources of Firm Preference for National Health Reform'. Unpublished paper. Boston University.

Martiniello, Marco (1993) 'Review of Marilyn Hoskin' *New Immigrants and Democratic Society'*, *International Migration Review*, vol. 27, pp. 204–5.

Martinussen, Willy (1977) *The Distant Democracy: Social Inequality, Political Resources and Political Influence in Norway*. London: Wiley.

Martinussen, Willy (1994) 'Velferdssamfunnet på hell?', in Anders Todal Jenssen and Willy Martinussen (eds), *Velferdsstaten i våre hjerter*. Oslo: Ad Notam Gyldendal, pp. 135–66.

Micheletti, M. (1990) *The Swedish Farmers Movement and Government Agricultural Policy*. New York: Praeger.

Micheletti, Michele (1994) *Det civila samhället och staten. Medborgarsammanslutningarnas roll i svensk politik*. Stockholm: Fritzes.

Milbrath, Lester W. and Goel, M.L. (1977) *Political Participation*, 2nd edn. Chicago: Rand McNally.

Miles, Robert and Dietrich Thränhardt (eds) (1995) *Migration and European Integration: the Dynamics of Inclusion and Exclusion*. London: Pinter Publishers.

Miller, Mark J. (1989) 'Political Participation and Representation of Noncitizens', in William R. Brubaker (ed.), *Immigration and the Politics of Citizenship in Europe and North America*. Lanham, MD: University Press America, pp. 129–43.

Ministry of Interior (1995) *Rådet for etniske minoriteter* (The Council of Ethnic Minorities; pamphlet).

Møller, Iver Hornemann (1995) 'Some Empirical and Theoretical Perpectives on Labour Market Marginalisation', in Nils Mortensen (ed.), *Social Integration and Marginalisation*. Copenhagen: Samfundslitteratur, pp. 114–46.

Moore, William J. and Newman, Robert J. (1988) 'A Cross-Section Analysis of the Postwar Decline in American Trade Union Membership', *Journal of Labor Research*, vol. 9, no. 2 (spring), pp. 111–25.

Mørkeberg, Henrik (1985) *Sociale og helbredsmæssige konsekvenser af arbejdsløshed*. First published 147. Copenhagen: Socialforskningsinstituttet.

Morris, Lydia (1994) *Dangerous Classes. The Underclass and Social Citizenship*. London: Routledge.

Mouffe, Chantal (1991) 'Democratic Citizenship and the Political Community', in Miami Theory Collective (eds), *Community at Loose Ends*. Minneapolis: University of Minnesota Press, pp. 70–82.

Mouffe, Chantal (1992) 'Preface: Democratic Politics Today', in Chantal Mouffe (ed.), *Dimensions of Radical Democracy*. London: Verso, pp. 1–14.

Mouffe, Chantal (ed.)(1992) *Dimensions of Radical Democracy*. London: Verso.

Mulhall, Stephen and Swift, Adam (1992) *Liberals & Communitarians*. Oxford: Blackwell.

Müller, Wolfgang (1992) 'Austria', in Richard S. Katz and Peter Mair (eds), *Party Organization: a Data Handbook*. London: Sage, pp. 21–120.

Müller-Jentsch, W. (1988) 'Industrial Relations Theory and Trade Union Strategy', *International Journal of Comparative Labour Law and Industrial Relations*, vol. 4, no. 3, pp. 177–90.

Munk Christiansen, Peter (1993) *Det frie marked – den forhandlede økonomi*. Copenhagen: Jurist- og Økonomforbundets Forlag.

Nannestad, Peter and Paldam, Martin (1994) *The Egotropic Welfare Man: a Pooled Cross-Section Study of Economic Voting in Denmark, 1986–92*. Memo 1994-2. Institute of Economics and Statistics, University of Aarhus.

Narud, Hanne Marthe and Valen, Henry (1996) 'Decline of Electoral Turnout: the Case of Norway', *European Journal of Political Research*, vol. 29(2), pp. 235–56.

Nie, Norman H. With Andersen, Kristi (1974) 'Mass Belief Systems Revisited: Political Change and Attitude Structure', *Journal of Politics*, vol. 36, pp. 540–87.

Neumann, George, Pedersen, Peder J. and Westergård-Nielsen, Niels (1991) 'Long-run International Trends in Aggregate Unionization', *European Journal of Political Economy*, vol. 7, pp. 249–74.

Niedermayer, O. and Sinnott, R. (eds) (1995) *Public Opinion and Internationalized Governance*, Beliefs in Government, vol. 2. Oxford: Oxford University Press.

Nielsen, Hans Jørgen (1976) 'Politiske Meninger og vaelgeradfaerd', in Ole Borre et al. (eds), *Vælgere i To'erne*. Copenhagen: AkademiskForlag, pp. 122–75.

Nielsen, Hans Jørgen (1992) 'Vælgersamtalerne', in Jørgen Goul Andersen, Hans Jørgen Nielsen, Niels Thomsen, Jörgen Westerståhl (eds), *Vi og vore politikere*. Copenhagen: Spektrum, pp. 272–324.

Nielsen, Hans Jørgen (1999a) 'De individuelle forskydninger 1994–98', in Johannes Andersen, Ole Borre, Jørgen Goul Andersen and Hans Jørgen Nielsen (eds), *Vælgere med omtanke – en analyse af folketingsvalget 1998*. Aarhus: Systime, pp. 49–60.

Nielsen, Hans Jørgen (1999b) 'Tilliden til politikerne', in Johannes Andersen, Ole Borre, Jørgen Goul Andersen and Hans Jørgen Nielsen (eds), *Vælgere med omtanke – en analyse af folketingsvalget 1998*. Aarhus: Systime, pp. 239–48.

Nieto, Lourdes Lopez (1994) *Local Elections in Europe*. Barcelona: ICPS.

Nørregaard, Carl (1996) *Arbejde og tilbagetrækning i 90'erne – og fremtidens pensionister*. Copenhagen: Socialforskningsinstituttet.

NOSOSKO (1999) *Social tryghed i de nordiske lande 1997*. Copenhagen: Nordisk Socialstatistisk Komité.

NOU (1988) *Nye mål og retningslinjer for reformer i lokalforvaltningen*. Olso: Kommunal- og Arbeitsdepartementet.

Nozick, R. (1974) *Anarchy, State and Utopia*. Oxford: Blackwell.

Nygaard Christoffersen, Mogens (1995) *Sandsynlige sociale konsekvenser af arbejds-løshed*, Working Paper 1995: 4. Copenhagen: Socialforskningsinstuttet.

OECD (1997) *Implementing the OECD Jobs Strategy*. Paris: OECD.

OECD (1998) *Employment Outlook*. Paris: OECD.

OECD (2000) *Employment Outlook*. Paris: OECD.

Oldfield, Adrian (1990a) 'Citizenship: an Unnatural Practice', *The Political Quarterly*, vol. 61, no. 2, pp. 177–87.

Oldfield, Adrian (1990b) *Citizenship and Community: Civic Republicanism and the Modern World*. London.

Olsen, Johan P. and Sætren Harald (1980) *Aksjoner og demokrati*. Oslo: Universitetsforlaget.

Olson, Mancur E. (1965) *The Logic of Collective Action*. Cambridge, Mass.: Harvard University Press.

Oskarsson, Maria and Oscarsson, Henric (1994) 'De unga väljarna 1968–91', in *Ungdomars välfärd och värderingar*. SOU 1994: 73. Stockholm: Fritzes, pp. 357–90.

Panebianco, Angelo (1988) *Political Parties: Organization and Power*. Cambridge: Cambridge University Press.

Pannekoek, (1946) *Arbejderråd*. Copenhagen.

Parry, Geraint, Moyser, George and Day, Neil (1992) *Political Participation and Democracy in Britain*. Cambridge: Cambridge University Press.

Pateman, Carol (1970) *Participation and Democratic Theory*. Oxford: Oxford University Press.

Pedersen, Lars, Pedersen, Peder J. and Smith, Nina (1995) 'The Working and the Non-working Populations in the Welfare State', in Gunnar Viby Mogensen (ed), *Work Incentives in the Danish Welfare State: New Empirical Evidence*. Aarhus: Aarhus University Press/The Rockwool Foundation, pp. 45–79.

Pedersen, Mogens N. (1979) 'The Dynamics of European Party Systems: Changing Patterns of Electoral Volatility', *European Journal of Political Research*, vol. 7, pp. 7–26.

Pedersen, Mogens N. (1989) 'En kortfattet oversigt over det danske partisystems udvikling', *Politica*, vol. 21(3), pp. 265–78.

Pedersen, Nikolaj (1975) *Folket og udenrigspolitikken*. Copenhagen: Gyldendal.

Pedersen, Peder J. (1989) 'Langsigtede internationale tendenser i den faglige organisering og den politiske venstrefløj', *Økonomi og Politik*, vol. 62, no. 2, pp. 91–101.

Pedersen, Peder J. (1990) 'Arbejdsløshedsforsikring og faglig organisering, 1911–85', *National Økonomish Tidsshrift*, vol. 128, pp. 230–46.

Petersson, Olof (1977) *Väljarna och valet 1976*. Stockholm: SCB.

Petersson, Olof (1991) *Makt. En sammanfattning av maktutredningen*. Stockholm: Almänna Förlaget.

Petersson, Olof, Hermansson, Jörgen, Micheletti, Michele, and Westholm, Anders (1997) *Demokrati över gränser*. Demokratirådets rapport 1997. Stockholm: SNS Förlag.

Petersson, Olof, Westholm, Anders and Blomberg, Göran (1989) *Medborgarnas makt*. Stockholm: Carlssons.

Pettersen, Per Arnt (1988) 'Hjemmesitterne: Hvor – Hvem og Hvorfor?', *Norsk Statsvitenskapelig Tidsskrift*, vol. 4

Pettersen, Per Arnt (1989) 'Comparing Non-Voters in the USA and Norway – Permanence Versus Transience', European Journal of Political Research, vol. 17, no. 3, pp. 351–9.

Philip, Alan Butt (1994) 'European Union Immigration Policy: Phantom, Fantasy or Fact?', *West European Politics*, vol. 17, no. 2, pp. 168–91.

Pierre, Jon and Widfeldt, Anders (1992) 'Sweden', in Richard S. Katz and Peter Mair (eds), *Party Organizations*. London: Sage, pp. 781–836.

Pixley, Jocelyn (1993) *Citizen and Employment: Investigating Post-Industrial Options*. Cambridge: Cambridge University Press.

Plasser, F. and Ulram, P.A. (1992) 'Überdehnung, Erosion und rechtspopulistische Reaktion', *Österreichische Zeitschrift für Politikwissenschaft*, vol. 16, pp. 214–58.

Plovsing, Jan (1973) *Funktionær: Organiseret eller uorganiseret?* Copenhagen: Danish National Institute of Social Research.

Pontusson, J. (1992) *The Limits of Social Democracy: Investment Politics in Sweden*. Ithaca, NY: Cornell University Press.

Potterfield, Thomas A. (1999) *The Business of Employee Empowerment – Democracy and Ideology in the Workplace*. Westport, Conn: Quorum Books.

Pressman, J. and Wildavsky, Aaron (1973) *Implementation*. Berkeley: University of California Press.

Przeworski, Adam and Sprague, John (1986), *Paper Stones: a History of Electoral Socialism*. Chicago: University of Chicago Press.

Putnam, Robert D., Leonardi, R. and Nanetti, R. (1993) *Making Democracy Work: Civic Traditions in Modern Italy*. Princeton, NJ: Princeton University Press.

Raaum, Nina (1999) 'Politisk medborgerskap: nye deltagere, nye værdier', in Christina Bergavist (ed.), *Likestilte demokratier? Kjønn og Politik i Norden*. Oslo: Universitetsforlaget/Nordisk Ministerråd, pp. 46–61.

Ragsdale, Lyn, and Rusk, Jerrold E. (1993) 'Who are Nonvoters? Profiles from the 1990 Senate Elections, *American Journal of Political Science*, vol. 37(3), pp. 721–46.

Rasmussen, Erik (1971) *Komparativ Politik 1*. Copenhagen: Gyldendal.

Rasmussen, Søren Hein (1997) *Sære alliancer. Politiske bevægelser i efterkrigstidens Danmark*. Odense: Odense University Press.

Rath, J. (1988) 'Political Action of Immigrants in the Netherlands: Class or Ethnicity', *European Journal of Political Research*, vol. 16, no. 6, pp. 623–44.

Rawls, John (1971) *A Theory of Justice*. Cambridge, Mass.: Harvard University Press.

Rawls, John (1985) 'Justice as Fairness: Political not Metaphysical', *Philosophy and Public Affairs*, vol. 14, no. 3, pp. 223–51.

Rawls, John. (1988) 'The Priority of Rights and the Idea of the Good', *Philosophy and Public Affairs*, 17.

Ringen, Stein et al. (eds) (1987) *The Scandinavian Model: Welfare States and Welfare Research*. Armonk, NY and Hove: M.E. Sharpe.

Roche, Maurice (1992) *Rethinking Citizenship: Welfare, Ideology and Change in Modern Society*. London: Polity Press.

Rokkan, Stein (1970) *Citizens, Elections, Parties*. Oslo: Universitetsforlaget.

Rosenstone, Steven J. and Hansen, John Mark (1993) *Mobilization, Participation and Democracy in America*. New York: Macmillan.

Rothstein, B. (1987) 'Välfärdsstat, implementering och legitimitet', *Statsvetenskapligt Tidsskrift*, vol. 90, pp. 21–37.

Rothstein, B. (1990) 'Marxism, Institutional Analysis and Working Class Strength: the Swedish Case', *Politics & Society*, vol. 18, no. 3, pp. 317–45.

Rothstein, B. (1992) *Den korporativa staten*. Stockholm: Norstedts.

Rothstein, B. (1996) *The Social Democratic State. The Swedish Model and the Bureaucratic Problems of Social Reforms*. University of Pittsburgh Press.

Rothstein, B. (1998) *Just Institutions Matter*. Cambridge: Cambridge University Press.

Rothstein, B. and Bergström, J. (1999) *Korporatismens fall och den svenska moddellens kris*. Stockholm: SNS Förlag.

Rudebrandt, S. and Thörn, S.(1979) 'Barn på daghem, familjedaghem och hemma – en uppföljingsstudie', *Rapport från ped. inst. vid Lärarhögskolen i Stockholm. 1979/6.*

SAMAK(1989) 'Fornyelse i den offentlige sektor'. *LO-bladet*, no. 5.

Samfunnsspeilet (2/1995) *Innvandrere i Norge*. Oslo: Statistisk sentralbyrå.

Sartori, Giovanni (1987) *The Theory of Democracy Revisited*. vols 1–2. Chatham, NJ: Chatham House Publishers.

Sänkiaho, Risto (1972) 'A Model of the Rise of Populism and Support for the Finnish Rural Party', *Scandinavian Political Studies*, vol. 6, pp. 27–47.

Sauerberg, Steen (1992) 'Politisk kommunikation under TV-konkurrence', in Lars Bille, Hans Jørgen Nielsen and Steen Sauerberg (eds), *De uregerlige vælgere – valgkamp, medier og vælgere ved folketingsvalget 1990*. København: Columbus, pp. 86–106

Schaffer, B. and Huang, W.H. (1975): 'Distribution and the Theory of Access', *Development and Change*, vol. 6, no. 2, pp. 32–64.

Scheuer, Steen (1984) *Hvorfor stiger den faglige organisering?* Copenhagen: Nyt fra Samfundsvidenskaberne.

Schiller, B. (1977) 'Industrial Democracy in Scandinavia'. *Annals, AAPSS*, 431, May 1977.

Schlozman, Kay Lehman and Verba, Sidney (1979) *Injury to Insult. Unemployment, Class and Political Response*. Cambridge, Mass: Harvard University Press.

Schlytter-Berge, A. and Ulveson, E. (1984) *Regler och praxis vid fördelning av barnomsorgsplatser*. (D nr.83:40:20). Nordisk institutet för Samhällsplanering.

Schmidt, V.A. (1997) 'European Integration and Democracy: The Difference Among Member States', *Journal of European Public Policy*, vol. 41, pp. 128–45.

Schmitt, Hermann and Holmberg, Sören (1995) 'Political Parties in Decline?', in Hans-Dieter Klingemann and Dieter Fuchs (eds), *Citizens and the State*. Oxford: Oxford University Press, pp. 95–133.

Schnapper, Dominique (1994): ' The Debate on Immigration and the Crises of National Identity', *West European Politics*, vol. 17, no. 2, pp. 127–39.

Schumpeter, Joseph (1944) *Capitalism, Socialism, Democracy*. London: Allen & Unwin.

Schweizer, Steven L. (1995) 'Participation, Workplace Democracy, and the Problem of Representative Government'. *Polity*, vol. 27, no. 3 (spring), p. 359ff.

Selle, Per and Svåsand, Lars (1991) 'Membership in Party Organizations and the Problem of Decline of Parties', *Comparative Political Studies*, vol. 23, no. 4, pp. 459–77.

Sen, A. (1982) *Choice, Welfare and Measurement*. Cambridge, Mass.: MIT Press.

Søllinge, Jette (1992) 'Pressens dækning af finanslovsforligene i 1965 og 1991', in Jørgen Goul Andersen, Hans Jørgen Nielsen, Niels Thomsen and Jörgen Westerståhl (eds), *Vi og vore politikere*. København: Spektrum, pp. 325–41

Sørensen, R. (1988) 'Ønsker kommunerne større lokalt sjelvstyre', in F. Kjellberg (ed.), *Nytt inntektssystem*. Oslo: Kommuneforlaget.

SOU (1990) *Demokrati och makt i Sverige*. Stockholm: Maktutredningens huvudrapport.

Statistiska Centralbyrån (SCB) (1985) *Förskolor, fritidshem och familjedaghem*. Stat. Meddelanden S. 10 SM 8601.

Statistika Centralbyrån (SCB) (1993) *Almanna valen 1991. del 3*. Örebro, Sweden: Statistika Meddelanden.

Statistiska Centralbyrån (SCB)(1995) *Valdeltagande bland utländska medborgare vid kommunfullmäktigvalen 1994*. Örebro, Sweden: Statistiska meddelanden.

Statistiska Centralbyrån (SCB)(1998) *Allmänna valen 1998, del 4*. Örebro, Sweden: Statistiska meddelanden.

Sterum, Line (1992) 'Flygtninge og indvandreres politiske deltagelse i Danmark'. Unpublished MA. thesis, Department of Political Science, University of Aarhus.

Sturmthal, (1977): 'Unions and Industrial Democracy', *Annals, AAPSS*, no. 431, May 1977.

Stymne, B. (1982) 'Union and Management Strategies for Handling Changes in the Social Environment: the Case of Codetermination in Sweden', EFI Research Paper 6245. The Economic Research Institute at the Stockholm School of Economics, Stockholm, Sweden.

Sundberg, Jan (1987) 'Exploring the Case of Declining Party Membership in Denmark: a Scandinavian Comparison', *Scandinavian Political Studies*, vol. 10, pp. 17–38.

Sundberg, Jan (1989) 'Premisser för politiskt massmedlemskap: Partierna i Danmark i en nordisk jämförelse', *Politica*, vol. 21, pp. 288–311.

Sundberg, Jan and Gylling, Christel (1992). 'Finland', in Richard S. Katz and Peter Mair (eds), *Party Organizations: a Data Handbook*. London: Sage, pp. 273–316.

Svallfors, Stefan, Halvorsen, Knut and Goul Andersen, Jørgen (2001) 'Work orientations in Scandinavia: Employment Commitment and Organizational Commitment in Denmark, Norway and Sweden, *Acta Sociologica* (forthcoming).

Svåsand, Lars (1992) 'Norway', in Richard S. Katz and Peter Mair, *Party Organizations*. London: Sage, pp. 732–80.

Svensson, Palle (1989) 'Vælgernes syn på det danske demokrati', in Jørgen Elklit and Ole Tonsgaard (eds), *To folketingsvalg. Vælgerholdninger og vælgeradfærd i 1987 og 1988*. Aarhus: Forlaget Politica, pp. 357–81.

Svensson, Palle (1996) *Demokratiets krise? En debat- og systemanalyse af dansk politik i 1970'erne*. Aarhus: Politica.

Svensson, Palle and Togeby, Lise (1986) *Politisk opbrud. De nye mellemlags græsrodsdeltagelse*. Aarhus: Politica.

Svensson, Palle and Togeby, Lise (1991) *Højrebølge?* Aarhus: Politica.

Taylor, Charles (1990) *Sources of the Self*. Cambridge: Cambridge University Press.

Tchernia, Jean-François (1991) 'The Factual Data from Eurobarometer Surveys: How they Help in Describing the Member States', in Karlheinz Reif and Ronald Inglehart (eds), *Eurobarometer: the Dynamics of European Opinion*. London: Macmillan, pp. 355–76.

Tema Nord (1996) *Ungdomsarbetslösheten i Norden*. Copenhagen: Nordiska Ministerrådet.

Teorell, Jan and Westholm, Anders (1999) 'Att bestämma sig för att vara med och bestämma. Om varför vi röstar – allt mindre', in Erik Amnå (ed.), *Valdeltagande i förändring. Demokratiutredningens forskarvolym XII*. Stockholm, pp. 137–204.

Thaulow, Ivan (1988) 'Arbejdsløshedens psykiske og sociale konsekvenser', Working paper. Copenhagen: Socialforskningsinstituttet.

Thomsen, Niels (1992) 'Det politiske rodnet', in Jørgen Goul Andersen, Hans Jørgen Nielsen, Niels Thomsen and Jörgen Westerståhl (eds), *Vi og vore politikere*. København: Spektrum, pp. 26–97.

Thomsen, Søren Risbjerg (1984) 'Udviklingen under forholdstalsvalgmåden (1920–1984)', in Jørgen Elklit and Ole Tonsgaard (eds), *Valg og vælgeradfærd. Studier i dansk politik*. Aarhus: Politica, pp. 39–69.

Thomsen, Søren Risbjerg (1987) *Danish Elections 1920–79: a Logit Approach to Ecological Analysis and Inference*. Aarhus: Politica.

Thorsrud, E. and Emery, F.E. (1970) *Mot en ny bedriftsorganisasjon*. Oslo: Tanum.

Tingsten, Herbert (1937) *Political Behavior: Studies in Election Statistics*. London: P.S. King & Son.

Tocqueville, Alexis de (1835/40) *De la Démocratie en Amerique*. Danish ed. 1981.

Togeby, Lise (1991) *Ens og forskellig. Græsrodsdeltagese i Norden*. Aarhus: Politica.

Togeby, Lise (1992) 'The Nature of Declining Party Membership in Denmark: Causes and Consequences', *Scandinavian Political Studies*, vol. 15, pp. 1–19.

Togeby, Lisa (1994) *Fra tilskuere til deltagere*. Aarhus: Forlaget Politica.

Togeby, Lise (1997) *Fremmedhed og fremmedhad i Danmark*. Copenhagen: Columbus.

Togeby, Lise (1999a) 'Et demokrati, som omfatter alle, der bor i Danmark?', in Jørgen Goul Andersen et al. (eds), *Den demokratiske udfordring*. Copenhagen: Hans Reitzels Forlag, pp. 133–53.

Togeby, Lise (1999b) 'Hvem sagde videnskabelighed, *Politica*, vol. 31, no. 4.

Tonsgaard, Ole (1989) 'Vælgervandringer og vælgerusikkerhed', in Jørgen Elklit and Ole Tonsgaard (eds), *To folketingsvalg*. Aarhus: Forlaget Politica, pp. 134–156.

Topf, Richard (1995a) 'Electoral Participation', in Hans-Dieter Klingemann and Dieter Fuchs (eds), *Citizens and the State*, Belief in Government, vol. 1. Oxford: Oxford University Press, pp. 27–51.

Torp Hege, (ed). (1999) *Dagpengesystemene i Norden og tilpasning på arbeidsmarkedet*. Tema Nord 1999:592. Copenhagen: Nordiska Ministerrådet.

Topf, Richard (1995b) 'Beyond Electoral Participation', in Hans-Dieter Klingemann and Dieter Fuchs (eds), *Citizens and the State*, Beliefs in Government, vol. 1. Oxford: Oxford University Press, pp. 52–92.

Touraine, Alain (1981) *The Voice and the Eye: An Analysis of Social Movements*. London: Cambridge University Press.

Torpe, Lars (2000) 'Foreninger og demokrati', in Jørgen Goul Andersen, Lars Torpe and Johannes Andersen (eds), *Hvad folket magter. Demokrati, magt og afmagt*. Copenhagen: Jurist- og Økonomforbundets Forlag, pp. 79–122.

Tøssebro, Jan (1983) 'Fagorganiseringa av arbeidarklassen: Strukturelle forklaringsfaktorar', *Tidsskrift for Samfunnsforskning*, vol. 24, pp. 331–54.

Touraine, Alain (1986) 'Unionism as a Social Movement', in S.M. Lipset (ed.), *Unions in Transition: Entering the Second Century*. San Francisco: ICS Press, pp. 151–76.

Touraine, Alain et al. (1987), *The Workers' Movement* (Michel Wieviorka, François Dubet; transl. by Ian Patterson). Cambridge: Cambridge University Press

Troy, Leo (1986) 'The Rise and Fall of American Trade Unions: The Labor Movement from FDR to RR', in S.M. Lipset (ed.), *Unions in Transition: Entering the Second Century*. San Francisco: ICS Press, pp. 75–109.

Troy, Leo (1990) 'Is the U.S. Unique in the Decline of Private Sector Unionism?', *Journal of Labor Research*, vol. 11, no. 2 (spring), pp. 111–43.

Turner, Bryan S. (1993) *Citizenship and Social Theory*. London: Sage.

Valen, Henry and Aardal, Bernt (1983) *Et Valg i perspektiv. En studie av Stortingsvalet 1981*. Oslo: Statistisk Sentralbyrå.

Valen, Henry, Aardal, Bernt and Berglund, Frode (1996) *Velgervandringer og sviktende valgdeltakelse. Kommune- og fylkestingsvalget i 1995*, Rapport 96: 13. Oslo: Institutt for Samfunnsforskning.

van Deth, Jan W. (1989) 'Political Interest', in M. Kent Jennings and J.W. Van Deth et al., (eds), *Continuities in Political Action: a Longitudinal Study of Political Orientations in Three Western Democracies*. Berlin and New York: De Gruyter and Aldine.

van Deth, Jan W. (1991) 'Politicization and Political Interest', in Karheinz Reif and Ronald Inglehart (eds), *Eurobarometer: The Dynamics of European Public Opinion. Essays in Honour of Jacques-Rané Rabier*. London: Macmillan.

van Deth, Jan (1997) 'Introduction: Social involvement and democratic politics', in Jan W. van Deth (ed.), *Private Groups in Public Life. Social Participation, Voluntary Associations and Political Involvement in Representative Democracies*. London: Routledge, pp. 1–23.

van Gunsteren, Herman (1994) 'Four Conceptions of Citizenship', in Bart van Steenbergen (ed.), *The Condition of Citizenship*. London: Sage, pp. 36–48.

Verba, Sidney and Nie, Norman H. (1972) *Participation in America: Political Democracy and Social Equality*. New York: Harper & Row.

Verba, Sidney, Nie, Norman H. and Kim, Jae-On (1978) *Participation and Political Equality: Seven-Nation Comparison*. Cambridge: Cambridge University Press.

Verba, Sidney, Schlozman, Kay Lehman and Brady, Henry E. (1995) *Voice and Equality: Civic Voluntarism in American Politics*. Cambridge, Mass.: Harvard University Press.

Visser, Jelle (1990) *In Search of Inclusive Unionism. Bulletin of Comparative Labour Relations 18/1990.* Deventer and Boston: Kluwer Law and Taxation Publishers.

Visser, Jelle (1991) 'Trends in Trade Union Membership', in OECD, *Employment Outlook*, July 1991, pp. 97–134.

Visser, Jelle (1993) 'Works Councils and Unions in the Netherlands: Rivals or Allies?', *The Netherlands Journal of Social Sciences*, vol. 29, no. 3, pp. 64–92.

Vogel, Joachim (1994) 'Politiska resurser', in SOU, *Ungdomars välfärd och värderingar.* Stockhom: Fritzes, pp. 347–56.

Walker, K.F. (1977) 'Towards the Participatory Enterprise: a European Trend', *Annals, AAPSS*, no. 431, May 1977.

Wallerstein, Michael (1989) 'Union Organization in Advanced Industrial Democracies', *American Political Science Review*, vol. 83, no. 2 (June), pp. 481–501.

Walzer, Michael (1983) *Spheres of Justice.* New York: BasicBooks.

Wattenberg, Martin P. (1990) *The Decline of American Political Parties 1952–1988.* London: Harvard University Press.

Weiler, J. (1999) *The Constitution of Europe.* Cambridge: Cambridge University Press.

Wessels, B. (1995) 'Development of Support: Diffusion or Demographic Replacement?', in O. Niedermayer and R. Sinnott (eds), *Public Opinion and Internationalized Governance*, Beliefs in Government, vol. 2. Oxford: Oxford University Press.

Western, Bruce (1993) 'Postwar Unionization in Eighteen Advanced Capitalist Countries', *American Sociological Review*, vol. 58 (April), pp. 266–82.

Westerståhl, Jörgen (1992) 'Mediernas roll – TV-avisen', in Jørgen Goul Andersen, Hans Jørgen Nielsen and Jørgen Westerståhl (eds) *Vi og vore Politikere.* Copenhagen: Spectrum/The Rockwool Foundation, pp. 98–126.

Westerståhl, Jörgen (and Folke Johansson) (1981) *Medborgarna och kommunen: studier av medborgerlig aktivitet och representativ folkstyrelse.* Stockholm: Kommundepartementet.

White, M. (1990) *Against Unemployment.* London: Policy Studies Institute.

Wiberg, Matti (1991) *The Public Purse and Political Parties: Public Financing of Political Parties in Nordic Countries.* Helsinki: The Finnish Political Science Association.

Widfeldt, Anders (1995) 'Party Membership and Party Representativeness', in Hans-Dieter Klingemann and Dieter Fuchs (eds), *Citizens and the State.* Oxford: Oxford University Press, pp. 134–82.

Williamson, Peter J. (1985) *Corporatism in Perspective: an Introductory Guide to Corporatist Theory.* London: Sage.

Withol de Wenden, Cathrine (1994) 'Immigrants as Political Actors in France', *West European Politics*, vol. 17, no. 2, pp. 91–109.

Wolfe, Alan (1989) *Whose Keeper? Social Science and Moral Obligation.* Berkeley: University of California Press.

Wolfinger, Raymond and Rosenstone, Steven (1980) *Who Votes?* New Haven: Yale University Press.

Yearbook of Nordic Statistics 1991.

Young, R. (1986) *Personal Autonomy: Beyond Negative and Positive Liberty.* London: Croom Helm.

Index